Crime and Defoe seeks to recover something of the original excitement, challenge, and significance of Defoe's four novels of criminal life by reading them within and against the conventions of early eighteenth-century criminal biography. Crime raised deeply troubling questions in Defoe's time, not least because it seemed a powerful sign of the breakdown of traditional social authority and order. Arguing that Defoe's novels provided ways of facing, working through, as well as avoiding, certain of the moral and intellectual difficulties that crime raised for him and his readers, Lincoln Faller shows how the "literary," even "aesthetic" qualities of his fiction contributed to these ends. Analyzing the various ways in which Defoe's novels exploited, deformed, and departed from the genre they imitate, this book attempts to define the specific social and political (which is to say moral and ideological) value of a given set of "literary" texts against those of a more "ordinary" form of narrative.

Moll Flanders, Colonel Jack, and *Roxana* are given extended readings in individual chapters. Other topics considered at length include the vexed question of Defoe's realism, his own version of reader response theory and how he deploys it, the novels' structural imitation of providential design, and his recurrent, almost obsessive effort to blunt or deny the commonly held notion that trade was somehow equivalent to theft.

CAMBRIDGE STUDIES IN EIGHTEENTH-CENTURY
ENGLISH LITERATURE AND THOUGHT 16

Crime and Defoe

Crime and Defoe

A New Kind of Writing

LINCOLN B. FALLER

Professor of English, University of Michigan

CAMBRIDGE
UNIVERSITY PRESS

Published by the Press Syndicate of the University of Cambridge
The Pitt Building, Trumpington Street, Cambridge CB2 1RP
40 West 20th Street, New York, NY 10011–4211, USA
10 Stamford Road, Oakleigh, Melbourne 3166, Australia

First published 1993

Printed in Great Britain at the University Press, Cambridge

A catalogue record for this book is available from the British Library

Library of Congress cataloguing in publication data
Faller, Lincoln B.
Crime and Defoe: A New Kind of Writing / Lincoln B. Faller.
p.   cm. – (Cambridge studies in eighteenth-century English
literature and thought)
ISBN 0 521 42086 5
1. Defoe, Daniel, 1661?–1713 – Criticism and interpretation.
2. Crime – England – History – Eighteenth century – Historiography.
3. Criminals – Biography – History and criticism.
4. Social problems in literature.
5. Criminals in literature.   6. Crime in literature.
I. Title.   II. Series.
PR3408.C76F35   1993
823'.5–dc20   92-17642 CIP

ISBN 0 521 42086 5 hardback

For my mother and father,
EVELYN *and* LINCOLN A. FALLER

and in memory of my grandparents,
LOUISE *and* ERNST STAHL
BERTHA *and* ALEXANDER FALLER

Contents

Preface

Perhaps the major problem in attempting to place Defoe in his time involves a more precise definition of Defoe's relation with his audience ... we may never discover in the fragmentary records we have what enabled Defoe to find a style which his contemporaries recognized as original and exciting and which brought the end of the romance and the beginning of the novel.

> Maximillian Novak, "Defoe," in *The English Novel: Select Bibliographical Guides*, ed. A. E. Dyson (London, 1974), p. 30

To understand the true Meaning of any ancient Writing, we ought to be acquainted with the Usages and Customs of the Time and Nation in which it was wrote, those Accidents and Circumstances which occasioned the writing of it, and (since the Sense of Words is continually changing), the Meaning in which such and such Words were used at the Time when the Author flourished.

> ?Defoe, *A Collection of Miscellany Letters Selected out of Mist's Weekly Journal* (1722–7), 2: 114

Discourse in the novel is structured on an uninterrupted mutual interaction with the discourse of life.

> M. M. Bakhtin, "Discourse in the Novel," in *The Dialogic Imagination*, ed. Michael Holquist, tr. Caryl Emerson and Michael Holquist (Austin, Tex., 1981), p. 383

Poetry ... is perpetual confrontation of lexicon with the world of things.

> Jan Mukařovsky, "Poetic Reference," in *Semiotics of Art*, ed. Ladislav Matejka and Irwin R. Titunik (Cambridge, Mass., 1976), p. 162

Defoe lived in a period notably troubled and greatly fascinated by crime. Jailed several times, he likely knew criminals on intimate terms and, after his great success with *Robinson Crusoe*, turned to writing their lives. This book will say little about the biographies of actual criminals attributed to him, which of their kind are not all that remarkable, nor of the rather anomalous, indeed nearly *sui generis History of the Pirates*; its main object is the criminal novels.[1] Though there is nothing quite like them in English

---

The place of publication for all seventeenth- and eighteenth-century texts cited in these notes is London, unless otherwise specified.

[1] Students of literature seeking a balanced overview of recent scholarship on crime in the period are best served by J. A. Sharpe, *Crime in Early Modern England, 1550–1750* (London, 1984). My

literary history before or after, *Moll Flanders* and *Roxana* offer the first full
or at least ponderable characters in all its prose fiction, and even *Captain
Singleton* and *Colonel Jack* have to be allowed their special virtues. But what
these virtues are, or may be, has been a topic much debated. How ironic is
Moll Flanders? How well is it structured? What does it say for the level of
Defoe's social consciousness, or its bent? With the increase of scholarly
publication over the last several decades such questions have been turned
on Defoe's other novels as well, making it all the more apparent – even
before "theory" established this as a general principle – that the texts by
themselves will never yield up definitive answers. Critics who read Defoe's
fiction because of its undeniable historical importance but without close
attention to its original context can easily misvalue it, reading into it,
among other things, meanings (or absences of meaning) it could never
have had for him and his original audience.

For that audience the experience of reading Defoe's four novels of
criminal life would have been shaped as much by centripetal as centrifugal
pressures. His narratives spun their meanings out against the force of the
discursive conventions they denied or put to their own use. No text comes
innocent into the world. There is always, as literary theorists have almost
tiresomely come to insist, a text *avant le texte*. Each act of reading is
committed under the influence of previous acts of reading. If not the sum
total or "construct" of all they have so far read, readers must nonetheless
ply their craft within the boundaries of certain historically determined
"formations," "fields," or "horizons," must accept, reject, chafe at, be
soothed, shaped, or chivied by the "reading positions" the texts before
them provide. As scholarship of a very different kind has made clear,
Defoe's audience came to his fictions equipped with habits of reading
shaped by a variety of genres, each with its characteristic themes and
techniques, its particular patterns of thought and expectation. These
included not only the usual works of philosophy, theology, law, and
political history, but also "secret" history, spiritual biography, conduct
books, travel literature, picaresque novels, women's novels, projectors'
pamphlets, advice columns in weekly papers, and journalism or "popular
writing" in general.[2] One aim of this book is to continue this line of study.

decision to keep to Defoe's fiction and not include the actual criminal biographies attributed to
him gets recent reinforcement from P. N. Furbank and W. R. Owens, *The Canonisation of Daniel
Defoe* (New Haven, 1988). Furbank and Owens make a powerful case for suspecting all these
attributions, which, along with a great many others, have been made on dubious, often wholly
intuitive grounds and not sufficiently argued.

[2] For the relation of Defoe's novels to many (though not all) of these genres, see especially Arthur
Secord, *Studies in the Narrative Method of Defoe* (Urbana, Ill., 1924), Maximillian Novak,
Economics and the Fiction of Daniel Defoe (Berkeley, 1962), *Defoe and the Nature of Man* (London,
1963), and *Realism, Myth, and History in Defoe's Fiction* (Lincoln, Neb., 1983), G. A. Starr, *Defoe
and Spiritual Autobiography* (Princeton, 1965) and *Defoe and Casuistry* (Princeton, 1971), J. Paul
Hunter, *The Reluctant Pilgrim: Defoe's Emblematic Method and Quest for Form in Robinson Crusoe*

In situating Defoe's pseudo criminal biographies within and against the forms and conventions that governed the writing and (presumably, too) the reading of actual criminals' lives, it will speculate on what, or rather how, they may have meant to their original audience – an audience whose needs, values, concerns, and habits of reading (for readers, too, play a role in the creation of literary genres) encouraged the "rise" of what we've come to call the novel.

In a previous book I've argued that the two earliest forms of criminal biography owed their wide popularity as well as most of their distinctive features to a powerful array of social, political, religious, and moral concerns specific to the late seventeenth and early eighteenth centuries. Criminals raised deeply troubling or at least deeply troublesome questions, and the function of criminal biography within the larger culture was to provide means for addressing, allaying, ignoring, even obscuring the impact or import of such questions.³ Defoe's novels, too, provided ways of facing, as well as avoiding, certain of the moral and intellectual difficulties crime could raise for him and his readers, but – exploiting, deforming, and in a variety of ways departing from the genre they purported to represent – they sought to better its "work." Written at a time, moreover, when the authenticity and social effect of much criminal biography had come under attack, Defoe's novels sought also to deal with the problems the forms themselves presented, with all their distortions, constrictions, and obsessions, their willful ignorance and special pleading. In shaping and ordering actual criminals' lives, both forms employed fictions masquerading as truth. Each had its special structures, ironies, and sympathies, as well as its special subject matter. Defoe shared their subject matter, but against their structures, ironies, and sympathies he proposed his own. Ranging his overt but seemingly more authentic and "truer" fictions against, particularly, the fragile, often dubious assurances offered by the one – and, too, against the other's jokey, sometimes grotesque whistlings of hanged men down the wind – Defoe took an already remarkably complex reading experience and made it still more complicated, producing, I shall be arguing, novel readers as well as novel criminals. Coming upon his fiction when it was new, the tensions animating it so much more apparent, so much more present, must have been exciting, challenging, and – I'll confess this bias right now – in some ways edifying.

(Baltimore, 1966), and Ian A. Bell, *Defoe's Fiction* (London, 1985), as well as relevant chapters in Robert Alter, *Rogue's Progress: Studies in the Picaresque Novel* (Cambridge, Mass., 1964), Richard Bjornson, *The Picaresque Hero in European Fiction* (Madison, Wis., 1977), Walter L. Reed, *An Exemplary History of the Novel: The Quixotic versus the Picaresque* (Chicago, 1981), and Paula R. Backscheider, *Daniel Defoe: Ambition & Innovation* (Lexington, Ky., 1986).

³ See Lincoln B. Faller, *Turned to Account: The Forms and Functions of Criminal Biography in Late Seventeenth- and Early Eighteenth-Century England* (Cambridge, 1987); hereafter cited in this book only by short title.

Recovering something of that challenge, excitement, and edification –
or, rather, recreating them as plausibly as possible – is a major aim of this
book. As Defoe and his readers cannot themselves be examined directly,
what will actually be attempted here is a limning out of something of the
shape of one (just one) of the "discursive formations" within which his
novels were written and first received; this involves drawing inferences
(and sometimes quite indirect inferences) from an assemblage of carefully
chosen collateral texts as well as the novels themselves. From the very first,
then, it ought perhaps to be specified that the "Defoe" who appears in this
book and the "audience" I'm supposing he had are, neither of them,
anything more in the vast scheme of things than hermeneutic constructs,
the one an "author function" or "utterance position," the other a "reception position" or "reading formation," and that I'm situating both within
a "horizon of expectations," a further hermeneutic construct.[4] This is
meant by way of explanation, perhaps I should further add, not apology;
as history itself is necessarily a hermeneutic enterprise, literary history
must especially be so.

Given the taint (formalism having become an F-word) that can nowa-
days attach to the close reading of texts, I want also to make it clear that in
arraying Defoe's "art" against the forms, concerns, and strategies of a
"popular" literature I am not trying merely to reproduce "aesthetic" or
"literary" categories. When Hans Robert Jauss speaks of determining the
"aesthetic value" of a literary work by taking its measure against its
"horizon of expectations," I would hope he does not mean to leave room
for the supposition that a literary work (however defined) might somehow
be extractable from its surround, that it can somehow exist independently
of particular social, historical, and political contexts. I believe with
Bakhtin that "literary scholarship is one branch of the study of ideologies,"
that "poetic structures [are] social structures," and that "the language of
art is only a dialect of a single social language." In literary studies there
can be no hard divide between the aesthetic and the pragmatic, which,
however, is not to say (again following Bakhtin) that the one is wholly
collapsible into the other. For too long Defoe's novels have been read as
relatively simple indices to the concerns and problems of the "rising"
middle classes in early eighteenth-century England, as vehicles for an

[4] For the meanings of Michel Foucault's "discursive formation" and "author function," see,
respectively, *The Archeology of Knowledge*, tr. A. M. Sheridan Smith (New York, 1972), and
"What is an Author?" in *Textual Strategies: Perspectives in Post-Structuralist Criticism*, ed. Josué V.
Harari (Ithaca, 1979); for "horizon of expectations" see Hans Robert Jauss, *Toward an Aesthetic
of Reception*, tr. Timothy Bahti, intro. Paul de Man (Minneapolis, 1982). For several incisive
pages on the "discursive positions" of "utterance and reception," see John Frow's chapter on
"Discourse and Power" in his *Marxism and Literary History* (Oxford, 1986), especially pp. 73ff.
"Reading formation," a term apparently owing to Foucault though he goes unmentioned, is
deployed by Tony Bennett in "Texts in History: The Determinations of Readings and Their
Texts," in *Post-Structuralism and the Question of History*, ed. Derek Attridge, Geoff Bennington, and
Robert Young (Cambridge, 1987), pp. 63–81.

emerging, particularly "bourgeois" ideology. Such "sociologism," to cite
Jauss again, actually diminishes the "specific ... historicity of literature"
by ignoring the forgotten mass of works that once surrounded the now
canonized text, works far less interesting than the "great work" in its
"solitary novelty" but at least equally (if not more) valuable for their
"social index."[5]

Though I'm not about to make any elaborate argument for the
"greatness" of Defoe's novels, their "literariness" seems to me of the utmost
importance, for it was only as "literature" that they were able to deal with
social and political problems in ways that other, more obviously ideological texts were not. I put "literature" in quotes, by the way, to mark the
problematic status of the term, expecially in relation to Defoe. To my way
of thinking, the term indicates a "use-category," a "literary" text being a
text read in some ways and not others, according to a more or less
elaborate set of conventions or protocols, which of course themselves are
historically determined. Defoe's novels are not "literature" except retrospectively; they stand as objects of study because they've come to be
included in the category of "literature," not because they were considered
"literature" to start with. Still, I will be arguing, even in their own time
they invited being read in "literary" ways, i.e., in full awareness of their
fictiveness and with considerable attention to their novelty of form.

As a wide variety of critics and theorists have pointed out, one of the
most significant features of literary discourse is its ability to connect ideas
up extracognitively, through metaphor, symbolism, even mere patterns of
imagery, or by attaching them together along a narrative line, more or less
allegorically. It can do this because, by convention, it stands at something
of a remove from reality (this is a function of its self-evident fictiveness),
because it is not tied to the "logic" of more "rational" or "practical" forms
of discourse, and because it may come to closure in ways other discourses
cannot (e.g., through weddings, deaths, having its protagonist go home or
light out for the territories, all conclusions in which, as Dr. Johnson might
say, nothing much is concluded). Literary texts are thus able to escape or
smooth over strongly felt contradictions in belief or practice that other
kinds of texts have difficulty dealing with. This can make them powerful
instruments for "solving" social and political problems (for the moment at
least), or, alternatively, for exposing the insufficiency in the face of such
problems of other, supposedly more reality-oriented forms of discourse –
e.g., philosophy, theology, the various forms of moral and political
economy, the "human" sciences generally, all sorts of "common-sense"
analysis, description, argument.

[5] Jauss, *Aesthetic of Reception*, p. 25; P. N. Medvedev / M. M. Bakhtin, *The Formal Method in Literary
Scholarship: A Critical Introduction to Sociological Poetics*, tr. Albert J. Wehrle (Baltimore, 1978),
pp. 1, 30, 36 (though originally published under Medvedev's name only, this work is now
assumed to be entirely Bakhtin's); Jauss, ibid., pp. 12–13.

It is the problem-solving, problem-creating dimension of Defoe's novels
that interests me most. I see them as remarkable instances of how
thoroughly literary discourse can be implicated by the socially and politically problematic, and how, too, such problematics can provide an
"occasion" for literature, starting it off and spurring it on, sometimes in
quite new, even "novel" directions. For all its pointing to vanished
attitudes, values, and structures of feeling and thinking, Defoe's criminal
fiction is still more interesting for the ways in which it diverges from and
resists, contends with and against mere ideological simplifications. Inasmuch as the vast body of surviving criminal biographies allows those
simplifications to be defined independently of Defoe's novels, this book can
get beyond the large, fuzzy questions of whether or not they are "representative" of their age, of whether they "reflect" or "refract" (and to what
extent) the world in which they were written. Because it can be, this book
hopes to be more solid and precise. In gauging Defoe's criminal novels
against a particular "discourse of life" – their closest, collateral non-
literary form – it will attempt to define in one concrete instance, at one
historical moment, the specific social and political, which is to say moral
and ideological value of a "literary" discourse vs. a specific kind of
"ordinary" or "standard" discourse.

This last juxtaposition of terms – "literary" vs. "ordinary" or "standard"
– derives from the Russian Formalists and the Prague Structuralists. We do
not need them or Bakhtin, however, to tell us the novel was born in
opposition, or that it gains its peculiar power by marking out its difference
from seemingly similar kinds of narrative. The novel's great practitioners
from Cervantes onward have always known this, and – a particular source
of comfort, given this project's "historicist" ambitions – it was nowhere
more clearly understood than in eighteenth-century England. Insisting,
thus, that *Clarissa* was no "light Novel, or transitory Romance" but "a
History of Life and Manners," Richardson quite explicitly played his great
work off against all three of these narrative genres, for he was concerned to
make the point, too, that his text was not actually a history but only to be
read like one, i.e., with a "Historical Faith." Fielding was still more
self-conscious about the peculiar status of his "new Province of Writing"
vis-à-vis other, less special kinds of narratives, repeatedly encouraging
readers of *Tom Jones* to compare it to biographies, romances, or the sort of
stories that appeared in newspapers. Such comparisons, he appeared to
hope, would show how much more closely his own text conformed to the
"Book of Nature," that ultimate and (we post-moderns might cleverly
think to add) ultimately unwritable text of "Facts as they are."[6]

---

[6] Richardson, "Author's Preface" to *Clarissa, or the History of a Young Lady* (Everyman, 1962),
p. xv, and letter to Warburton, 19 April 1748, in *Selected Letters of Samuel Richardson*, ed. John
Carroll (Oxford, 1964), p. 85; Fielding, *Tom Jones*, 2: 1 and 7: 12.

Fielding here is as good in his own way as Bakhtin commenting on the "mutual interaction" of novelistic and real-life discourse. As he is, too, at a point in *Tom Jones* when he expects readers might object to a seemingly implausible turn of events: "I am not writing a System, but a History," he says, "and I am not obliged to reconcile every Matter to the received Notions concerning Truth and Nature." This is to speak, according to Bakhtin, as the artist should, wanting "nothing to do with prepared or confirmed theses," nor with "the aesthetics of the ready-made and completed." Truth and Nature, exceeding received notions, stand beyond or at least resist systematization (thus the culpable stupidity of Thwackum on the one hand, Square on the other). There may be "Philosophers, who can reduce all the Matter of the World into a Nut-Shell," but the novelist, wiser than this, knows better. The value of his "new Province of Writing" – not history actually, as Fielding points out elsewhere, nor romance either (though he allows at times it might be) but some third thing he sets against them both as well as against the "Book of Nature" – its value is that it is peculiarly suited to raise a similar knowledge in its readers.[7]

Not so much inventing as stumbling on *his* version of the "new" kind of writing, Defoe shows nowhere near the narrational self-consciousness of Fielding or Richardson nor anything like their solicitude for readers. Still, by disturbing, displacing, deforming, and opening up the complete and ready-made "aesthetics" of criminal biography, by failing to advance the "prepared theses" it typically confirmed, he, too, explored the ways words relate, or fail to relate, to "the world of things." And he, too, encouraged new forms of reading. The English novel (and if not a founding father Defoe was certainly its midwife) may be said to have been born when English prose fiction entered into and enlarged "poetry" as Mukařovsky defines it, which is to say literary practice, which is to say reading as well as writing. If, as once again we've come to suspect, "reading" does indeed "maketh the man," the advent of the novel may have brought with it new modes of consciousness. Not the least of Defoe's contributions to "novel reading," then, might have been the boost his fiction gave to characteristically modern forms of subjectivity. Though it is not possible to speak of these matters as concretely, as precisely, or with as much certainty as I'd like, they, too, will from time to time form a major concern of this book.

Most of what follows was first drafted out between 1980 and 1982. The intervening years of rethinking and rewriting have been spent awaiting the appearance of its predecessor, a protracted and at times agonizing process; the author was also distracted by Africa. All this bears mention only because in the meanwhile something of its original impulse and some

---

[7] Fielding, *Tom Jones*, 12: 8; Bakhtin, *The Formal Method*, p. 19, and *Rabelais and His World*, tr. Helene Iswolsky (Cambridge, Mass., 1968), p. 25; Fielding, *Joseph Andrews*, 2: 2.

few of its ideas have been anticipated by other writers; more than one of us were breathing in the same zeitgeist. I have gained a great deal from these writers in revising and rethinking earlier drafts, and I hope my notes sufficiently indicate this as well as the ample contributions of other scholars and critics to the substance and shape of my thinking. Some debts, however, are best indicated here.

First, I wish to express my gratitude to the Horace G. Rackham School of Graduate Studies at the University of Michigan and to its Dean, John D'Arms, for a most timely contribution to the publishing costs of this book. For permission to include as part of chapter 2 material that appeared in *Comparative Literature Studies*, I thank the editors of that journal and the Pennsylvania State University Press. For her continuing love, faith, and financial generosity (until close to the end she was the only foundation supporting this book), I once again celebrate my wife. Tom Toon and John Richetti are owed special thanks for wading through this text in some of its more unseemly manifestations, Richetti at least twice and Toon despite far more compelling interests in French cookery, skindiving, and the sociolinguisitics of Old English dialects. And, too, I continue to owe more general debts to friends, students, and colleagues at the University of Michigan, to the libraries of that institution, and to the British Library. I need to thank as well my students and colleagues at the University of Yaounde for all they taught me about the specific social and political importance of literature in West Africa, Western as well as African, at and in this highly particular, highly interesting historical moment; I suspect I have a better knowledge of eighteenth-century England and its literature as a consequence. (In the at first unconscious pun appearing chapter 4, note 7, they – and only they – will detect the depth of their influence.) Finally, at the threshold of this book – something else learned during my year in Africa – I pay tribute to the ancestors and greet (oh, how you suffer for me!) those who are owed more than any praise singer might sing.

Abbreviations

The following abbreviations and editions have been used when citing works by Defoe in the main text and the notes:

FI   *The Family Instructor, The Novels and Miscellaneous Works* (Oxford, 1840–1), vols. 15, 16

RC   *The Life and Strange Surprizing Adventures of Robinson Crusoe*, ed. J. Donald Crowley (London, 1972)

RC2   *Farther Adventures of Robinson Crusoe*, pub. as *Robinson Crusoe. Part II, The Works of Daniel Defoe*, ed. G. H. Maynadier (New York, 1903–4), vol. 2

SRC   *Serious Reflections of Robinson Crusoe*, ibid., vol. 3

CS   *The Life, Adventures, and Pyracies, of the Famous Captain Singleton*, ed. Shiv K. Kumar (London, 1973)

MF   *The Fortunes and Misfortunes of the Famous Moll Flanders*, ed. G. A. Starr (London, 1971)

CJ   *The History and Remarkable Life of The Truly Honourable Col. Jacque, Commonly Call'd Col. Jack*, ed. Samuel Holt Monk (London, 1970)

R   *Roxana, the Fortunate Mistress*, ed. Jane Jack (London, 1969)

CET   *The Complete English Tradesman*, 2nd edn, 2 vols. (London, 1727)

CEG   *The Complete English Gentleman*, ed. Karl D. Bülbring (London, 1890)

1

Romancing the real: the "field" of criminal biography

It is something strange, that a Man's Life should be made a kind of a Romance before his Face, and while he was upon the Spot to contradict it; or, that the World should be so fond of a formal Chimney-corner Tale, that they had rather a Story should be made merry than true.

> ?Defoe, *The Life and Actions of the Late Jonathan Wild* (1725), p. [iii]

As no person ... perhaps, in any condition of life whatever had so many romantic stories fathered upon him in his life, or so many fictitious legendary accounts published of him after his death .... [i]t may seem a low kind of affectation to say that the memoirs we are now giving ... are founded on certainty and fact.

> *Lives of the Most Remarkable Criminals* (1735), ed. Arthur L. Hayward
> (New York, 1927), p. 247

Thus have we given the World a faithful account of this Poor Wretches Crime and Behaviour, and what she declared and persisted in to the last; with the great Remorse she expressed for all sin, and the mighty work of God upon her soul .... All which we leave to each Readers consideration and reflection, to Credit or Disbelieve her Asseverations, and make such judgment thereof as he shall think fit.

> *Warning for Servants ... Or, the Case of Margret Clark, Lately Executed for*
> *Firing Her Master's House in Southwark* (1680), pp. 30–1

When a Man becomes remarkable in Life, though it be only on the Score of Villainy, he generally becomes a Topick of Conversation .... Truth is made to subside for the Diversion of a Company, and many Things are advanced as Facts, which never had Existence. I will therefore, to prevent the Publick being imposed on by false Accounts, either in Conversation, or in Print, here set down a true and impartial Account of my Life, from my Birth, to my unhappy Exit, where not a Villainy I have committed shall be lessened by my Narrative, but it shall be set in all its Glare of Light!

> Henry Simms, *The Life of Henry Simms, Alias Young Gentleman Harry* (1747),
> pp. 1–2

Many things are true in it, but most are false, & many material things are omitted.

Beware reader this son of a bitch the composer of the following [dying] speech has impos'd upon the world by calling it my Lord Strafford's.

1

ms. notes in Antony Wood's copies of G[eorge] F[idge], *The English Gusman; or the History of That Unparallel'd Thief James Hind* (1652) [Bodleian Library press mark Wood 372 (2)], and *The Two Last Speeches of Thomas Wentworth Late Earle of Strafford . . . May, the 12. 1641* (t.p. missing; n.p., n.d.) [Wood 366 (4)]

I am giving an account of what was, not of what ought or ought not to be.

Moll Flanders, p. 98

Almost by definition we expect novels somehow to be "new," to effect transformations of what is "old," of what has "always already" seemed "there." "Inherited narrative paradigms," says Fredric Jameson, "are the raw material on which the novel works, transforming their 'telling' into its 'showing,' estranging commonplaces against the freshness of some unexpected 'real,' foregrounding convention itself as that through which readers have hitherto received their notions of events, psychology, experience, space, and time." In the large style of many recent arguers for (and against) the powers of literature, Jameson goes on to claim that the novel's "critical, analytic, corrosive mission" has played "a significant role in what can be called a properly bourgeois cultural revolution." That is, its "undermining and demystification" of the "traditional" has helped along "that immense process of transformation whereby populations whose life habits were formed by other, now archaic modes of production are effectively reprogrammed for life and work in the new world of market capitalism."[1] Perhaps so. Believing myself in a possibly more old-fashioned way that "forming a counterenvironment is one of the major functions of literature in any age," and that this alone sufficiently argues for its worth, I'm more inclined to think the novel emerges to serve the needs of readers not any Onward March of History.[2] Readers' needs, to be sure, are necessarily defined by their place in history, but history itself, especially as Marxists have tended to define it, has more than enough of other kinds of writing to do its business. And, writing aside, there are handier, far more direct and enduring ways of shaping experience and forging consciousness to specific social and political ends; art is short, life is long.

It seems a peculiarly modern condition – the consequence of our living in a large, diverse, decentered world where anything may happen and often does – that, as Roberto Unger says, "our ideas suffer from an incurable instability: we may always discover at the next moment something that is not just novel but incompatible with our assumptions. Not only may we have ignored this truth before, but we may have ignored the whole way of thinking, or seeing, or talking that its full exploration requires." If the novel prepares readers for anything, I'd argue, it is for

---

[1] Fredric Jameson, *The Political Unconscious: Narrative as a Socially Symbolic Act* (Ithaca, 1981), pp. 151, 152.

[2] Northrop Frye, "Varieties of Eighteenth-Century Sensibility," *Eighteenth-Century Studies*, 24 (1990): 161.

living in just such a world, a perpetually "novel" world where "no practical or imaginative ordering of human life represents the definitive, complete form of personality or society, nor do all the orderings that have ever existed, when put together." "Made up of distinct selves, each with its power to resist submission and disclosure," such a world may seem mysterious and unintelligible, "recalcitran[t] ... to complete mastery by the imagination and the will"; still, it also allows "a strange freedom from any given finite structure." "We are not governed *fully*," Unger points out (my emphasis), "by the established imaginative and institutional contexts of our societies"; though we "never overcome [such] context dependence .... we may loosen it."[3]

Defoe's criminal novels, as I see them, do "reprogram" readers but not necessarily in ways that would make them better, more compliant instruments of "market capitalism." His fiction, rather, is a great "context loosener," and, too, in its own way, a provider of "a strange freedom" from preestablished imaginative and institutional constraints. This book starts by sketching out something of those constraints. In describing the commonplace notions and narrative paradigms of criminal biography – arguably the most substantial, significant component of the "always already" that defined attitudes and feelings about crime in Defoe's era – it seeks to delimit part of the "horizon of expectations" within which his novels would first have made their estranging "freshness" felt. How would readers have been positioned within that "horizon" – how would that "horizon" have positioned them – as Defoe's fiction hove into view? Or, rather – since a reader "is not an entity existing prior to the [reception] positions which it fills" but "a process within the network of signifiers" – how would the reading of Defoe's novels have been constrained by a particular interpretive "regime" or "semiotic institution"?[4]

A "horizon of expectations," as Jauss defines it, is "the objectifiable system of expectations that arise for each work in the moment of its appearance, from a pre-understanding of the genre, from the form and themes of already familiar works, and from the opposition between poetic and practical language." Such a "system," of course, can never be fully delineated. Even the completest possible description of criminal biography would fail to give a full "synchronic cross-section" of the expectations governing the original reception of Defoe's novels.[5] A host of other literary and non-literary genres would also have to be factored into consideration,

3 Roberto Mangabeira Unger, *Social Theory: Its Situation and Its Task. A Critical Introduction to "Politics," a Work in Constructive Social Theory* (Cambridge, 1987), pp. 34, 23, 16, 21. For a useful, brief account of Unger's thinking, which challenges the totalizing assumptions of "conservatives, liberals and Marxists alike," see Perry Anderson, "Roberto Unger and the Politics of Empowerment," *New Left Review*, No. 173 (January/February 1989), pp. 93–107.
4 John Frow, *Marxism and Literary History* (Oxford, 1986), pp. 76–7, 185–6.
5 Hans Robert Jauss, *Towards an Aesthetic of Reception*, tr. Timothy Bahti, intro. Paul de Man (Minneapolis, 1982), pp. 22, 36–8.

and, practically speaking, one would never get to the end of describing them or their possible impact. Jauss's idea is better taken as a source of inspiration than a possible blueprint for action, or so at least I take it here. My reading of Defoe's criminal novels against the background of criminal biography means, at best, to provide new vantage points on the matters Defoe's fiction addressed, agitated, reordered, and advanced, new insight into his craft as a writer and the possible effects of his texts on active and attentive readers; it intends no global account of his work's "surround." Though it starts by tracing out similarities and differences between his fiction and criminal biography, it will move increasingly beyond such matters, at times even stretching comparison. It aims not at cataloguing Defoe's deviations and divagations for their own sake but to focus on and follow up the questions they raise.

For Defoe and his original audience, criminal biography was a well-established but relatively recent phenomenon, not something of long inheritance. A "new province of writing" all of itself, it had become a regular feature of English popular culture only in the middle of the seventeenth century; perhaps this made its commonplaces all the more easily "estrangeable." Previously, there had been broadside accounts of certain notable executions and pamphlets on horrendous murders, to say nothing of the "cony-catching" chapbooks of the late sixteenth century. But it was only during the political upheaval of the Interregnum – a point of some significance, I'd argue – that writing about actual crimes and criminals began to organize itself around, typically, the life histories, characters, and deeds of specific individuals rather than, say, the stratagems, tricks, and knaveries of criminals in general, or their affront to good order, or the sufferings of their victims, or the manifest signs their crimes, capture, and punishment might display of God's displeasure, providence, or both.

Even the earliest criminal biographies seem to have been highly popular and widely read. By the 1670s, public interest in the lives, crimes, and fates of even rather ordinary criminals had grown great enough to sustain the printing of regular accounts of the trials at the Old Bailey (these were called "sessions papers"), as well as the so-called "ordinary's *Accounts*," which were reports by the chaplain "in ordinary" at Newgate prison on the last behaviors and dying words of the convicts hanged at Tyburn. Both these began as broadside publications, the sessions papers listing defendants trial by trial, the substance of their indictments, and the disposal of their cases, and the ordinary's *Accounts* giving no more than a paragraph or two to each criminal mentioned. By the second decade of the eighteenth century, however, the ordinary's *Accounts* had become six-page pamphlets, and by the 1730s both they and the sessions papers could stretch to more than fifty pages. Even trivial criminals could by then get as many as 2,000 words from the Newgate chaplain, and trial accounts, taken down in shorthand and presented as spoken dialogue, might run five double-columned pages or more. It was during the second decade of the eighteenth century, it ought also to be noted, that the first great collections of criminals' lives began to appear. The forerunners of the later Newgate Calendars, these are gatherings, often rewritings, of previously published materials interspersed with commentaries and narratives of their compilers' own invention. In editions of two, three, even four volumes, at prices of as much as ten shillings the set, they mark not only the full arrival of criminal biography as an English cultural institution but also the money that could be made of it. Though he had no particular liking for the institution, Defoe, who would soon begin writing novels, would likely have been attracted by the money.

Criminal biography was only one of a multitude of popular narrative genres that, developing along with and shaping an increasing, practically insatiable appetite for "news" of all kinds, is generally seen as the seedbed of the novel.[6] It is intrinsically one of the most interesting of these genres, but there are other reasons to give it special attention. Criminal biography developed in England when and how it did, it has been suggested, because people in an age of increased individualism and anomie liked identifying with outlaws, masterless men, and other defiant disturbers of the social order. Reading about a criminal's crimes would have given them vicarious experiences of the extremest kind of freedom from social control, and reading about his punishment would, in a sense, have consoled them for their own actual lack of freedom. It might also, according to the standard Freudian model, have allowed readers the psychic relief of focussing and discharging the various guilts aroused by their fantasizing on the heads of those who were, after all, scapegoats as well as surrogates. Criminals thus would have paid not only for the reader's wish to be autonomous and to do the most terrible things but also for his own felt lack of autonomy and perhaps, too, his sense of powerlessness in a too rapidly changing (to shift from psychology to sociology), increasingly "distantiated" world.[7] From this standpoint, criminal biography would be powerfully important for the

---

6 For recent contributions to this view, see Lennard J. Davis, *Factual Fictions: The Origins of the English Novel* (New York, 1983), Michael McKeon, *The Origins of the English Novel, 1600–1740* (Baltimore, 1987), and J. Paul Hunter, "'News, and new Things': Contemporaneity and the Early English Novel," *Critical Inquiry*, 14 (1988): 493–515, as also chapter 7 of his *Before Novels: The Cultural Contexts of Eighteenth-Century English Fiction* (New York, 1990), pp. 167–94. A recent survey of prose fiction preceding the "rise" of the novel may be found in Paul Salzman, *English Fiction, 1588–1700: A Critical History* (Oxford, 1985).

7 I borrow the quoted term from Anthony Giddens, who uses it in conjunction with "low presence-availability" to describe the "large-scale, industrialised societies" that begin to develop with capitalism (see *A Contemporary Critique of Historical Materialism* [Berkeley, 1983], pp. 65–7, 90–108, 115–17).

insight it might give into readers' needs, feelings, and expectations at the time our first important novels were written, and so, very likely, the ends their authors aimed at. One writer has even gone so far as to suggest that "the whole project of the novel, its very theoretical and structural assumptions, were in some sense criminal in nature," that it "seems almost to demand a criminal content," and that, conversely, "there seems to have been something inherently novelistic about the criminal."[8]

Though such efforts at explaining the peculiar popularity of criminal biography and its potential relation to the early novel are frequently plausible and sometimes quite sophisticated, they can easily seem too vague, too abstract, too timelessly "psychologistic," too insufficiently attached to practical, historically bound realities.[9] They tend, moreover, to obscure important differences between the two main forms of narratives about actual criminals: the morally serious and quasi-realistic on the one hand, a kind of spiritual biography, and the generally frivolous, overtly romantic and often fantastic on the other, which was modeled on the picaresque novel and seems primarily to have wanted to entertain. Both forms of criminal biography are best seen and understood, I've suggested elsewhere, as a kind of cultural practice, as socially determined and socially sanctioned discourses which, in one way or another, "glossed" or made tolerable sense of criminals, their crimes, and the punishments they had to suffer. And it was important to make such sense of criminals in Defoe's era, for a variety of historically specific reasons. These reasons, and the narrative forms or "myths" they prompted, will be the main concerns of this chapter, along with the reading habits such narratives would have tended to encourage.

Defoe was not the first to write novel-length accounts of criminals' lives in England, nor even the first to fashion these "lives" out of the whole cloth of fiction. Richard Head, Francis Kirkman, Elkanah Settle, and the anonymous "autobiographer" of Mary Frith, for instance, anticipated him by decades.[10] None of these writers, however, was much if at all

---

[8] Davis, *Factual Fictions*, pp. 123–5.

[9] From this specific criticism, however, I'd particularly exempt Michael McKeon and J. Paul Hunter, each of whom – in his very different way – grounds his book on the origins of the novel in an impressive and skillfully deployed knowledge of English social, political, and cultural history.

[10] Thus see *The Life and Death of Mrs. Mary Frith. Commonly Called Mal Cutpurse* (1662); Richard Head and Francis Kirkman, *The English Rogue Described in the Life of Meriton Latroon*, originally published in four parts, 1665–71 (New York, 1928); F[rancis] K[irkman], *The Counterfeit Lady Unveiled. Being a Full Account of the Birth, Life, and Most Remarkable Actions, and Untimely Death of Mary Carleton, Known by the Name of the German Princess* (1673); Elkanah Settle, *The Life and Death of Major Clancie, the Grandest Cheat of This Age* (1680) and, by the same writer, *The Complete Memoirs of the Life of that Notorious Imposter Will. Morrell* (1694). A rather basic problem with seeing these texts as precursors to Defoe's fiction, however, is their relative unavailability in the early eighteenth century. If the British Library Catalogue is an accurate indication, none had been reprinted within two decades or more of the publication of Defoe's novels. Radical

concerned with the "real" deficiencies of criminal biography, by which I mean the problematics of its relation to the "reality" it purportedly but – even at its most serious and seemingly authentic – never quite adequately described. Defoe's "enlarged" versions of criminal biography aim at greater adequacy to the actual and, being novels, they achieve it (or, rather, *seeming* to achieve it, they *become* novels, indeed begin to define the very genre "novel"). Our concern here must be, then, not only the aims and conventions of criminal biography at the time Defoe's novels were written and first read but the strains and tensions it displayed, its felt insufficiencies and consequent vulnerability to criticism. These last made it a genre – or set of genres – highly ripe for rewriting.[11]

Though it seems now that crime was actually declining in early eighteenth-century England, contemporary observers were sure it was catastrophically on the rise. This perception can be explained in a variety of ways, but the fears it called forth came (as in our own day) from crime's seeming importance as a sign of the breakdown of traditional social authority. "All Thieves and Murderers," the Newgate ordinary preached, were "Rebels."[12] Given the rumblings and dislocations in the English polity since the Civil Wars, this was only to say that criminals were part of a much larger trend. Defoe's interest in the new politics of his changing age extended from the highest matters of state down to the arrangement and conduct of the workplace and the household. The new rules and practices obtaining between husbands and wives, parents and children, masters and servants, as well as between businessmen, their customers, and their employees, provide the main impetus for his conduct manuals. Again and again these manuals stress the disorder, even chaos, that can occur when traditional authority is called into question or fails to exert itself with sufficient confidence and power. Children defy their fathers, wives leave their husbands, apprentices scheme against their masters, shoppers and shopkeepers eye each other with deep mistrust, and housemaids preach sedition in the kitchen.[13] Money would not have been Defoe's only motive in writing about criminals; they stood as rich signs of the times.

Criminal biography was almost exclusively concerned with convicts

abridgements of the original accounts of Frith and Carleton appear, however, in Alexander Smith's *Lives of the Highwaymen* (5th edn, 1719), and it is likely that this would have been the source of Defoe's and his readers' knowledge of them.

11 Though it incorporates new materials, most of what follows in this chapter is very closely based on *Turned to Account*. Readers familiar with the earlier work should feel free to skim, or, possibly, skip forward to the next chapter.

12 Paul Lorrain, Ordinary Account, 6 June 1707.

13 See, respectively, *The Family Instructor*, vol. 1, pt. 1 passim and vol. 2, pt. 2 passim; *The Complete English Tradesman*, 1: 12–17, 85–96, 146–61, 2 (pt. 1): 31–2, 44–6, and *Religious Courtship* (Glasgow, 1797), pp. 236–7.

safely and permanently put away. In more than 150 years there are only a handful of exceptions to this rule. Criminals not yet captured or who had escaped, whose death sentences were commuted to transportation, or who had reformed and taken up honest lives, practically never got biographical treatment. Criminal biography was in a sense, then, a supplement to execution, which was itself an effort to impose, once and for all, a socially acceptable signification on criminals. Each form differed radically, however, in the kind of "supplement" it offered. Serious criminal biography sought to extend and enhance the significance of executed criminals, giving plot and substance to their lives as it traced their fall from grace and good action, dwelt on the depths of their depravity, and charted their climb back toward God and a proper respect for their fellow men. The other, sedulously non-serious kind tended, however, to do quite the opposite. Indeed, contracting criminals into rogues of one kind or another, caricaturing their victims, making their lives seem series of disjunctive, implausible episodes, it might even be said to have offered a "negative" supplement. But let us begin with positives.

At least as far back as the Tudors, public executions in England offered criminals – or could impose upon them – the opportunity to speak to the assembled crowd. By Defoe's time these speeches had become highly ritualized affairs. "Oh take warning by my sad Example," said a servant girl hanged in 1680 for firing her master's house, "pray get some good to your selves by my Sin, and shameful Death." "Good People," a burglar declared in 1703, "take warning by my Fall; you see I am a young Man, who by my Sins have shortened my Days, and brought my Self to this Shameful but deserved Death .... Live not as I have done, lest you come to the like sad and untimely End."[14] Though such dying declarations were often put into criminals' mouths by helpful clergymen, or other well-meaning prison visitors, they were by no means empty formulae.

Criminals' confessions, according to a Bishop of Oxford, were "a Satisfaction they ow'd their Country," and the satisfaction looked for was actually of several kinds.[15] In France and other places on the Continent, the purpose of public execution was simply and totally to humiliate and erase the criminal, often literally to crush him, and so to chasten and subdue the watching crowd with an overpowering display of state authority. Though they also were expected to make highly ritualized apologies before being put to death, criminals in France were not of much interest in

[14] *Warning for Servants: And a Caution to Protestants. Or, the Case of Margret Clark, Lately Executed for Firing Her Masters House in Southwark* (1680), p. 13; N. B., *A Compleat Collection of Remarkable Tryals of the Most Notorious Malefactors, at the Sessions-House in the Old Baily, for near Fifty Years Past* (1718–21), 2: 186–7.

[15] William Talbot, later bishop of Salisbury and finally of Durham, in *The Truth of the Case. Or, a Full and True Account of the Horrid Murders, Robberies and Burnings, Committed at Bradforton and Upton Snodsbury ... Worcestor* (1708), p. 36.

and of themselves; criminal biography there tended, correspondingly, to be brief, undeveloped, and infrequent. In England, however, where the body politic was far more active, divided, and complicated, the execution of criminals could be a far more richly nuanced affair. Nowhere else was it expected they would play so central a role in the social drama staged to exploit their dreadful ends; nowhere else were their voices given so much scope; nowhere else were their lives and fates potentially so dense with social, political, and religious implication. Serious criminal biography was particularly concerned with drawing out, developing, and broadcasting these implications.

In the first place, as men slated imminently to meet their maker, condemned criminals were ripe objects for religious curiosity and manipulation. How had they fallen away from God, what made them succumb to their own worst impulses, what exactly had they done, and how had they felt, what were their thoughts, before, during, after? How had they been caught, and what did they feel then, when first put in prison, and during their trial, and now as they prepared to meet a shameful death? Were they hopeful or confident of salvation, and if so on what grounds? The worse their crimes and the greater their state of sin, the more these questions were asked, and the more criminals were pressed to give appropriate answers. Of course what counted for appropriate answers depended on the religious orientation of the clergymen who were charged with the care of the condemned, or of those who came forward voluntarily (not all of them clergy) in hopes of exhorting them into an appropriate frame of mind. Most of the earlier criminal biographies of the serious kind are Calvinist and fundamentally Protestant in their emphases, but after the Interregnum they become more orthodox and latitudinarian. The clergy who report the behavior and testimony of condemned criminals (a behavior and testimony, to be sure, which they've done a good deal to shape) now put less emphasis on the power of individual grace descending unaided and freely from God, and emphasize more the kind of "talking cure" they've effected by getting their patients to accept and consider certain key doctrines, and to perform certain standard religious exercises. Over time condemned criminals meet death with less "rapture and extasie," and become more "sensible."[16]

Criminals cured by priestly exhortation or the sudden influx of the Spirit, or both, were powerful advertisements for whatever brand of religion was on offer. During the latter half of the seventeenth century, when religious factionalism was particularly acute in England, criminals

[16] Randolph Yearwood, compiler, *The Penitent Murderer. Being an Exact Narrative of the Life and Death of Nathaniel Butler* (1657); Paul Lorrain, Ordinary Accounts, 25 October 1704, 16 December 1709, 17 March 1710. "Stupid" was the opposite of "sensible" in the ordinary's lexicon; see, for instance, his account of Susan Perry (13 March 1713), hanged as a child murderer; more will be said about Perry in chapter 2.

could become instruments to advance particular religious persuasions (this was true in the latter half of the eighteenth century as well, during the Methodist revival). It is hardly an accident that criminal biography should have started flourishing during the Interregnum. The general effect of criminals' great and surprising conversions, however, was to testify to the great and redeeming power of Christian faith, whatever the sect, sincerely held after all. A "friend" (probably Calvinist), visiting a murderer shortly before he was hanged in 1657, proposed (hypothetically, to be sure) that he be set at liberty, but "clapping his hand on his breast" this new recruit for God declared, "Really, Really, Really . . . if I know my own heart, I would not for ten thousand worlds lose the opportunity of this morning. I am now going where I shall never sin again." His "dark Dungeon" was "the best Room that ever I came in; and [his] contemptible Bed, the best that ever I lay in!" "May you be strong and courageous, and bear up," said another murderer's spiritual advisor in 1680, "taking comfort, that you are a monument of divine Justice; and that in and thorow you, God sheweth the consequences of a sinful and wicked life." The more temperate language here suggests a quieter, more orthodox point of view. But whatever the case, the important point is the persistent hope that God (or rather His servants) could show, too, in and through the converted criminal, the pure, even ecstatic benefits of unalloyed faith. Thus, to cite a spread of instances from the late seventeenth through the mid-eighteenth century, a penitent burglar could claim that his execution would be "the happiest Minute of my Life," a forger could go to the gallows "happy" and "smiling," and an arsonist could rhapsodize, "Oh! the Transcendent Joys, I am not able to express the Joys I have since I have been condemned." Even a man innocent of the murder for which he was hanged – or so he and some few others claimed – could show "a well satisfied Acquiescence in his Disposal, whatever it might seem to Flesh and Blood."[17]

Such dying behavior was reassuring from more than one angle. Crime always raises doubts, but in Defoe's time these could be peculiarly unsettling. At its worst of course, as in cases of unreasoning murder, crime could seem to impugn God's justice. How could parricide, fratricide, the murdering of children or of husbands, be allowed to happen in a justly ordered universe? It had always been believed that God intervened in cases of murder, taking special pains to mark murderers out so they might be punished in this world. In Defoe's day, the age of miracles being past,

---

[17] Yearwood, *The Penitent Murderer*, pp. [xxix-xxx]; *A Full and True Account of the Penitence of John Marketman* (1680), pp. 14–15; N. B., *Compleat Tryals . . . for near Fifty Years Past*, 3: 61; *Select Trials for Murder, Robbery, Burglary, Rapes, Sodomy, Coining, Forgery, Pyracy, and Other Offences and Misdemeanours* (1764), 4: 172; *Warning for Servants*, p. 29; *Mistaken Justice: Or, Innocence Condemn'd, in the Person of Francis Newland, Lately Executed at Tyburn, for the Barbarous Murder of Mr. Francis Thomas* (1695), p. 17.

such interventions had ceased taking supernatural form. Now, it was believed, God struck invisibly, going straight to the murderer's heart and mind. Typically, then, murderers were expected to say they had suffered a sudden, unaccountable disordering of their intellects or a failure of will almost immediately after their crime, and that this not only prevented them from concealing it, or even fleeing the scene, but as much as declared their guilt to all who saw them. Such testimony was hardly necessary in the cases of less threatening, less shocking criminals, but even relatively ordinary crimes, inasmuch as they, too, indicated the general depravity of human nature, could raise disturbing questions. For one thing, why was it that men continued to violate the law, given its growing harshness and the terrible risk they ran?

In the absence of an appropriate abnormal psychology or any concept of a separate criminal class, the criminal impulse could seem utterly mysterious and highly threatening. The very language of criminal indictments caught something of this mystery, criminals being routinely accused of having committed their crimes "not having the fear of God before their eyes, and being seduced thereunto by the instigations of the Devil." Given the inherent, general depravity of human nature, the original sinfulness of us all, it could seem, moreover, that everyone was susceptible to these instigations; all of us were thieves by nature, and we all had murder in our hearts. Crime was thus in a sense a "normal" phenomenon; the wonder was not that there was so much of it, but that there was not more. Though criminal behavior was understood to have an etiology – it was held as a maxim that "no man becomes excessively wicked all at once," i.e., that criminality proceeded by gradations – the whole terrible drift toward crime could start with something so trivial, or so some writers quite seriously claimed, as failing to observe the sabbath or staying out late at night. From such beginnings criminal biographers could detail, step by step, the dreadful progress of parricides, poisoners, servants who murdered fellow servants or even their masters, bullies who killed passersby in the street, mothers who smothered their infants, and, most severely punished of all, wives who did in their husbands.[18]

Other, less Calvinistic writers offered more sophisticated etiologies of crime, anticipating (in a small way) modern theories of psychological and social disadvantage; these "theories," however, hardly covered all cases. Every time a more than usually heinous crime was committed by someone who, until that moment, had not seemed especially wicked, the inference was all too plain; none of us could trust our impulses or count ourselves

---

[18] The maxim may be found, for instance, in *Memoirs of the Life and Times of Sir Thomas Deveil ... One of His Majesty's Justices of the Peace* (1748), p. 49; Deveil was Fielding's predecessor as Bow Street magistrate. Women who murdered their husbands were burned at the stake over most of the eighteenth century.

secure. And when hitherto honest tradesmen, impecunious gentlemen, or even menials with a taste for living above their means slipped into supporting themselves by thefts and robberies, the inference was much the same. Only God's grace could keep us from a shameful death on the gallows and, possibly (though by no means certainly), a good education. But if criminals showed more luridly than other men that any of us might become chief of sinners, and that the wages of sin is death, they could stand, too, among God's most notable instances of grace and mercy. Hanging was a "great Affliction" and "more than Human Nature can bear," yet some bore up remarkably well. "From the Time that he was committed last to *Newgate*, to his dying Hour, he devoted himself to Religion," we read of a murderer hanged in 1708; "He had compos'd his Thoughts so much from the very first, that he seem'd to have conquer'd Death with greater Ease than most People imagine it to be done." Or, as another writer said of a similarly "composed" murderer some fifty years earlier: "He reads by his example, a lecture of consolation."[19]

Very much the same sort of consolation was squeezed out of penitent criminals in New England; there, too, a high emphasis was placed on their individual capacity to find God at last. In France, where the real star of an execution was often not the criminal himself but his confessor, the most important element in an appropriate dying behavior was of course the good offices of the Church. What made English criminal biography distinctly different from that of both France and America was not, then, that it pursued either or even both these ends but its pursuit of a third; it sought a satisfaction in criminals' glad deaths that, though moral, was not especially religious. A peculiar generosity of spirit could sometimes be made to imbue – or seem to imbue – the putting to death of criminals in England. The dying man was encouraged not only to play an active role in the affair, but to participate in what seems, almost, an exchange of compliments. Consider, for instance, this long and approving account by a Newgate ordinary of the last reflections of a wife murderer named Dramatti:

without any desire of justifying himself in anything he was not to be justify'd in, he ... declar'd, that he was in charity with all Mankind; wishing all Mankind were so with him. And here he again begg'd Pardon and Forgiveness of *God*, whom he had so very grievously offended: And he thought it his Duty also to ask Pardon of the *Queen*, whose Land he had defil'd with Blood; and of the *Church of God*, which he had given so great a scandal to; of his *Lord*, that he had prov'd to him such an unhappy Servant: and of the whole *World*, for having set before them such an

19 Henry Harrison, *The Last Words of a Dying Penitent: Being an Exact Account of ... His Being Concerned in the Bloody Inhumane Murder of Dr. Clinch* (1692), p. 30; *The Life and Penitent Death of John Mawgridge ... Executed for the Murder of Captain Cope* (1708), p. 10; R[obert] Boreman, *A Mirrour of Mercy and Iudgement. Or, an Exact True Narrative of the Life and Death of Freeman Sonds Esquier* (1655), p. 30.

Instance of Sin as (considering all the heinous and aggravating Circumstances of it) was never seen before. But his hope is, That all Men, instead of imitating him in that his Crime, will abhor and detest it, and take such a Warning by his Fall, as carefully to avoid both his Sin and his Punishment. This he repeated at the Place of Execution, and desired me to give it from him, to the People.[20]

The fulsomeness of Dramatti's apology, and the ordinary's self-effacing willingness to act as his conduit, are no less remarkable than their ultimate audience: "the People," who, as another murderer observed, expected just such a confession "always at the time of any Mans Execution." In paying his respects to all the powers that be – God, the sovereign, the Church, his master, and, last but not least, the people – Dramatti exerts a certain power or authority of his own; there is a positive force in his holding himself up as a negative example, and, too, certain powerful political implications. In England, as elsewhere, crime was regarded as an act of lèse majesté, but more than this, more than merely a disturbing of the king's peace, it was an act of "war against all mankind," a violation of the social contract that preceded royal sovereignty. In apologizing to the people at large, in hoping they might get some "good" out the evil he had done and the bad end he'd come to, the criminal was, among other things, recognizing their part in the body politic. "If we . . . consider Mankind, as . . . naturally ally'd, and politically combin'd in Societies, for their mutual Defence," an assize sermon declares, "it is certain, that those who violate this Precept, endeavour to loose the strongest Bands of human Society, and, as much as in them lies, to weaken the Sinews of Government; and are the common Disturbers of the Good Order and Welfare of Both."[21] Dramatti, at the end, tries to undo some of the social damage he has done; serving the public now in the only way he can, he disinterestedly assents to his own death in the most dramatic way possible, for the good it may do others.

The importance of this gift to the public, of the criminal's dying "in charity with all Mankind," can easily be underestimated. "All Men are by Nature equal," an assizes preacher declared, "how wide soever the Distance may seem to be, which Birth and Fortune has made between [them] . . . they are still substantially all alike." In addressing himself to "all Men" – and not to some specific criminal subclass or to those, say, inclined to fly off the handle – Dramatti reminds his audience that anyone can fly off the handle and become a criminal. This was not only sobering in late seventeenth- and early eighteenth-century England, but potentially scandalous.

[20] Paul Lorrain, *The Confession of John Peter Dramatti, a Frenchman, Executed . . . for the Barbarous Murther of Frances His Wife* (1701), sing. sheet fol.
[21] Harrison, *Last Words*, p. 1; Locke, *An Essay Concerning the True Original, Extent and End of Civil Government*, chapter 2, para. 11; George Atwood, *The Rule of Doing as We Would Be Done Unto Stated and Recommended. A Sermon Preach'd at the Assizes Held at Taunton . . . Somerset . . . April 2d 1723* (1723), p. 22.

Because crime seemed all too clearly to confirm the worst suspicions about human nature, it carried with it a certain embarrassment for those who (shall we call them "liberals"?) wanted to take a more hopeful view of themselves and their fellow beings. For if the generality of men were indeed inherently and, in effect, often inexplicably wicked, the only politics possible were those of Calvin or Hobbes; men would need some divinely inspired or sanctioned authority to keep their vicious, anarchic impulses in check (and if not the rule of the saints, then perhaps Stuart absolutism). Hobbes, particularly, was the great *bête noire* of the age, a "fanciful" modern whose "absurd Scheme" was to "represent the World as no better than a wide Wilderness; and all Mankind, like Beasts of Prey, devouring one another in it." The truth (according to this same writer) was instead that the golden rule – "so necessary ... for the upholding Society" – was "originally *written by the Finger of God* upon the *Hearts* of Men." Conscience itself stirred them to feel "natural Obligations" toward each other.

Across the ocean, hearing such talk and ascribing it to "a Detestable Generation of men, who go under the Name of *Deists*," Cotton Mather didn't like it at all. In his outrage and disgust, he put *his* finger on exactly what it was all about. "These Dangerous Wretches pretend unto a kind of *Moral Vertue*," bad enough given his Calvinism, but, still worse, this so-called virtue amounted to nothing more than mere "civility." "All the *Bonds of a Good Behaviour*, that these Baptised Infidels are sensible of," he writes with scathing sarcasm and no small sense of what is at stake, "is this; A man expects the *Civilities* of his Neighbours; his Condition would be insupportable should his Neighbours count him unworthy of their *Civilities*. Now, that a man may not Lose the *Civilities* of others, he must then treat them with *Civilities*." Given the monstrosity of human nature, he cannot understand how anyone could believe "this is all, that keeps [them] from Stealing, and Lying, and Murder."[22] Mather's faith in God spared him the necessity of having much faith in his fellow human beings.

If Hobbes or Calvin were right, sovereignty could never inhere in the ruled rather than the ruler; "civility" could never be the basis of a truly "civil" government. The importance of the dying man's speech at the gallows was that it could work for or against this bleak view of the polity. Dramatti's speech, on balance, probably did more to lift than dash the spirits of those he left behind. This is yet another reason why public execution in England – as it almost never did in France – could aim at exalting the criminal rather than debasing him. If he who had done the

---

[22] George Bell, *A Sermon Preach'd at the Cathedral Church of St. Peter in York ... at the Assizes* (York, 1722), p. 18; Atwood, Assize Sermon, pp. 21–22; Cotton Mather, *The Curbed Sinner. A Discourse upon the Gracious and Wondrous Restraints Laid by the Providence of ... God .... Occasioned by a Sentence of Death, Passed on a Poor Young Man, for the Murder of His Companion* (Boston, 1713), pp. 12–13.

worst of things could now act in the best imaginable manner, could rise to a heroic, disinterested goodness, why not others less morally compromised? Murderers who had turned on their closest relations, as Dramatti had, made for this reason the very best sort of penitent dying criminal. Providing the sharpest before-and-after contrasts, they made the strongest case that "Conscience" (to quote a Newgate ordinary) was the "Natural Magistrate in every Man's Heart," and so lifted hearts in general. The extraordinary, but nonetheless typical claims made for the good and hopeful effect of John Marketman's moral conversion is a case in point. Marketman was a brutal wife murderer, too, but

the behaviour of this poor Creature when he came to die, was so very exemplary, that it was surprising to most that came to see him, and begot an equal pity and astonishment in the numerous spectators, as well it might; to behold a Man who not a month before had given up himself to all manner of sins, those in particular which even human nature it self abhors, and which undermine the well being of it: I say to behold this Man carrying himself in such an humble and submissive manner, exerting such acts of Faith and Charity; giving such wholesom and good advice to all that were round about him, and that with all requisite earnestness and Zeal, declaring his utter detestation of every thing whereby God's Authority was any ways lessened or abused, was enough indeed to raise an admiration in the Breasts of all those who attended this Execution.[23]

Where Marketman's crime was surprising in the worst possible way, his behavior here surprises in the best. What is more, it surprises the spectators on their own account as well as his, for, just as he shows charity to them, they show a wonderful (i.e., admiring) pity toward him. "One must want humanity and be totally void of that tenderness which demonstrated both a man and a Christian," one of the more important criminal biographers writes some fifty years later, "if we feel not some pity for those who are brought to a violent and shameful death from a sudden and rash act." "The Cement that unites Mankind, the Bond that holds Communities together," a preacher at an assizes declared at about the same time, is "mutual Love and Kindness."[24] Here at Marketman's execution we have a display of that tenderness and pity which demonstrates one's humanity, of that mutual love and kindness which, one would like to think, is actually what holds the world together. It is not only the redeemed criminal's goodness at the end which shows these things, but – rallying point that he is for others' generosity of spirit – the goodness of those "round about him" as well. He makes them feel good, but so, too, does their response to him.

[23] Samuel Smith, Ordinary Account, 26 January 1690; *The Penitence of Marketman*, sigs. A1v-A2r.
[24] *Lives of the Most Remarkable Criminals Who Have Been Condemned and Executed for Murder, the Highway, Housebreaking, Street Robberies, Coining or Other Offences*, 1st pub. 1735 in 3 vols., ed. Arthur L. Hayward (New York, 1927), p. 209; Richard Newcome, *A Sermon Preach'd in the Cathedral Church of Winchester . . . at the Assizes Held There . . . March 13, 1727/28* (1728), p. 9.

All this would have carried readers a great distance away from the sordid, ugly, and, in some cases, loathesome facts of individual crimes to say nothing of their direst implications. Crime not only "made sense," it could make the best possible, the most morally and socially useful sense. By making accidental or unusual discoveries of especially horrific crimes seem providential, writers of criminal biography could show that God still intervened to punish the wicked in this world, as He also still helped them to grace – thus criminals' unaccountable changes of heart, which could show, too, that there was marvellous goodness to be found in even the worst of men. Nor – inasmuch as such accounts made it plain that nobody became wicked at once, that delinquency grew through a predictable series of stages over time – would the "good" people who read them have to worry too much about their own, notional, proclivities toward committing punishable crimes. Could they not in any case *feel* their own goodness, as they generously pitied the about-to-die but born-again convict? Such criminal biography "glossed" the real in more than one sense, giving it a high lustre as well as "meaning." A very different kind of romance was offered by the other kind of criminal biography.

If every hanging was, or might be made to seem, an experiment in human nature, it is important to note, too, that many experiments failed or gave ambiguous results. Few criminals exited the world in the best possible fashion, many fewer, indeed, than reporters of dying speeches and last behaviors cared to admit. Thieves often thought it "very hard" their lives should be taken merely for offences against property, and elements of the public apparently agreed. Such complaints were typically discountenanced by "serious" criminal biographers, on the grounds that hanging thieves was absolutely necessary to the maintenance of social order; criminals failing to realize this had yet to make a full moral recovery. But this was a desperate argument, a good deal of evidence suggests, and not at all easily sustained. Neither natural nor Mosaic law countenanced the death penalty for property offences, nor was it justified in any obvious way by its practical effect, given the seemingly high continuing incidence of crime. But even those content to argue for the hanging of thieves on practical grounds could feel, at times, that English law was notably cruel. "What a lamentable case it is to see so many Christian men and women strangled on that cursed tree of the gallows," Coke writes in the epilogue to the third of his *Institutes*, "insomuch as if in a large field a man might see together all the Christians, that but in one year, throughout England, come to that untimely and ignominious death, if there were any spark of grace, or charity in him, it would make his heart to bleed for pity and compassion." Proposing to make public executions more solemn and terrible, and so more effective deterrents to crime, Bernard Mandeville begins by speaking of "the Multitude of unhappy Wretches, that every Year are put to Death for Trifles in our great Metropolis." This state of affairs, he says without a trace of his infamous cynicism, "has long been afflicting to Men of Pity and Humanity; and continues to give great Uneasiness to every Person who has Value for his Kind."[25]

Both kinds of criminal biography, as I've argued elsewhere, owed a good deal of their specific concerns to the "uneasiness" Mandeville describes; where the one sought to allay this uneasiness, or to transform the feeling behind it into something sublime, the other made it more or less impossible to feel. If thieves, like murderers, could be made to seem happy to be dying for their crimes, grateful, even, for the opportunity they were now given to do some positive service for their fellow men, and certain – as certain as any sinner could be – that they were bound for a better place, why, then, should men of pity and humanity find anything at all afflicting in their executions? Readers and writers of criminal biography could nonetheless, it seems to me, still find the hanging of thieves bothersome, or at least embarrassing, however "well" they died. Thus there was a curious tendency over time to "forget" or suppress the moral and religious lessons that might be drawn from thieves' cases and to deemphasize what they had come to at last. Many thieves' biographies were in fact rewritten, constructed along entirely new lines, the information provided in previous, "serious" accounts discarded to make room for adventures, pranks, tricks, and jokes. Most of these are amusing, often at the expense of the criminals as well as their victims, but some seem quite horrific. Murderers' biographies almost never get rewritten in this manner. Rather than making thieves' lives into a kind of (Christian, to be sure) tragedy, this other form – which I call criminal rogue biography – presents at most a kind of "Tragi-Comedy." Generally, though, it hardly rises above farce, burlesque, or Grand Guignol. Its primary aim, it seems to me, was not to evoke serious, sustained consideration of criminals, their crimes, or their punishments, indeed rather to prevent it. Such biographies empty their subjects out, deleting from them most or all of the qualities that serious criminal biography emphasizes in its efforts to reconcile them with God, to reintegrate them into the social, to reattach them to their fellow beings. In the "several characters" of those he writes about, says the most notable of Defoe's contemporaries to practice criminal rogue biography, "the reader will find the most unaccountable relations of irregular actions as ever were heard." Or, as another practitioner of the genre emphatically declares, a

---

25 Henry Fielding, *The Journal of a Voyage to Lisbon* in *Jonathan Wild and The Journal of a Voyage to Lisbon*, ed. A. R. Humphreys (Everyman, 1964), p. 195; Sir Edward Coke, *The Third Part of the Institutes of the Laws of England: Concerning High Treason, and Other Pleas of the Crown, and Criminall Causes* (1644), sig. Kk1r; Bernard Mandeville, *An Enquiry into the Causes of the Frequent Executions at Tyburn; and a Proposal for Some Regulations Concerning Felons in Prison, and the Good Effects to Be Expected from Them* (1725), p. 36.

famous thief of the seventeenth century was "remarkable" because she "was like no body, nor could not be *Sorted* by any *Comparison*."[26]

The "irregular actions" or, as they could also be called, "uncommon Adventures" of highwaymen, housebreakers, shoplifters, pickpockets, and other thieves may well have given a certain attractive license to readers' imaginations. From the first, criminal rogue biography offered readers trips to "Nonesuch," i.e., to a fantasy world where normal social and political relations were turned upside down or otherwise put into a happy disarray. In such a world, freedom, power, and glory might be had simply for the taking. "Jack," one famous highwayman says to a recruit, "if thou wilt live with me thou shalt have money at comand or any thing thou wantest." Or as another, equally famous robber reflects, the highwayman's "way" was "the best that ever he could have fallen into; yea better than an Estate in Land ... For now, if he wants Money, 'tis but taking his Horse and riding out." Indeed "any brisk young Fellow might easily make his Fortune," it could seem, "and live like a Gentleman, by going upon the Highway." All one needed was the requisite courage. "He did what all that saw him fear'd to do," says an epitaph proposed for a notorious burglar, and there was little room to doubt this claim in a world where everyone, it seemed, naturally sought his own advantage. In his own way the thief did what all men would do, could they free themselves from social constraint. "Till there were instituted great Common-wealths," observed Hobbes, "it was thought no dishonour to be a Pyrate, or a High-way Theefe; but rather a lawful Trade." Nor was there all that much difference between trade and crime in the present age either, according to some. "Trade is almost universally founded upon Crime," Defoe could say nearly as a matter of course, and he felt obliged, in the midst of celebrating the "compleat" English tradesman, to admit "some difference between an *honest man* and an *honest Tradesman*." All sorts of common commercial practices – e.g., concealing defects in goods, using false weights and measures, wearing sellers down so they felt forced to sell, holding back wages after they were due, to say nothing of usury and engrossing – all these were seen as violations of the commandment "Thou shalt not steal."[27] Theft from this standpoint might seem the pursuit of economic

26 [Defoe], *Street-Robberies, Consider'd: The Reason of Their Being So Frequent, with Probable Means to Prevent'em . . . . Written by a Converted Thief (1728)*, p. 70: Alexander Smith, *A Complete History of the Lives and Robberies of the Most Notorious Highwaymen, Footpads, Shoplifts, & and Cheats of Both Sexes*, 5th edn in 3 vols. pub. 1719, ed. Arthur L. Hayward (London, 1933), p. 1; *Life and Death of Frith*, sigs. A3v-A4r.

27 Appendix to James Guthrie, Ordinary Account, 13 January 1742; *No Jest like a True Jest: Being a Compendious Record of the Merry Life, and Mad Exploits of Capt. James Hind, the Great Rober of England*, 1st pub. 1657, (London, 1817), n.p.; ibid.; *The Life of Deval* (1669[/70]), p. 4.; *Select Trials, for Murders, Robberies, Rapes, Sodomy, Coining, Frauds, and Other Offences. At the Sessions-House in the Old-Bailey*, 2nd edn (1742), 1: 300; *The Triumph of Truth: In an Exact and Impartial Relation of the Life and Conversation of Col. Iames Turner* (1664), p. 31; Hobbes, *Leviathan*, ed. C. B.

individualism by other, easier, often more stylish, and frequently more amusing means.

Given this possible affinity between so-called honest men and thieves, it is hardly surprising that some of those who figure in this other form of criminal biography could also rise to a kind of nobility; here, though, the phenomenon is harder to interpret. The most notable highwaymen rob with gallantry and panache and sometimes are shown doing a certain rough justice to various kinds of social parasites. More than eighty years after he was executed one still "much talk'd of" highwayman was remembered for "his Pleasantry in all his Adventures; for he never in his Life robb'd a Man, but at the same Time he either said or did something that was diverting." In his own time this same highwayman famously claimed never to have robbed honest men but only "the Caterpillars of the Times, viz. *Long-gown men, Committee-men, Excize-men, Sequestrators*, and other *Sacrilegious persons.*" His successors singled out landlords, lawyers, clergymen, politicians, less than scrupulous businessmen, and Whigs of all kinds. Such behavior may have helped to "legitimate" readers' fantasies of power and revenge, but the criminals in question seem to have been more than mere stalking horses for vicariously experienced extremes of economic and social individualism. Thus, for all their seeming embodiment of such an ethos, they can, at the same time, attack it. "I follow the general way of the world, sir," a highwayman explains to one of his victims, a world, he regrets, "which now prefers money before friends or honesty."[28]

The political tendency of certain highwaymen is also difficult to explain in terms of readers' vicarious involvement. Many of the most famous flaunt Royalist, Jacobite, or Tory sympathies, and they display, concomitantly, a marked disposition to prey on Republicans, Williamites, Whigs, and Hanoverians (depending on who, at the time, is in power). In Defoe's

Macpherson (Penguin, 1968), pp. 156–7; Defoe, *CET*, 2 (pt. 2): 108, 1: 226; e.g., Gabriel Towerson, *An Exposition of the Catechism of the Church of England, Part II. Containing an Explication of the Decalogue or Ten Commandments* (1681), pp. 416–20. The term "Nonesuch" comes from G[eorge] F[idge], *Hind's Ramble, or, the Description of His Manner and Course of Life* (1651), which says of its highwayman hero, arguably the first of his type, that "He may be likened to a place called, *Nonesuch* ... for all the Histories in the World cannot afford the like president" (pp. [5–6]).

28 Capt. Charles Johnson, *A General History of the Lives and Adventures of the Most Famous Highwaymen, Murderers, Street-Robbers, &c. To Which Is Added, a Genuine Account of the Voyages and Plunders of the Most Notorious Pyrates* (1734), p. 86; *We Have Brought Our Hogs to a Fair Market: Or, Strange Newes from New-Gate; Being a Most Pleasant and Historical Narrative of Captain James Hind* (1651[/2]), p. 1 (cf. *Life and Death of Frith*, p. 150, where Mary is made to say that she helped plan Hind's attacks on "Committee-Men and Parliament People," "both of us concurring to be revenged ... by those private assaults, since publique combating of them would not prevaile"); Smith, *Lives of the Highwaymen*, p. 452. See also *The Speech and Deportment of Col. Iames Turner at His Execution ... January 21. 1663* (1663), p. 7, the protagonist of which harks back nostalgically to a world of "Hospitality, loving friendship, peace and quietnesse," now utterly displaced by a "new world, a world of malice and indifference" where "all people are in Combustion, none tied in love and unity."

day these last three groups, at least, were associated with the rise of a new, moneyed, increasingly commercial and increasingly corrupted society. It ought to seem quite curious that thieves like these should be made, despite their marked individualism, to seem such explicit and open enemies of the prevailing social and political order, and that they should hark back to the more hierarchical and authoritarian regime of one or another Stuart. Some of this, to be sure, was stimulated by fact. A few highwaymen did actually parade Royalist or Jacobite sympathies, hoping perhaps to seem "political" criminals and not mere common thieves. The presentation of such sentiments in criminal biographies, however, would have owed less to actual fact than the disposition of certain writers and presumably their readers at a time when, as one historian has put it, "political life in England ... had something of the sick quality of a 'banana republic.'" In being made to attack Republicanism and Whiggery, such criminals contributed their part to an ongoing critique of the new regime brought in by William and sustained by the Hanoverians. Or else, and this seems equally plausible to me, they parodied and so diminished the impact of such discourse, thus gratifying those who might well have felt vulnerable to more cogent, focussed criticisms of the social and political order. Probably they performed both functions, being, as I've argued, symbols with multiple and contestable meanings.[29]

The complicated and even contradictory significance of the sympathetic or noble robber is not a topic that can detain us here, nor are the nearly as rich and complicated implications of theft as a symbol or metaphor for commercial activity in early eighteenth-century England. What I do want to emphasize is that most of the subjects of criminal rogue biography were not presented in so interesting or attractive a light as were certain of the leading highwaymen, and that even the most attractive (or at least entertaining) of these could drop into grotesque buffoonery or awesomely casual cruelty. Though this, too, may have offered readers vicarious pleasure, I would see in such declensions, and in the general unattractiveness of criminal rogues, something more specifically historical. For whatever criminal rogue biography may have done to stimulate

---

[29] E. P. Thompson, *Whigs and Hunters: The Origins of the Black Act* (London, 1975), p. 197; on the political implications of criminals' attacks on Republicans and Whigs, see *Turned to Account*, pp. 120–3, 177–8, 186–8, 209–11, and the accompanying notes. At their simplest, these attacks would have been an expression of what Michael McKeon's *Origins of the English Novel* terms a "conservative" reaction against "progressive" ideology (which itself was opposed to "aristocratic" ideology) or, to use Isaac Kramnick's famous term, part of "the politics of nostalgia" (see *Bolingbroke and His Circle: The Politics of Nostalgia in the Age of Walpole* [Cambridge, Mass., 1968]). Much of this "conservatism" or "nostalgia" would have been stimulated by what J. G. A. Pocock calls "a basically hostile perception of early modern capitalism" (*The Machiavellian Moment: Florentine Political Thought and the Atlantic Republican Tradition* [Princeton, 1975], p. ix, and especially chapter 14, "The Eighteenth-Century Debate: Virtue, Passion, and Commerce," pp. 462–505).

readers' imaginations in certain respects, in others it did a great deal to limit or close them down. By emphasizing the "irregular" and "unaccountable" qualities of the thieves it portrayed, by asserting they were "like no body" and exiling them to "Nonesuch," criminal rogue biography would have done a great deal to counter or displace the general assumption, basic to the culture, that criminals were indeed our semblables, our *frères*; it did this by "anticknesse" of form as well as content. "It is no great matter how I place my words and matter," Mary Frith explains at yet another disjunctive point in her story, "since there was nothing serious in the whole course of my life." Transformed into highly improbable heroes or, more often, into fools or monsters, the men and occasional women who had been put to death for arguable reasons and a dubitable purpose were made into objects hardly worth thinking about. "What has been said," it is claimed at the end of one rogue's life, "is not intended to blacken his Memory, or deprive him of the Pity which naturally arises in every Man's Mind, on those who fall Victims to Justice and Law." Such an assurance (or is it a denial?) gives away the game. The "Rumors without Foundation," the "formal Stories" that get foisted on criminals in this kind of criminal biography, seem indeed to have aimed at preventing "Compassion," as a doomed highwayman is reported to have complained. He thought such efforts "to blacken one already overthrown" came either from a "Cruelty of Disposition, or a Barbarous Levity of Mind."[30]

One cannot say for sure this highwayman was wrong, but the "levity" he complains of may have actually owed less to "barbarousness" than to its opposite. That is, the often derisive and even "sick" humor of this kind of criminal biography may have worked to mask, and so defend against, the "uneasiness" Mandeville mentions. Behind its all too apparent cruelty and inhumanity there may have been a certain embarrassment or disturbance of mind – just as there often is (or so one would like to hope) behind the nervous, guilty giggles evoked by obscene jokes. But whatever the case, the "re-presentation" of the criminal as an insouciant, irregular, and unaccountable rogue would certainly have served to establish an emotional or at least affective distance between him and the reading public; this was recognized at the time. If Jack Sheppard "had been as wretched, and as silly a Rogue in the World as upon the Stage," said a review of a play purporting to represent his escapes from Newgate, "the lower Gentry, who attended him to Tyburn, wou'd never have pittied him when he was hang'd."[31]

[30] *Life and Death of Frith*, p. 116; appendix to Guthrie, Ordinary Account, 13 January 1742; the highwayman is William Gordon, quoted in *Select Trials* (1742), 4: 61–2.
[31] Mist's *Weekly Journal; or Saturday's Post*, 5 December 1724.

Though my synoptic account of the main concerns and leading strategies
of criminal biography has necessarily omitted a great deal in the way of
evidence, nuance, and further argument, two main points should by now
be clear. First, criminals were powerfully important cultural symbols at
the time Defoe wrote, and of great interest to the reading public; they were
a "hot" topic. Second, in attempting to deal with the problematics of
crime and punishment, each form of criminal biography emphasized
themes peculiar to itself and followed a specific set of protocols; each had,
as it were, a specific agenda. In writing his criminal fictions, Defoe could
thus count on having not only an audience but one with certain known
tastes and expectations. Picking up his novels, they would have expected
one or another set of topics, organized (or disorganized) into one or
another "plot," colored by one or another tonality or point of view. That
is, to use Moll's turn of phrase, they would have known "what ought, or
ought not to be" in one or the other kind of criminal biography. Seeking to
communicate a sense of the "what was" or "is" as opposed to any "ought
to be," Defoe was thus provided not only with highly specific sets of
conventions to play with and against but with highly defined genre
expectations as well. The general value of these expectations to Defoe as a
writer – the general value of *any* such expectations to *any* writer – should be
obvious enough. What requires to be emphasized, however, is the particularly rich set of opportunities criminal biography would have provided
Defoe, given its strong encouragement to particularly complex habits of
reading.

Shaping and patterning, or alternatively disordering and distorting the
real, endowing it with certain meanings and depriving it of others,
criminal biography was very much in its own right a kind of fiction. This
was the source of its power, for unless it manipulated the facts of cases –
enlarging some, suppressing others, often simply inventing what was
needed – it could not achieve its ends. But this also made it highly
vulnerable to a variety of criticisms. Defoe certainly disliked it for its
fictitiousness, which is to say for what he took to be its unwholesome
distortion of the truth of crime and criminals. Where the one kind of
criminal biography turned "Vagrants" and "ungodly Knaves" into
"Saints," the other made "a Jest of [their] Story" and showed them "in
such an amiable Light, that vulgar Minds are dazzled with it." What was
"a Tragedy of itself" ought not to be presented in "a stile of Mockery and
Redicule" but "in a Method agreeable to the Fact." Criminals were to be
taken seriously, but even the soberest-seeming criminal biography did not
take them seriously enough. By shipping "Loads of *Saints* to Heaven" the
Newgate ordinary and writers like him not only compromised "the
Churches Dignity" but trivialized the whole matter of repentance and
salvation. If the executioner's ladder was "the *Shortest Way*" to "Ascend

the Skys," it could well be asked, "what need we mortifie and pray"?[32] For all its apparent, reiterated concern with morality, criminal biography even at its most serious set a bad moral example. It was, moreover, of dubious authenticity. Defoe advances this point in *Moll Flanders*, where the Newgate ordinary is a drunk who "extort[s] Confessions from Prisoners, for private Ends, or for the farther detecting of other Offenders." "All his Divinity run upon Confessing my Crime," Moll complains, "making a full Discovery, and the like without which he told me God would never forgive me." Not the sort to move prisoners to "such freedom of Discourse" as might either disburden their minds or profitably inform the public, he doesn't even know why she is in prison, nor does he ask. Moll gets "no manner of Consolation from him" and neither, presumably, should any of the readers of his *Accounts* (*MF*, 277–8, 288).

Defoe's criticisms are not at all unique. Almost from its inception, in fact, criminal biography could seem – far more than almost any other popular narrative form – an especially fragile and suspect discourse. Thus the signatories of one of the earliest full-scale treatments of a properly penitent murderer were worried that their text might make readers "apt to encourage themselves in sin," repentance for even the worst of sins seeming easy and glorious; and this was a concern to be regularly voiced over the next hundred years. Nor is Defoe's attack on the Newgate ordinary at all unusual, the man and his office having been something of a joke for more than two decades by the time *Moll Flanders* appeared. Scorn for the chaplain's office was so widespread, in fact, that at the death of the incumbent in 1719 a correspondent wrote to one of the weekly papers to complain of the tone it and others had taken. "For God's Sake," he asked, "wherein lies the Infamy of assisting some of the unhappiest Men in the World in their Passage to Eternity, and endeavouring to save their Souls?" The infamy, he might have been answered, was not in the enterprise but its execution. The mere fact the Newgate ordinary's name was "set" to an account of a criminal's life, declared one inmate of the prison, was "sufficient reasons for the World to suspect the Truth of it."[33]

Suspicions did not stop with the ordinary. There was reason to doubt the accuracy, sincerity, and provenance of much of the writing that, taking criminals seriously, focussed on the state of their souls. The

---

[32] The phrasings come from *A Hymn to the Funeral Sermon* (1703), n.p.; *Street-Robberies, Consider'd*, pp. 48–9; *Augusta Triumphans: Or the Way to Make London the Most Flourishing City in the Universe* (1728), pp. 47–8; and H. D., *The Life of Jonathan Wild, from His Birth to His Death* (1725), p. [4]. It ought to be noted, however, that the attributions of the first and last of these texts to Defoe rest on unargued assumptions (see P. N. Furbank and W. R. Owens, *The Canonisation of Daniel Defoe* [New Haven, 1988], pp. 38–9, 78–82, 184–7).

[33] *A Serious Advice to the Citizens of London . . . . Upon Occasion of the Horrid Murder and Dreadful Death of Nathaniel Butler* (1657), p. [8]; Mist's *Weekly Journal*, 14 November 1719; Charles Newey, *Captain Charles Newy's Case Impartially Laid Open* (1700), p. 14.

Newgate ordinaries themselves were not above (or below) criticizing their rivals and fellow practitioners. Warning against "false Accounts" of "the Confession and Dying Speeches of Malefactors at Tyburn," one Newgate ordinary declared that "Some Criminals who have Dyed *Penitentiary's*, have several times been Mis-represented to have been hardened in a State of Sinning, of whose Happiness after their Death, the *Ordinary* hath had (in Charity) a fairer Prospect." Still "other Dying Criminals," he went on, "have been affirmed to be very Penitent, who have been insensible of the particular Crimes for which they Suffer'd, and in a manner persisted in the Denyal of the Perpetuation of them. So that it was very difficult for any to Judge Positively, as some Pamphleteers did, of the truth of their Repentance." Another ordinary published similar statements at least nine times in the space of six years, complaining that the "several Sham-papers some Persons have lately assumed the liberty of putting out ... are so far defective and unjust, as sometimes to mistake even the Names and Crimes of those [who were executed]." Such complaints, such warnings, given the highly suspect status of the ordinary's own discourse, could only have served to undermine the public's trust in *any* writer of criminal biography. The more strenuously they assured their readers that "here is no Fiction, as is commonly used in Pamphlets of this Nature," the more they claimed that all other accounts were "spurious," "false," "scandalous," and "fictitious," the more they would have aroused doubts about the authenticity and authority of the genre as a whole.[34]

The strength and prevalence of such suspicions is more than amply indicated by the measures taken to allay them. It was not uncommon, for instance, for readers to be assured they might visit the publisher's office to consult the original documents on which specific accounts were based, along with various depositions attesting to their authenticity. Some of these papers, of course, would have been written in the criminal's own, now dead hand. "I Thomas Billings," declared one condemned murderer in a newspaper advertisement, "do hereby inform the World, that what Confession or Account I shall leave of myself, and of my Conduct and Behaviour, I shall only leave to be Publish'd by Mr. John Applebee in Black Fryers, as witness my Hand this 29th Day of April, 1726." The "Original" of this document was to be "seen at Mr. Applebee's," the criminal's signature to it having been witnessed by his victim's brother. Another criminal strove to validate his purported autobiography by warning readers "not to give credit to what [the ordinary] shall publish concerning me, if it shall be in contradiction to what I have here related,"

---

[34] Samuel Smith, Ordinary Account, 23 May 1684; Lorrain, ibid., 13–14 October 1703 for the one passage quoted; *The Life and Infamous Actions of That Perjur'd Villain John Waller, Who Made His Exit in the Pillory, at the Seven-Dials ... the 13th ... of ... June* (1732), p. [3]; the adjectives have been gathered out of announcements in Applebee's *Original Weekly Journal*, 13 May and 22 July 1721.

because "notwithstanding all his Importunities to be apprized of my most intimate Secrets, I always industriously avoided entring upon Particulars." But this account itself was thought to be of dubious provenance, indeed wholly "fictitious" except for "a few Hints borrowed from the Sessions-Paper and" – ironically, for all it says to the contrary – "the *Ordinary*'s Account." There could be counterclaims, too; thus Dean Bryant disavowed a "Declaration" printed in the *Daily Advertiser* over his name, saying "it is possible I might set my Hand to a Paper, not knowing the Contents thereof, I being at that time in a *High Fever*, and consequently might be *light-headed*." Those who urged him to sign it, he adds, "were not my Friends," and "that Paper . . . is an Imposition on the Publick." All this is attached to the ordinary's account of Bryant, and meant to authenticate – or rather, *re*authenticate – that writer's version of the dying criminal against any possible competitors.[35] But amidst such claims and counterclaims, who could know which writer, which text, was actually telling the truth?

Some writers sought to enhance the authority of their texts by making claims for authenticity on internal grounds. Thus the "abrupt breakings off" in one malefactor's dying speech, "and other expressions not so smooth as might have been," were offered as proofs that these were the "very words that the Gentleman delivered then." "I . . . have tyed my self to his own Expressions," this writer insisted, "that I may neither abuse the World, or the dying man, or my self." An interesting variation on this theme is found in the printer's advertisement to the life of a murderer. That "no great Art is shown [in the] drawing up this short History," it says, indicates that "we are much more solicitous about Truth than Language." The author of the text that follows was chosen not for his literary skills, but because he was "that Person" best "acquainted with . . . Mr. *Stanley*'s Life." Internal evidence could also suggest that a particular text was not to be trusted. The Bishop of Oxford judged that a letter he got from two convicted murderers retracting their confessions was written not by them but by some third person, and concluded, once he saw "their pretended Dying-Speeches," that these, too, had been written by someone else. One of his collaborators undertakes a detailed analysis of these same speeches to prove the point. The fact was that a text's coherence, or relative incoherence, could be read either way. "I have not had time to digest [my confession] into Method, because Time is precious with me now," a condemned murderer purportedly wrote, begging "the Reader to make no Nice Construction of my words, but to take the real honest meaning." The author of an account of another murderer, however,

---

[35] Applebee's *Journal*, 7 May 1726; James Carrick, *A Compleat and True Account of All the Robberies Committed by James Carrick, John Malhoni, and Their Accomplices* (1722), pp. 24, 1; *Select Trials* (1742), 1: 215; Guthrie, Ordinary Account, 20 and 22 December 1738.

invites readers to compare his "authentick" account against the "several Fictitious Trials, or rather incoherent Accounts" emanating from other, less authoritative sources.[36]

Given the problematics of such comments and claims, readers of course could hardly have avoided making "nice constructions." They were bound to sift and second guess, even if, indeed, they were willing to take the good faith of the texts they read for granted. For quite apart from the intentions of the writers of criminal biography, or the fidelity of their accounts to the manifest facts of any particular case, the criminal's dying behavior itself could be suspicionable. "I have observed many dolorous complaints of Criminals against themselves to vanish away," one Newgate ordinary wrote, "upon slender Hopes of a Reprieve." Criminals, he pointed out, could be mistaken about their true state of mind, believing that "a slight sorrow for Sin" was actually "a thorow Conversion." A writer might give the actual details of a dying behavior accurately enough, but one might doubt the interpretation he gave it. Thus an account of a parricide describes him showing "Signs of the greatest Horror" as he was led through the large crowd that had come to see him hanged, "as [if] being ashamed, after such an Action to be seen by so many who had been his Neighbours and particular Acquaintance." But the man may just have been afraid of dying, for indeed "he expressed the utmost Reluctance at parting with Life, driving off the fatal Minute, and desiring the Officers and Executioner to defer it as long as possible." Even more powerful doubts could be raised when convicted criminals went to execution protesting their innocence. A murderer hanged in 1692 presented such a case, showing "great Devotion and Penitence, after his *Condemnation*," but also making "repeated Protestations of his Innocence, to the last Moment of his Life." He thus managed "to startle and stagger a great many tender Ears; it being a little hard to conceive, that any Dying Man, especially with his professions of Piety, could look Eternity in the Face, with so many repeated Asseverations, to the Pledging of his Salvation upon the Truth of his Innocence, if really Guilty." Such cases have nonetheless occurred, this writer points out, and he goes on to cite some.[37]

Other writers, enmeshed in and seeking to sort out similar circumstances, tried to suggest criteria by which disturbing claims to innocence might be judged. "The Words of dying Men are of weight, when all their Actions before have been of a piece," insisted one such writer, and he sought to explain the phenomenon of criminals denying their obvious guilt

---

[36] John Hinde, *A True Copy of Sir Henry Hide's Speech on the Scaffold, Immediately before His Execution .... Taken in Short-Hand from His Mouth* (1650), p. 3; *The Life of Mr. John Stanley* (1723), p. v; [William Talbot], *The Truth of the Case*, pp. 50–2; Harrison, *Last Words*, p. 1; *The Genuine Trial of Charles Drew, for the Murder of His Own Father*, 2nd edn (1740), p. 3.

[37] Samuel Smith, Ordinary Account, 28 February 1694; *Trial of Drew*, pp. 3, 40; Robert Rowe, *Mr. Harrison Proved the Murtherer ... of Dr. Andrew Clench* (1692), pp. [i-ii].

by theorizing about their state of mind. "Condemn'd Men may hope to obtain a Pardon," he thought, "by denying a Guilt too black to be forgiven by Men, when own'd, and after denying it so long, may be asham'd to own it at last." Though such suggestions were plausible and even flattering, perhaps, to the increasingly favored notion that all human beings have some inherent sense of morality, the idea that one could somehow see into the minds of criminals – or indeed into anyone's mind – was a highly debatable proposition. Criminals could not be judged on the basis of "humane appearance," one writer insisted, "the heart God only can judge." In doubtful cases, said another, elaborating the point, "He only can judge who is acquainted with the secrets of all hearts"; we "who are confined to appearances and the exterior marks of things" are easily deceived, "His penetration [being] utterly unknown to us." Still, said a third writer concerned (sometimes) with penetrating the minds of criminals, this was no reason to abandon the attempt, for "tho' we cannot impartially Guess at other Men's Thoughts, their Actions [do] frequently discover their Intentions and Imaginations." One could know something if not everything of criminals' thoughts, intentions, and imaginations, but, then, too, one might be teased by the prospect – and the practical impossibility – of knowing still more. As one writer had to say about a more than usually problematic thief, "there are questionless some Concealments and Depths, which will never be fathomed here by any Life or Research, unless Providence by its All-seeing Eye shall unfold the Mystery." Despite all this – or perhaps rather because of it – the impossibility of knowing for sure what went on in criminals' minds was no bar to eager writers. Thus one author of a highwayman's life was moved to offer his version of things not only because the "Accounts publish'd by such People themselves, or their profess'd Friends" were "partial in the Relations of Facts" but, too, because they were "defective in that Part of the Narrative, in which the Publick is chiefly interested, *viz.* the secret Springs and Motives of Actions."[38]

Doubts about the tendency, sincerity, veracity, or even mere adequacy of criminal biography – even at its most serious – suggest that the "supplement" it sought to provide the facts of actual cases often seemed a fragile and precarious thing. Defoe may have wanted to achieve better, solider, more truly serious effects in his fiction. If so, it would seem, too, that he had a fairly sophisticated audience waiting for him – one which, for a variety of reasons, would have read anything purporting to be a criminal's life story with no small degree of critical attention. The great

---

[38] *The Truth of the Case*, pp. 51–2; Rowe, ibid.; *Lives of the Most Remarkable Criminals*, pp. 33–4; Johnson, *Lives of the Highwaymen*, p. 193; *The Life and Death of James Commonly Called Collonel Turner* (1663[/4]), p. [iii].; *A Complete History of James Maclean, the Gentleman Highwayman* (1750), p. 4.

social importance that attached to the true states of criminals' hearts would have made for readers disposed to ponder what they were reading, that is, for "nice" or what we'd call "close" reading. One might never know for sure what went on in a criminal's mind, if he or those about him were telling the truth, but one might guess by paying careful attention to the text. "The less ornament there is in a dying persons discourse," it was suggested, "the less it will be suspected of hypocrisy .... the words ... are not chosen, but flow naturally." Though "we meet [very seldom] with an Accomplice in such Rogueries willing to give a true Account," another writer asserted, "in the following Sheets ... the Reader ... will certainly find a genuine Relation of *Facts* only: and we are the more Confident therein, because the Evidence, from whose Mouth it was taken, throughout the whole Narrative never varied, but related it with such an air of Veracity! with such Perspicuity! and in such Chronological Order, that Fiction could never support."[39]

Still it would not do to be too credulous, too sure of one's ability to judge what was plausible and so possibly or likely true. The close examination of criminals' confessions was no more certain a path to sure knowledge than the close examination of their actions. Thus, after giving a highly circumstantial and seemingly likely account of a sailor's recruitment into a pirate crew, taken from the man's own pocket journal, the writer of his life warns that "it is very probable this Journal might be a Contrivance, to confront the Evidence against him if ever he should be taken." Readers accustomed to such appeals and such warnings – "let the Reader judge" was no uncommon injunction in criminal biography – would have come to Defoe's novels prepared to raise a variety of questions, to make all sorts of "nice" inferences and "constructions."[40] Readers would even have been ready at times to practice a kind of textual criticism, or so certain writers expected. Thus the Newgate ordinary at one point hopes to "satisfy the Reasonable Reader" by getting him to distinguish his own work from "the various (and often contradictory) Reports made of [the condem'd Malefactors] by others," and on another occasion "the Reader" of an anthology of criminals' lives is invited to "observe the Variation" between similar exploits attributed to two different criminals "by comparing them together." "There are several facts which have happened in the world, the

[39] Gilbert Burnet and Anthony Horneck, *The Last Confession, Prayers and Meditations of Lieuten. John Stern* (1682), p. 12; Guthrie, Ordinary Account, 5 October 1744.

[40] Johnson, *Lives of the Highwaymen*, p. 303. For "judge," etc., see *The Truth of the Case*, p. 34 (also pp. 3, 12); for a sampling of comparable invitations or commands, see Lorrain, Ordinary Accounts, 7 February 1705, 28 April 1708, 24 June 1709; N. B., *Compleat Tryals ... for near 50 Years Past*, 1: [viii]; *The History of the Lives and Actions of Jonathan Wild, Thief-Taker. Joseph Blake alias Bleuskin, Foot-Pad. And John Sheppard, Housebreaker* (1725), pp. 61–2; Johnson, *Lives of the Highwaymen*, p. 193; *Select Trials* (1742), 1: 244, 4: 63; Select Trials (1764), 1: 4; and a certain Dr. Allen's *An Account of the Behaviour of Mr. James Maclaine, from ... His Condemnation to ... His Execution* (1750), p. 27.

circumstances attending which, if we compare them as they are related by one or other," yet a third eminent criminal biographer observes, "we can hardly fix in our own mind any certainty of belief concerning them, such equality is there in the weight of evidence of one side and of the other." Simpler appeals to the reader's capacity to sift texts could be made as well. Thus, though "the paper" Mary Hanson "left behind her" was "very agreeable to the nature of her case," readers were expected to see "it is penned in the manner not likely to come from the hands of a poor ignorant woman."[41] This is not quite the higher criticism or even much in the way of philology, but it does show that readers of criminal biography were by no means the passive, uncritical *naifs* some have claimed them to be.

Questions of accuracy and authenticity hardly if at all impinged on the second form of criminal biography. It was widely known to be fictive and, besides, no great questions hung on its truth or not. Still, in at least one way it, too, would have provided Defoe with a useful precedent. Its shocking leaps and jumps, its winking claims to be factual, were more than enough all by themselves to make readers wary of anything remotely resembling it. As the main alternative to serious criminal biography, it may, too, have made readers particularly wary of *any* narrative that diverged from the ordinary ways of writing seriously about criminals. Such accounts parcel their information out in a highly predictable fashion, which means their discourse is relatively easy to follow; narrators present themselves as little more than conduits for the facts, their moral commentary being much the same any sober-minded person might make. Writers portraying criminals as rogues of one or another kind stand in a much more complicated relation to the reader. Mocking and ironic, satirical but sometimes simply serious, they are altogether more "difficult." The relative looseness of their narrative form would also have put readers at a certain disadvantage. One could never quite tell where the story might go because, set "free" from the prescriptive plotting of serious criminal biography, it might at any moment take any one of several directions.

There would of course have been a certain heady pleasure in this, as one surprising turn built upon another, and especially too, perhaps, as nothing much was at risk. The form remained essentially familiar and, after all, was nothing to take seriously. Defoe, too, departs from the usual way of taking criminals seriously, but his novels nonetheless mean to be taken quite seriously. Venturing out of the strict and predictable confines of the one form of writing and reading about criminals, finding themselves in a looser, more highly textured and surprising form which, however, was not the other customary form, Defoe's audience would have been prepared for his leaps and jumps but not for his seriousness. That is to say, in preparing

---

[41] Lorrain, Ordinary Account, 31 January 1713; Johnson, *Lives of the Highwaymen*, p. 55; *Lives of the Most Remarkable Criminals*, p. 211; ibid., p. 220.

readers to be surprised as they read, this second form of criminal biography would have given Defoe an opportunity to pile surprise upon
surprise in an unforeseen and therefore highly "readable" mixture of
claims upon their attention, imagination, and sense of morality.

Fiction, among other things, creates a "space" inside our minds, a "field"
in which our imaginations are more or less free to "play," i.e., move within
certain limits. The idea is by no means so new as some might think. Sydney
spoke of "narration" providing "an imaginative ground-plot" for
"profitable invention," and a mid-seventeenth-century translation of a
picaresque novel recommended itself to readers as a "delightful Grove ...
a Meadow of Mirth, wherein ingenious Head-pieces may recreate themselves" while following its "ingenious Paths."[42] Defoe himself took up the
metaphor, proposing that the "various Turns" of *Colonel Jack* might serve
as "a delightful Field for the Reader to wander in; a Garden where" –
"recreation" understood almost literally, as therapy – "he may gather
wholesome and medicinal Plants, none noxious or poisonous" (*CJ*, 2).
The "fields" of Defoe's novels are complex and various, charged (to shift
the metaphor from horticulture to physics) with all sorts of subtle and
mysterious currents. But as "fields" they nonetheless stand within larger
and still larger "fields" – stretching toward but never quite reaching the
"unsurveyable" Jaussean "horizon" – and these "fields," too, have their
tensions and complications, whatever they may seem to lack in subtlety.
Because the energies that went into criminal biography were especially
powerful and its tensions and complications peculiarly rich, it provided
Defoe's novels with more than just a set of issues to take up and consider,
or a set of conventions to be manipulated, played with, or cleared away.
Defoe's novels are concerned, to be sure, with the consciousness and even
the psychology of criminals, with the operations of providence and the
uneasy, even vexing equation of trade with theft. But for all this they move
in their own ways to their own peculiar ends. They are not so much
extensions or rewritings of criminal biography as exploitations or culti-
vations of the discursive "field" it provided, "workings" of the possibilities
and needs it marked out and opened up.

   "As it is a very ordinary case for fiction to be imposed on the world for
truth," the compiler of one collection of criminal lives observes, "so it
sometimes happens that truth hath such extraordinary circumstances
attending it, as well nigh bring it to pass for fiction." This is no unhappy
circumstance for a novelist, especially as criminal biography produced a
readership ready to agree – particularly in the cases of anomalous crimi-

---

[42] Sir Phillip Sydney, *Defence of Poesy*, ed. Dorothy M. Macardle (London, 1963), p. 33; *The
   Rogue: Or, the Excellencie of History Displayed, in the Notorious Life of that Incomparable Thief, Guzman
   de Alfarache, the Witty Spaniard ... Epitomiz'd into English*, by A. S. Gent (1655), sig. [B6r].

nals – that "too much care cannot be taken to sift the truth, since appearances often deceive us and circumstances are sometimes strong where the evidence, if the whole affair were known, would be but weak."[43] Defoe's novels play upon this alert and complex disposition by differing from actual criminal biography in ways both obvious and highly subtle. They are longer, range widely outside the limits of mere criminal activity, and leave their protagonists unpunished; one protagonist, Roxana, may not even seem to have committed a hangable offense.[44] They allow their readers to treat them as fictions, rather than pretending to be literal renderings of the actual truth. Their meanings (or intentions) are to a large extent mysterious, as they tend neither to the simple, clear moralism of the one form of criminal biography, nor to the hectic but equally simple-minded "meaninglessness" of the other. Finally, because they have no actual preexisting referents, no connection to events already brought into and so "processed" and "fixed" by the operations of public discourse, they allow their readers a peculiarly private, highly idiosyncratic – i.e., "fresh" and "novel" – encounter with the stories they tell. All in all, Defoe's novels are more teasing, provoking, and capacious than actual criminal biography, and more taking and inviting. Encouraging strategies of reading far more complicated than anything required by their putative genre, they can put readers into highly complicated, highly self-conscious, highly abstracted "reading positions." They have the advantage, too – and it is this that will engage us first – of seeming more authentic.

[43] *Lives of the Most Remarkable Criminals*, pp. 525, 374.

[44] Bigamy was a felony, and so punishable by death, but no one so far as I know was actually hanged for it. Roxana's potential criminal liability is darker, more ambiguous, and far more dangerous. If, as it appears, Amy has murdered her daughter, and that crime were to come to light, Roxana would have a very hard time staying clear of suspicion and might easily be charged, along with her servant; more of this in chapter 3.

2

Defoe's realism: rough frames, strange voices, surprisingly various subjects and readers made more present to themselves

[In novels] the Author sits down and invents Characters that never were in Nature: He frames a long Story or Intrigue full of Events and Incidents, like the Turns in a Comedy; and if he can but surprise and delight you enough to lead you on to the End of his Book, he is not so unreasonable to expect you should believe it to be true.

?Defoe, *A Collection of Miscellany Letters Selected Out of Mist's Weekly Journal* (1722–7), 4: 124–5

The way I have taken ... is entirely new, and at first perhaps it may appear as something odd, and the method may be contemned; but let such blame their own more irregular tempers, that must have everything turned into new models; must be touched with novelty, and have their fancies humoured with the dress of a thing; so that if it be what has been said over and over a thousand times, yet if it has but a different coloured coat, or a new feather in its cap, it pleases and wins upon them.

The Family Instructor, 15: 2

The success the former part of this work has met with in the world ... is acknowledged to be due to the surprising variety of the subject and to the agreeable manner of the performance.

Preface to *Farther Adventures of Robinson Crusoe*, p. vii

The life of MOLL FLANDERS has been so notorious, that a Man can go into no Company, but they are talking of her: Some will have it that there never was any such Person in the World, and that it is all Fable and Romance; others affirm, that there was such a Woman, and won't stick to swear, that they knew her personally, and have convers'd with her: But be that as it will ...

"To the Reader," *Fortune's Fickle Distribution: In Three Parts. Containing First, The Life and Death of Moll Flanders ... Part II. The Life of Jane Hackabout, Her Governess ... Part III. The Life of James Mac-Faul, Moll Flanders's Lancashire Husband* (Dublin, 1730), sig. A3r

All the Exploits of this Lady of Fame, in her Depredations upon Mankind stand as so many warnings to honest People to beware of them .... all give us excellent Warnings in such Cases to be more present to Ourselves in sudden Surprizes of every Sort.

Preface to *Moll Flanders*, p. 4

Making readers conscious in various ways of the "prodigious pitch of wickedness, rapine and cruelty, human nature is capable of reaching unto, when people abandon themselves to a desire of living after their own wicked inclinations," criminal biography worked to shape their sense of what was socially and politically possible, and of how they themselves should act. Even the most frivolous writers in the genre fall frequently into moral exhortation. Though at such moments they often sound patently insincere and might easily be disregarded, the dirty and debasing ends of even the most attractive and sympathetic outlaws must have prompted readerly reflection on the "dreadful" cost of their "tinsel" and all too transient "splendour."[1]

In their different ways and to their different degrees, both kinds of criminal biography encouraged readers to measure their own characters, their own inclinations and ambitions, against the characters and histories of those whose life trajectories ended at the gallows. "You see in me what sin is," said an adulterer and infanticide with the rope around his neck, encouraging spectators (and readers) to look into their own hearts for anything similar lurking as dangerously there. That this particular criminal was a clergyman who lived honored and respected almost to the end made him all the more powerful a force to encourage introspection. Providing occasion for cruel and sneering comments on their self-fancying pretensions, showing how "vulgar" and "false notions of courage" lead to "ignominious death," countless dashing thieves served to give a somewhat different dimension to readers' self-consciousness. The message of their lives was clear. Even in situations of extremity one should "try every honest method ... rather than commit dishonest acts," the "ill-natured world" waiting ready to "charge all upon ... the poor wretch" who falls into "disgrace." "At most," such writers warned, the world "will spare [its] pity till it comes too late." This argument for circumspection – "prudence," as Fielding's Allworthy would call it – is particularly directed to "young persons, and especially those in a meaner state," who, it is presumed, "make up the bulk of my readers."[2]

In promoting a self-monitoring self-awareness both forms of criminal biography can be seen as contributing to "the civilizing process," as Norbert Elias grandly calls the development and spread of "civility," or – to use Foucault's more complicated, more somber characterization of the same shift away from "sovereign power" toward self-control and the internalization of social norms – "the government of individualization."

---

[1] Lives of the Most Remarkable Criminals Who Have Been Condemned and Executed for Murder, the Highway, Housebreaking, Street Robberies, Coining or Other Offences, 1st pub. 1735 in 3 vols., ed. Arthur L. Hayward (New York, 1927), pp. 128, 28.

[2] Charles Johnson, A General History of the Lives and Adventures of the Most Famous Highwaymen, Murderers, Street-Robbers, &c. To Which Is Added, a Genuine Account to the Voyages and Plunders of the Most Notorious Pyrates (1734), p. 317; Remarkable Criminals, p. 73; ibid., pp. 27–8.

Foucault finds ominous what Elias thought salutary, but the development of "the bourgeois superego" (as both might agree to call it) can be seen as neither one nor the other, only a practical social necessity.[3] In all societies, according to Anthony Giddens, "all (competent) actors ... are expected to 'keep in touch' with why they act as they do, as a routine element of action, such that they can 'account' for what they do when asked to do so by others." As "traditionally established practices" lost their "moral bindingness" in the "open," "fluid," "competitive," and "acquisitive" society that came with an increasingly urbanized, increasingly commercial England, such "reflexive monitoring" and "rationalization" of action gained particular importance. "Town life," as P. J. Corfield points out, "depends upon a degree of trust, that numerous daily contacts with complete strangers can be conducted with reasonable safety."[4]

How could such trust be sustained? Alluding to "reforms in the nature and administration of justice that were ultimately political in their implications," Corfield speaks of the "insistent self-scrutiny" of "mass, urban society." Apparently he means to refer to the various social institutions developed to monitor, control, and discipline behavior in the great towns and cities, but, before this happened – before, to quote Giddens again, there was "a massive expansion of the surveillance activities of the state and ... radical alterations in modes of handling crime and 'deviance'" – the cultural institution of criminal biography was doing all it could to make individual self-scrutiny seem – naturally and normally though at times a bit tardively – a sufficient basis for all the inhibitions that make society possible. "What is to hold the passions in check when the moral

[3] See Norbert Elias, *The History of Manners* and *Power and Civility*, vols. 1 and 2 of *The Civilizing Process*, tr. Edmund Jephcott (New York, 1978, 1982), the latter of which is especially relevant here, and, among Foucault's late work, *Discipline and Punish: The Birth of the Prison*, tr. Alan Sheridan (New York, 1977), *The History of Sexuality, Volume 1: An Introduction*, tr. Robert Hurley (New York, 1978), and "Afterword: The Subject and Power," in Hubert L. Dreyfus and Paul Rabinow, *Michel Foucault: Beyond Structuralism and Hermeneutics* (Chicago, 1982). The "government of individualization" is a phrase appearing in the last of these texts. It describes, much as does Foucault's concept of "biopower," the means by which individuals have been "integrated" into "the modern state," i.e., "under [the] one condition ... that [their] individuality would be shaped in a new form, and submitted to a set of very specific patterns." Abandoning the straightforward, direct repressiveness of what Foucault elsewhere calls "sovereign power," which is exercised typically through the centralized authority of a more or less absolute ruler, these patterns "structure" and so limit the "possible field of action" of "free subjects" by facing them with a "field of possibilities in which [only] several ways of behaving, several reactions and diverse comportments may be realized" (pp. 212, 214, 221). Elias, whose ideas in some ways anticipate Foucault's, is concerned with, among other things, the "sociogenesis" of "self-control," i.e., how, with the rise of the modern state, "the interdependence of larger groups of people and the exclusion of physical violence from them" leads to the establishment of "a social apparatus ... in which the constraints between people are lastingly transformed into self-constraints" (*Power and Civility*, pp. 242–3).

[4] Anthony Giddens, *A Contemporary Critique of Historical Materialism, Vol. 1: Power, Property, and the State* (Berkeley, 1981), pp. 35–6, 154; P. J. Corfield, *The Impact of English Towns, 1700–1800* (Oxford, 1982), pp. 124, 145, 144.

community on which tribal [or traditional] society depends has fallen apart?" asks Roberto Unger. "The greater the independence of the passions from the common culture, the more urgent the need to find an alternative basis for order among and within men."[5] Responding to something like this question, seeking to satisfy something like this need, criminal biography repeatedly displays not only the fatal consequences of independent passions but also the happy intervention of "the Natural Magistrate in the heart." This superego-by-another-name is nearly as powerful a countervailing force for social and moral order as God's providence, and certainly more visible. In representing it as a "natural" force at work in its subjects, criminal biography hopes also to evoke and sustain it in its readers.

Looked at from this angle, criminal biography may seem to have worked as a "dominant" or "hegemonic" discourse. But this would be to consider it apart from or outside its own "horizon of expectations"; it would be to take it, so to speak, at its own word. Though to a large extent the writers of criminal biography did seek to speak with a near "sovereign" authority, and did in a variety of ways "set the agenda of the thinkable" about criminality, "clos[ing] off alternative discursive possibilities," it is hard to see them working clearly or exclusively to the advantage of any specific "class" or group.[6] Criminal biography could be read and "used" from a number of different vantagepoints, to a number of different social and political ends. Insofar as it argued for the essential uniformity of human nature and the widespread distribution of a moral sense, it raised a clear challenge to aristocratic privilege. As Elias points out, "civility" is a banner under which the bourgeoisie seeks to advance its status. Still, as he also points out, the values it represents are aristocratic in origin. The situation of criminal biography is even further complicated by the fact that the "natural magistrate" argument could be used with equal force against Calvinist *or* Stuart absolutism, against the hegemonies that extreme factions of the middle-classes *or* the gentry would want to impose.[7] The ideological tendencies of criminal rogue biography are still more difficult to pin down, as it can be read as simultaneously satirizing *and* celebrating both bourgeois *and* aristocratic values.

The whole question of how or whether class models ought to be applied to early eighteenth-century England is a vexed one. As E. P. Thompson

---

[5] Giddens, *Critique*, p. 12; Corfield, *English Towns*, p. 145; Roberto Mangabeira Unger, *Law in Modern Society: Toward a Criticism of Social Theory* (New York, 1976), pp. 145–6.

[6] This particular description of hegemonic strategies comes from John Frow, *Marxism and Literary History* (Oxford, 1986), p. 63.

[7] Elias, *Power and Civility*, pp. 312–16. Pointing out that aristocratic codes of manners and morals are inevitably hegemonic, Elias has some very interesting things to say here on how they can be wrested away from and turned against an aristocracy by a bourgeoisie that not only adopts them but makes them their own.

points out, the presence of a generally shared culture and a certain respect
for "the rule of law" tended to damp down some of the grosser effects of
socioeconomic stratification. There was, too, the lingering aftermath of
the previous century's rebellions and revolutions. The presence of a king
over the water as well as another upstream at Westminster, the persistent
threat of Jacobite uprisings and the memory of a time the world was
turned upside down – a memory supposedly kept alive at the feasts of
"calvesheads clubs" on the anniversary of Charles I's execution – all
tended to prevent the establishment of a single, unquestionably legitimate,
natural-seeming social hierarchy.[8] There were competing "centers" of
authority (or would-be authority), and multiple points of resistance to
such claims for authority. Given this situation, the claims criminal biography made for itself as "a true prospect of things" were neither readily
nor simply accepted at face value; it was itself a highly challengeable
discourse.[9]

    Realizing this, some criminal biographers made light of their situation.
Allowing that readers might find some of his stories "very odd, and
perhaps a little improbable," one writer begged their indulgence. "A
Reader that cannot relish these Passages," he hoped, "will find enough for
his Diversion without them, and those who have a pretty deal of Faith may
easily stretch it to our Standard." "At least," he continued, "what will not
pass for real Truth, may please by the same Rules as many of our modern
Novels, which are so much admired."[10] This is charming, but it is a
confession to irrelevance; it is to concede one's own insignificance. Defoe
makes no such apologies or appeals. Nor could he, if (as I read him) he too
was concerned with promoting a self-reflexive self-consciousness in his
readers that would compensate for the loss of moral certainty and moral
community that marked his age. Breaking the rules of criminal biography
as well as the "rules of novels" as his contemporaries would have understood them, he wrote narratives so full of "real truth" that to this day there
are those who believe there must have been a "real" Moll Flanders, that is,
an actual person who served as her model. Such is the continuing vitality
of the liveliest of Defoe's characters, "nothing appertaining to her," as was
said with much less justice of another Moll, "being to be matcht

---

[8] On questions of class, see Edward P. Thompson, "Patrician Society, Plebeian Culture,"
   Journal of Social History, 7 (1974): 382–405; "Eighteenth Century English Society: Class
   Struggle Without Class?" *Social History*, 3 (1978): 133–65; and *Whigs and Hunters: The Origin
   of the Black Act* (London, 1975), pp. 258–69; also R. S. Neale, *Class in English History, 1680–1850*
   (Oxford, 1981), pp. 68–99, 154–66. The "calvesheads clubs," whether actual or fabled,
   show that public imagination still retained a significant trace of the mid-seventeenth-century
   radicalism portrayed by Christopher Hill in *The World Turned Upside Down: Radical Ideas
   During the English Revolution* (New York, 1972); for quotes from contemporary accounts of these
   "clubs," see John Ashton, *Social Life in the Reign of Queen Anne* (London, 1883), pp. 180–2.
[9] *Remarkable Criminals*, p. 28.
[10] Johnson, *Lives and Adventures of the Most Famous Highwaymen*, p. 114.

throughout the whole Course of History of Romance."[11] But Defoe's other criminals have a richness as well. Even Singleton, the least interesting of them, invites far more consideration than most protagonists do in actual criminal biography, and even his story has stimulated discussions of Defoe's realism.[12] Without realism, without a strong claim to be speaking "real truth," no narrative of criminal life could claim to be much more than a mere entertainment.

For so long his chief claim as an artist, then, and his chief distinction as one of the "inventors" of the novel, Defoe's realism is important, too, for the authority it would have given him in his own time. What are (or were) its salient features? How, particularly, might it have prompted readers to an enhanced, moralizing (if not moral) self-consciousness? And – before going any further – what can I mean in bandying about so highly loaded, so notoriously tricky a term?

The customary way of describing and assessing Defoe's realism has been to quote long passages from the novels, all the while commenting on the sense they give of "an actual physical environment," of "solid" objects, and of the flow of experience as it registers on the consciousness of more or less plausible narrators.[13] This, however, does not seem to me an especially useful way to account for the powerful sense of authenticity projected by Defoe's novels, particularly the criminal novels. There is, for one thing, often less concrete particularity in them than in many of his other, non-fictive writings. Crusoe's island, to be sure, is as vivid and present to us as H. F.'s London; we hardly need a map to trace the outlines of either, and could easily draw our own maps of the island. But the London

---

[11] For a survey of these claims, see G. A. Starr's introduction to *MF*, pp. xii–xv. In Defoe's own day the author of *The Highland Rogue* (1723) was certain that *Robinson Crusoe, Moll Flanders*, and *Colonel Jack* were "romantic Tale[s]" about "meer imaginary Person[s]," and not "real History" (p. [iii]). A 1722 sale catalogue, however, lists *Robinson Crusoe* and *Moll Flanders* as "English Lives" rather than as "Novels, Romances, &c."; this puts them into company with Burnet's *Rochester*, Locke's *Life of Christ*, a life of Cromwell, and various biographies of English and European monarchs (*Bibliotheca Sturbitchiana. A Catalogue of Curious Books Bought at Sturbitch-Fair* [1722], pp. 26, 37). This same catalogue, it is also worth noting, lists an account of the actual but fabulous Mary Carleton among its novels and romances. The other "Moll" is Mary Frith, for which see *The Life and Death of Mrs. Mary Frith. Commonly Called Mal Cutpurse* (1662), sig. A3v.

[12] Gary J. Scrimgeour, "The Problem of Realism in Defoe's *Captain Singleton*," *Huntington Library Quarterly*, 27 (1963): 21–37.

[13] The quoted terms are from Ian Watt's *The Rise of the Novel* (Berkeley, 1957), pp. 26, 97; see also pp. 26–7, 96–7. Other writers making similar points include Alan Dugald McKillop, *The Early Masters of English Fiction* (Lawrence, Kan., 1956), pp. 28–33; Maximillian E. Novak, "Defoe's Theory of Fiction," *Studies in Philology*, 61 (1964): 659–62; and James Sutherland, *Daniel Defoe: A Critical Study* (Boston, 1971), pp. 183–92. Samuel Holt Monk enters a significant demur to these notions in his preface to *CJ*, pp. xix–xxi, and, more recently, Novak emphasizes the mistakenness of "Watt's argument that Defoe was the inventor of circumstantial detail in fiction" (*Realism, Myth, and History in Defoe's Fiction* [Lincoln, Neb., 1983], p. 7).

inhabited by Moll, Jack, and Roxana is not so precise and specific. For all
their frequent naming of streets and places, their city is hardly more
definite in outline than Crusoe's Barbary or the Africa or Ceylon of
Singleton, the Virginia visited by Moll and Jack, or the Europe of Jack's
adventures and Roxana's intrigues. That Defoe had not visited these
exotic locales (he probably had traveled in Europe) is not to the point, for
of course neither had he visited (actually, that is) Crusoe's "Isle of
Despair."[14]

Concrete particularity was a fairly cheap commodity in Defoe's day.
His travel writing, for instance, contains examples of it far exceeding
anything to be found in his fiction; thus the following passage from *A Tour
Through Great Britain*:

From this town of Guilford, the road to Farnham is very remarkable, for it runs
along west from Guilford, upon the ridge of a high chalky hill, so narrow that the
breadth of the road takes up the breadth of the hill, and the declivity begins on
either hand, at the very hedge that bounds the highway, and is very steep as well
as very high. From this hill is a prospect either way, so far that 'tis surprising; and
one sees to the north, or N.W. over the great black desert, called Bagshot-Heath
. . . one way, and the other way south east into Sussex, almost to the South Downs,
and west to an unbounded length, the horizon only restraining the eyes. This hill
being all chalk, a traveller feels the effect of it in a hot summer's day, being
scorched by the reflection of the sun from the chalk, so as to make the heat almost
insupportable; and this I speak from my own experience. This hill reaches from
Guilford town's end to within a mile and half of Farnham . . . . and at the top of the
ascent from the town stands the gallows, which is so placed respecting the town,
that the towns people from the High-Street may sit at their shop doors, and see the
criminals executed.[15]

Describing a view for each of the compass points, this passage takes pains
to orient its reader in space and then gives that space an affective quality;
thus the heat radiating up from the chalk underfoot, the emptiness that
slopes away on either side of the road as it follows and entirely occupies the
top of the ridge. Then, moving the reader through its space, up the hill to
the crest, it looks back to Guildford where citizens sitting in their doorways
can look up the mile and a half to the gallows that reader (and text) have
just passed by. This passage (it is indeed a passage) *conducts* us from
Guildford to Farnham, makes us feel a progress; should we ever walk that
road again, we'd know it.

There is nothing in Defoe's criminal fiction to match this solidity and
precision, a fact made all the more curious because criminal biography is

[14] For the care with which Defoe reconstructed pre-Fire London in *The Journal of the Plague Year*,
see Manuel Schonhorn, "Defoe's *Journal of the Plague Year*: Topography and Intention," *Review
of English Studies*, n.s. 19 (1968): 387–402.
[15] *A Tour Through Great Britain*, abr. and ed. Pat Rogers (Penguin, 1971), pp. 158–9; the
paragraph quoted has not itself been abridged.

rich in accounts that take readers similarly, step by step, through all sorts of extraordinary events, giving a sense of solid objects occupying equally solid environments, and where the piling up of significant details simulates plausible movements of mind.[16] Holding that confession "in general" was not a sufficient "acknowledging" of guilt, serious criminal biographers leaned hard on criminals to get them to "come to Particulars." Criminals who admitted their guilt without giving "any particular Account" of their lives and crimes could still be reckoned "stubborn" or reproved for their "stiffness" and "obstinacy." The criminal who "disburthen'd his whole Conscience" by confessing "all the Particulars of his Life," however, was valued for the "Opportunity" he thereby gave his audience "to observe all his Motions, and to dive even into the Bottom of his Soul, and all his Intentions."[17] This concern for "particulars" and the pressures exerted on criminals to get them – as well as the frequent disposition of writers to invent particulars when they couldn't be gotten – made for a good many riveting accounts of just how crimes were planned and committed, and just how criminals felt during and after their crimes, when faced with what they had done. Harmon Strodtman's *Confession*, supposedly written by himself, provides a classic example of just such an account.

Strodtman, who was apprenticed to two German tobacco merchants headquartered in London, murdered a fellow apprentice because, he claimed, the man had long been mistreating him. What follows are just a few excerpts from a relatively long but often spellbinding text. Here, for instance, is Strodtman's description of the crime itself:

... and coming to his Bed-side, [I] open'd the Curtains, and with my Tobacco-beater knockt him on the Head, giving him four or five Blows on the left side of it, and another on the right. When I had given him the first Blow, then my Heart failed me; yet being afraid to be discover'd by the Noise he made with groaning, I followed close this first Blow with three or four others; and then had not Courage enough to go on with giving him any more. Therefore to stop his Groans, I took his Pillow, and laying it on his Mouth, pressed it hard upon it with my Elbow, as I was sitting on the side of his Bed; and by this means stopp'd his Breath and stifled him.[18]

---

16 John Robert Moore makes an interesting comparison between the *Tour* and *Moll Flanders*, observing that both cover, though "in reverse order," some of the same ground (*A Checklist of the Writings of Daniel Defoe*, 2nd edn [Hamden, Conn., 1971], p. ix). A look at the relevant passages, however, shows that Moll is nowhere as solidly descriptive as Defoe was when writing in his own person; see especially the description of Colchester, Harwich, and the places between them in the *Tour*, pp. 57–63. Moll simply doesn't travel in Defoe's shoes, or he in hers, as much as some critics would claim.

17 Paul Lorrain, Ordinary Accounts, 24 June 1709 and 27 October 1708; *The Life and Penitent Death of John Mawgridge, Gent. . . . Executed for the Murder of Captain Cope* (1708), p. [2].

18 For this and subsequently quoted passages from "The Life, Tryal, and Behaviour, under Condemnation, and Confession of Harman Strodtman," see N. B., *A Compleat Collection of Remarkable Tryals of the Most Notorious Malefactors, at the Sessions-House in the Old Baily, for near Fifty Years Past* (1718–21), 2: 205–9.

Dense and highly detailed descriptions of Strodtman's behavior and state of mind, before and after, bracket these shocking sentences. Thus, as his narrative continues, it tells how he searched through his victim's effects, gathered what he wanted up into a bundle, set the house on fire, fled, and returned to his lodgings to change clothes.

"Going then to the Sweeds Church in Trinity-lane," Strodtman "heard the Bill of Thanks read which my Masters had put up for their own and Neighbours Preservation" from the fire, the murder apparently not yet being discovered:

At which my Heart sunk down, and I had great Checks of Conscience, and could not forbear shedding of Tears, which I hid, (all I could) from an Acquaintance of my Masters, who was in the same Pew with me, and told me, that my Masters House was like to have been burnt the last Night, it being set on Fire by an Accident yet unknown; but the mischief which it might have done, was (through God's Mercy) happily prevented, by the *Dutch* Maid, who first smelt the Fire, and saw the Smoak, and thereupon called her Master, and fetch'd up a Pail of Water; by which means it was presently put out.

Acting normally, Strodtman accepts his companion's invitation to meet at another church that afternoon. But then the man fails to show up and, without saying why, Strodtman goes off "alone" to yet a third church:

And after Sermon walked in the Fields towards *Mile-end*, where I saw at a distance two *Dutch* Men that were hang'd there in Chains. Then I was struck with some Remorse and Fears, and said to my self, *Thou may'st come to be one of them, and be made a like Spectacle to the World.* After this, as I went on, I came to *Blackwall* (as I think) and there saw another Person (a Captain of *French* Pirates) who also hang'd in Chains in that Place. Then the same Thoughts again returned upon me, *viz.* That it may come to my lot to have such a shameful End.

As indeed it does.

In its way quite as fascinating as any novel, Strodtman's *Confession* is also more than a bit extraordinary. Crimes like his were rare, and there were few occasions for such excited, and exciting, writing. Still, even when working with far less spectacular materials, criminal biographers could frequently convey a noteworthy sense of particular settings, of sets of actions, or of sequences of feeling. Consider, for instance, this account of a witness's testimony at a more or less ordinary murder trial:

The first Evidence was a Neighbor, who deposed, That the Morning after Mr. *Norris* was murder'd, he having Occasion to go near the said Ditch, which ran at the back part of his House, and casting his Eye on the Water, espied a Toe of a Boot standing out above the Water; that thereupon he getting a Pole with a Hook at the End of it, took hold of it, and rais'd it a little higher, and then saw a whole Boot, and on the upper Part, a Scarlet Stocking about the Knee, and raising it higher, found it was the Body of a Man; wherefore getting Help, they got out the body, and found his Throat had been cut in a most barbarous manner.[19]

Or, as another example of more or less "ordinary" writing, this account of a burglary discovered in progress. The intruders included a former servant whose

Associates, two Men and a Boy, rush'd out at the Fore-door and escaped, but she being in a Place where she could not slip by her Master without being apprehended, went backwards, and before she was taken, chose rather to jump into the Necessary House, and suffocated with Stench. Mr. *Rode* look'd about and found the House of Office broke, and looking down, found something moving; he called up some of the Neighbours to his Assistance, who opening the upper Part of it with an Axe, they with Difficulty took it up, not Knowing whether it was Man, Woman, or any other Creature; they laid it upon the Ground, and at last discover'd it to be a Woman; they put her into a Sack, washt her with Water, gave her Drams, or what they thought most proper, till she came to herself, and told of the two Men and the Boy escaping, and how they were packing up the Things mentioned in the Indictment, together with some Eatables, but being Interrupted, they could not carry 'em off.[20]

As efforts to give a sense of "real, particular" happenings (to use Ian Watt's phrasing) and as plausible emanations of mind, even these passages stand up well in comparison to Defoe. Mr. Norris's body emerges from the watery ditch bit by bit, just as it did for the man who found it. Gradually it takes shape before our eyes, first the toe of a boot (perhaps it's only a boot, not the missing Mr. Norris), then the whole boot, then a scarlet stocking, then (horribly!) a knee. It is a man's body, about to become Mr. Norris's body, and his throat has been slashed. Though less charged emotionally, the second passage is no less interesting for the sense it gives by its density and careful construction of a highly specific occasion. We share Mr. Rode's bepuzzlement as, looking for burglars, he finds "something" stirring at the bottom of his latrine. He is kept from "knowing whether it was man, woman, or any other creature" until, being washed, this extraordinary, disgusting *thing* "comes to herself" and makes all clear. The mention of "eatables" at the end provides a nicely ironic closing touch.

Many more instances of concrete particularity could be cited from Defoe's nonfictional writing, and examples from criminal biography fished up almost endlessly. The point to be made is that Defoe's criminal novels do not stand out from other texts of their day – either his, or those they purport to resemble – for their close attention to the bits and quiddities of concrete experience. Defoe's readers are not prevented from fleshing out the physical environment of his criminal protagonists, or even from insert-

[19] N. B., *Compleat Tryals*, 1: 258–9.
[20] James Guthrie, Ordinary Account, 24 November 1740.

ing themselves into it, but the novels themselves seem not especially
concerned with promoting such responses. To understand how Moll could
have seemed "real" to early readers of *Moll Flanders* – and can still seem so
to us – we shall have to focus on other aspects of her narrative.

For many modern readers, the essence of Defoe's realism is that his
novels "[imitate] the randomness" of actual experience. Or, as Ian Watt
says, "Defoe flouts the orderliness of literature to demonstrate his total
devotion to the disorderliness of life." This is somewhat more sophisticated
than the "solid object" argument and carries us beyond the limits of
talking merely about the plausible representation of consciousness. It
presents, nonetheless, two main problems. In the first place, it makes it
difficult to see much art in Defoe's disorderliness. Watt's assessment is not
altogether approving. He finds *Moll Flanders* riddled with "confusion" and
"discontinuities," which make much of its "vividness" and "authenticity"
seem "curiously incidental." His consequent "doubts about the completeness of Defoe's control over his narrative" prevent him giving Defoe
much credit as a conscious artist.[21]

The second problem with the view that Defoe is somehow a naive realist
is more basic. In claiming he wrote the way life "is," it makes too big an
assumption about life and overestimates the ease with which life may be
compared to literature. We may believe that life is random and disorderly,
and even (along with Watt and other "undeconstructed" critics) that one
of the higher goals of art is to project a compensatory "orderliness." But
these assumptions would have been entirely foreign to Defoe's original
audience and, most likely, to him as well.[22] Defoe's culture provided, in
any case, a ready made "order" for the narrating of criminals' lives that, so
it liked to think, was the order of those lives as they were actually lived.
Alternatively, it allowed for a maximally disordered narrative, one which
was self-consciously and often avowedly unreal and fantastic. Inasmuch as
Defoe's novels of criminal life accept neither of these culturally provided
forms – neither the "orderliness" of the one nor the equally programmatic
(and so in a sense orderly, too) disorder of the other – they would not have
imitated life as his contemporaries normally (or normatively) conceived it.
Watt's dictum ought perhaps to be reversed: Defoe flouts the orderliness
not of literature, but of life itself.

Yet the paradox is not so neat as it seems. Watt's terms are not discrete
opposites, the truth being that life and literature are often indiscreetly and
embarrassingly inopposite. Penetrating each other, they promiscuously
intermingle. Nor can life itself be directly compared with or contrasted to

[21] Laura Brown, *English Dramatic Form, 1660–1760* (New Haven, 1981), p. 189; Watt, *Rise of the Novel*, pp. 106, 97–9.
[22] On this subject see Martin C. Battestin, *The Providence of Wit: Aspects of Form in Augustan Literature and the Arts* (Oxford, 1974).

literature. However we define our terms (and inevitably we begin defining them as soon as we start talking about them), in speaking of life the thing we have before us is not life itself (whatever that may be) but life as we, within all the limits imposed on us by our particular culture, are able to describe it in our discourse. In other words, all we are doing is setting one particular book (or our notion of it) against our redactable notions of life, i.e., the larger "book of nature" as Fielding called it.

A current term that might stand as a rough equivalent to "book of nature" is "code," inasmuch as it is vis-à-vis a code or codes that texts come to seem realistic. Roman Jakobson sets the whole matter out with characteristic clarity and elegance.[23] There are basically two kinds of realism, he points out, that in which a text conforms to a generally accepted model of reality (this might be called academic realism, and would include socialist realism) and that in which a text challenges such a model on the grounds of its inadequacy to the full rich nature of things as they really are (this might be called avant-garde realism, and would include, in our own century, futurism, surrealism, even abstract impressionism). In eighteenth-century English terminology the difference between the two realisms lies in the very different implications of the terms "just" and "lively," between, that is, the upholding of various "decorums" or the departing from them in search of literal accuracy rather than strict propriety.[24] Jakobson explains that either kind of realism can, over time, take on the character of the other. Eventually the avant-gardists may subvert and even seize the academy, institutionalizing in one way or another some version of their own set of values; their program of deviation from previously established norms for the representation of reality may then itself become a norm for the representation of reality. Once these new norms have been established, the displaced and forgotten norms of earlier academies may well come into vogue again, seeming to the new avant-gardists much more appropriate to the full-rich-nature-of-things-as-they-are than those proposed by their immediate and (as they see them) now ossified rivals. Realism, then, is a value conferred on a text by the dispositions of its readers as well as the intentions of its author, as the one and the other situate it with respect (or disrespect) to conventional notions or codes of the real.[25]

---

[23] Roman Jakobson, "On Realism in Art," in *Readings in Russian Poetics: Formalist and Structuralist Views*, ed. and tr. Ladislav Matejka and Krystyna Pomorska (Cambridge, Mass., 1971), pp. 38–46.

[24] See, for instance, Dryden's use of "just" and "lively" in *An Essay of Dramatic Poesy.*

[25] "No literary text relates to contingent reality as such," to quote Wolfgang Iser, "but to models or concepts of reality" (*The Act of Reading: A Theory of Aesthetic Response* [Baltimore, 1978], p. 70). This point is developed at length with reference to the visual arts by E. H. Gombrich's great *Art and Illusion: A Study in the Psychology of Pictorial Representation*, 2nd edn (New York, 1961), which remains powerfully suggestive for the study of literary texts.

Obviously a novel like *Moll Flanders*, which has persuaded readers for more than two and a half centuries that it is in one way or another realistic, must employ powerful and subtle strategies for evoking such notions or codes, and for getting readers to play these against its text in ways that either confirm them or else suggest the possibility of something not entirely encodable looming beyond them, "realer" still than any mere *notionable* reality. Any account of Defoe's realism ought first to realize that his characters would not have seemed "real" in the eighteenth century for exactly the same reasons they do to us. Its next concern ought to be the various strategies by which, then and now, his texts invite being set vis-à-vis a code or codes of the "real." Finally, it ought to be alert to the ways in which any such code, in saying (or providing for the saying) that "reality" is "naturally" and "actually" thus and so, carries with it a great deal of ideological freight. One's "sense of reality" powerfully constrains one's thoughts and feelings, but, as Raymond Williams for example points out, for all that this may seem "simple" it is not simply given. "The pressures and limits of simple experience and common sense" – necessary things to defer to, or so it may seem – are themselves shaped by "the pressures and limits of . . . a specific economic, political, and cultural system" working to sustain "relations of domination and subordination."[26]

Even the simplest, most straightforward-seeming accounts of the actual "truth" as it was (or might be) experienced can be laden with social and political implication. Excluding Strodtman's confession as too obvious a case to need explication, we might consider Mr. Rode's discovery of his ex-servant – at least as we have it recounted – at the bottom of a privy. This gives a comedic turn to a frightening and bothersome event, showing the criminal who would have betrayed her master cast down and utterly debased, he all the while retaining, as multiply privileged observer, the status her behavior has challenged. The horrific discovery of Mr. Norris's body, told in all its excruciating detail, testifies to the sensibility of the witness who was there then and is now here, in court, doing his civic duty as all good citizens should, and doing it by showing – however some "barbarous" person or persons may have acted – that *his* heart was and is

26 Raymond Williams, *Marxism and Literature* (Oxford, 1977), p. 110. "It is indeed a peculiarity of ideology," says Althusser, "that it imposes (without appearing to do so, since these are 'obviousnesses') obviousnesses as obviousnesses, which we cannot *fail to recognize* and before which we have the inevitable and natural reaction of crying out (aloud or in the 'still, small voice of conscience'): 'That's obvious! That's right! That's true!'" (Louis Althusser, *Lenin and Philosophy and Other Essays*, tr. Ben Brewster [New York, 1971], p. 172). According to Fredric Jameson, one of the "objective" functions of the "realistic" novel is to contribute to the ideological needs of "market capitalism" by producing just the sort of obviousnesses appropriate to the new "life world" of the "commodity system" (see *The Political Unconsciousness: Narrative as a Socially Symbolic Act* [Ithaca, 1981], p. 152); it is hard to see within the terms of his subtle and interesting argument, however, how novels would do better at this than other, simpler, "realistic" forms of prose narrative, like, for instance, criminal biography.

in the right place. The careful noting of actual detail in both accounts
works at more than merely gaining credence; it says the people involved in
these events are themselves important and worthy of note. In France,
where such people were not important, and where there was no particular
concern with achieving wide participation in the processes of the law,
similar events got only vague and anonymous description if they got
described at all.[27] It is possible, too, to find a kind of social as well as
physical geography in something as apparently neutral as Defoe's account
of the road between Guildford and Farnham. This narrow, rocky, steeply
bounded way leads to the gallows, a place the good folk of Guildford may
contemplate with all the complacency of the just taking a well-earned rest
from their labors – but only from their shopdoors, industry scrupulously
preserving its difference from idleness even here. The writer, curiously,
minds other business, seeks other prospects, and, venturing out on the road
– is there further allegory here? – leaves the comfort, safety, and presumably the complacency of town behind.

No code of the real, no measure or representation of "what was" or "is,"
can be free of notions of "what ought to be," and both play important roles
in the power relations of any given society.[28] It follows that any tampering
with or playing about with a particular code of the real – anything that
reconstructs or deconstructs "obviousness" – is likely to be engaged in
some kind of political work. It is with these points in mind that, over the
rest of this chapter, we shall start comparing certain aspects of Defoe's
pseudo criminal biographies to the "real" thing, by which of course I
mean not criminals' lives as they were actually lived but rather as they
were said – or written – to have been lived. Whatever the reasons for
Defoe's criminals seeming realistic to us, one powerful reason for their
seeming so to his original audience, I'd suggest, was their standing out so
sharply from the stereotypes into which actual criminals were regularly
(and often ruthlessly) cast.

Though recognizable within the terms of criminal biography, Moll and
the rest – to use the terms of Russian Formalism – are somehow "made

---

[27] For information on the representation of crime and criminals in France, see *Turned to Account*,
pp. 232, 248–9. The peculiarity of English practice in these matters might be explained from
Elias's perspective by "the fact that in England … the constraint which the individual had to
exert on himself, particularly in all matters related to the life of the state, grew stronger and
more all-round than in the great Continental nations" (*Power and Civility*, p. 363).

[28] Consider, for instance, Roberto Unger's observation that "the last defining attribute of liberal
society" is "its tendency to destroy the foundations of the idea that what ought to be somehow
inheres in what is. The loosening of the ties of community fosters a particular mode of
consciousness and is fostered by it. This outlook begins with the insight that conventions of
behavior are shaped by history; it goes on to the denial of their intrinsic goodness; and it ends
in the conviction that they are based upon the naked acts of will by which people choose
among conflicting ultimate values" (*Law in Modern Society*, p. 169). Defoe's fiction may well
prefigure our arrival at such a state of mind, but, I'll be arguing, it does not necessarily help it
along.

strange," their qualities and contours "roughened," their stories presented in ways that "retard" or "impede" easy or "automatic" comprehension.[29] In "deautomatizing" standard images and conceptions of criminality, I'll eventually suggest, in disturbing and perturbing the "horizon" within which they were read, Defoe's texts work at heightening and shaping their readers' sense of themselves and where they themselves stand. The very great difference between the "true prospect" of criminal biography and Defoe's view of things, it seems to me, is that *his* "what is" becomes something by or against which readers can define – or feel they are defining – their *own* "ought to be."

On a number of occasions Defoe's novels invite explicit comparison to well-known criminal biographies. Roxana says, ruefully, that she "might as well have been the *German Princess*" (271), and Moll claims to have been as "impudent a Thief, and as dexterous as ever *Moll Cut-Purse* was, tho' . . . not half so Handsome" (201). She is less reserved in praising Jemy, her favorite husband, who "had committed so many Robberies, that *Hind*, or *Whitney*, or the *Golden Farmer* were Fools to him" (281). Singleton hears how Captain Avery stole the Great Mogul's daughter, and temporarily joins forces with him; elsewhere he mentions a certain "Captain Kid" (154, 179).[30] Such comparisons serve to heighten the differences between

29 The main collection of Russian Formalist writings in English is *Readings in Russian Poetics*, ed. Matejka and Pomorska; see also *Russian Formalist Criticism: Four Essays*, ed. and tr. Lee T. Lemon and Marion J. Reis (Lincoln, Neb., 1965). For a compendious overview of the Russian Formalists, see Victor Erlich, *Russian Formalism: History-Doctrine*, 3rd edn (New Haven, 1981), and, for a stimulating "metapoetic" analysis of its "poetics," Peter Steiner, *Russian Formalism: A Metapoetics* (Ithaca, 1984). Essays by the Prague Structuralists are collected in *A Prague School Reader on Esthetics, Literary Structure, and Style*, ed. and tr. Paul L. Garvin (Washington, D.C., 1964); *Semiotics of Art: Prague School Contributions*, ed. and tr. Ladislav Matejka and Irwin R. Titunik (Cambridge, Mass., 1976); and *The Prague School: Selected Writings, 1929–1946*, ed. Peter Steiner and tr. John Burbank (Austin, 1982). In *Semiotics of Art* see especially Jan Mukařovsky's two essays, "Art as Semiotic Fact," and "Poetic Reference." Garvin offers part of an essay by Mukařovsky on "Standard Language and Poetic Language," but see also "On Poetic Language" in Mukařovsky, *The Word and Verbal Art*, ed. and tr. John Burbank and Peter Steiner (New Haven, 1977). A lucid and useful overview of Prague Structuralism is offered by F. W. Galan, *Historic Structures: The Prague School Project, 1928–1946* (Austin, 1985).

30 For "Moll Cut-Purse," see The *Life and Death of Frith*; there is a powerful irony (more likely Defoe's than hers) in Moll's concession that she's less "Handsome" than her predecessor, for according to the standard contemporary account of her life, Moll Cutpurse always wore men's clothes and was "so ugly in any dress as never to be wooed nor solicited by any man" (Alexander Smith, *A Complete History of the Lives and Robberies of the Most Notorious Highwaymen, Footpads, Shoplifts, & Cheats of Both Sexes*, ed. Arthur L. Hayward [London, 1933], p. 284; first published in 1712, this work achieved a fifth edition by 1719). The German Princess was Mary Carleton, the subject of a good many accounts, the longest of which is Francis Kirkman's *The Counterfeit Lady Unveiled* (1673). James Hind, James Whitney, and the Golden Farmer were all legendary but actual highwaymen. The most substantial account of Hind is George Fidge's *The English Gusman* (1652), and two "lives" of Whitney survive from 1693 (for the latter see my "King William, 'K. J.,' and James Whitney: The Several Lives and Affiliations of a Jacobite Robber," *Eighteenth Century Life*, n.s. 12 [1988]: 88–104). All five criminals get attention in

the novels and their (supposedly) non-fictional analogues; they are indications, as are practically all such self-conscious intertextualities, that the text at hand is not quite to be read in the same way as all those other texts.

Such effects, of course, can also be achieved without explicit reference to criminal biography. Thus, though there is no particular mention of any previously famous criminals in *Colonel Jack*, its chief character quite obviously is made to stand out against two other "Jacks," the Captain and the Major, who represent types commonly found in texts like Alexander Smith's *Lives of the Highwaymen*. The Captain is like any one of a number of basically brutish thieves; though not without charm, he commits a number of ugly crimes and comes to the usual bad end. The Major is more like the gallant, even heroic highwaymen that Hind, Whitney, and the Golden Farmer were reputed to be, but, broken on the wheel in France, he comes to a worse end.[31] *Colonel Jack* shares neither their temperaments nor their fates. Moll similarly stands out in contrast, not only to the earlier Moll, whose story was so well known, but also to Jemy whose story, if told, would likely proceed along familiar lines. Amy serves a similar role as Roxana's foil, though, to be sure, she is not at all the typical murdering servant found in criminal biography.[32] Singleton, of course, is quite different from Avery, the most famous pirate to sail the Indian Ocean. He creates no kingdom on Madagascar but retires to England where, for his own safety, he must act a stranger in his native land.

Defoe's protagonists are thus foregrounded against some highly specific background, but they stand out in certain general ways as well. Two of

---

Smith's collection, and it and the plagiarisms it inspired would have been the main source of information on all five up through the end of the century. Avery, the most famous pirate of his day, is the subject of two anonymous biographies, *The Life and Adventures of Capt. John Avery, The Famous English Pirate* (1709) and *The King of the Pirates* (1719), which has been attributed to Defoe. Avery figures as well in Charles Johnson, *A General History of the Robberies and Murders of the Most Notorious Pyrates*, vol. 1 (1724), also attributed to Defoe. William Kid (or Kidd) appears in the second volume of that same work (pub. 1728); hanged for piracy in 1701, he was the occasion of several pamphlets published that year.

[31] For a "typology" that sets out three kinds of thieves – hero, brute, buffoon – see *Turned to Account*, pp. 125–48; Defoe apparently had no interest in buffoons.

[32] Murderous servants typically rebel against their masters and mistresses, harming, if not them, their children or other servants. Though Amy's claiming to know what Roxana wants better than she does herself might be accounted an act of rebellion, she nonetheless does what she believes is Roxana's will. Further complications arise from the fact that Susan is Roxana's former servant as well as abandoned child, so when Amy murders her she is, as it were, committing her own version of two highly conventional crimes at once. Harmon Strodtman offers a good example of the servant-to-servant kind of murder; a good example of the other is provided by Charity Philpot, who "on a sudden without cause given rushed in upon her Mistress, who was in a Room with her Child," saying she would kill her and burn down the house. When the woman fled, leaving the child behind, Charity cut its throat (see *A True and Wonderful Relation of a Murther Committed . . . . By a Maid Who Poysoned Her Self* [1681]).

them are women, which merely statistically would make them different
from the average thief and murderer.[33] But women were exceptional
criminals by virtue of their natures, too, which could be a source of
particular interest. Thus a reviewer of the *History of the Pirates* called
readers' attention to the fact it includes the biographies of two female
buccaneers, and remarked on "the Strangeness of two Women's engaging
in a Life of Blood and Rapine." He himself, though, was "most entertained
with those Actions, which give me a Light into the Nature of Man." The
nature of woman was of itself an altogether peculiar thing. Having "not so
large a Portion of Reason ... as Men," possibly the same writer specified
elsewhere, women "are more easily seduc'd into Vices, as well as preserv'd
within the Bounds of Modesty, and all Sort of Example is more catching
and prevailing amongst them." Women might be easily controlled, or they
might be especially dangerous. "When once the Modesty of a Woman is
gone," the preface to a reworked version of *Moll Flanders* declares, echoing
an old maxim, "she is capable of any Mischief the Devil can put her upon,
there being no Creature in the World so voracious as a wicked Woman."[34]

[33] Only fourteen of the 135 criminals mentioned in the table of contents to the 1719 edition of
Smith's *Lives of the Highwaymen*, for instance, are women. For a historical perspective, see J. M.
Beattie, "The Criminality of Women in Eighteenth-Century England," *Journal of Social
History*, 8 (1975): 80–116, and *Crime and the Courts in England, 1660–1800* (Princeton, 1986),
pp. 105–6, 113–24, 237–43, 436–9, 481–3, 534–8.

[34] ?Defoe, *A Collection of Miscellany Letters Selected Out of Mist's Journal* (1722–7), 4: 198, 237;
*Fortune's Fickle Distribution: In Three Parts. Containing First, The Life and Death of Moll Flanders ...
Part II. The Life of Jane Hackabout, Her Governess ... Part III. The Life of James Mac-Faul, Moll
Flanders's Lancashire Husband* (Dublin, 1730), sig. A4r. Essentially the same notion about
women is advanced by *A Collection of Miscellany Letters*, 4: 236; Alexander Smith, *The School of
Venus* (1716), 2: sig. A3r; George Lillo, *The London Merchant; or the History of George Barnwell*
(1731), 1: 3; *Lives of the Most Remarkable Criminals*, ed. Arthur L. Hayward (New York, 1927),
p. 205; and Guthrie, Ordinary Accounts, 3 March 1736/7 and 12 June 1741. According to
Johnson's *Lives of the Highwaymen* (1734), the relative rarity and essential difference of women
criminals made them more interesting than men: "'tis certain, [whether] a Woman always
discovers more Art and Cunning than a Man ... or whatever else," that "a female Offender
excites our Curiosity more than a Male"; thus, "we must still acknowledge ... that the Tricks
of a *German Princess* leave stronger Impressions than the open Robberies of *Hind* and *Duvall*"
(p. 327). The opening number of a courtesan's life, which was to be published in parts, makes a
comparable point and can almost seem a prospectus for *Moll Flanders* or *Roxana*. Noting that
"the celebrated History of *Robinson Crusoe* [has] met with great and deserved Success," the
supposed first-person narrator comments that, having read it, "I could not but flatter myself,
that if my Story were faithfully pen'd, it would be read with the same fond Eagerness, and
impatient Curiosity. For, thought I, if the Life of a Man, who had by Misfortune pass'd his
Time alone, had such Charms in it, what would be the Pleasure in reading the Adventures of a
Woman, who had, by a still greater Misfortune, past her Life in publick?" (*The Narrative: or,
The Delightful and Melancholy History of Leucippe*, No. 1 [12 November 1719]; no additional
numbers are to be found in the British Library). Defoe's reasons for writing two novels about
female criminals may have been more than merely opportunistic, however. "Women," he
wrote in a not inapposite context, "when once they give themselves leave to stoop to their own
circumstances, and think fit to rouze up themselves to their own relief, are not so helpless and
shiftless creatures as some would make them appear in the world" (*CET*, 1: 303). For a highly
interesting account of some of the period's worst and consequently most fascinating female

All this threatens the normal etiology of crime, making it more irritable, less predictable. Consider, for instance, Moll's sudden and shocking temptation to murder the child whose necklace she steals. This is something "the Devil put me upon," she says, recalling the maxim herself (194). It is only her second theft, and already she is on the brink of doing the worst thing she could ever do: "a Piece of Barbarity," as the Newgate ordinary called a similar crime that did end in the death of a child, "as no Age can hardly parallel." No one was supposed to become "superlatively wicked at once," but Moll very nearly does.[35]

Defoe's men are not quite so exciting. As a pirate, of course, Singleton stands outside the usual run of redacted criminals, and, even though Jack's early life in many ways resembles standard criminal biography, he is (rather remarkably) never brought to law. Defoe's protagonists, moreover, are situated in contexts that suggest other popular narrative genres as well. Jack goes on to a variety of careers as slave, planter, leisured Londoner, soldier, Jacobite, and merchant. Singleton takes holidays from pirating, traveling across Africa and through Ceylon; at times his story reads like a travelogue or captivity narrative, just as Jack's sometimes reads like the memoirs of a soldier or private gentleman. Before she commences thieving, Moll leads a romance-life of seduction, betrayal, and intrigue, by turns whore and housewife, shrewd bargainer and wide-eyed fool; there is, too, something of the conduct books in parts of her narrative. Almost all Roxana's story reads like a "secret history" of the kind, say, written by Delarivière Manley (Roxana herself uses the phrase twice, pp. 317, 326) – at least until it appears she is partly responsible for the murder of her daughter. Cobbled up as they are, Defoe's novels stick to no single last.

But even were they trimmed or otherwise abridged so as to include only criminal doings, Defoe's novels would still in one way or another surprise

criminals, see Margaret Anne Doody, "The Law, the Page, and the Body of Woman: Murder and Murderesses in the Age of Johnson," *The Age of Johnson*, 1 (1987): 127–60.

[35] Lorrain, Ordinary Account, 13 March 1713; *Lives of the Most Remarkable Criminals*, p. 451. According to John Richetti ("The Family, Sex, and Marriage in Defoe's *Moll Flanders* and *Roxana*," *Studies in the Literary Imagination*, 15 [1982]: 23, 33), Moll's and Roxana's difference from Defoe's "male adventurers" leads in Defoe's last novel to the implication that "female identity in a normal social order is so limited and fragile that once ordinary conditions are altered, a woman is turned into a pure opportunity for free-floating selfhood." For remarks on Roxana's unpredictability, her danger and mysteriousness as a female "monster," see Paula Backscheider, *Daniel Defoe: Ambition & Innovation* (Lexington, Ky., 1986), pp. 188–90, 208–12, and for a description of Moll as an "unfamiliar social hybrid," see John Rietz, "Criminal Ms-Representation: *Moll Flanders* and Female Criminal Biography," *Studies in the Novel*, 23 (1991): 403–15. For rather a different view of Moll, one which sees her as being, finally, for all her deviance, rather narrowly "constructed" into a "normative female subject with a sexuality dedicated to the production of domestic tranquillity," see John P. Zomchick, "'A Penetration which Nothing Can Deceive': Gender and Juridical Discourse in Some Eighteenth-Century Narratives," *Studies in English Literature*, 29 (1989): 535, 547–53.

expectation. They simply fail to conform to – or even be congruent with – the two main structures of criminal biography. The lives they describe are never quite reducible to the aimless meanderings of criminal roguery, but neither can they quite be made to fit the strict fall and rise of serious criminal biography. The curve of Jack's career may be "plotted" in a variety of ways (for which see chapter 6), and Roxana falls merely, in an ever deepening, widening gyre of degradation. Moll's life may seem to incorporate both the downward and upward movements of serious criminal biography, but its pivot point – her repentance in Newgate – is riddled with troubling ambiguities (more on this in chapters 3 and 4). So, too, is the worldliness of her final prosperity. The general diffuseness and episodic character of Singleton's career may seem more in keeping with criminal rogue biography, but its primary comparison is to pirates' lives, a rather different and relatively rare genre of criminal biography.

From the standpoint of "ordinary" criminal biography there is an inordinacy about Defoe's novels, an incompleteness or overrepletion. They go too far or not far enough. They dilate or reflect or digress, or jump from one thing to another. They leave out or put in too much, and none comes to a proper ending. Indeed, in terms of the conventions of criminal biography, they aren't yet ready to be made into stories. Thus, writing about four criminals hanged early in 1723, the Reverend Mr. Lee, Curate of Croyden, saw no reason "to give any particular Account" of those merely "ordered for Transportation ... they not having finished their Courses."[36] From the point of view of someone steeped in the forms of their purported genre (like myself, of course) the "openness" and seeming "incoherence" of Defoe's novels are both dizzying and fascinating; the terrain they cover, both familiar and strange, not wholly but only partially anomalous, makes for maximal curiosity and a high sense of novelty. Such curiosity, such novelty, are important for the strain they put on readers' cognitive and affective apparatuses. I'll start explaining what I mean by focussing on two sets of features that particularly mark these narratives out: their beginnings and endings, and the voices that relate them. For these novels are anomalous in what might be called their textures, too, their first-person narratives failing to achieve the simple, unambiguous clarity of first-person narrative in standard criminal biography.

Though only one of the two kinds of conventional criminal biography may be said to have a proper "middle" (that is, one linked to its beginning and end), the beginnings and ends of both kinds are similar enough to establish a general rule: criminal biographies begin by locating their subjects in society – place of birth, occupation or status of father, edu-

---

[36] Rev. — Lee, "An Account of Behaviour, Confessions and Last Dying Words of the Four Malefactors ... Executed at Croyden ... the 27th of April, 1723," in Applebee's *Original Weekly Journal*, 4 May 1723.

cation and early experience – and end by describing the circumstances of their execution, which firmly establishes their final relation to society. Defoe leaves his readers hanging, not his protagonists. Singleton returns home to England where, if discovered, he will probably die; all his future safety is entrusted to what has to seem a harebrained and easily penetrated disguise. Moll escapes with Jemy to Virginia, the two of them relatively unscathed and increasingly prosperous, for reasons God only can know. Then, in a further complication, she returns to England, soon followed by her husband. Moll notes that the terms of her transportation have been fulfilled, but leaves us in the dark about her husband, who barely thirty pages before was banned from England "as long as he liv'd" (311). If Defoe is not merely forgetting what he had earlier written, then Jemy returns home at the risk of discovery and certain death.[37] Jack's story, too, ends curiously. The one-time thief turned Jacobite has repented of this latter, willful folly, and shares in the king's general pardon. His plantations in Virginia have made him wealthy, and he returns to England made all the more wealthy by illegal trade with the Spaniards in the Caribbean – a trade which, however profitable to himself, is inimical to the interests of English commerce in general.[38] Roxana's is perhaps the most curious case of all. Her all too obsequious servant has disappeared with her all too troublesome daughter, and – though she will not say for certain – it appears the daughter has been murdered. At the very end of her narrative Roxana discloses that Amy finally followed her over to Holland, but she "can say no more now," except to note that after some few years of flourishing they both "fell into a dreadful Course of Calamaties .... the Blast of Heaven seem'd to follow the Injury done the poor Girl, by us both" (329–30).[39]

There is no need to rely merely on my sense of these things. The endings of *Moll Flanders* and *Roxana* prompted several eighteenth-century efforts at emendation, presumably because of perceived inadequacies. Thus,

[37] Some indication of the risk that Jemy and Singleton incur by returning home as they do is provided by two actual and more or less contemporary events. "Grecian habits," not Persian, were the favored disguise of a pair of highwaymen who "went publicly about the streets" after escaping from Newgate, but they were caught all the same (Narcissus Luttrell, *A Brief Historical Relation of State Affairs* [Oxford, 1857], 4: 466–7 [31 December 1698]). Almost exactly eight months after *Moll Flanders* was published Applebee's *Journal* notes an "unusual Number of Persons executed this Week" and explains that "their Crimes ... were such, as ... could hardly admit any Mercy." Three murderers and seven "notorious" robbers were hanged, along with "two for returning from Transportation" (29 September 1722).

[38] Maximillian Novak, *Economics and the Fiction of Daniel Defoe* (Berkeley, 1962), pp. 121–7; this topic will be addressed at length in chapter 6.

[39] Most modern students of Defoe see the abrupt ending of *Roxana* as just another instance of his flawed art. Robert Hume, however, makes an interesting and (to me) persuasive argument in defence of the novel's ending in "The Conclusion of Defoe's *Roxana*: Fiasco or Tour de Force?" *Eighteenth-Century Studies*, 3 (1969): 475–90. For a balanced consideration of the question see also Sutherland, *Defoe* (1971), pp. 205–16.

though the hugely popular chapbook version of *Moll Flanders* very much abridged the original text, it nonetheless made space to have her tell how she and her husband, "in sincere penitence for the bad lives we had lived," resolved to spend their last days in Virginia "being hospitable and generous, pious and charitable, relieving many from want and slavery." It closes with a third-person account of her death, which she greeted with "the greatest piety and devotion," and of her bequeathing "several legacies to charitable uses." Two somewhat more sumptuous abridgements of *Moll Flanders* allow Moll (and Jemy) to return from exile in America, but situate her in Ireland rather than England. They, too, have her die a pious death, preceded by a repentance that far outdoes in its explicitness and lack of ambiguity her earlier repentance in Newgate. We get details of Moll's funeral and an opportunity to read some "witty" verses composed for the occasion by young gentlemen from Trinity College. It is probably significant that aspects of this interment recall the conclusion of *The Life and Death of Mrs. Mary Frith*, the chief biography of Moll Cut-Purse. Moll in any case is put away, safely among her kind.[40] All three of the extant revisions of *Roxana* also add on to its story, continuing to a decent denouement rather than breaking off in full, but unrealized catastrophe. Roxana's further adventures, as these texts give them, have her variously coming to better terms with her abandoned children, perishing miserably in a debtor's prison, or dying in the best sentimental fashion – repentant, redeemed by her suffering, and lamented by all around her. In none of these subsequent versions does it turn out that her daughter has actually been murdered, and in one of them the crime is not even hinted at; the reader is spared any such concern, even momentarily.[41]

---

[40] *The Fortunes and Misfortunes of Moll Flanders* (1750?), p. 23; *The Life and Actions of Moll Flanders, Containing her Settlement in Ireland* (1723), and *Fortune's Fickle Distribution*. A much later, still more curious version of the novel takes still greater pains to make Moll a more presentable personage; see *The History of Laetitia Atkins, vulgarly called Moll Flanders* (1776). Needless to say, these revisions belie the reason given in the novel's preface for its ending short of Moll's death, i.e., that "no Body can write their own Life to the full End of it" (5). There was in fact no particular convention requiring Defoe to stick to the first person; cf., for instance, *The Matchless Rogue: or, An Account of Tom Merryman* (1725), in which Tom tells his story in the first person, and then, as a third-person narrator informs us, is hanged.

[41] See E. Applebee's edition of *The Fortunate Mistress* (1740); *The Life and Adventures of Roxana* (1765); and *The History of Mademoiselle de Beleau; or, The New Roxana* (1775). *Captain Singleton* appears never to have attracted sufficient attention to be abridged or revised; at least no such text survives to my knowledge. Nor, so far as I know, do any copies of the three-penny edition of *Colonel Jack* survive (see advertisements in Applebee's *Original Weekly Journal*, 24, 31 July and 7 August 1725). This pamphlet, however, may have been the basis for the abridgement of *Colonel Jack* which appears in Johnson, *Lives of the Highwaymen*, pp. 117–26, at about one-tenth the length of the original. This abridgement, we might note, gives disproportionate attention to Jack's life as a thief (about two-thirds of its total), and shrinks his trading voyages at the end to a few parenthetical phrases (for a still shorter abridgement, see *A General and True History of the Lives and Actions of the Most Famous Highwaymen, Murderers, Street-Robbers, &c.* [Birmingham, 1742], pp. 220–30).

The beginnings of Defoe's novels are not so odd as their endings, but here, too, they deviate significantly from standard criminal biography. Basically, too much or too little information is offered about the origins of Defoe's protagonists for them to be seen in the usual emblematic way. Singleton and Jack are, essentially, without social background. Singleton offers what he can of his "pedigree"; it is part of his effort to conform to biographical convention or, as he says, to be "methodical." But all that he knows is that he lived somewhere near Islington as a child and that his parents could afford to keep him "very well drest." At least this much is true if he "may believe the Woman, whom [he] was taught to call Mother" (1). Jack says, "my original may be as high as any Bodies, for ought I know," but he and we have this "by oral Tradition" only; he, too, knows only what he has been told by the woman who raised him (3). At the very start of their narratives, then, Singleton and Jack lose a great deal of their emblematic potential; they are insufficiently rooted in the social order. If they cannot be seen as members of a class (and I mean the word taxonomically as well as socially), how can they be seen as types? The other two novels achieve a similar effect by opposite means. That is, they give too much information about the origins of their protagonists for them to be "typed" or otherwise relegated to standard social categories.

Moll knows exactly where and to whom she was born, information later confirmed by the narrative. Her parentage and place of birth are, to be sure, rich in emblematic possibilities; in fact I cannot recollect another criminal of the period, actual or fictitious, who was born in Newgate of a thief and who came (as Moll nearly does) to end at her beginning. But the simple, rich, and luminous facts of Moll's birth are hedged about with other information, and this has a complicating effect. In the first place, before she tells us where and to whom she was born, she asks us to consider the provision made in France, she thinks, for the children of convicted criminals. "Had this been the Custom in our Country," she says, her life would have taken a happier turn (8). This remarkable statement is somewhat perplexing, as it keeps the reader from any simple response as she goes on to situate herself vis-à-vis society. Is she implying the world is at fault? Is it? Is she trying to excuse herself or even, rather cleverly, to solicit pity? Emblems have to be taken in at a glance, and people who are to serve as emblems ought not to raise such questions; it makes them too engaging. Though similar questions are sometimes raised in criminal biography, they tend to occur toward the end of the text, after readers' attitudes have had a chance to harden.[42]

---

[42] Actually, judging from the many cases coming to public notice involving the maltreatment of orphans and other parent-less children, Moll would seem to have been moderately lucky; she doesn't get all that she should by way of a proper upbringing, but things could have been worse. "The case of Orphans and Bastards is deplorable," says *Fair Warning to Murderers of*

But even were it not for this curious remark, which occupies the whole
third paragraph of the novel, the simple facts of Moll's birth would still
escape easy translation into the conventions of criminal biography for the
equally simple but far more pregnant fact that she has more than one
point of origin. Like Singleton and Jack, Moll is raised by strangers, but
unlike them by several different sets of strangers. First there is some
unspecified relation of her mother's, then a band of gypsies (it is here that
Moll begins to have recollections of her own), and then first one and then
another household in Colchester. Moll does not coalesce out of thin air, as
Singleton and Jack seem to do, but begins again and again. Indeed this
can seem the story of her whole life; without a definite beginning or end,
Moll in a sense is always beginning, always starting over, unendingly vital.
It is interesting that here, also, at least one of Defoe's admirers thought he
could do better and made "improvements" on the original.[43]

Roxana is quite a different case, but she, too, supplies more information
than we need or would like in order to see her emblematically. Roxana's
origins are the most defined of all Defoe's criminal protagonists. She
belongs not only to a specific social class, but to a specific and highly
visible ethnic group, the Huguenots of Soho. She tells how she was raised
and gives the sad history of her marriage, of her going into keeping, of her
intrigues in Europe and England, and then finally the events leading up to
her daughter's apparent murder. The anomaly here from the standpoint
of criminal biography is that the text is all front matter, all etiology but no
crime and punishment. The effect of this is all the more powerful because
the text has seemed, as one reads through it, not a criminal biography at
all but a secret history. Only in retrospect does it become the story of a
woman's child killed to preserve her reputation, or at least the start of such
a story. This was no uncommon tale in Defoe's time, but typically the
victim was a newborn infant, smothered by its mother to conceal an illicit
pregnancy.[44] *Roxana* introduces a new twist into an old tale by killing (or
hinting at the killing) of a legitimate child, and by waiting until that child
has grown up and come to love and seek out her mother. Those of us who
know the relevant genres – i.e., both secret history and criminal biography
– find to our surprise that we have been reading its narrator's disclosures
"wrong"; suddenly, as her story takes a different shape, we have to revise

---

Infants: Being an Account of the Tryal, Co[n]demnation and Execution of Mary Goodenough (1692):
"Parishes indeed, take care to place them out where they may learn a slavish way of living at
the cheapest rates, but seldom consider whether they'll be carefully instructed in the Fear, and
piously conducted in the ways of God" (p. [iii]).

[43] Cf. *Fortune's Fickle Distribution*, which gives Moll a detailed (and significantly altered) family
history.

[44] For the historical background on women killing infants legitimate or not, see R. W. Malcolm-
son, "Infanticide in the Eighteenth Century" in *Crime in England, 1550–1800*, ed. J. S.
Cockburn (Princeton, 1977), pp. 187–209, and Beattie, *Crime and the Courts*, pp. 113–24.

our view of it and her.[45] Our first, sustained impression doesn't quite fade
away, however, for the genre expectations appropriate to secret histories
have been too strongly evoked. Thus Roxana becomes at the very least a
compound figure, and all the more remarkable because the elements
which form this compound – the secret history character and the murderer
– are neither in themselves complete nor encased in fully worked out
versions of the appropriate forms. If readers accustomed to "completed"
and "ready-made" aesthetics (and of course the ethics that accompany
such aesthetics) want such forms, either here or in Defoe's other criminal
novels, the working them out and the filling them out is up to them.[46]

We moderns are used to having our characters seem whole and entire in
all but the most contemporary fiction. What can easily seem a deficiency
from our point of view, however, may well have enhanced the reading
experience of Defoe's original audience. Criminal biography offered them
characters that were either entirely or not at all of a piece, either over-
determined sinners or fractured, unintelligible rogues. Defoe's protagonists are not unemblematic, but neither are they swallowed up by their
function. Their names themselves intimate as much, being particular
enough to serve as normal proper names but quasi-allegorical as well. The
commonness of Jack survives in terms like lumberjack and steeplejack; it is
a fit name for your ordinary sort of guy, a kind of everyman who, after all,
is a jack of many (though not all) trades. Singleton, too, is an apt name, its
bearer being a social isolate in more than one sense. Practically though not
actually an orphan, he becomes a pirate who never quite affiliates with the
"anti-society" of other pirates and, even after reforming, is obliged to keep
to himself. Moll and Roxana, for their part, seem nearly trade names. The
first, a diminutive for Mary, was as common a name among female
criminals as Jack among the general male population. Roxana did not
have as clear a connotation, so far as I can tell, but the text makes it seem a
synonym for your highest class of doxy. Thus speaking of her reputation
after a three-year affair with an exalted person she does not name, Roxana
says "it began to be publick, that Roxana was, in short, a meer *Roxana*,
neither better nor worse; and not that Woman of Honour and Virtue that

---

45 Ian A. Bell, *Defoe's Fiction* (London, 1985), pp. 70, 184, 186, also makes something of this point.
   In retrospect, however, the novel's leap from one genre to another may not seem so abrupt
   after all. Thus the murdered daughter first appears slightly after the middle of the novel, and,
   if we see her murder as the culminating point of Roxana's moral, social, and psychological
   decay, all that precedes this appearance is relevant to her final, terrible disappearance.
46 Reader expectation may have been similarly complicated by Roxana's self-comparison to the
   German Princess. She seems to have started down the same slippery slope, though from a
   higher initial position, without having yet bottomed out as the German Princess did, who was
   finally hanged for theft after an abortive career of playing herself on stage. By the end of the
   novel, of course, Roxana is implicated in far more terrible events than the German Princess
   ever was, and represents far greater moral corruption.

was at first suppos'd" (182).[47] That Moll and Roxana are not their real
names only further complicates their status; behind the quasi-emblematic
words lurk their real, undiscoverable identities. That Moll's real given
name may be Elizabeth, and Roxana's Susan, makes the mystery of their
true identities all the more teasing.

Unlike other redacted criminals, Defoe's are neither immediately nor
easily categorizable. The peculiar quality of his "realism" vis-à-vis that of
criminal biography, then, is not merely that his texts simulate plausible
movements of mind in their narrators but that they agitate their readers,
too, to just such movements as they confront those narrators. This is true
even at the most basic level of the text, as it moves forward phrase-by-
phrase, sentence-by-sentence. It is not so much *what* Defoe's criminals say,
as *how* they say it that marks them out from ordinary, actual criminals.
That is, they speak in voices peculiar to themselves, not at all like the
first-person narrators occasionally found in criminal biography. By this I
don't mean that each speaks in a voice characteristic of him or her as an
individual, for Defoe is actually not much concerned (and perhaps
unable) to represent the consciousness of idiosyncratic individuals. He is,
however, very much concerned with presenting a variousness of consciousness, both in and around the voice of his narrators. In standard criminal
biography there is essentially no difference between first and third-person
narrative, as can be shown by a simple test. Thus all that is required to
shift a text from one mode to the other is an alteration of the appropriate
pronouns.[48]

---

[47] For a discussion of the rich implications of "Jack," see David Blewett, *Defoe's Art of Fiction*
(Toronto, 1979), pp. 94–5, 104. The disreputableness of "Moll" was of long standing. "Seeke
all *London* from one end to t'other," says a character in Thomas Middleton and Thomas
Dekker's *The Roaring Girle, or Moll Cut-Purse* (1611), "More whoores of that name, then of any
ten other" (sig. E2v; for this reference – and much else – I am indebted to the late Arthur
Friedman). A mid-century pamphleteer explains the generic use of the term "Moll" on the
grounds that "the far greater Number (of any other Name) of loose and disorderly Women are
called by the Name of Mary" (*Reasons Offered for the Reformation of the House of Correction in
Clerkenwell* [1757], p. 21n.). Though "Roxana" could not have had a comparable currency,
some commentators see an allusion back to the (literally) poisonous character of the same
name in Nathaniel Lee's *The Rival Queens* (1677); for this suggestion and others, see Maximillian E. Novak's "Crime and Punishment in *Roxana*," *Journal of English and Germanic Philology*, 65
(1966): 260–2, "The Unmentionable and the Ineffable in Defoe's Fiction," *Studies in the Literary
Imagination*, 15 (1982): 98, and *Realism, Myth, and History in Defoe's Fiction*, pp. 115–16, where
Novak also finds some play on names in *Moll Flanders*, pp. 84–5. There may also be some hint in
Roxana's name of the dialect word "rox," first recorded in the nineteenth century, meaning to
decay, rot, soften, or slacken; the adjective form, "roxy," was typically applied to fruit or
cheese (see the *Oxford English Dictionary*).

[48] Several instances of narratives switched from first to third person in fact survive. Cf., for
instance, Smith's account of Moll Cutpurse in *Lives of the Highwaymen*, especially p. 285, to his
source, *Life and Death of Frith*, especially p. 43. Cf. also the account of John Everett in *Lives of the
Most Remarkable Criminals*, pp. 512–19, to that appearing in *The Tyburn Chronicle: Or, Villainy
Display'd in All Its Branches* (1768), 2: 308–33. *In The Life and Adventures of Gilbert Langley* …

Turn back a few pages and try the experiment with the bits quoted from Harmon Strodtman's *Confession*, or consider the following, supposedly Bernard Fink's own account of how, having been arrested on suspicion of several earlier robberies, he went on to commit two more:

After I was Discharg'd, I had not Grace enough to leave off my wicked Courses. I with *Hugh Morris*, going a long *Piccadily* one Evening, we attack'd a Gentleman, and as soon as we attack'd him, he cry'd out; we reply'd to him, Sir, *do not be Frighted, Money we want, and Money we must have*; so we took from him fifteen Shillings; the Watchmen coming their Rounds, we bid the Gentleman go about his Business, and not to speak one Word, and if he did, he was a dead Man; upon which he said, upon my Word, I will not; as he was crossing the way, he said Gentlemen, Will you have any thing else? I having a very indifferent Hat, I call'd him back, and made an Exchange with him, and told him *an Exchange is no Robbery*, Gentlemen says he, *will you have my Wigg also*; *Hugh Morris* Swore he wou'd shoot the Gentleman if he did not go back and shew him where his Watch was; the Gentleman reply'd, he had not any Watch about him, or any where else; so took his Leave of us, and wish'd us better success. The same Night going along we met a Man, who was very much in Liquor, whom we attack'd, when we bid him Stand, [said he] *you Rogues, I value you not*; we made no more to do, but took our Pistol and put it to his Nose, and bid him smell to it, which somewhat surpriz'd him; *I thought Gentlemen, you were but in Jest*; Sir, says I, *you shall see that we are in Earnest*, for we took from him his Watch, and some Silver, but what quantity I cannot well Re-member.[49]

This is more interesting than most such passages, and many of its details ring true. The men robbed behave rather like people do in such circum-stances, the second with stunned disbelief and the first with a giddiness that makes him all too obliging. "Gentlemen, Will you have anything else?" he asks, "will you have my Wigg also?" And as he finally leaves he wishes them "better success"! A sense of authenticity is also contributed by the text's occasional ungrammaticality; it sounds as if it might be based on a shorthand copy of Fink's own discourse. Nonetheless, there is no essential difference between the language registered here and that which any prison chaplain or other "ordinary" provider of criminal biography might use to describe the same two events. Only the recurring "I," instead of "he" or Fink's name, identifies this as the discourse of a specific individual sup-posedly speaking from personal experience. In the very next paragraph, Fink will describe yet another robbery. Here, when the victim resists, Fink swears an oath that he will shoot him unless he submits – "which God forgive me," Fink interpolates in a parenthesis. In a confession of some 1,800 words, only these four do not readily translate into third-person

Written by Himself (1740), we catch such switching in mid-flight, for after beginning with approximately 600 words in the third person, the narrative shifts to the first in the middle of a sentence, and stays there (see p. 3).
49 Guthrie, Ordinary Account, 26 July 1731.

narrative. The difficulty, moreover, comes not from the diction or sentiment of the phrase, but from its syntactical relation to the sentence in
which it is embedded. Its sentiment and diction, like the text as a whole,
align Fink entirely with the official values of his culture; the parenthesis is
still no more than the speech of a ventriloquist's dummy.

This excerpt from Fink's confession might usefully be compared to
almost any similar description in Defoe's four criminal novels. (Finding a
close match in *Roxana* might be difficult, but I would suggest her account
of how she played the bawd to Amy, forcing her into bed with the London
jeweller, the first of her several lovers.) In most cases, if not all, shifting
Defoe from first- to third-person narrative would require substantial
rewriting merely to avoid awkwardness, and even a bare minimum of such
changes would significantly alter his meaning. Roxana's description of
how she made Amy a "whore" like herself, for instance, would become
downright pornographic: e.g., "and with that, [she] sat her down, pull'd
off her Stockings and Shooes, and all her Cloaths, Piece by Piece, and led
her to the Bed to him," etc. (46).[50] The other three novels offer closer
comparisons to Fink's confession, as each contains first-hand descriptions
either of robberies or of violent, or potentially violent, encounters. Here,
for instance, is Jack telling how he and his partner Will mugged an
unwary apprentice:

The next Adventure was in the dusk of the Evening in a Court, which goes out of
Grace-Church-street into *Lombard-street*, where the *Quaker's-Meeting House* is; there
was a young Fellow, who as we learn'd afterward was a Woolen-Drapers Apprentice in *Grace-Church-street*; it seems he had been receiving a Sum of Money, which
was very considerable, and he comes to a Goldsmith's-Shop in *Lombard Street* with
it; paid in the most of it there, insomuch, that it grew Dark, and the Goldsmith
began to be shutting in Shop, and Candles to be Lighted: We watch'd him in
there, and stood on the other Side of the way to see what he did. When he had paid
in all the Money he intended, he stay'd still sometime longer to take Notes, as I
suppos'd, for what he had paid, and by this time it was still darker than before; at
last he comes out of the Shop, with still a pretty large Bag under his Arm, and
walks over into the Court, which was then very Dark; in the middle of the Court is
a boarded Entry, and farther, at the End of it a Threshold, and as soon as he had
set his Foot over the Threshold he was to turn on his Left Hand into *Grace-Church-
street*.

Keep up, says *Will* to me, be nimble, and as soon as he had said so, he flyes at
the young Man, and Gives him such a Violent Thrust, that push'd him forward
with too great a force for him to stand, and as he strove to recover, the Threshold
took his Feet, and he fell forward into the other part of the Court, as if he had

---

[50] This is as good an indication as any of the way Defoe's narrative "I" in this and the other
novels intervenes between the reader and any "clear" sense of the action; the deletion of the
"I" here is like the removing of a screen, allowing us simply to "see" what is happening, thus
the sudden, voyeuristic, pornographic effect. For more on this topic see chapter 7.

flown in the Air, with his Head lying towards the *Quaker's-Meeting-House*; I stood ready, and presently felt out the Bag of Money, which I heard fall, for it flew out of his Hand, he having his Life to save, not his Money: I went forward with the Money, and *Will* that threw him down, finding I had it, run backward, and as I made along *Fen-Church-street*, *Will* overtook me, and we scour'd home together; the poor young Man was hurt a little with the fall, and reported to his Master, as we heard afterward that he was knock'd down, which was not true, for neither *Will*, or I had any Stick in our Hands; but the Master of the Youth was it seems so very thankful that his young Man was not knock'd down before he paid the rest of the Money, (which was above 100l. more) to the Goldsmith, who was Sir *John Sweetapple*, that he made no great Noise at the Loss he had; and as we heard afterward, only warn'd his Prentice to be more careful, and come no more thro' such Places in the Dark; whereas the Man had really no such Deliverance as he imagined, for we saw him before, when he had all the Money about him, but it was no time of Day for such Work as we had to do, so that he was in no Danger before.   (57–8)

This passage communicates a subjectivity rarely if ever found in criminal biography. That there is an individual voice speaking here is indicated not only by the use of "it seems," "as I suppos'd," and "as we learn'd/ heard afterward" but also by the recurring references to the growing dark, which not only sets the stage for the robbery but, eventually, means that the money dropped by their victim must be located by the sound it makes falling and "felt out" by Jack's groping hand. But more than merely Jack's particular sense of the event is communicated here; his subjectivity is located among other subjectivities. Their victim reports to his master that he was knocked down, "which was not true," says Jack, because he and Will did not use sticks. Does their victim think they did? Or is he embroidering his story to be better believed, and perhaps also in a bid for his master's sympathy? Or perhaps it is Jack who is cavilling, hoping to mitigate the hurt he admits he did this "poor young Man"? The victim's employer has his point of view, too. Glad that the largest part of his money was safely paid out, he finds a lesson in the event, warning his apprentice to be more careful of dark places in future. This seems sensible and useful, until Jack undercuts it, though only partially, by pointing out that the master simply does not know the whole affair. Sir John Sweetapple (a real goldsmith, by the way) is the only person mentioned that isn't heard from, but doubtless he, too, would have had something to say.[51]

There is an intimation here not only of the speaking subject's processes

---

[51] For the reality of Sir John Sweetapple, and the appearance of his name along with a number of other actual London goldsmiths, see *CJ*, p. 313, n. 1. In this novel and *Roxana*, Defoe curiously involves real people in his fictitious plots. This was a common phenomenon in the fictionalized accounts of highwaymen and other notorious thieves – thus, in Smith's *Lives of the Highwaymen*, Oliver Cromwell gets robbed four times in all – but Defoe is not aiming at the usual (and cheap) satiric effect. The complications that ensue from his practice are far more teasing and implicative.

of mind, then, but of the processes of mind of other, potentially speaking, subjects around him. Though the event is described from Jack's point of view, it is possible to reimagine it from others. At the end of the first quoted paragraph there is even something of a push in that direction, when the physical setting of the crime is described as the victim himself is about to encounter it, i.e., "and as soon as he had set his Foot over the Threshold he was to turn on his Left Hand." But even by itself Jack's point of view is no simple thing, for there is a difference between what he saw and remarked on at the time, and what he later "heard" or "learn'd." The difference between these two separate awarenesses sets up a potentially interesting dynamic for the reader to contemplate, as does Jack's consciousness generally in its various juxtapositions to those of his divers victims. When Defoe spoke of "the surprising variety of the subject," he could almost have been speaking phenomenologically.

This proliferation of points of view is typical of all Defoe's novels, but especially noticeable in *Colonel Jack*. Its many dialogues might themselves be the subject of an essay, providing as they do a context for Jack's discourse, qualifying it in a number of ways but most importantly by offering an alternative, more "normal" point of view to be set next to his. It is not difficult to imagine what the apprentice or master in the passage just quoted might have thought or said about the robbery, because we have already heard Jack's victims speaking in conversations with him, his confederate Will, and certain of their friends, as they respond to the problems his thefts cause not only them but Jack as well. (Their loss has been his gain, which in various ways – first financially, then legally, and finally morally – comes to embarrass him.) For eighteenth-century readers, of course, Jack would stand out from other criminals because he fails to measure up (or down) to the conventions of criminal biography, his "deviation" made all the more striking by the close resemblance of the opening part of his narrative to certain actual biographies.[52]

But Jack stands out as well – and in ways that transcend the immediate historical context of the novel – because, inevitably, his attitudes and feelings get measured against those of the good-natured customs house broker who unwittingly helps him to his first big haul, the Jewish diamond merchant whose pocket he picks, and, finally, the Kentish Town widow whose mite he robs and then returns with interest. So much experience with other characters' direct speech prepares readers to imagine, on rather slight hints, the discourse and point of view of characters whose speech is reported only indirectly and briefly at that; this is rather a nice trick for Defoe to have accomplished in a first-person narrative, and more will be

---

[52] Thus, yet another reason for quoting from Bernard Fink's confession is its resemblance, overall, to Jack's account of his all-night crime spree with Will and a gang of other young robbers, and which includes his robbing the Kentish Town widow.

said on the subject in the next several chapters. Here it is enough to say that Jack becomes all the more substantial, complex, and interesting because of the "otherness" readers are led to sense around him. The more alert one grows to Jack's particular subjectivity, the more aware one becomes that the world at large is composed of subjectivities. This, though, isn't something Jack himself knows; one's own subjectivity can mask or screen the presence of others and so prevent such an awareness.

Defoe uses dialogues elsewhere to similar effect. Not a husband or lover of Moll's is without at least one speech giving his point of view as against hers. Moll doesn't always understand as much of these transactions as any moderately alert reader might, but her husbands and lovers practically never know just what is on her mind. Moll's victims often speak up as well (more on this in chapter 5). Roxana, too, is hedged about with dialogues, one of the most memorable occurring when she refuses the Dutchman's offer of marriage, her wild feminism contrasting strangely with the reasoned views of a man who wants – against her will and all the conventions of secret history – to do right by her. Other dialogues in that novel shade Roxana's voice more darkly, particularly those between her and Amy, the Quaker confidante who replaces Amy, and her terribly importunate daughter (for more on this topic, see chapter 7). Singleton has his Quaker, too, and the frequent dialogues between him and William introduce a most curious ambivalence into the text, setting Singleton's ignorant and to some extent innocent brutality (or what passes for such) against William's casuistical combination of decency and greed. For Defoe's original audience Quakers would have been ambivalent figures in themselves, envied for their business acumen yet scorned for not only their curious habits but the equivocations by which they continued to live – and prosper – in a world they nonetheless affected to reject.[53]

Defoe's first-person narratives differ from those to be found in criminal biography, then, in that they offer a variety of voices. This variety stretches out to include points of view beyond those of the putative narrator, but of course the voices of the narrators themselves are complicated. Thus all make distinctions between what they knew or felt at the time, and what they later found out or felt as a result of subsequent experience, and/or upon reflection. This gives Defoe's novels a complex

[53] For a typical attitude toward Quakers, see Tom Brown, *The Works of Mr. Thomas Brown*, 5th edn (1720–1), 4: 119–20. A similar ambivalence is on offer when the diamond merchant robbed by Jack and Will is described as both a Jew and – the term appears some two dozen times without irony – a "Gentleman" (45–54). The text fails to recognize even the possibility of a discrepancy between these terms, and, in negotiating with Will, the Jew proves a decent, honorable, and civil man. Still, many of Defoe's readers would have despised Jews – cf. the repulsive Jew who threatens Roxana in Paris – and even those not especially anti-Semitic may have been puzzled at this episode's implications.

temporality, no small part of which is the sense they give of *lived* lives.[54] The criminal characters, moreover, recollect their pasts with a split sensibility, speaking of it at times with penitence and chagrin, but at other times with no such embarrassment, even almost or actually with delight, caught up again in the thrill of the reimagined event. Defoe's criminal protagonists are nothing if not ambivalent – or perhaps I should say polyvalent – about their pasts. The second term might be necessary to make the distinction between them and the protagonists of actual criminal biographies sufficiently clear. The typical criminal turned into "chiefest of sinners" is often proud of his new preeminence and of two minds about his "shameful-happy" history. Defoe's characters, however, are often of several minds, and their disparate points of view, to say nothing of the tensions between them, are never consolidated or resolved into the over-arching whole of serious criminal biography, which above all looks for pattern and coherence in its subject's life, for the one true meaning of each event considered as part of a series of plainly significant events, the whole series itself having one clear meaning. Sure at the end of his life that "within a few Hours" he will "sing with the blessed Saints above," Harmon Strodtman exactly fits the Newgate ordinary's description of him as "that once *unfortunate*, but *now*, and *for ever Happy* Young-man."[55]

Parts relate to whole transparently and unequivocally in such bi-ography, not only for the audience but also, later if not sooner, for the criminal who figures in it. Looking back at the entire sweep of his life, he knows surely and simply what it all means and has meant; that meaning, moreover, is congruent with official morality, and the criminal is able to articulate it in the simplest of terms – terms in fact identical with those a magistrate or priest might use, the two chief spokesmen of official morality. That Defoe's criminals at times approximate this mode makes their falling away from it all the more surprising and problematical. Not only their lives, but their views of their lives, are no simple things. Neither they nor their readers can easily interpret the entire sweep of their experience; in fact it is hard to take in that sweep in a single glance, and as hard for readers as it is for them to be of a single mind about it. These are not lives to be recollected in tranquillity, which is more or less the aim of most criminal biography, whether serious or not; these are lives to agitate and unsettle readers, to put them to a variety of tests.

Another way of setting out the special challenge that Defoe's novels

---

[54] On this subject see particularly Paul K. Alkon, *Defoe and Fictional Time* (Athens, Ga., 1979).

[55] For "shameful-happy" see Robert Franklin, Thomas Vincent, Thomas Doolitel, James Janeway, and Hugh Baker, *A Murderer Punished and Pardoned: Or a True Relation of the Wicked Life, and Shameful-Happy Death of Thomas Savage* (1668); Savage was one of the most famous murderers of the seventeenth and eighteenth centuries. For Strodtman's and Lorrain's comments, see N. B., *Compleat Tryals . . . for near Fifty Years Past*, 2: 214, and Paul Lorrain, *Harmon Strodtman's Last Legacy to the World* (1701).

would have posed readers accustomed to "ordinary" criminal biography is to point out that, even when narrated in the first person, the latter suggests no real difference between author and narrator; both speak in the same voice. And because the author typically speaks in an officially sanctioned voice, there is, presumably, no real difference between him and his audience. This is not the case in Defoe's novels – even *Robinson Crusoe* takes steps to insert a wedge between its narrator's consciousness and that of its audience – and it most especially is not the case in his novels of criminal life. Because the narrators here are criminals, and not subsumable within the categories their culture prescribes for criminals, there is always and inevitably a tension between what they say and what they ought to be saying. Often, indeed, they are so far from knowing what they are actually saying, so unaware of the impact of their voices, that listening to them can be irritating, unsettling, even chilling and eerie. Moll's account of how she waylaid "a pretty little Child" is a case in point, and so, too, Roxana's description of her daughter's trip to Greenwich with Amy. Both episodes have about them a kind of menacing obscenity, not so much for what happens as what might have happened, not so much for what is said as what should have been said and is not. The light of conscience, that "Natural Magistrate in every Man's Heart," shines only intermittently through their speech, flickering just enough to show how truly dark they are – and this is much darker, to be sure, than criminal biography would allow any of its criminals to be or show themselves to be.

"A pretty little Child had been at a Dancing-School, and was going home, all alone," says Moll,

and [the Devil,] my Prompter, like a true Devil, set me upon this innocent Creature; I talk'd to it, and it prattl'd to me again, and I took it by the Hand and led it a long till I came to a pav'd Alley that goes into *Bartholomew Close*, and I led it in there; the Child said that was not its way home; I said, yes, my Dear it is, I'll show you the way home; the Child had a little Necklace on of Gold Beads, and I had my Eye upon that, and in the dark of the Alley I stoop'd, pretending to mend the Child's Clog that was loose, and took off her Necklace and the Child never felt it, and so led the Child on again: Here, I say, the Devil put me upon killing the Child in the dark Alley, that it might not Cry; but the very thought frighted me so that I was ready to drop down.

Turning the child around and sending it home, Moll flees down a series of streets, lanes, and passages, their names following one upon the other as she gives them in giddying succession. She doesn't stop until, plunging finally into a "Crowd of People," she feels "it was not possible to have been found out" (194).

Before telling this story Moll warns it's "of a dreadful Nature indeed," and, as it unfolds, it's clear she's not mincing words. Her fright, her fleeing, her wanting to lose herself in a crowd, all of it seems an appropriate response to her having teetered for a moment, vertiginously, at the edge of the abyss. All that stood that moment between that "innocent Creature" and the worst the Devil might offer was Moll, weak vessel that she is. But then Moll seemingly shrugs off the whole affair: "[It] left no great Concern upon me," she says, "for as I did the poor Child no harm, I only said to my self, I had given the Parents a just Reproof for their Negligence in leaving the poor little Lamb to come home by itself, and it would teach them to take more Care of it another time." And she goes on to speculate that the necklace belonged to the child's mother, that she was wearing it because of her mother's vanity (she wanted her daughter to "look Fine at the Dancing School"), and that the maid who ought to have been with her "was taken up perhaps with some Fellow that had met her by the way, and so the poor Baby wandred till it fell into my Hands." "I did the Child no harm," she insists, "I did not so much as fright it, for I had a great many tender Thoughts about me yet, and did nothing but what, as I may say, meer Necessity drove me to" (194–5).

The irony of Moll's special pleading has been noted by many modern readers, some finding a certain wry pleasure, even a kind of comedy in it.[56] Sputtering and fuming against the child's parents, imagining a feckless maid distracted by "some fellow," she pities the child for falling into her very own hands. She gives no thought to her own miserable record as a parent or to the fact that she, too – though no longer a maid, alas! – has herself been "taken up" by a "fellow" (and he the worst of them all). Defoe's contemporaries may well have read this passage a good deal less disinterestedly, however, taking less pleasure in its ironies and even finding them more than a bit horrific. Though criminal biography in my experience contains nothing quite like Moll's description of this encounter in the alley, children were not infrequently robbed by adults, especially of their clothing; this was chiefly a women's specialty, apparently because they more easily gained the confidence of their victims. Violence was rarely used, but it was still considered a dangerous and particularly loathesome crime. "This ... robbing and stripping young Children," wrote a Newgate ordinary less than twenty years after the publication of *Moll Flanders*, "has [often] been attended with the most dismal Consequences, a favourite Child being in this manner taken away, has perhaps been the Loss of a Parents Senses or Life. Other Times perhaps the Child by being left all Night almost naked by these barbarous Wretches in the Fields, has lost its Life."[57] Parents hearing Moll's account of her "second Sally into the World" – or those who could imagine how parents felt –

[56] E.g., most recently, Ian Bell, *Defoe's Fiction*, p. 140.
[57] Guthrie, Ordinary Account, 14 September 1741. For analogous passages in Defoe's other writings, and a pertinent newspaper advertisement, see Starr's edition of *MF*, p. 388, n. 3 for p. 194.

would inevitably have been reminded that theirs was a world (like ours) where children could not safely be left alone in public for a minute. How could such readers not have felt anger, fear, and disgust at Moll's self-serving rationalizations? Loading guilt onto the child's parents, she all too easily sloughs off her own.

Not quite nine years before the publication of *Moll Flanders* there was in fact a case of a child being left naked in the fields. Susan Perry, alias Dewy, about twenty-two years old, was "condemn'd for Stripping naked, Robbing and Murdering ... *John Peirce*, an Infant of 4 Years of age."[58] Perry's account of herself is worth noting if only for its rough congruence with Moll's own history. She, too, might have claimed that "Poverty ... hardened my Heart, and my own Necessities made me regardless of any thing" (194). Certainly the response she and her story got suggests something of what contemporary readers might have felt as, with "no great Concern," Moll tells how she robbed and was tempted to kill another "pretty little child." Apprenticed to a mantua maker but finding no work in that trade, Perry first became a seamstress and then peddled newspapers and fruit in the streets. Convicted of a felony (probably theft, she doesn't say) and whipped for it (which was lucky; she could have been hanged or transported), she "liv'd a poor, miserable, wretched Life" after her release from Newgate. "Which [Life]," says the ordinary of that place without the least bit of sympathy, "as she had then no Thought to render better by honest Means, so she was easily tempted to make it worse, as she did by committing the Fact she is now to die for."

His coldness is prompted by her bad attitude. Failing to appreciate "the horrid Enormity" of her "Inhumane and Barbarous" crime, she does not seem "sensible of her great Guilt." Refusing to admit the murder, she claims that "she never laid violent hands upon the Child, only took off his Cloaths from him, and left him (otherwise) untouch'd and unhurt." The ordinary simply cannot believe her; why should anyone else have come along after "to strangle a Child that lay stark naked in the Fields"? "She who had the cruel Heart to do such a barbarous thing, as to leave a poor innocent Babe in that manner, and in such a place" – it was the midst of winter, darkness coming on – "must naturally be thought," he admonishes her and assures his readers, "to be the bloody Person that committed the Murder also." And even if she hadn't actually strangled the child, leaving him naked in so cold and damp a season was the same as killing him. Perry does not "at first appear to be much mov'd" by these representations; "so great was her Stupidity, that she express'd no Concern nor Remorse for the great Evil she had done." Though later she does weep and show "Expressions of Grief," the ordinary still cannot in the end be sure she was

---

[58] For this and subsequent quotes pertaining to Perry, see Lorrain, Ordinary Account, 13 March 1713.

"truly sensible," that she'd overcome her "Ignorance" or "obstinate and harden'd Disposition."

Perry doesn't behave as she ought, but she behaves far better than Moll. At least she gropes toward the proprieties, and might be said to have met the demands of her audience half way. Moll does nothing of the sort. Blaming her crime on "the Devil" and her "Necessities" without seeing how her own dishonesty opens her to both, impugning the character of the child's parents and their maid instead of her own, she claims that despite her "harden'd" heart "I had a great many tender Thoughts about me yet." It is of course her hardened heart – or, as the ordinary would say, her "stupidity" and "ignorance" – that makes this claim. No conventional criminal biographer would permit Moll to say such things uncontradicted. His voice would come down hard on hers, as the Newgate chaplain's does on Perry's, or he would suppress such talk altogether. In allowing Moll to speak unchallenged, Defoe burdens his readers as no ordinary criminal biographer ever would. In the absence of some third, safely authoritative voice to say where and how she is wrong, it is up to the reader himself to challenge her; and what she is saying is so provoking that the reader *must* challenge her, there is no keeping his peace.[59]

The effect of Roxana's telling how Amy lured Susan down to Greenwich, with a view to killing her there "among the Woods, and Trees" (314), is altogether more subtle and delicate. Here, too, Defoe's narrator speaks in several opposing voices. She calls Amy's scheme a "fatal and wicked Design" (311) and pauses in her description of it to say how, later, remonstrating with Amy, she told her to her face "she was a Murtherer, and a bloody-minded Creature," and that her daughter "was in the right." She "had nothing to blame [Susan] for"; whatever trouble "the Girl" was causing "was owing to the Wickedness of my Life." "I wou'd not murther my Child," she tells Amy on that later occasion, "tho' I was otherwise to be ruin'd by it." And when Amy says for her part she would, "if she had an Opportunity," Roxana is "horribly disturb'd" and tells her to clear out (312–13). Set against this outburst of stern morality, however, is the tone Roxana takes as, before and after, she recreates the scene at Greenwich. Amy's may be a "wicked Design," she says, "but we were all hamper'd to the last Degree, with the Impertinence of this Creature; and in particular, I was horribly perplex'd with it." Perplexed and disturbed must the reader be, too, as, continuing her narrative to its most climactic moment, Roxana takes Amy's point of view. Thus when Susan "boldly" refuses Amy's offer to walk in the woods – "she did not know but she might

---

[59] Rewritings of the novel smooth these difficulties over, *Fortune's Fickle Distribution* omitting Moll's temptation to kill the child and the chapbook version cutting the whole incident down to less than a sentence: "... I inveigled a little child from whom I took a gold necklace; but I did not kill it, but put it in its way home again" (*Fortunes and Misfortunes of Moll Flanders*, p. 11). This awkward denial says a great deal about audience expectation.

murther her" – Roxana finds this "very provoking." "But however," she goes on with considerable sympathy for her servant's predicament, "Amy kept her Temper, with much Difficulty, and bore it, knowing that much might depend upon it" (311–12, 314).

Is Roxana sincere in her outrage? Does she side with Amy or not? The answer of course is that she is and isn't, that she does and doesn't. The variety of voices within Roxana's voice, and the contradictions they embody, make her one of the most interesting characters in eighteenth-century fiction – especially as all these voices are not her own. As she describes the expedition to Greenwich, we hear Amy's and Susan's voices, too, and these are also various, expressing through their own contradictions the complex motives behind them as well. The episode all by itself is dense with implication (with what kinds, and how, will be a concern of chapter 7) but read against the conventions of criminal biography it gains a further overlay of meaning. This luring of troublesome females away into "the woods, and trees" to murder them would have been an old idea to readers of criminals' lives. It was what one did, on occasion, when seduced girls or cast-off women refused to be abandoned, and made demands. It is what Christopher Slaughterford did in 1709 when he drowned his ex-sweetheart in a pond near Guildford, and what Dramatti did in 1703 when he bludgeoned and stabbed his estranged wife to death in the fields between Chelsea and Kensington.[60]

Such crimes gained prominence not from any great frequency, for in fact they were relatively rare. It is likely they fascinated the public because of the element of betrayal in them, especially given the well-known danger of women in lonely places. In these instances it was no stranger who threatened, but men who normally ought to have been their protectors. The not incidental resemblance between such crimes and the crime halfheartedly attempted by Amy gives an odd and especially unhealthy tinge to the whole episode. It is not a man who lures Susan away and threatens her, but her mother's loyal friend and servant. Susan's love for her mother is utterly unrequited, but Amy, also loving Roxana, treats her like a dangerous rival; it is as if Susan were endangering Amy's own happiness with her desperate importunities. There is an ill-defined but nonetheless powerfully felt perversity in all this, an effect enhanced by Amy's odd power over Roxana, as well as by Susan's immediate, fully justified suspicion that Amy means to do the worst. Something curiously obscene is on view in this love triangle, for that in fact is what it is, something darker and dirtier than any ordinary passion-fraught murder in the woods. Certainly the sense of betrayal it gives is greater, for a daughter

---

60 Dramatti has been discussed in the previous chapter; for Slaughterford, see William Price, *The Birth, Parentage, and Education, Life and Conversation of Mr. Christopher Slaughterford, ... Executed at Guilford in Surry for ... the Barbarous Murther of Jane Young His Sweetheart* (1709).

ought not to fear her own mother or her mother's servant, or a woman another woman in dark and lonely places. And how could any mother retell this tale as Roxana does, with only an occasional, intermittent sense of what is properly at stake?

Roxana is far more guilt-ridden than Moll, but the depth of her guilt is not so deep as her sin. "The Caniballs that eate one another will spare the fruites of their owne bodies," says an early seventeenth-century account of a woman who had murdered two of her own children, "the Savages will doe the like, yea every beast and fowle hath a feeling of nature, and according to kinde will cherish their young ones." "Shall [a] Woman," it asks, "nay a Christian woman, Gods owne Image, be more unnaturall then Pagan, Caniball, Savage, Beast or Fowle"? How was it "that the blood of her owne body should have no more power to pearce remorse into her Iron naturd heart"? Nearly a hundred years later the language is less colorful and urgent, and seemingly more sympathetic. Hanged for killing her bastard infant, Christian Russel appeared "at the first ... very little concern'd for what she had done," says the Newgate ordinary, "she confessing her Sins, without apparent Signs of true sorrow for them." "But this might, in some measure," he adds in a spirit of charity, "be attributed to her dulness and slowness of Capacity, she being very stupid and ignorant, and a poor simple Creature, that knew little of Religion."[61] Roxana warrants no such charity, being neither dull nor slow, nor very stupid and ignorant. She is sensible enough to know her daughter is in the right; she says as much herself, and she dismisses Amy for wanting to murder her. Even so, she can still speak afterwards of "that vexatious Creature, *my Girl* .... who hunted me, as if, *like a Hound*" (316, 317). Her heart remains unpierced and iron-natured to the end.

However sympathetic Moll and Roxana may seem at times, however excusable or even admirable certain of their actions, neither they nor Jack nor Singleton ever quite speak in the socially sanctioned voices of their bleached and laundered *confrères*. The opposition between their several voices and what might be termed the official voice of society is, moreover, all the more emphasized when Defoe occasionally lays aside his impersonation of the narrator-protagonist to speak in his own voice (or at least in what we take to be his own voice). Readers are alerted to the possible presence of this voice by the prefaces to each of the novels. These not only claim that the books that follow are in some way morally (i.e., socially) valuable, but suggest their texts have been edited or otherwise reworked by the person (not the narrator) responsible for their publication. Defoe's

---

[61] *A Pitilesse Mother. That Most Unnaturally at One Time, Murthered Two of Her Owne Children ....* *Beeing a Gentlewoman Named Margret Vincent* (1616), sig. B1r-v; Lorrain, Ordinary Account, 28 January 1701.

criminal novels thus exhibit, albeit crudely, a situation much discussed by modern theorists of prose fiction: the text implies an author standing behind its narrator and speaking through him or her to an audience which, at some level aware of its complex relation to the text, is encouraged to respond critically; to perform, in other words, a variety of interpretive acts.

This of course is not the situation in serious criminal biography, where author, narrator, and reader are presumably at one, and where (ideally) no occasion is given to the reader to second guess the text. All those invitations to "judge" are extended in full confidence that the reader will see things as the writer himself does. Nor are readers of criminal rogue biography much encouraged to second guess its texts. Though here one's situation is not quite so simple – witness the abundance of sarcasm and irony – things are in so confused a state that second guessing is hardly worth the trouble. Basically the criminal is a joke shared, collusively, by author and audience; for this reason, perhaps, very few of these narratives are presented in the first person. Unlike the thieves debased by rogue biography, Defoe's criminals have to be taken seriously – but they will not submit to being taken seriously according to the prescriptive terms of the other, supposedly more meaningful form of criminal biography. Because they stand beyond socially sanctioned redaction, Defoe's criminals never quite get absorbed into the social; but then neither do they ever seem so incoherent and strange as to stand insolubly beyond it.

Such an odd and shifting liminality makes them both fascinating and provoking, almost scandalous in their anomaly. Criminal biography presents very strange or very "sociable" criminals, repairing the breach they made in the social order by expelling them into some extra-social "space" (the realm of "Nonesuch"), and so demolishing their status as fellow human beings (they are like "no body" and cannot "be sorted by any comparison"), or by bringing them firmly back into the fold, reconstructed along the most socially acceptable lines ("good" people speaking to "good people"). In following neither course, and in abandoning the mechanisms that allowed readers a comfortable distance from, or oneness with, their subjects, Defoe's novels present criminals that would have not only seemed fresh and new but put readers peculiarly on the spot. These, to borrow Shklovsky's famous phrasing, would have been *stony* stones indeed. Faced, for instance, with the sheer obscenity of Moll's temptation to kill that child or Roxana's indifference to her daughter's pain, readers would have had no one to turn to but themselves. There is no ironic commentary here safely teasing them away from the thing itself, no morally authoritative voice to tell them what and how to think and feel; there is only the voice of the criminal herself speaking free of social sanction, possibly penitent but even then insufficiently de- or reconstructed.

The powerfully disturbing effect of voices like Moll's and Roxana's on readers trained up in the conventions of criminal biography can easily be imagined, but so, too, can its likely consequence. Readers may well have sympathized, even identified, with Defoe's criminals for all the reasons, psychological and social, that modern critics have advanced. The absence of a "normalizing" context for their narratives would in some ways have made this all the more likely. But what those criminals say could at times be so provoking, I'd suggest, that readers would have felt obliged to draw back and demur, unable otherwise to keep their readerly peace. Defoe was working, I suspect, along lines sketched out in his preface to *An Essay on Projects*. Preparing his audience for some future discomfort, he says that in order "to expose the Vicious Custom of Swearing" he will be "forcing the Reader to repeat some of the worst of our vulgar Imprecations, in reading my Thoughts against it." He sees no real problem in this, "for [though] of necessity it leads the Hearer to the Thoughts of the Fact," it does not mean he shares in "the Morality" – or, rather, immorality – "of [the] Action."[62] Indeed, the hoped for effect would appear just the opposite, to make readers recoil from the viciousness they are forced to mouth.

"Whenever I read," says Georges Poulet, "I mentally pronounce an *I*, and yet the *I* which I pronounce is not myself."[63] Feeling this "strange displacement," feeling, too, the absence of criminal biography's safely contextualizing, safely distancing, safely numbing voice, Defoe's readers would have been put in a difficult but negotiable position. They were "speaking" someone *not* themselves *in* themselves, someone saying things that sometimes simply cried out for contradiction (and all the more as elsewhere that speaking voice might have seemed, and might seem again, attractive or sympathetic). Who was there to speak up against that someone, to put that someone in his or her place, if not the someone who was, or could seem, *truly* them? Identity is defined as much, perhaps more, by denial and rejection as it is by sympathy and affiliation. "Leav[ing] ... Readers to their own just Reflections" on "Decency" and "Vice," Moll at one point says she does so because she expects "they will be more ... effectual than I, who so soon forgot myself, and am therefore but a very indifferent Monitor" (126). Against the strangely familiar yet strangely strange "*I*" of Defoe's criminals, readers would have had a chance at this and at many other, unmarked, moments in his texts to "remember" and assert the "*I*" which was, or ought to be, themselves – the "monitoring," self-regarding "*I*" that linked them up with and made them fit for society. Surprising, shocking their readers, Defoe's texts do more, then, than just warn against criminal behavior; they seek, as the preface to *Moll Flanders*

[62] *An Essay upon Projects* (1697), pp. xiii-xiv.
[63] Georges Poulet, "Criticism and the Experience of Interiority," in *The Structuralist Controversy: The Languages of Criticism and the Sciences of Man*, ed. Richard Macksey and Eugenio Donato (Baltimore, 1972), pp. 60, 62; see also p. 63.

says, "to make us more present to Ourselves." Like hanging, like criminal biography, they, too, can seem experiments in human nature. Here, though, the experiment would have turned on the reader, not the criminal, rising to the occasion.

Because readers were put into a position where their heart's "natural magistrate" ought to have spoken up does not mean, of course, that it did; or that, if it did, it had anything particularly noteworthy or valuable, original or idiosyncratic to say. The "pregiven" discourse of criminal biography would have been ready to hand, either to supply "properly" moral or ironic sentiments or itself to be ironized or reversed into a "counter-discourse." Either way, the reader's assertion of his own "ought to be" would be aligned, positively or negatively, with the values of the larger culture; this, of course, is what having a superego is all about. The important thing would have not have been the conclusions readers came to, but their freedom – or seeming freedom – to become (or seem) a source of authority in and of themselves. Defoe's novels in this way represent a significant departure from criminal biography not only in form, subject matter, and technique, but in political tendency as well. Though supposedly left to their own reflections, readers of criminals' lives are pressured again and again to hew to a preestablished program leading to already formulated conclusions. Criminals mark out the paths to perdition and salvation, says a voice sounding as if it had the full faith and credit of all moral and social authority behind it, take heed! Or else readers are told not to think much at all about the actual humanity of people hanged for crimes against property, even though the hopes and ambitions, the fears and necessities that animated and compelled them, may bear some strong resemblance to their own.

Defoe frees readers of such narrow constraints, creating narratives that resist such simple construings. Staunch Protestant that he was, he believed in the peculiar need and privilege of us all to agonize for ourselves over matters affecting salvation and grace, and, individualist that he was, of individuals generally to work out their own epistemologies and ethics. "'Tis not worth while," says Locke dismissively, "to be concerned, what he says or thinks, who says or thinks only as he is directed by another."[64] In the world he and Defoe helped inaugurate, individuals value themselves only insofar as they think (or think they are thinking) for themselves; this is the ostensible (and hidden) foundation of any "liberal" political order. Defoe was highly sensitive to the matters raised within these parentheses, highly aware of the ways in which the seemingly free opinion of seemingly free people could be jostled and nudged toward certain views and away from others, or otherwise kept within bounds. He was quite good at it

[64] Locke, "Epistle to the Reader," *An Essay Concerning Human Understanding*, ed. Peter H. Nidditch (Oxford, 1975), p. 7.

himself, despite occasional mishaps, and had rather an intriguing metaphor to describe how it was done.

Complaining, thus, in *The Secret History of the Secret History of the White
Staff* that booksellers hire hack writers to argue back and forth on all sides
of a political question just to sell books, and with a cynical disregard for
the issues at hand, he tells how the public gets taken in. They buy the
books, analyze and discuss their arguments, stake out positions and construct arguments of their own, thinking all the while they're actually
participating in political life. What is really happening, Defoe says, is that
the booksellers are putting a "Trick . . . upon the Town" and "causing the
deceiv'd People to Dance in the Circles of their drawing." Of course, on
this specific occasion, Defoe's claim that no real political matters are in
question is itself a subterfuge; he is doing very much the same sort of thing
he's accusing others of doing, only more so, attempting to control opinion
by seemingly freeing it to come to its own conclusions. And yet it would be
hard, too, to say he is simply "covering a Fraud with a greater Fraud,"
practicing an "*Ambodexter* Scuffle" of his own. It was not merely in a
narrowly religious sense that Defoe wanted to "regularize" dissent, i.e., to
stimulate and yet keep it within socially valuable, responsible bounds. The
complicated rhetoric of *The Secret History of the Secret History* cannot be
studied here, but, piling voice upon voice to great dialogic effect, it argues
against simply accepting without evidence – and without weighing and
judging the force of that evidence for oneself – the assertions of any single
authority. "This is Popery," its chief voice says, and "Protestants are come
to a Point in such Things, *viz.* to believe nothing, without some Proof."[65]

The nature and extent of the freedom Defoe allows his readers will be a
recurrent theme of this book. For the moment, however, I want only to
suggest that his novels abandon criminal biography's attempts at speaking
with a kind of "sovereign power" without, in my view, quite moving on to
the sort of "government of individualization" discernible in the fiction of
later boosters and modelers of the superego, most notably Richardson and
Fielding. Defoe's readers reap none of the abundant sensations of "goodness" that shower down on those who respond "correctly" to Richardson's
novels, powerfully shaping their sense of self, nor do they quite become
what Fielding's readers are meant to be, the author's "subjects" as he

---

[65] *The Secret History of the Secret History of the White Staff, Purse and Mitre* (1715), pp. 6, 8, 33, 39.
The main source of information supporting the point of view Defoe is advancing in this text is a
man "who appear'd as a Quaker, and spoke as a Quaker, altho' as I afterwards understood, he
was not a thorough Quaker." A conversation this Quaker – another Quaker "full of double
Meanings"! – has with someone else in a coffeehouse "stir'd up my Curiosity," says the putative
author of the piece, an anonymous "Person of Honour," and he goes on to have "a little
Friendly Discourse with him" (pp. 9, 12). As a result of this dialogue supra dialogue, the
"Person of Honour" is persuaded of the position that Defoe seeks to advance with his readers.
Similar strategies of persuasion through or by indirection, it seems to me, are very much at
work in the novels.

establishes his own, new version of sovereign authority as the "founder" of his own, "new province of writing."[66] To the extent Defoe establishes authority over his readers, it is oblique, indirect, hardly noticeable. It seems to me paradigmatic of his method (to cite Althusser's fable of "interpellation") that in his novels it is no "policeman" that "hails" the reading self into "subjecthood," but a crook.[67] Challenged by voices from the alleyways and margins, readers are prompted (and long before there actually was any such thing in England) to become their *own* policemen. Lacking any visible authority to turn to, they present themselves to themselves.

All this may be seeming to claim too much for Defoe as a writer. Any text may be made to yield subtleties, but how much subtlety, after all, can he reasonably be credited with? So far I have tried to avoid the (to me) unprofitable question of whether Defoe was a "conscious" or "accidental" artist. Artists are always both, never intending everything they achieve in their work but moving, the best of them, serendipitously along. Defoe was sloppy, rarely if ever revising, and it seems to me that much of what he did, he stumbled upon, in both senses. The movement of his novels is typically the movement of all his longer works. Defoe veers and tacks his way through a subject matter, tending this way and that, gainsaying and reversing himself, frequently digressing, until at last he worries his way through to, usually, a more or less equilibrious or at least exhausted end. This was, I suspect, his way of writing long books.[68]

---

66 Contemporary responses to Richardson's fiction are richly set out in T. C. Duncan Eaves and Ben D. Kimpel, *Samuel Richardson: A Biography* (Oxford, 1971); Diderot's description of the effect of *Clarissa* on him – "Combien j'étais bon! combien j'étais juste! que j'étais satisfait de moi!" (quoted pp. 101–2) – might be taken as paradigmatic. Fielding's description of his sovereignty over his readers appears in *Tom Jones*, 2: 1: "As I am, in reality, the Founder of a new Province of Writing," he says, "so I am at liberty to make what Laws I please therein. And these Laws, my Readers, whom I consider as my Subjects, are bound to believe in and to obey." The passage admits of more extensive quotation – it playfully mixes arguments for absolute and contractual sovereignty – but it would be a mistake to think it entirely ironic. In this novel as well as in *Joseph Andrews* (the effect is less obvious in *Amelia*), Fielding does all he can to encourage "good" (or "good-natur'd") reading – which, among other things, is reading that recognizes, honors, and respects authorial intent – and to prevent, discourage, or discountenance a variety of inappropriate or incorrect readings (see, for example, *Joseph Andrews*, 4: 12 and *Tom Jones*, 6: 1, 10: 1). Though their methods differ, it isn't at all difficult to see the power that Richardson and Fielding achieve over their readers in terms of Foucault's "government of individualization"; both propose a field of possible responses to their texts, making some seem "easier" and others "more difficult" (Foucault, "Afterword: The Subject and Power," p. 220).

67 Althusser, *Lenin and Philosophy*, pp. 173–5ff.

68 This is not to say that Defoe wrote this way on purpose, but rather that, knowing he wrote this way, he took no great pains to correct himself. "I must beg my Reader's Indulgence," he says in the midst of *Augusta Triumphans* (1728), "being the most immethodical Writer imaginable; 'tis true, I lay down a Scheme, but Fancy is so fertile I often start fresh Hints, and cannot but pursue 'em; pardon therefore kind Reader my digressive way of Writing, and let the Subject,

Defoe was canny enough to know that in order to fill up five or six shillings worth of text (the price range of all his novels), he had not only to choose hot topics but to find means of drawing them out, all the while sustaining audience interest. He could afford to scorn novelists who framed "long" stories "full of Events and Incidents, like the Turns in a Comedy" (to quote possibly his own words) because he himself was so skillful at it, and not only in novels. Witness, for example, *The Family Instructor*, *Religious Courtship*, and *The Complete English Tradesman*, all of which not only stretch their subject matters out but even endow them with a modicum of suspense. Though criminal biography was highly popular, as a genre it was typically brief. While in theory the episodic japeries of thieves could be spun out indefinitely, most writers of such narratives wisely chose to quit early. If they wanted long books, they strung together a series of relatively brief lives, getting in and out of each before it began to get boring; and even then their work rarely fetched more than two shillings or half a crown the volume. The more serious kind of criminal biography was even more constrained by its given form. It had so highly developed a structure that it could be expanded only by magnifying its individual elements; each of the necessary episodes could be drawn out and made more detailed, but there was not much room for adding new kinds of episodes. Defoe's "opened" texts are a way of making such room, and – most important – of making his narratives interesting and engaging over the long haul (and presumably to the writer as well as his readers).[69]

All this Defoe may have done unconsciously or incidentally, but, if it were all that he did, we would not still be reading him. *Moll Flanders* and the other novels would be mere parasite forms on the larger body of eighteenth-century criminal biography and would not have survived its decline. This, in fact, is a central problem with the Russian Formalists' view of literature; they cannot explain how a literary text outlives the conventions it deforms. As Mukařovsky and others writing in the wake of the Formalists came to see, a literary text owes its survival to its autonomy.[70] Though inevitably defined against other literary forms and other redactions of life, it survives by virtue of the claims it can make on its readers as a thing considerable in and of itself, though – necessarily – it stands amidst and inevitably connects with other things. The "confusion"

not the Stile or Method engage thy Attention" (p. 38). For interesting comments on how Defoe's sentence-construction "keeps taking a new lease on life," see P. N. Furbank and W. R. Owens, "Defoe and the 'Improvisatory' Sentence," *English Studies*, 67 (1986): 157–66, and also their *The Canonisation of Daniel Defoe* (New Haven, 1988), pp. 125–33.

[69] "As I am quick to conceive," says Defoe, "I am eager to have done, unwilling to overwork a Subject; I had rather leave part to the Conception of the Readers, than to tire them or my Self with protracting a Theme" (*Augusta Triumphans*, p. 8).

[70] Mukařovsky, "Art as Semiotic Fact" in *Semiotics of Art*, ed. Matejka and Titunik; P. N. Medvedev / M. M. Bakhtin, *The Formal Method in Literary Scholarship: A Critical Introduction to Sociological Poetics*, tr. Albert J. Wehrle (Baltimore, 1978), especially pp. 159–70.

and "discontinuities" Watt finds in Defoe's fiction cannot all be explained away as distortions of "standard" criminal biography; not all of them are that clever. But even the shrewdest of such distortions would by themselves seem stupid or, at best, merely opaque to modern readers, who cannot be expected to know anything of how Defoe's criminals ought – or ought not – to have lived and talked.

Defoe's novels survive because he found means to bound the confusions and discontinuities in his fiction, to stimulate his readers to make connections even where possibly (or probably) he intended none, to find meanings and intuit wholes that excuse – or persuade us to overlook – his unfinished prose and seeming lack of authorial purpose. Defoe's novels invite interpretation, so much so that even modern readers can find them stimulating, surprising, and even – in one way or another – realistic and so morally challenging. Nor, for all the crudeness of his writing, should Defoe's realism seem naive or primitive; as I'm about to show, he had a good basic grasp of what we'd call narrative theory and purposively – very probably even consciously – exploited the complexities inherent in the tale-telling situation.

3

The copious text: opening the door to inference, or, room for those who know how to read it

The Brother argued, That, as the End and Use of every Fable was in the Moral, so a Fiction, or what they call'd a Romance, told only with Design to deceive the Reader ... that the Fact related was true must be ... criminal and wicked, and *making a Lye* .... But on the contrary, when the Moral of the Tale is duly annex'd, and the End directed right ... Fables, feigned Histories, invented Tales, and even such as we call *Romances*, have always been allow'd as the most pungent Way of writing or speaking; the most apt to make Impressions on the Mind, and open the Door to the just Inferences and Improvement which was to be made of them.

Defoe, *A New Family Instructor* (1727), pp. 51–3

The pretended Abridgement of this Book ... consists only of some scatter'd Passages incoherently tacked together; wherein the Author's Sense throughout is wholly mistaken, the Matters of Fact misrepresented, and the Moral Reflections misapplied.

Advertisement for *Robinson Crusoe*, the *Daily Courant* and Applebee's *Original Weekly Journal*, 8 August 1719

This work is chiefly recommended to those who know how to Read it, and how to make the good Uses of it, which the Story all along recommends to them ... it is to be hop'd that such Readers will be much more pleas'd with the Moral, than the Fable; with the Application, than the Relation, and with the End of the Writer, than with the Life of the Person written of.

Preface to *Moll Flanders*, p. 2

The Moral indeed of all my History is left to be gather'd by the Senses and Judgment of the Reader; I am not Qualified to preach to them, let the Experience of one Creature compleatly Wicked, and compleatly Miserable be a Storehouse of useful warning to those that read.

Moll Flanders, p. 268

Here's Room for just and copious Observations.

Preface to *Colonel Jack*, p. 1

Some time after the publication of Robinson Crusoe's *Adventures* and *Farther Adventures*, we are to suppose, he meets "a serious old lady," one of his readers. They begin a conversation on religion during the course of which she reminds him of several events described in one of his books. He allows that her memory is accurate but fails to see what she is getting at. "Well, madam," he says, "I grant all this; pray what do you infer from it?" "O sir," the lady replies, "I have many inferences to draw from it," but these, she adds somewhat archly, are "for my own observation; I do not set up to instruct you." Crusoe finds the encounter puzzling but also curiously exciting, and it starts him on a long inquiry into "the present state of religion in the world" (*SRC*, 115). Texts have an independent status, this encounter suggests. A book can say more than its writer knows, for more may be inferred from it than he can understand. Once a piece of writing goes out into the world, its meaning, in any case, is up for grabs. *Roxana* must "speak for itself" (1), says Defoe, or as he writes in the preface to *Moll Flanders*, "we must be content to leave the Reader to pass his own Opinion upon the ensuing Sheets, and take it just as he pleases" (1).

This last, in effect, is just what the "serious old lady" has done with Crusoe's two books, and to all appearance quite appropriately. She gives no indication of being one of those "envious and ill-disposed" readers mentioned in the preface to the *Serious Reflections* (ix), seeming instead the sort of "sober as well as ingenious reader" commended at the start of the *Farther Adventures* (vii). She seems, in short, one of "those who know how to Read." She seems also an effective composer of her own (albeit oral) text, inasmuch as her refusing to spell out exactly what she has in mind sets Crusoe to thinking and, not incidentally, to writing a new text. "I thought," says Crusoe, "this serious old lady would have entertained a farther discourse with me on so fruitful a subject, but she declined it, and left me to my own meditation, which, indeed, she had raised up to an unusual pitch" (*SRC*, 115–16). Thus one text leads to another, which produces yet a third; thus it is that readers can lead writers back into further conversation with themselves, as writers of course do readers.[1]

There is a sly power in the obliquity of this old lady's enigmatic style, and perhaps it is not too far-fetched to see in this – and in Crusoe's

---

[1] Defoe's staging this encounter between his hero/author and a reader may owe something to his having read (and resented) the Pirandellian confrontation Charles Gildon enacts in *The Life and Strange Surprizing Adventures of Mr. D— De F— of London, Hosier* (1719). Robinson Crusoe and Friday suddenly appear to Defoe late one night on his way home, having "come to punish" him for making them "such Scoundrels." They make him eat his own words, i.e., vols. 1 and 2 of *Robinson Crusoe*, then toss him in a blanket until the "Dose" befouls his breeches (pp. viii–ix, xvii–xviii). Appropriating the strategy of Gildon's insult but turning it to his own ends by showing an unknown reader praising him rather than his own characters attacking him, Defoe, then, would be writing against a misreading he's read of something he'd written, pushing the appropriation of his text back in a more "normal" or at least plausible direction. This is more than dialogue; it is an act of psychic and professional self-defense. And why "a serious *old* lady"? "There is not an old woman that can go to the Price of it," Gildon has his pseudo-Defoe tell Crusoe, "but buys thy Life and Adventures, and leaves it as a Legacy, with the *Pilgrim's Progress*, the *Practice of Piety*, and *God's Revenge against Murther*, to her Posterity" (pp. ix-x). Here, too, Defoe gets back his own.

response to it – a metaphor for Defoe's intended effect on his own audience. Defoe often advocated a plain style, believing that "that speech, or that way of speaking which is most easily understood, is the best." But he also recognized a need at times to be indirect, even "hieroglyphic." "There is no instructing you without pleasing you," he tells readers of *The History and Reality of Apparitions*, and as there is "no pleasing you but in your own way, we must go on in that way; the understanding must be refined by allegory and enigma."[2] Readers who would not abide being sermonized might, nonetheless, be "led by the Hand" to "serious Inferences" by books like *Moll Flanders* – assuming, of course, that their "infinite variety" (as the common phrase went), their "abundance of delightful Incidents" (another come on), was "carefully garbl'd [i.e., sifted] of all . . . Levity, and Looseness" (*MF* 4, 2–3). They might even be prompted – as Crusoe is by his "serious old lady" – into an extended reexamination of things they wouldn't otherwise have thought about.

Defoe's writing may too often bring the modern sense of "garbled" to mind. Not only is he frequently inattentive to the finer details of his narratives, but, as one of our earliest novelists, he can seem not to have the technical skills (one could almost say technology) to keep readers from what he calls (albeit in another context) "the whimsical building of erroneous structures on my foundations" (*SRC*, 289). Fielding and Richardson make far greater efforts at keeping readers in line, Fielding with an artfully contrived narrative voice that, in effect, makes the author the chief "character" of his tale and the reader's trusted governor, advisor, and friend, and Richardson by using a multiplicity of narrative voices to suggest an overall point of view which he, as putative editor, buttresses with occasional footnotes and highly directive prefaces and postscripts. Readers needn't follow such authorial direction – from the first, Richardson's have been remarkably recalcitrant and not everyone finds a friend in Fielding – but, clearly, in both authors' works it is there to be accepted or rejected.

Defoe's novels – especially the criminal novels – are far more ambiguous. Given his practice in certain of his overtly didactic fictions, and certain things he said about story-telling in general, it seems safe to assume that he expected readers would respond to this ambiguity with a high degree of critical awareness. The mere fact, of course, that the criminal novels imitate so suspect and second-guessed a form should itself indicate as much. But, quite obviously, the criminal novels are not "horizon"-bound; they don't entirely depend on their original context to engage readers in complex acts of interpretation. Readers knowing nothing of eighteenth-century criminal biography find them powerfully ambiguous,

---

[2] *CET*, 1: 26; the *Review*, 7: 25 (11 April 1710); *Romances and Narratives by Daniel Defoe*, ed. George A. Aitken (London, 1895), 13: 43.

teasingly inviting still; these are no accidental qualities. Defoe's novels *mean* to play a cagey game; behind them, and working in them, is a partly conscious, partly implicit "theory of fiction" even current theorists might admire, and the practical effects of which modern (or postmodern) readers are particularly well positioned to appreciate.

Presenting themselves as redacted versions of events supposed actually to have occurred, all Defoe's novels, and the criminal novels especially, show a high self-consciousness of their status as discourse. What we have in our hands as we read, they remind us regularly, is an artifact standing as a sign for things both obscure and important in the world, things which any given discourse can only partly reveal, and which we, as readers, must conjure up for ourselves by exercising our imaginations and interpretive skills. Read only within the limiting surround of criminal biography, Defoe's criminal novels might still seem merely more complicated, more elaborate, and cleverer ways of bringing readers back to the same old home truths. Read within the field they create for themselves, however, they seem especially significant for the distance they put between readers and social convention, for the empowering isolation they thereby allow them. The "room" readers get – reading Defoe's fiction with all the privacy that novel reading entails – is very much a room of their own. Readers of criminal biography could never have achieved a comparable solitude, if only for the fact that it recounted events they might already have witnessed in a courtroom or at the place of execution, or, at the least, have heard about and discussed in the company of other people.[3]

The general elements of Defoe's "theory of fiction" have been set out elsewhere, in a ground-breaking article that gathers together most of his important pronouncements on fiction writing.[4] Here I want to explore two aspects of that "theory" which (quite understandably, given its date of publication) that article tends to overlook. The first has to do with the partiality of "relators," that is, story-tellers or narrators. The second has to do with Defoe's highly developed awareness of "reader response." The novels themselves give few clues on either of these subjects, apart from their frequent urgings that readers should come to their own conclusions. Defoe's collateral, quasi-fictive writings, however, are far more illuminat-

---

[3] On the solitude of novel reading and the move of the genre away from the "communal," see J. Paul Hunter, "The Loneliness of the Long Distance Reader," *Genre*, 10 (1977): 455–84, and his still wider-ranging remarks in chapters 3–6 of *Before Novels: The Cultural Contexts of Eighteenth-Century English Fiction* (New York, 1990). Roger Chartier also has a good deal of interest to say on the implications for individual self-consciousness of increased reading during the early modern era, both in private and in company, in "The Practical Impact of Writing," *A History of Private Life, III: Passions of the Renaissance*, ed. Roger Chartier, tr. Arthur Goldhammer (Cambridge, Mass., 1989), pp. 111–59.

[4] Maximillian E. Novak, "Defoe's Theory of Fiction," *Studies in Philology*, 61 (1969): 650–68.

ing, particularly *The Serious Reflections of Robinson Crusoe* (1720), *The Family Instructor* (1715; 1718), and *Religious Courtship* (1722). The first of these, a gloss on the *Adventures* and *Farther Adventures of Robinson Crusoe*, might serve as a window into Defoe's mind (though never more than semi-translucent) at almost exactly the same time he began writing his criminal novels.[5] The second and third are interesting because they show an occasional intrusion by an authorial voice which comments on the meaning of the story as it unfolds and, sometimes, on the means by which it is being unfolded. Such commentary indicates a consciousness of audience that makes the absence of any similar commentary in the novels all the more curious; indeed, it makes that absence seem a clear abdication of authorial responsibility and, consequently, a considerable part of their technique.

The *Family Instructor* and *Religious Courtship* are for the most part comprised of dialogues, a form Defoe credits with a "taking elegancy." "The story being handed forward in short periods, and quick returns," he says, "makes the retaining it in the mind the easier, and the impression the more lasting as well as delightful." He chose this form with some care, he explains, his first intention being to make *The Family Instructor* "a dramatic poem; but the subject was too solemn, and the text too copious, to suffer the restraint on the one hand, or the excursions on the other, which the decoration of a poem would have made necessary" (*FI*, 15: ix). As if to show, however, that even so carefully chosen a form is not entirely adequate to his purpose, Defoe at times interrupts his interlocutors to speak in his own (or at least an authorial) voice. Some of these comments are made for the sake of clarity or economy, and others seem designed to assure the reader the story is still under control. "The last two dialogues," he writes at one point in *The Family Instructor*, "are to be understood to be a recapitulation of what had been acted some time past, in order to introduce this part, and preserve the connection of the history" (15: 326–7). In *Religious Courtship*, just as an important meeting is about to take place between a young woman and her suitor, the description of the event is postponed, the author saying "it will be necessary here to leave this part a while, and bring forward the story of the young gentleman as far as it is needful to the co-herence of things; the story also," he hastens to assure his readers, "will be very short."[6]

Defoe seems afraid that his writing will get away from him, and not without reason. Jailed twice already because readers had failed or refused to understand what he meant (misprision with a vengeance), he had openly – and on occasion combatively – distrusted his audience for more than a decade. Readers of the *Review* "often" mistook his meaning, he complained, and "dislik'd" what he wrote. His efforts to "pursue unbias'd

---

[5] *Captain Singleton* was published 4 June 1720, and *Serious Reflections* on 6 August of the same year.
[6] *Religious Courtship* (Glasgow, 1797), p. 123; further references in the text.

and impartial Truth" were often wasted, as "what ought to oblige you does not, nay sometimes rather disgusts you." Aware that his readership included "Opponents . . . ready to object against every thing they see," he felt himself "oblig'd to make long Digressions, and place needless Cautions in the Front of almost every Paragraph" so as to block their "importunate Cavils."[7] Perhaps it was to forestall similar criticisms and misinterpretations that Defoe took pains in *The Family Instructor* to identify what is salient and important in his speakers and their actions. Thus in one instance a family is thrown into turmoil when the parents experience a sudden religious awakening. The elder daughter resists the new rules of conduct they impose on their children, but the younger obeys and arouses her sister's anger and jealousy. After showing this in a dialogue between them, Defoe pauses to observe that what they've said "needs no observation, save on the different temper between children dutifully submitting to family government, and affectionately complying with their parents' just desires; and on the other hand, children obstinately adhering to the dictates of their passions; and this," he adds, "will appear to every common reader" (15: 94).

This may seem just another example of Defoe's notorious verbosity. Without such guidance, or "Cautionary Exception," however, some readers might well have read the passage differently, giving it a "false Construction." Such readers might be ill-disposed or stupid – "clowns" and "fools" Defoe could call them – but not necessarily so. "Impatient" readers, too, were his bane, it seeming "something hard" to him that they

---

[7] The *Review*, 7: 257 (26 August 1710), 4: 485 (22 November 1707), 5: 49 (27 April 1708), 1: 145 (27 June 1704), pref. to vol. 1 (1705), p. [4]. On Defoe's imprisonments for his writing, see John Robert Moore, *Daniel Defoe: Citizen of the Modern World* (Chicago, 1958), pp. 104–49, 352–3, and Paula R. Backscheider, *Daniel Defoe: His Life* (Baltimore, 1989), pp. 106–35, 322–8. For more on Mr. Review's sense of audience, see Laura A. Curtis, *The Elusive Daniel Defoe* (London, 1984), pp. 103–13. *Jure Divino* (1706) also shows a high awareness of the extent to which readers might misunderstand an author's meaning or intention; thus, among many notes on this theme, Defoe's reference to "the captious Distemper of the Age, which is apt to condemn a Work for a Word, not because it merits the Censure, but because they do not understand it" (bk. 2, p. 15n.). The shock of the authorities' response to *The Shortest Way with Dissenters* had taught Defoe a hard and indelible lesson (see his letter to William Paterson, April 1703, in *The Letters of Daniel Defoe*, ed. George Harris Healey [Oxford, 1955], pp. 4–5), a lesson to be repeated in 1713 despite Defoe's wariness (see his letter to Robert Harley, 12 April 1713, ibid., pp. 406–7, and also, for Chief Justice Parker's interpretive obtusity, pp. 410–11n.). In 1718 Defoe would yet again be misread and threatened with punishment, on grounds now that must have seemed utterly unforeseeable, even bizarre (see his letter to Charles De la Faye, 10 May 1718, ibid., pp. 454–5). Gildon's stupid and malicious misreading of *Robinson Crusoe* would only have been icing on the cake, but from it Defoe may possibly have learned still more about keeping his cards close to his vest (or at least about not wearing his heart on his sleeve). For examples of Defoe himself as a careful, or not so careful but nonetheless critical, reader of other writers, see the *Letters*, pp. 92–3 (in response to an anonymous political tract) and pp. 433–8 (a gathering of inferences from several pieces by Richard Steele), as well as Paula R. Backscheider, "Daniel Defoe as Solitary Reader," *Princeton University Library Chronicle*, 46 (1985): 178–91 (this last concerns Defoe's marginalia in a copy of Bacon's *Advancement of Learning*).

could not "refrain their Conclusions before I come to mine."[8] Defoe is always careful in *The Family Instructor* to make his conclusions clear and to keep them clearly before his reader's eye. This is particularly important in the case of the two daughters, for, on any grounds but the strictest Protestantism, the elder might seem legitimately angry with her parents and the younger all too smarmy. Thus, as the dialogue between them begins, the elder has just had her ear boxed for answering her father saucily. She didn't see why she shouldn't have gone riding in the park on Sunday, when she'd always been allowed before. While she was out, moreover, her collection of plays and novels had been taken away and burnt. Daughters mustn't speak saucily to fathers, but this daughter can seem provoked. Knowing that some of his readers would be readers of plays and novels, too, and so sympathetic to the elder daughter's display of temperament, Defoe appeals to the "common" reader's common sense, offering an "observation" where, supposedly, none should have been necessary. Or so I would suggest; one cannot always be sure that certain things will go without saying unless, of course, one actually *says* they go without saying. "Readers are strange Judges," Defoe once observed, "when they see but part of the Design" – especially, he might have added, "our *English* Readers, who are not over-stocked with Patience in Books, and do not love a long Story, let it never be so well told."[9]

Where *The Family Instructor* consistently stresses parental authority, *Religious Courtship* may at one point seem to be undermining it. Three daughters are to be married, and the father, a widower whose head is filled with business, puts the matter into the girls' own hands. One of them makes the terrible mistake of marrying a closet Catholic because, despite certain suspicions, she accepts her father's assurance that the man is indeed a Protestant. "If you are satisfied," she says to her father, "I shall do as you would have me; I do not suppose you would have me have him, if he was not a very sober man." At this point Defoe breaks into the dialogue to comment, in brackets: "She has nothing in her but the same

---

[8] The *Review*, 1: 145 (27 June 1704), 5: 49 (27 April 1708), 5: 18 (8 April 1708), 1: 153 (4 July 1704).

[9] Ibid., pref. to vol. 1 (1705), p. [4], 1: 46 (1 April 1704). Another significant point at which Defoe intervenes in the moral dialogues of *The Family Instructor* occurs after a young child asks his father who made him. This sets the father to thinking on a variety of religious questions and, eventually, leads him to re-order his whole way of life. In "the inquiries of the Child," Defoe points out, one may see "how [all things] essential to our salvation ... lie so plain so natural, and in so exact an order, that nature seems to direct the child, who knows nothing of them, to force them from the father, by the power of the most innocent, uninstructed inquiries" (15: 37–8). This situation has much the same significance as Friday's simple but profound religious questioning in *Robinson Crusoe*; here, too, a naive inquiry leads a supposedly wiser man to a much better knowledge of God and Christianity than he had before. One reason Defoe glosses this passage, I suspect, is that he wants to step back from the notion that the child's question originates in a natural goodness, still present in him but somewhat spoiled in the father. The child, in a manner of speaking, merely pulls his father's string.

dull story of doing everything her father would have her do" (168). This too easy complaisance seems, on the face of it, exactly opposite to the insolence Defoe condemns in *The Family Instructor*. A little thought, however, shows no real contradiction between the two texts; parents are not to be blindly obeyed, except when they are right. Because this is no simple notion and may seem to contradict conventional opinion, it needs commentary all the more. "It may be seen by [her] dull and empty discourse," says Defoe of this conventionally obedient daughter,

that this poor young lady went on ... like the ox to the slaughter, not knowing or considering, that it was for her life. She resolved all her scruples into that weak way of answering, I leave it all to you, Sir, I hope you are satisfied, Sir; and I'll do as you would have me, Sir; and the like; not considering that she had a father that laid no stress upon any thing but the money; his whole care was for the settlement, and the estate, not inquiring into the principles of the person, and therefore his answers are as silly for a father, as hers were for a wife.   168

In this particular instance, Defoe wants his readers to see conventional discourse with a critical eye, perhaps even to experience a certain shock of recognition. His paraphrase of the daughter's "weak way of answering" might have been shortened, but I think the repetitions forcefully communicate the insipidity of her speech and thought. Still, these are phrases Defoe's readers might have heard any day from a too complaisant child, or themselves have spoken in an all too placid, unthinking eagerness to please, if not their parents, then someone else in authority.[10]

Such efforts to undermine the discourse of specified speakers ought to seem relevant to the first-person novels, especially the criminal novels. Though no authorial voice breaks into Crusoe's narrative, he is so careful a considerer of what he has thought, felt, said, and even dreamt, that all by himself he encourages readers into critical habits of thought. Crusoe is aware that all too often he has been unthinkingly confident of his own power, too sure in what he had taken to be knowledge but which, after all, was only a finer kind of ignorance. His ongoing relationship with God, in which he reaches what he thinks to be certainty only to find he's been overconfident again, or wrong, is the quintessential case. Crusoe's efforts to answer Friday's religious questions, for instance, start a dialogue that

10 There is a similar effort in *The Family Instructor* to get readers to look beneath the surface level of an individual's discourse, and to find it not what it seems to be. At the very beginning of the work, Defoe alerts us to the deficiencies of the parents' speech and point of view. The father is "one of those professing Christians who, acknowledging God in their mouths, yet take no effectual care to honour him with their practice"; he is "a kind of negative Christian ... sound in knowledge, but negligent in conversation; orthodox in opinion, but heterodox in practice." The mother is "likewise a formal, loose-living Christian": "she is a professor, one that knows how to talk of religion, and makes a show to belong to it; but – alas for the rest!" The text that follows, Defoe points out, is "calculated to reprove and admonish" such people, by showing them "their own pictures drawn: may the sight of it have the same healing, convincing efficacy, as appears upon the persons here" (15: 3).

shows him and the reader both how much there is yet to know, and yet is beyond knowing.[11] None of the criminal narrators is as self-conscious as Crusoe, nor as reflective.

Given Defoe's practice elsewhere, it might well be asked why he refrained from intervening in the first-person narratives of his criminal novels, especially as the form makes for so much ambiguity. But this, too, is beyond knowing. Perhaps he found himself unable to write these novels otherwise because, had he once begun commenting, he would have felt obliged to disapprove almost constantly of nearly everything his criminals said and did. "Clog'd with Moral Reflections," such stories would never get off the ground.[12] Certainly the tendency of his comments in *The Family Instructor* and *Religious Courtship* is heavily moralistic, guiding interpretation of the text always toward conformity with conventional proprieties. Defoe's own emphasis on the need for fiction to justify itself on moral grounds might well have cramped his style, allowing him to write about "negative" characters only within the explicit didacticism of his conduct books or by silencing the authorial voice altogether. Perhaps he resolved to write much as he'd traveled through hostile territory for Harley, "Incognito," because it gave him "Room for Many Speculations."[13] All this, however, remains itself the sheerest speculation. To put our inquiry on a more solid footing we ought to ask not *why* Defoe wrote his novels as he did, but *how* he could have done so, given his strong sense of moral responsibility as an author. What could he have hoped to achieve with first-person narration? It is here that Defoe's views on the partiality of narrators become important.

We have already seen how Crusoe's "serious old lady" suggests herself as the best sort of reader. Just before that encounter, Defoe (or Crusoe) writes at length on "the liberty of telling stories, a common vice in discourse." While he seems primarily concerned with defending *Robinson Crusoe* from the charge that it is a worthless pack of lies, he has some interesting things to say about narrative. Distinguishing between "chimney-corner romance" and "parable or ... illusive [*sic*] allegoric history," Defoe explains that the latter is "always to be distinguished from this other jesting with truth" inasmuch as "it is designed and effectually turned for instructive and upright ends, and has its moral justly applied." Though such "history" involves "invention," it has nothing to do with "the sport of lying" and so "the selling or writing" of it (how like him to see the

---

[11] We are not meant to be so critical of the narrator of *The Journal of the Plague Year*, for that novel is not so much about H. F. as London in general. It might be interesting to ask why readers tend to accept H. F.'s point of view, rather than second guess it, but such a study would lie beyond the bounds of this book.

[12] Gildon, *Life of De F—*, p. 30; the context is Gildon's claim that *Robinson Crusoe* was "clog'd" with such reflections in order "to swell the Bulk up to a five Shilling Book" (p. 31).

[13] *Letters*, ed. Healey, p. 385.

commercial side!) is not to be condemned. *Robinson Crusoe*, its author claims, is in a class with "the historical parables of Holy Scripture," as well as *The Pilgrim's Progress* and his own (though modestly he doesn't identify it as such) *Family Instructor* (*SRC*, 103, 106–8). The most interesting part of this argument, from the standpoint of the criminal novels, is what leads up to it. Defoe has some shrewd things to say about the genesis of "chimney-corner romance," and these have teasing implications for the novels.

Even a true story can be made as good as a lie, Defoe explains, by being overembellished "till not only it comes to be improbable, but even impossible to be true; and the ignorant relater is so tickled with having made a good story of it, whatever it was when he found it, that he is blind to the absurdities and inconsistencies of fact in relation, and tells it with a full face even to those that are able to confute it by proving it to be impossible." Defoe finds it "a strange thing that we cannot be content to tell a story as it is, but we must take from it on one side or add to it on another till the fact is lost among the addenda, and till in time even the man himself, remembering it only as he told it last, really forgets how it was originally." The consequence is that "nothing is more common to have two men tell the same story quite differing one from another, yet both of them eye-witnesses to the fact related." Indeed, though some men "tell the same story over and over, till the jest is quite worn out," even they "seldom tell it the same way twice." Eventually the truth gets lost, "what begun in forgery ends in history," and even "real stories . . . become as romantic and false as if they had no real original." For Defoe "this supplying a story by invention" risks more than just the truth. It "is a sort of lying that makes a great hole in the heart"; it is "to play at shuttlecock with your soul." There is, besides, "a spreading evil in telling a false story as true, namely that you put it into the mouths of others, and it continues a brooding forgery to the end of time . . . . we make our lies be told for truth by all our children that come after us" (*SRC*, 103, 104–5, 108–9).

Quite apart from the question of truth value, though linked to it, is a further point of difference between "chimney-corner romance" and what, for the sake of concision, might be called "parabolic" history.[14] The latter not only offers a moral to be "drawn" but, once "published," it is "once for all related . . . the history remains allusive only as it was intended." I take Defoe to mean here that redacted narrative, whether literally or figurat-

---

14 Thus the use of the term by Defoe's schoolmate, Timothy Cruso, who speaks of "a third sort" of story which goes a "*middle way*" between "*Parable*" and "*History*" and is a "mixture of both; i.e. a kind of *Parabolical History*, or *Historical Parable*," and which "may be partly a Narrative of matter of fact and partly illustrated with *circumstantial additions*, which are not to be look'd upon as real things, nor stretch'd too far beyond the *main design*" (*Discourses upon the Rich Man and Lazarus* [1697], pp. 1–2). Citing Cruso, J. Paul Hunter observes that many others used the same terminology (*The Reluctant Pilgrim: Defoe's Emblematic Method and Quest for Form in Robinson Crusoe* [Baltimore, 1966], p. 118).

ively true, or even if neither, has this major advantage over oral narrative: because its form has been fixed, its meaning is stable. Now this may seem to contradict what he indicates elsewhere, that meanings are to a certain extent generated by readers, and that these meanings can exceed the conscious knowledge of the writer. But the contradiction is more apparent than real, for Defoe does not suggest that "sober" or "serious" readers generate meanings out of nothing, rather they find them in the text, nor does he imply that such meanings will contradict the overall intentions of the author. Robinson Crusoe may not know what his "serious old lady" has in mind particularly, but they share, apparently, a common point of view.[15]

What I want especially to stress, however, is the advantage Defoe sees in the written and published text. Its meaning – and most important, its truth – cannot be lost or obscured by the various additions and subtractions of successive relators wanting to make it a "good" story. Implicit here is the notion (though I would not attribute it necessarily to Defoe) that writing powerfully impinges on the story-telling process, for it "hardens" narratives; they lose the "plasticity" that comes with successive retellings and which allows them to meet a variety of circumstances by altering and shifting their meanings. If the meaning of a written story is to change, say, as social circumstances around it change, this will have to be a product of the way it is read. Writing is definite and final; all manuscripts are, as it were, found in bottles. It follows that "smart" writers will take pains to fashion texts to be read in their absence. Though not as obviously as Richardson or Fielding, Defoe too was much concerned with shaping his readers' responses along certain wished for lines. Nor was he blithely unconscious of the problems his audience might face in interpreting a fictive text.

In Defoe's day much of what Bakhtin calls "the discourse of life" was no better than chimney-corner romance, criminal biography especially so. Like all such romance, the stories it told bore little relation to the facts they purportedly described, and their relators were not particularly to be trusted. The fact that such stories were redacted rather than oral is not so significant as the fact that they were continually being re-redacted. The revisions, borrowings, and plagiaries of individual criminal biographies – consumed, discarded, soon forgotten, some of them literally worn out by the sweaty palms of those who read them – made them hardly less ephemeral than the spoken word. Defoe's novels, I suggest, are efforts to

---

[15] "I think ... plainness of expression ... will give no disadvantage to my subject," says Defoe speaking through Crusoe, "since honesty shows the most beautiful ... when artifice is dismissed ... likewise the same sincerity is required in the reader, and he that reads this essay without honesty, will never understand it right .... If prejudice, partiality, or private opinions stand in the way, the man's a reading knave, he is not honest to the subject; and upon such an one all the labour is lost" ("An Essay Upon Honesty," *SRC*, p. 27).

rise above this process. Turning criminal biography into something more than chimney-corner romance by exploiting its two main faults – facticity and the unreliability of its narrators – they take full advantage of its "writtenness." Rather than trying to mitigate or suppress these faults in their own, more fictive versions of criminal biography, Defoe's novels stimulate consideration of them, almost homeopathically one might say, curing the disease by calling attention to it; but this is to get a bit ahead of ourselves.

To return to Defoe's three main points about "telling stories": First there is the distinction, highly important, between the "facts" and the story they generate, between what he elsewhere calls "the Thing it self" and the words used to describe it.[16] Second, there is the idea that more than one story can be told out of any given set of circumstances, for individual human imaginations are often at variance with each other and not in themselves to be trusted. The human mind is inconstant, and frequently the temptation to tell a "good" story gets in the way of the "true" story. Finally there is the intriguing suggestion that story-tellers can be "ignorant relaters," blind not only to the "absurdities" and "inconsistencies" of their discourse and the effect these have on their audience but also to the "great hole in the heart" that opens as they speak. The novels give ample evidence of the impact of these notions, being rich in circumstances that suggest their narrators are not to be trusted or, at least, not to be taken at their own valuation. They conceal important facts, engage in special pleading, and often show a remarkable lack of proper emotional or intellectual response. In this respect they are in actuality not much different from texts typically generated by supposedly penitent criminals, whose protestations were frequently suspect. A major difference between such narratives and Defoe's, however, is that rather than seeking to allay such suspicion – as criminal biography so often and ineffectually did – Defoe's rouse it up. But there is more here than merely this simple reversal. Defoe's novels are not in any sense elaborate parodies of criminal biography, nor are his narrators sly liars. Moll and the others often simply do not know all they are telling us; at other times they do not, or cannot, know what we and even they themselves would like them to tell us. *Pace* to all irony hunters, Defoe's novels are not brought into greater focus or resolution by the application of any fixed and simplifying ironic lens.

Presenting the case of a criminal who "seem'd to be very sensible" and full of "Charity ... for all Mankind," the Newgate ordinary endorsed what he said as "the Words of a Dying Man, that has done with the World and now speaks without Disguise." But not all criminals' confessions were or could

16 The *Review*, 7: 25 (11 April 1710); more will be made of this distinction in chapter 7.

be so easily credited. Defoe was well aware of the situation and ready to exploit it for his own ends. "I shall use freedom in what I am about to write," says the ex-criminal supposedly the author of *Street-Robberies, Consider'd*, "being I am not afraid I shall be call'd to an Account for any of my past Pranks." The narrators of the novels speak with a similar lack of constraint, free not only from all fear of prosecution but, too, of all the "official" apparatus that surrounded the confessions of executed criminals. Here there is none of the inhibiting influence of the ordinaries or other supposedly well-meaning redactors, pressing them to say certain things and not others, shaping and filtering their discourse. The account he was giving of his charges' "Past Lives, Present Dispositions, and Hopes of a Future State," one Newgate chaplain frankly admitted, contained only "so much as I have judg'd proper to impart here to the World."[17]

Nor, given their cloak of anonymity, need Defoe's narrators be inhibited by those "Principles of Honour implanted in our Nature" that make even the worst human beings so regardful of their "Character, as to be willing to leave a good Name behind [them]." Even the Newgate ordinary could sympathize with this "Regard to the good Opinion of Posterity" and allow it to affect what he said. Thus, on one occasion, he made it clear that what he was "impart[ing] to the Publick" of "these Dying Persons respective Confessions" was only "so much, and no more, than they themselves were willing should be inserted in this Paper." It is also significant that Defoe's narrators, unlike actual criminals, speak as if they had all the time in the world. "It may be expected," said one burglar and attempted murderer, "that I should make a long Narration in Detestation of my Crime: But Time and my own Inability abridges you of that Satisfaction." Writing in a "Hurry, and under ... great Fatigue," the Newgate ordinary, too, could apologize more than once for not offering "so full and so congruous" an account "as [the reader] might desire," pleading the "deal of Work I have had to dispatch in a few Days."[18] Defoe's narrators face no hangman's rope as they write; no deadline dangles in their eyes.

If this makes their discourse seem more authentic, it also encourages readers to take an especially critical view of what they are saying. It may be freer and fuller than any criminal confession they've read before, but this means also that it remains "unprocessed," the "just Inferences and Improvement," to use Defoe's phrasing, requiring yet to be made. The open-endedness of the novels alone ought to have alerted readers to the

---

[17] Lorrain, Ordinary Account, 25 October 1704; *Street-Robberies, Consider'd* (1728), p. 3; Lorrain, ibid., 13 March 1713.

[18] Charles Johnson, *A General History of the Lives and Adventures of the Most Famous Highwaymen, Murderers, Street-Robbers, &c.* (1734), p. 304; *Select Trials, for Murders, Robberies, Rapes, Sodomy, Coining, Frauds, and Other Offences* (1742), 1: 37; Lorrain, Ordinary Account, 28 January 1701; John Benloes, quoted by Samuel Smith, Ordinary Account, 26 January 1690; Lorrain, Ordinary Accounts, 19 September 1712 and 17 December 1707 (see also 24 June 1709).

possibility that what they were reading (or had just read) was somehow not "right," for above all else a criminal's confession was validated by his submitting to death as a well-earned punishment. Lacking the conclusion usual to criminal biography, Defoe's criminal narratives come unendorsed by any authority save what appears in their prefaces, and these send readers off to the main text in a curious frame of mind. (*Captain Singleton* has no preface, which is yet one more of its anomalies, and possibly the consequence of its being the first in a series.)

To begin with a relatively benign example, there is at the end of the preface to *Colonel Jack* a powerful imputation that what we have before us may be more verisimilar than strictly veridical. It is not "of the least Moment," says Defoe, "to enquire whether the Colonel hath told us his own Story true or not; If he has made it a *History* or a *Parable*, it will be equally useful" (2). This may be, but such a declaration is not itself without "moment." For one thing, by alerting readers to the possibility that all that follows may not be literally true, it prevents the greatest danger of story-telling in Defoe's eyes, that fictions may become lies. "The description of a lie is, that it is spoken to deceive," and if such a deception is prevented, "then the essence of lying is removed" (*SRC*, 106). For another, by waiving the claim that everything that follows has actually happened, Defoe finesses the whole bedevilling problem of authenticity. In suggesting the text may be either "history" or "parable," he excites a different set of questions, encouraging readers to approach it in an inter-pretive frame of mind.

This is highly important, for, as with *Robinson Crusoe*, so too with Defoe's other novels: the "inferences" and "applications" made by the reader "must legitimate all the part that may be called invention or parable in the story" (*RC2*, vii). By warning that specific details may not be true, and so are not to be valued in and of themselves, the preface to *Colonel Jack* prompts inference, making Jack's "history" or "parable" something to be closely examined *and* seen through. The prefaces to *Moll Flanders* and *Roxana* achieve similar effects, the first by splitting the "Application" and "Moral" off from the "Relation" and "Fable," and making the former seem the more important (*MF*, 2), and the second by speaking of the "Noble Inferences" that "abundantly justifie" publication of the text, even though the literal truth of the whole narrative cannot "so well be vouch'd" (*R*, 2).

Defoe's prefaces condition his readers in still more sophisticated ways by suggesting that the narratives which follow are highly provisional renderings of realities that lie somewhere behind or beyond them. It is difficult to fix the status or provenance of any of these narratives; they are somehow peculiar and extra-categorical. The last is signalized by the distinctions proposed between "history," "story," and "parable" in the prefaces to *Colonel Jack* and *Roxana*. As the usage of these terms here and elsewhere indicates, a "history" is a narrative that is literally true, a "story" is a mere fiction, and a "parable" is a fiction told to illustrate a moral truth.[19] Thus the preface to *Roxana* claims that her "*Story* differs from most of the Modern Performances of this Kind" in that its "Foundation ... is laid in Truth of Fact; and so the Work is not a Story, but a History" (1). It is left open, of course, whether *Colonel Jack* is either a "history" or a "parable," but then it really doesn't matter, as all its details, true or not, are "equally useful." Here, it is interesting to note, Defoe suggests a distinction only to withdraw it. For insofar as a history illustrates moral truth, it is in essence a parable; whatever difference remains is trivial. Something similar occurs in the preface to *Roxana*, for, after specifying that its narrative is a history and not a story, Defoe goes on to use the two terms interchangeably, calling the novel a "story" seven times and a "history" only twice.

I would suggest that what we are seeing here is more than mere confusion or inattentiveness. Fielding shows an analogous imprecision in using words like "history," "system," and "romance" to describe what he is trying to achieve in *Tom Jones*. None of these terms quite defines Fielding's novel, and, though all are mutually exclusive, all (even the discreditable "system") are in some way relevant to the kind of text he is writing. Fielding is bolder and clearer-minded than Defoe, and far more conscious that the terms he is using to describe his new genre are metaphors and approximations. Nonetheless, in similarly advancing his own terminology and then partially retracting it, Defoe, too, is signaling his readers that here they have come upon something *sui generis*, which shall have to be read carefully. Are these purported autobiographies actual histories, mere stories, or parabolic fictions? By marking out the ambiguous status of his texts, Defoe alerts his readers to move through them with maximal curiosity. Trying to sift the actual out from the invented is not so important as looking for the meaning that stands behind both, and which makes both "equally useful."

The prefaces to *Moll Flanders* and *Roxana* give even greater stimulus to the reader's critical capacities by suggesting, teasingly, that behind their text is another, racier, less morally useful but potentially more diverting narrative, which the present text has toned down. For, as the prefaces to both novels take pains to indicate, neither is a literal transcription of the actual woman's memoirs. This is so blatant a reversal of the increasing tendency to advertise a criminal's life as utterly authentic, printed verbatim from his own text or just as it was written down using his own words, that the effect must have been startling. Here is no invitation to come to the printer's office to see the actual manuscript (as if that proved any-

[19] As well as *SRC*, pp. ix–x, 102–9, see *FI*, 15: 4, 192–3.

thing), but an admission that Moll has been "made to tell her own Tale in modester Words than she told it at first; the Copy which came first to Hand, having been written in Language more like one still in *Newgate*, than one grown Penitent and Humble, as she afterwards pretends to be" (1). (The question of Moll's repentance, and the meaning of that problematic "pretends," remain to be considered.) Nor is Roxana's narrative given exactly as she wrote it; a "hand" has intervened here as well. Indeed, this "hand" goes so far in calling attention to itself that it fulsomely apologizes for what it may have done to "the History of this Beautiful Lady." For "if it is not as Beautiful as the Lady herself is reported to be," the preface begins, "if it is not as diverting as the Reader can desire, and much more than he can reasonably expect; and if all the most diverting Parts of it are not adapted to the Instruction and Improvement of the Reader, the *Relator says*, it must be from the Defect of his Performance; dressing up the Story in worse Cloaths than the *Lady*, whose Words he speaks, prepar'd it for the World" (1).

Rather than trying to erase the gap between his speaking subject and the audience, which is what criminal biography at its most serious tries to do, Defoe introduces intervening and supervening subjects and makes sure his reader is alerted to their silent interposition between him and the actual subject of the story. In the passage just quoted, for instance, one may detect not only a "relator" standing between Roxana and the reader, but also possibly – in the "I" who subsequently surfaces – the writer of the preface. (It is simply unclear whether this "I," who speaks also of "the Writer" of the text, is supposed to be either the "relator" or "writer" himself, or some third person.) The important thing in any case is that, for all its seeming freedom from all the usual conventions, Roxana's story does not come straight from the whore's mouth; the text presents an "authorized" version, and more. Roxana's story has been rewritten (or re-related), and then offered for publication to someone who may or may not have written the preface but is in any case the sponsor of the book.[20]

Here again we see Defoe's great complication of a relatively simple discursive situation: there is a narrator, an editor, possibly a publisher,

---

[20] Cf. the preface to *Robert Drury's Journal*, which may have been written by Defoe. While much abridged and "put ... in a more agreeable Method" than the original version of Drury's manuscript, this text takes pains to assure readers that it nonetheless authentically represents its source, Drury having "constantly attended the Transcriber, and also the Printer" (*Madagascar; or, Robert Drury's Journal, During Fifteen Years' Captivity on that Island*, ed. Pasfield Oliver [London, 1890], p. 29). This, along with a variety of other assurances that the text represents the unvarnished truth and so can be read without the sort of skepticism that keeps readers second guessing, makes a nice contrast to Defoe's agitation of doubts in the prefaces of his novels. Drury's is a text *not* to be read "parabolically." More might be made of this juxtaposition had the "transcriber" (as it seems right to call him) not "scruple[d] to own, and confess ... putting Some Reflections in the Author's Mouth" when "such remarkable and agreeable topics" as religion and the origin of government came up (p. 31).

and certainly an author (for no one could really believe these are actual histories), and all are speaking at the same time with different effect to a reader whose role, he is told, is to read for both "Profit and Delight" (*R*, 3).[21] The reader's task is made all the more difficult – and exciting – because all these speakers communicate through a single "channel," the supposed voice of the narrating subject. What is not said becomes as important as what is said, for both presumably reflect on the functioning and intention of the editor, who, so as not to offend his public, has toned down, censored, and otherwise cleaned up Moll's and Roxana's discourse, and judged Jack's fit to print. How something is said (and even how certain things are not left unsaid) also becomes important, for this presumably reflects on the intentions of the actual author, who declares only so much of himself in the preface as is necessary to begin a cat-and-mouse game with the reader.

Why, the reader is encouraged to ask, are these criminals saying the curious things they do, and not the things they might reasonably be expected to say? What can they mean? And why are they being offered up as objects worth considering? Defoe and presumably his readers were well aware of the difference "between what men say of themselves, and what others say for them, when they come to write historically of their lives." What is that *other* saying about them, through what they are saying about themselves? The fact this "other" remains anonymous would, moreover, have kept readers' attention focussed all the more closely on the text itself. "If a Man writes to this Age," Defoe may once have complained, "it is not now enquir'd, *What does he say?* But *who is it says it?* Not, Is the Thing true? But do you like the Man that speaks it?"[22] In making it difficult to know just who or what is behind the text, Defoe's prefaces block immediate or easy recourse to the intentional fallacy; readers are put in a position to become *avant la lettre*, as it were, formalists as well as policemen.

Once beyond the preface and launched into the full stream of narrative, the critically alerted reader may well feel somewhat at sea. The "taking elegancy" of Defoe's moral dialogues is certainly not in evidence here, the story not moving forward in the "short periods" and "quick returns" that make "retaining it in the mind easier" but in an unremitting, practically undifferentiated flood of experience and observation. The tactic (if that is

---

[21] Even *Captain Singleton*, though it has no preface, nonetheless suggests a second hand was somehow involved in its composition. Thus the account of Knox's captivity on Ceylon – an "other Story" which Singleton introduces "to shew, whoever reads this, what it was I avoided" – is supposedly a précis of a longer text written by a "Friend" (238). The fiction is that Singleton and his "Friend" have swapped stories, but who is this writing "Friend," and what part (if only as potential audience) might he have played in the shaping of Singleton's larger text?

[22] ?Defoe, *The King of the Pirates*, in *The Works of Daniel Defoe*, ed. G. H. Maynadier (New York, 1903–4), 16: xv; the *Review*, 8: 581 (26 February 1712).

what it is) is not limited to the criminal novels, but its contribution to their overall effect is especially powerful for several reasons. In the first place, both the *Journal of the Plague Year* and *Robinson Crusoe* fall into clear and significant parts. In the *Journal*, for instance, the regular interruption of the bills of mortality not only allows readers to track the rise and fall of the disease, but serves to segment the narrative almost as chapter divisions might do. Less notable, but nonetheless significant, is the clear breakdown of Crusoe's narrative (at least in the first book) into four or five significant parts: his first sea voyages, his enslavement and escape from Barbary, his solitary sojourn on the island, the arrival first of Friday and then the others, and finally his rescue and journey home. But the criminal novels are not so easily divisible into large units of clear significance. The first half of *Captain Singleton* is about Bob's travels in Africa, and the second about his life as a pirate, but it is hard to see essential differences between the two, especially as his piracies often read like travelogue, and his trek across Africa – necessitated by a failed attempt to become a pirate – seems itself a species of buccaneering. One may tell Moll's and Roxana's days by the male company they keep (or rather which keeps them), and Jack's life may be measured by the various social roles he undertakes, but these modes of organizing the texts do not make them, either, any easier to retain in the mind. *Moll Flanders* and *Roxana* are clearly about larger things than the passing of women from hand to hand, and Jack's various transmogrifications show no clear pattern of rise and/or fall. It is not surprising that at least one contemporary abridgement of *Moll Flanders* did divide the text into chapters – apparently according to some protocol, for the chapters are of unequal length – and gave each chapter a summary heading, the better, perhaps, for it to be kept in mind.[23]

The criminal novels demand to be read differently from Defoe's other fiction, too, because their narrators are so obviously anomalous. The great difference between their discourse and that of conventional criminals puts special pressures on readers to organize the text, to make it coherent in ways they can understand. A term we might use for this process is Wolfgang Iser's "consistency building."[24] The reader begins looking for patterns, and of course begins to find them. Roxana's movement from man to man is not so significant, perhaps, as Moll's, and the lack of any clear

---

[23] See *The Life and Actions of Moll Flanders* (1723); thus, for instance, its heading for "chapter 2": "*Moll Flanders* sick for Love: Her Marriage (tho' unwillingly) with her Master's youngest Son, by whom she had two Children: Her second Marriage with a Linnen-Draper, who soon broke, went into the *Mint*, and thence into *France*; so that *Moll* became a Widow bewitch'd: Her third Marriage to her own Brother; Voyage to Virginia with him, by whom she had three Children: Cause of leaving him in *America*; and return again to *England*." We have here not only a "telegraphing" of the plot, but a pre-interpretation of it.

[24] Wolfgang Iser, *The Act of Reading: A Theory of Aesthetic Response* (Baltimore, 1978), pp. 16–18, 118–19, 122–30.

direction to Jack's sequence of careers can itself seem significant; but more of this in subsequent chapters. The point I want to develop here is that Defoe's texts require readers to work at understanding them. Again, in terms of the reading process they impose, they might be contrasted to *The Family Instructor* and *Religious Courtship*, where the objectives of the text are always made abundantly clear. Thus in *Religious Courtship*, for instance, before beginning the unhappy story of the second sister and her Catholic husband, Defoe pauses to describe their differing characters. "It is proper to the relish of the story," he says, "to have [its] general idea, that we may not be left to gather it up slowly among the particulars" (139). In the criminal novels, it would appear, he meant to have his story relished differently.[25]

To an audience aware of the conventions Defoe is manipulating, and faced with the task of "gathering up particulars into a general idea," the texts of the criminal novels can come to seem palpably deficient things. They stand between the reader and the world they adumbrate, and face him with an ongoing task of "revision" (a task much like the one Moll's editor claims to have accomplished, though along different lines, in an opposite direction). To borrow Crusoe's terminology, Moll, Jack, Roxana, even Singleton, all eventually come to seem "ignorant relators," unaware of the impression they give and of all their stories can mean. In Moll's case the point is made especially clear by the reference in the preface to her "original" version, but they all speak without knowing the full effect of what they say. So do we all, of course, but as readers we enjoy the advantage, *qua* readers, of having the text of their discourse before us, which in the privacy of our closets we may mark and consider, then remark and reconsider. Like Crusoe's "serious old lady," readers may notice things that never quite register on the narrators. Indeed, the narrators themselves often urge them to do as much.

Defoe's criminal protagonists are untrustworthy in peculiarly intriguing ways. They are not the usual sort of "unreliable narrator," for readers seem meant not so much to overturn or reject their points of view as to transcend them. They dissimulate through most of their lives, but there is no reason to believe they are lying here and now, as they speak. In fact when they don't want to talk about something, they say so. The reader is privileged as no one else in his access to their lives and minds, but their

---

[25] Something of Defoe's effect may be gauged by a later writer's effort to undo it. Thus in a preface to the last of the eighteenth-century revisions of *Roxana*, Defoe supposedly reconsiders the organization of his narrative: "I have thought proper, for the ease of the reader to throw [Roxana's history] into chapters; that he, like a traveller on the road, when he espies a good inn, may put up his horse, and rest both himself and his beast; may also when tired, lay down the book, at the several resting places, I before have appointed" (*History of Mademoiselle de Beleau; or, The New Roxana* [1775], pp. 5–6).

minds are often dark and what they know and can say of their lives is limited. They understand this, and thus their urgings that readers should build on their experience. "The Moral indeed of all my History," says Moll, "is left to be gather'd by the Senses and Judgment of the Reader; I am not Qualified to preach to them" (268). She carries this idea even further after describing how she felt when she first experienced a "real" repentance. Though "not capable of reading Lectures of Instruction to any Body," she says, "I related this in the very manner in which things then appear'd to me, as far as I am able; but infinitely short of the lively impressions which they made on my Soul at that time." "Indeed," she adds, "those Impressions are not to be explain'd by words, or if they are, I am not Mistress of Words enough to express them" (287–8).

Moll's insufficiency of insight, indeed her limited capacity for expression, impose an important task. "It must be the Work of every sober Reader," she declares, "to make just Reflections" on an experience which, though she is unable to describe it, "every one at sometime or other may feel something of" (288). Her readers are thus to plumb their own memories and imaginations, looking in "their Lives," as Jack says, for "any Similitude of Cases" (*CJ*, 309). Or as Moll says, making reflections "as their own Circumstances may direct" (288). Each of the novels advances some or all of these ideas. The narrators cannot know the whole truth of their situations, and cannot tell all they know; it is up to the reader to flesh their details out with meaning, to read not so much between as beyond their lines.[26] Occasions for such exertion are made especially plentiful as the novels repeatedly remind readers of the inherent limitations of story-telling as a way of representing the world. No story is ever quite adequate to the whole truth, and these stories do more than simply acknowledge this point, they enact it. Just beyond the boundaries of what they can and do say, they indicate the presence of much that is beyond saying or they just don't get around to saying.

Language itself is partly the problem; it is slippery and difficult, a powerfully and curiously limiting medium. Adverting to the "inexpressible" frequently, unable to do more than limn out what she felt at certain crucial moments, Moll is aware that much of her life exceeds her power to put it into words. Her first (and only) seducer talks her into marrying his brother in "much more moving Terms than it is possible for me to Express" (55), and she finds it "impossible to express the Horror of my Soul" when she commits her first theft (95). No one can "conceive aright" the dreadfulness of Newgate without having been imprisoned there, nor

---

26 Much of what follows could also be said about the style and presentation of *Robinson Crusoe* and *Journal of the Plague Year* (see, e.g., Mary E. Butler, "The Effect of the Narrator's Rhetorical Uncertainty on the Fiction of *Robinson Crusoe*," *Studies in the Novel*, 15 [1983]: 77–90). What might be called Defoe's epistemological incertitude has a very particular effect in the criminal novels, however, because the protagonists themselves are so deeply and obviously suspect.

how, after awhile, the place can become "not only tollerable, but even agreeable." Like much of her experience, this remains to her "a thing Unintelligible" (276). The same problem of fitting words to reality confronts Defoe's other narrators somewhat differently, though to much the same effect. Singleton often finds himself in situations where normal discourse is impossible. "We conversed with some of the Natives of the Country," he observes shortly after his arrival in Africa, "What Tongue they spoke, I do not yet pretend to know. We talked as far as we could make them understand us" (48). Such "conversation" and "talking" must proceed without words, for they and their interlocutors have none in common. "I spoke to him as well as I could by Signs," says Jack on a similar occasion (57). Throughout Singleton's narrative the same curious situation repeats itself almost obsessively.[27] Beyond the language readers share with him, there are whole worlds of other discourse, seemingly innumerable and certainly not English.[28]

[27] See also pp. 95, 276, 286, 292, and, for slight variations on this theme, pp. 231, 289.

[28] Nor is Singleton's English in and of itself entirely adequate to the story he has to tell, a point so repeatedly made by the novel as to warrant particular attention. As Singleton voyages to and across Africa, he is frequently unable to name or even describe all the things he sees. On Madagascar the woods are filled with "wild and terrible Beasts, which we could not call by their Names"; as they journey to the continent they trade with natives in canoes for some "large Fish, of which we did not know the Names"; and in Africa itself, besides seeing many more animals they cannot name, they eat "several Sorts of Fruits and Roots, which we did not understand" (23, 31, 68). And so on, all across Africa; there are too many instances to quote them all (see pp. 59–62, 65–8, 70–1, 73–5, 78, 82, 107, 117, 157, 160–1, 205, 222, 241; and, for variants, pp. 84, 90, 199, 207, 244, 269–70, 272, 277). Africa stands beyond the English language, beggaring it. The extent to which it exceeds Singleton's powers of description is never so clear as when he happens on a vivid, homely metaphor. Thus on a number of occasions he describes Africa in terms that are (or ought to be) familiar to Englishmen, but which make it seem only stranger. An unnamed river, for instance, shows at "a fair open Channel about as broad as the *Thames* below *Gravesend*." Two hundred miles later it has narrowed to a stream "not above as broad as the *Thames* is at *Windsor*," and one day's journey farther on it falls in "a great Water-fall or Cataract, enough to fright us" (64–5). If the presence of a great cataract just above "Windsor" is not enough to throw the comparison askew, then the distance between "Windsor" and "Gravesend" should be. Similarly incongruous references back to England occur in Singleton's narrative at regular intervals. When his camp is menaced by "multitudes" of animals for which he does have names – i.e., "Lions, and Tigers, and Leopards, and Wolves" – he describes them as "standing ... as thick as a Drove of Bullocks going to a Fair" (100–1). Long after leaving Africa, as he cruises the Indies, he and his men are threatened by a great crowd of savages curiously got up. They are half-naked and have "great high Things on their Heads, made, as we believed, of Feathers, and which look'd something like our Grenadiers Caps in England." When pursued, these half-naked "grenadiers" take refuge in the "prodigious great Trunk of an old Tree." There is no English name for this tree, either, "but it stood like an old decay'd Oak in a Park, where the Keepers in *England* take a *Stand*, as they call it, to shoot a Deer" (206–7; see also pp. 73, 97, 102, 113, 129, 171).

Discussing different but comparable examples, Pat Rogers finds in them a kind of psychological realism: "The general effect is that of men trying to accommodate themselves to an alien environment by invoking familiar, but also strained, comparisons" ("Speaking Within Compass: The Ground Covered in Two Works by Defoe," *Studies in the Literary Imagination*, 15 [1982]: 110–11). My point is that readers, too, would be "strained" and challenged by all these

Roxana has a very different problem with language. If anything, certain words all too readily fit her situation: adultress, whore, murderer. As her case will be considered at length in chapter 7, I'll limit myself here to several comments she makes in describing the onset of her first illicit affair. Amy, who argues the necessity of the relationship by painting "in their proper Colours" all the horrid consequences of saying no, "had but too much Rhetoric in this Cause," says Roxana (39). So, too, in a sense does her "Friend," who, by a variety of "Circumlocutions," persuades himself that their relationship is "Lawful" (41). Thus he claims they will in effect be "marry'd," and wants her to call him "Husband" as he calls her "Wife" (42–5). Roxana finds this rhetoric unbearable, and it is, I think, to shatter all such pretense that she forces Amy and her "Husband" to sleep together; this is a way of making it clear that his relationship with her is founded on no "other Terms than that of notorious Adultery," and that she herself is nothing more than a "whore" – a hard word she at first is not at all reluctant to use (38, 43). In this instance and repeatedly in *Roxana*, language comes to seem dangerously capable of falsifying the simplest moral truths. If not always adequate to the describing of the world, it can still be used all too well to describe things in ways that please our corrupted fancies, or at least obscure the plain truth of right and wrong. Roxana consents to prostitute herself "with open Eyes," "knowing it to be a Sin, but having no Power to resist." So "overcome" is her "Reason" that she willfully turns her back on "Faith," "Religion," "Conscience," "Modesty," "Duty to God," and "Virtue and Honor." These are no circumlocutions, but words as hard and true in their way as "whore." Roxana knows this and, as we shall see later, it serves to harden her. "When this had thus made a Hole in my Heart," she says, "and I was come to such a height, as to transgress against the Light of my own Conscience, I was then fit for any Wickedness, and Conscience left off speaking, where it found it cou'd not be heard" (44). Roxana is unique among Defoe's criminal protagonists – and indeed among all the actual, redacted criminals I know – in that the disparity between the world and the words used to describe it proves her undoing. As I shall eventually argue, she provides one of the richest examples to be found in her period of the psychology of deviance and, particularly, of the etiology of crime.

Jack, the most affable of Defoe's criminals, illustrates yet another problem in trying to represent the world through language: the impossibility of saying everything. Limitations of space and the need to be

awkward conjunctions of the "alien" and the "familiar." Singleton's situation in Africa, and its potential effect on readers, bears close comparison to Crusoe's on his island. Crusoe, to take just one instance, also encounters animals he has no names for, but then he names them, like Adam in the Garden. Where Singleton is only a buccaneer in a hurry, Crusoe is a sojourner, accommodating himself to his island, and the island to himself, making it good; Singleton finds – and makes – the alienness of Africa impenetrable even as he succeeds in traversing it.

coherent force one to omit or skip over matters of great intrinsic interest. Jack meets a goodly number of interesting people, most of whom have stories of their own that seem worth telling. The various "Pranks" of his foster brother Captain Jack are "very diverting" and would in themselves "make a Volume larger than this" (116, 88; also 184). He also mentions the stories of Major Jack; of his "tutor" in Virginia (which story could also "fill a book"); of his first wife after she turns up a slave on his plantation, and indeed of all the other Englishwomen who are slaves with her; and finally of the men on his trading sloop, who, after being wrecked on the Gulf Coast, make their way overland to South Carolina, "a Journey, which indeed deserves to have an Account to be given by itself" (16, 164, 258 and 252, 300). Jack in fact is so highly aware of other people's stories that he must frequently call himself back to "my own Story," a phrase (or its equivalent) which occurs at least eleven times over the course of the novel.[29]

The same locution appears twice in Moll's mouth, both times with respect to Jemy's story, which is "much brighter . . . than any I ever saw in print" (159). It is only "with great reluctance" that she declines the "relating" of his adventures, "but I consider that this is my own Story, not his" (301). Nonetheless, she has "thoughts of making a Volume of it by it self" (339). Her governess's life, too, might fill a book, or just the "Hundred Pranks" she played in Ireland alone (213). The preface to *Moll Flanders* goes so far as to suggest that both lives have already been written and only await publication.[30] Singleton, for his part, actually meets with the subject of several already published biographies, the famous Captain Avery, nor should we overlook the up and coming "young Captain Kid" (154, 179, 140). Singleton's narrative includes, moreover, a précis of Robert Knox's account of his captivity on Ceylon, a well-known work first published in 1681.[31] The story of the Englishman he encounters toward the end of his trek across Africa never gets told, however, except in a few brief pages. Though in itself it would make "an agreeable History . . . as long and as diverting as our own," says Singleton, "having in it many strange and extraordinary Incidents . . . we cannot have Room here to launch out into so long a Digression" (123). It perhaps befits Roxana's egoism that she only once comes close to telling another person's story (83). It is, appropriately enough, that of her "familiar" or doppelgänger, Amy.[32]

---

[29] See pp. 17, 88, 95, 96, 116, 117, 153, 167, 174, 215, 223.

[30] These lives do in fact appear, written by whatever hand, in *Fortune's Fickle Distribution: In Three Parts. Containing First, The Life and Death of Moll Flanders . . . Part II. The Life of Jane Hackabout, Her Governess . . . Part III. The Life of James Mac-Faul, Moll Flanders's Lancashire Husband* (Dublin, 1730).

[31] See Robert Knox, *An Historical Relation of the Island Ceylon: Together, With an Account of the Detaining in Captivity the Author and Divers Other Englishmen* (1681).

[32] For Roxana's mentions of other person's stories, see pp. 33, 95, 107, 109, 188–97, 204, 265.

Defoe's criminal protagonists move through a swirl of other sensibilities; though these are unrealized, they are nonetheless indicated. Almost everyone mentioned in any detail in these novels seems to have a story that might be told, even if the protagonists are not interested in it. In *Captain Singleton*, there is obviously Quaker William as well as the solitary Englishman, and also the Dutchman they rescue from Ceylon, to say nothing of the Africans who have seized their slave ship and left not a "Christian" on board. In *Moll Flanders*, characters with potentially interesting stories or points of view include, besides Jemy and the governess, Moll's first husband, Robin; her mother, who tells Moll one story and then tries to tell her another; her "honest citizen"; and several of her victims, particularly the woman whose bundle she steals in her first theft, the little girl she nearly murders in an alley (imagine the story she'll be telling when she gets home!), and the journeyman mercer who mistakenly arrests her (more of him in chapter 5). In *Colonel Jack*, beyond all those characters already mentioned, there are Jack's mother and father, with their story; his "nurse" and her husband, with their different stories; the customs-house broker who becomes his banker; the old woman from Kentish Town, chief among his victims; and of course wives two through four. Roxana's children, too, have stories that might be told, as does her runaway husband, as does the first of her "Friends," as do all her other lovers and no doubt the Quaker woman, too, whom she coopts into her nasty schemes to discourage her daughter. In all these novels, there is a rich sense that the text before us is only one of many possible texts.[33]

Even the stories that do get told, it is intimated, might have been told otherwise. Here, too, principles of selection and coherence necessarily

---

[33] The necessary partiality of any history, the exclusions implicit (or explicit) in any narrative, are also indicated in *Robinson Crusoe* and *Journal of the Plague Year*. Thus Friday has his story, too, though it never really gets told, as do also the Spaniards who come over from the continent, the ship's crew which mutinies, and, in the *Farther Adventures*, the colonists, most notably Will Atkins. The interpolation of the "journal" Crusoe keeps during his first months on the island also serves to heighten our sense of the text before us, and of other possible texts, as it differs significantly in tone and detail from the main narrative's description of the same experience. (Consider, for instance, the three significantly different accounts we get of Crusoe's arrival on the island.) Crusoe's actual experience is larger than any particular redaction of it. *The Journal of the Plague Year* also plays with a multiplicity of texts, all emerging from the same general phenomenon: H. F.'s own narrative, the story of the three men who flee into the countryside, and of course the bills of mortality. And if there are not eight million but, at most, only a few hundred thousand stories in H. F.'s naked city, the novel nonetheless suggests stories in abundance. An important difference between these two novels and the other four, however, is that the criminal protagonists come into much closer contact with other people than either Crusoe or H. F., and under circumstances highly likely to raise readers' curiosity, and suspicion, about those other people's motives and aims. The company of Defoe's criminals puts one far more "on edge." An interesting (well, not so interesting) counter-example to Defoe's leaving other characters' stories untold is Richard Head's and Francis Kirkman's *The English Rogue Described in the Life of Meriton Latroon* (1665–71), where such stories do get told – repeatedly and quite tediously.

come into play, along with something else. On no fewer than twenty-seven occasions Roxana cuts short her description of significant and potentially interesting events in her life, on the grounds that she has no space, or that these depart from her main concerns.[34] And of course we never do get the conclusion of her story. Moll similarly foreshortens her narrative, saying practically nothing of her five years of marriage to Robin, because it "concerns the Story in hand very little," nor does she say much more of the five years she was married to the "honest citizen" (58, 188). These omissions are especially teasing, as some knowledge of Moll's life as a bourgeoise gentlewoman might have offered richer insights into her later criminal career. When arrested, Moll "makes short this black Part of my Story" (272). Jack is too busy getting his own story out against the competition, perhaps, to feel much embarrassed by "surplus" detail, but he does, for instance, cut short his account of the French campaign in northern Italy on the grounds that "I am not writing a Journal of the Wars, in which I had no long Share" (215). *Captain Singleton*, for whatever reasons, does not employ this stylistic device. But again, perhaps its position as the first of the criminal novels is relevant; as Defoe goes on, he seems to pay increasing attention to the story-telling process.

Singleton and Jack do share with Moll and Roxana, however, a most intriguing reluctance to tell all. There are things they have done, or at least know about, which they would rather not speak of in detail. This has nothing to do with the exigencies of discourse in itself, by which I mean limitations of space and the need to be coherent, but rather with the constraints imposed on it by a self-censoring sense of decorum. Defoe's criminals are occasionally embarrassed by, even ashamed of, what they have to tell. Singleton omits the details of how he squandered his first fortune, for instance, saying "the rest Merits to be Conceal'd in Blushes" (137–8). A few pages later he hints, more darkly, at Captain Wilmot's cruel measures against English ships, "that they might not too soon have an Advice of him in England." One presumes that not a soul is left alive to testify, but Singleton only says, "this Part I bury in Silence for the present." Nor should suspicions be the least allayed when, soon after, he discounts the "many Stories" told in Europe about "how we murthered the People in cold Blood, tying them Back to Back, and throwing them into the Sea; one Half of which was not true" – one half! – "tho' more was done than it is fit to speak of here" (142, 144). On several occasions Moll and Roxana both note they are concealing things "not proper for a Woman to write," as Moll says (233). But the passing over such things speaks volumes.[35]

Roxana's reticence about the sexual practices of her last lover is par-

---

[34] For some examples see pp. 9, 10, 24, 29, 41, 44, 72, 99, 103, 106, 185.
[35] For other instances see *MF*, pp. 25, 58, 236, and *R*, pp. 64, 181, 199, 207.

ticularly striking, for it hints at practically unimaginable obscenities. "He grew worse and wickeder the older he grew," says Roxana, "and that to such a Degree, as is not fit to write of." His "capricious humours" made her "sick," a feeling the reader would share, she believes, "if I cou'd suffer myself to publish them . . . but that Part of the Story will not bear telling" (199, 207).[36] There is her three year-liaison as well "with a Person, which Duty, and private Vows, obliges her not to reveal, at least, not yet" (181). This may be the "K----," i.e., Charles II, from frequent hints in the book, or it may be his ill-fated natural son, "the D---- of M-------th," from another. This is not the only time Defoe infiltrates real people into his criminal fictions, their names blocked out or spelled in full, which is one more way his texts suggest a reality beyond themselves they cannot or do not choose fully to reveal. It is also a way of stimulating even the laziest reader's curiosity, for nothing so invites being seen through as the flimsy veiling of scandal in high places, except of course sex of any kind (the kinkier the better) and blood-curdling violence. The most striking omission in Roxana's narrative concerns an event of this last kind, for, though she hints darkly of Susan's eventual fate at the hands of Amy, we never know exactly what has happened. Such reticence here must have been especially teasing to eighteenth-century readers trained up in the conventions of criminal biography and used to being told, with horrifying exactitude, every bloody detail.

Finally, the novels indicate, we are getting only part of the actual story because the narrators themselves cannot know everything; their perceptions are necessarily limited, and so is their insight. At one point Singleton's ship is attacked by savages shooting fire arrows, a process Singleton describes as closely as he can (as would any true Defoe protagonist). But there is more to the process than it seems he can tell, for "I could not say," says Singleton, "whether they set their Cotton Rag on Fire before they shot the Arrow, for I did not perceive they had Fire with them" (235). Another time, he and his men land on an "Island, *if it was such, for we never surrounded it*" (206).[37] The physical features of the universe often escape our ken, but even more difficult to fathom are the actions and intentions of other people. Singleton has trouble with some natives on another island, "some of our Men having been a little too familiar with the *Homely Ladies* of the Country." That his men have "good Stomachs" for such stuff is not as interesting as the fact that he "could never fully get it

---

36 For more on this point, see Maximillian Novak, "The Unmentionable and the Ineffable in Defoe's Fiction," *Studies in the Literary Imagination*, 15 (1982): 85–102. James Maddox suggests that *Roxana* becomes increasingly "predicated upon . . . unspeakable events" ("On Defoe's *Roxana*," *ELH*, 51 [1984]: 679).

37 Cf. Crusoe, who discovers only during his second voyage to the island that the land on the horizon, which he thought was the South American continent, is actually only another island (*RC2*, p. 92).

out of [them] what they did," though he understands "in the main, it was some barbarous thing" (218). On two occasions Jack adverts to things similarly dark and beyond his knowledge. One involves the Captain's connection with a gang of kidnappers: "there was it seems some Villainous thing done by this Gang about that time, whether a Child was murther'd among them, or a Child otherwise abus'd; but it seems it was a Child of an eminent Citizen, and the Parent some how or other got a Scent of the thing, so that they recover'd their Child, tho' in a sad Condition, and almost kill'd." He cannot be more specific, because "I was too young, and it was too long ago for me to remember the whole Story" (11). The other has to do with the gang Jack joins for one night only, in an orgy of robbing right across London, and which the next night goes on "to commit a notorious Robbery, down almost as far as Hounslow ... where they wounded a Gentlemen's Gardiner so, that I think he dyed." The wounded gardener is mentioned again, but it is still not clear how badly he was injured, and whether in fact he did die (69, 81).[38]

There is nothing quite so teasingly indefinite in *Moll Flanders*, but this may be more a question of emphasis than of any radical departure in narrative technique. Thus Moll's early experience is beyond her knowledge, like Singleton's and Jack's, though she doesn't make so much of the matter as they. Nor is she as alert to things she does not know. Moll's world may seem relatively "hard-edged," in that it raises fewer of the basic phenomenological issues to be found in the other novels. But it may only be that she is not so curious or self-conscious as Defoe's other criminals, being more serene in her ignorance or, as is more likely, more careless. Thus there are a number of matters that might dog her consciousness and don't, as for instance the identity of her first victim, who, she thinks, "may be some poor Widow like me" (193), the whereabouts of her second, absconded husband, and the fate of all those children she's sloughed off. In the last two instances Roxana provides a sharp contrast to Moll, as in fact she does generally. Here it will only be noted that, like Jack and Singleton, she also bumps up against the boundaries of perception, cognition, and knowledge. Roxana "never knew" the identity of the "tall well-shaped Gentleman" who appears at the first of her balls, masked, and pays her so much attention (175, 176; see also 288). Nor, doing her "Turkish" dance for the lords and ladies of the court, does she ever notice she is under the worshipful, careful gaze of a little cookmaid, who, eventually and crucially, will prove to be her daughter (289; cf. 175–6). Sending Amy to Paris to inquire after the Dutch merchant, she asks, too, for information about the Jew who gave her so much trouble, but Amy is unable "to come at a Certainty what was become of him," though she does find he has got

---

[38] Note also Will's victim, who mysteriously disappears from the ditch where they have left him bound and immobilized (*CJ*, p. 64).

into some kind of trouble with the law (232). The murder of Roxana's first
lover is similarly tinged with uncertainty. She knows he was "stabb'd ...
into the Body with a Sword, so that he died immediately," but it can only
be "suppos'd" (the word is used twice) what his killers' motives were (53;
see also 54).[39]

Defoe's novels are rich in gaps, dark patches, all sorts of loose ends.
Though some of these are inadvertent, most, I would argue, originate in a
prevailing interest in the isolation of the individual subject in a universe it
cannot entirely fathom, surrounded by others with whom, for one reason
or another, it cannot fully communicate.[40] While this concern permeates
all the novels (and indeed many of Defoe's other texts), it is in the criminal
novels, perforce, that his protagonists are most isolated from other human
beings. All of them live by intrigue, sussing out their marks as best they can
and suspecting their marks are doing the same. They might all say with
Roxana, "we went upon Guesses at one another's Designs" (145). All of
them also share the curious circumstance of Jack, who cannot tell what
impression he gives, he says, "for I cannot see my own Countenance"
(227).[41]

What is the reader to see? Like all subjects of serious criminal biography, Defoe's protagonists are meant as case histories. "I am a Mem-
orial," says Roxana, "to all that shall read my Story" (161). The difference, and it is a great difference, is that here we no longer know quite how
to read their cases – and by "we," I mean all Defoe's readers, past and
present. We, too, are isolated, though in our case it is in texts we cannot
fully understand or comprehend. We are like Roxana's daughter, who,
though she had "but a broken Account of things," is nonetheless able to
piece together her mother's story because "she had receiv'd some Accounts
that had a reallity in the Bottom of them." And we are like Roxana and
Amy, too, who "pick" this knowledge "out of the Girl's Discourse,"
though "it all consisted of broken Fragments of Stories" (269).

That stories do not come whole but must be assembled is problematic
enough, but that they are broken and assembled again and again suggests,
first, that any getting at "a reallity in the Bottom" of things is bound to be
impermanent, and, second, that truth can come in a variety of not quite
identical versions. However much one may feel at any one point he's

---

[39] See also pp. 125, 127, 133, 269, and, as variations on this theme, pp. 135, 220, 251, 278, 293.
[40] The real-life basis of this interest is somewhat poignantly expressed in one of Defoe's letters to
Charles De la Faye, where – "Posted among Papists, Jacobites, and Enraged High Torys, a
Generation ... My Very Soul abhors" – he sounds like a spy (which of course he was) wanting
to come in from the cold. "I May one Time Or other," he writes asking for reassurance from his
masters, "Run the hazard of fatall Missconstructions" (26 April 1718, ed. Healey, p. 454).
[41] Cf. Roxana: "what my Face might do towards betraying me, I know not, because I could not
see myself" (284).

sleuthed out the truth of a particular case, that he's found the "real" story, it can only seem a whole and coherent story if he overlooks how he's patched it together. It is impossible, in any case, for him to pass it along to anyone else whole and entire. The "whole" truth is at best an artfully repaired artifact, something repeatedly cemented together. Defoe's "concrete" particularity is as much an aggregate as the thing itself, though – of itself – it never quite hardens into a fixed and enduring form.

To a remarkable degree, then, Defoe's criminal novels depend on their readers to give them meaning, which is to say, on what their readers are willing or able to bring to their texts by way of "reflection." Readers whose attitudes toward criminals had been shaped by criminal biography, I suspect, would have been far less moved by the plights of Moll and Roxana than many modern readers have been, and, possibly, a good deal more interested in the peregrinations of Singleton and Jack. I suspect, too, they would have been more susceptible to the "openness" of Defoe's texts, more inclined to feel the challenges and difficulties as well the special sense of discovery that such openness can produce. A brief look at Moll's repentance in Newgate will allow me to indicate something of what I mean, to show how differently Defoe could once have been read from the ways we read him now.

Most modern commentators assume that Moll's repentance is supposed to be taken as sincere and consequential. Read against the conventions of criminal biography, however, it seems instead rather dubious, including too many ups and downs to fit the proper paradigm. Moll is quite sure several times she is sorry for what she has done, but again and again her consciousness of her situation comes to seem insufficient. Despite the "real" repentance she claims to have achieved under the care of the kindly minister who visits her in Newgate, she never takes the full guilt of her crimes upon herself, nor does she transcend the prospect of death. She as much as lies in her plea for mercy to the court, saying amidst tears that "at the worst it was the first Offence, and that I had never been before any Court of Justice before." After sentence has been passed, however, and with the help of "this extraordinary Man," she is brought to feel she "cou'd freely [go] out that Minute to Execution, without any uneasiness at all, casting my Soul entirely into the Arms of infinite Mercy as a Penitent" (287, 286, 289).

This of course would be the best possible way for Moll to feel, "more desirous to die than to live," as a Newgate ordinary phrased it, taking "great Satisfaction and Comfort in dying."[42] Still, when the death warrant comes down, it is a "terrible blow" to her "new Resolutions": "indeed my Heart sunk within me, and I swoon'd away twice" (285–9). As

---

[42] Lorrain, Ordinary Account, 15 May 1706.

she is reprieved and then committed for transportation, her friend, the minister, shows on four separate occasions a concern that her repentance be and continue "unfeign'd and Sincere." Pressing her "to retain the same Sentiments of the things of Life, that [she] had when [she] had a view of Eternity," he warns her that she "must have more than ordinary secret Assistance from the Grace of God ... not [to] turn as wicked again as ever." In his final appearance, when he expresses "his fears of [her] relapsing into wickedness," Moll placates this "good Minister" by telling her Governess in front of him that his "fears were not without Cause." But then, just as soon as he leaves and as if to prove him right, the two of them start scheming how to get Moll to Virginia as comfortably as possible, with Jemy in tow, her stolen fortune intact (see 290–306).

Readers of criminal biography would have found it hard to know exactly what to make of Moll's "new Resolutions." More will be said about these in the next chapter; here my concern is not whether she should or would have seemed sincere, but the grounds – or lack of grounds – on which that question could have been decided. The one best way to be sure of Moll's repentance is of course to hang her, the ultimate (though by no means perfect) test of any criminal's repentance. The notion gets an airing as Moll addresses those of her readers who might be bored with all her moral talk. Realizing that they who were "pleas'd and diverted with the Relation of the wild and wicked part of my Story, may not relish this, which is really the best part of my Life, the most Advantageous to myself, and the most instructive to others," she asks to be allowed "the liberty to make my Story compleat." "It would be a severe Satyr on such [readers]," she adds, "to say they do not relish the Repentance as much as they do the Crime; and that they had rather the History were a compleat Tragedy, as it was very likely to have been" (291). There are actually two "tragedies" averted here, Moll dying as a doomed soul and Moll dying as yet another Newgate "saint." It is only at the cost of one or the other that one could be sure of Moll and make her story really "compleat." Should she die for being a thief? This is a question that could almost never be asked about actual criminals, for by the time their lives got written they were already dead, and the decision of the law required to be upheld. But Moll, a fictive character, is a different case; for this reason, it may be, Defoe and many of his readers felt they could afford to banish her to the green fields of Virginia, even allow her an eventual return.[43] But not all readers, as every one of the abridgements indicates by bringing Moll to a certain, unambi-

---

[43] In this way, then, Moll's story might have produced the "satisfaction" a writer confesses to in 1735 when he tells of a criminal who took warning "in time" and, like Jack, escaped without being arrested to a new and prosperous life in the New World (*Lives of the Most Remarkable Criminals*, pp. 200–4).

guously penitent death and, keeping her in Virginia or relocating her in Ireland, barring her forever from the greener fields of England.[44]

In shortening and simplifying Moll's story, disambiguating her repentance and describing her death, the later abridgements of the novel are in fact attempting to "complete" Defoe's purposefully open narrative. The preface claims that "the History is [not] carried on quite to the End of the Life of this famous *Moll Flanders* . . . for no Body can write their own Life to the full End of it, unless they can write it after they are dead" (1). But this, for all its superficial plausibility, is the ripest of red herrings. Why shouldn't "the Pen employ'd in finishing her Story" have actually "finished" it? This is what happens in the abridgements, a third-person narrator taking over after Moll, and there are many examples of such mixed narratives in both actual and fictive criminal biography.[45] Perhaps Defoe did not quite know how Moll's life might be brought, as criminal biographies always were brought, to a definite conclusion, that is, to some clear "application" or meaning in the end. Perhaps, believing that "a Man's Life will furnish Matter for many Memoirs," and that it was "scarce possible for any single Man to give a compleat History of his [own] Life" – or anyone else's – Defoe saw no alternative to leaving Moll's story unfinished. Perhaps (or so I believe) he didn't quite know himself what it all might have meant, and so escaped having to say so. "The Author can never be charg'd with Incoherence in the Story he tells," he sought to persuade impatient or otherwise unruly readers of the *Review*, "till the Gentlemen have heard it all told."[46] According to this logic, readers of *Moll Flanders* must content themselves with their own theories about the overall meaning of what they've so far read, even when it's all there is to read. Moll's story is never "all told." This may be burdensome, but the alternative is to be something less than the best sort of reader, i.e., one of the "severely satirizable" sort who, liking their stories "compleat," for just this reason never get the full and actual story.

Cut off from familiar ways of reading, repeatedly invited to come up with "their own just Reflections," Defoe's readers would have been placed

---

[44] *Fortune's Fickle Distribution* shows Moll going through only one cycle of despair and repentance in Newgate, not two, and she never grows accustomed to the place, as she does in the original before hearing herself sentenced to death. It might also be noted that the ordinary never visits Moll in this revision of her story, a further simplification of Defoe's complex consideration of what a supposedly penitent behavior in this prison might mean. The other abridgements of the novel are still more laconic, but all give Moll a last and wholly unambiguous repentance as she lies on her deathbed, indicating, I would think, some doubt in the minds of these "editors" about the efficacy and/or permanence of Moll's "pretended" reformation as Defoe himself presents it. Note also for its apparent seriousness, or at least unironic straightforwardness, the repentance of Meriton Latroon in a text otherwise remarkable for its lack of either quality (Head and Kirkman, *The English Rogue* [New York, 1928], pp. 228, 233, 234, 259, 264).

[45] See chapter 2, notes 40, 48.

[46] ?Defoe, *Memoirs of the Life and Eminent Conduct of ... Daniel Williams, D. D.* (1718), p. 85; the *Review*, 1: 293 (4 November 1704).

in a challenging but also potentially exciting situation. Given access to stories not yet compressed into the "ready-made" and "complete" pattern-ings of criminal biography, stories that would have been told quite differently had they ever reached the courts and the popular press, they may even have felt an occasional thrill of self-enhancing privilege and power. Exposed to the full glare of public attention, for instance, Roxana's "secret history" would necessarily have been made into something far less mysterious, subtle, and "juicy." Ambiguity would have been banished, or a damp blanket thrown over the whole affair. Though it is hard to know, really, just how deeply implicated Roxana is in the murder of her daugh-ter, or even that her daughter has actually been murdered, readers would have had no difficulty supposing what would have happened in "real life" were a young woman's corpse discovered and her mother's servant con-nected to the crime – especially if there were witnesses to come forward to say what a profound embarrassment that daughter had been to both mother and servant, and what a thoroughly corrupt life the two of them had led.

Men "ought to incline ... to an honest life," one criminal biographer advises, if only to avoid "the danger [they run] from being known to be of ill ... fame." A person can all too easily be "accused from his character ... of crimes which he [is] guiltless of," and "in such a case might find it difficult to get his innocence either proved or credited if any unlucky circumstance should give the least weight to the accusation." Recounting a number of cases where clearly this appears to have happened, this writer just as clearly feels that no particular injustice has been done.[17] Though very likely innocent of the particular facts for which they were hanged – other criminals said as much – these people shouldn't have allowed themselves to get into, or be put into, situations where guilt by association might taint them. Brought to trial, Roxana might have been convicted; the facts of her life, her close and unwholesome relationship with Amy, would be more than enough to make a murder charge stick, one way or another.

Were she hanged, of course, Roxana's story would become the usual – and I emphasize *usual* – public property. Cleaned up and straightened out according to the standard narrative models, it would lose most of what makes it truly interesting, the idiosyncratic smell of truth, its "novelty." Or else she might not be tried and convicted, and the truth of her case would remain too muffled and vague for imaginative reconstruction. The three men who in 1682 murdered Thomas Thynne, one of the richest men in

---

[17] *Lives of the Most Remarkable Criminals Who Have Been Condemned and Executed for Murder, the Highway, Housebreaking, Street Robberies, Coining or Other Offences*, 1st pub. 1735 in 3 vols., ed. Arthur L. Hayward (New York, 1927), pp. 303–4; see also the lives appearing pp. 288–92, 297–300, 303–6, all of which concern criminals hanged over the winter of 1725–6.

England, were almost certainly in the employ of the Swedish ambassador, but no hard evidence surfaced to confirm this as a fact; readers of the pamphlets describing the case were consequently barred from ever knowing all the writers themselves knew or seemed to suspect. Much the same thing happened in 1699 when Spencer Cowper and several other men were acquitted of drowning a young woman who, it appeared, had actually committed suicide. Still, there were dark suspicions that contemporary writers could only adumbrate.[48] Once news becomes a commodity, as it certainly had become in Defoe's lifetime, then what lies behind the news can seem a rarer, still more valuable commodity. "Inquiring minds want to *know*," the supermarket scandal sheet proclaims, endorsing even at this level the notion that knowledge is power.

Being "in the know" isn't the same thing as knowledge, of course, but it nonetheless confers a sense of power. The more readers worked at piecing together Defoe's criminals' stories out of their "broken" narratives, the harder they worked at finding "similitudes of cases" in their own life experiences, the more, in short, they poured their energies into seeing what was "really" there, beyond the incapacity of language itself to capture it, beyond all the usual, obfuscating conventions, the greater would have been that sense of power. No one else would – or could – have known quite what they knew about these dark and complicated lives, truth taking several shapes, none ever quite clear or fully communicable, and no one having exactly the same experience. Opening the door to inference, Defoe's novels privilege their readers not only as centers of judgment and authority but as gathering points for information. The story they assemble – all by themselves, it must be emphasized, for novel reading *is* a solitary sport, and behind these novels there is no already determined, already made meaningful set of events – such a story is not so much a preestablished "given" as something, seemingly, that takes its shape in and from them, that can become, in a sense, peculiarly their own.

Further discussion of the possible or potential meanings of *Moll Flanders* and the other novels will have to wait; this chapter is already long enough.

[48] For the murder of Thomas Thynne, see primarily *The Tryal and Condemnation of George Borowsky ... Christopher Vratz, and John Stern; for the Barbarous Murder of Thomas Thynn, Esq.; Together with the Tryal of Charles Count Coningsmark, as Accessory ....Who Was Acquitted* (1681), and Gilbert Burnet and Anthony Horneck, *The Last Confession, Prayers and Meditations of ... John Stern .... Together with the Last Confession of George Borosky* (1682). For the Spencer Cowper affair, see particularly *The Tryal of Spencer Cowper, Esq; John Marson, Ellis Stevens, and William Rogers, Gent .... for the Murther of Mrs. Sarah Stout, a Quaker .... of Which They Were Acquitted* (1699). Under the guise of fiction, Delerivière Manley gives thinly veiled accounts of both scandals, purporting to say what the full, actual, secret, so far undisclosed events and motives were in each. The Cowper–Stout affair, where the principals are disguised as Mosca and Zara, is traced in *Secret Memoirs and Manners .... From the New Atalantis* (1709), 1: 227, 229, 235, 237–44, and the Thynne murder, where Königsmark is called Count Alaric, in *Memoirs of Europe, Towards the Close of the Eighth Century* (1710), 1: 136–41.

We might conclude, however, by noting that Defoe's complaints about the abridgement of *Robinson Crusoe* – that it mistook and misapplied its author's meaning, that as a patching together of "scatter'd Passages" it lost its moral usefulness – may well have extended to the abridgements and revisions of the three most popular criminal novels. These not only simplify and tidy up the fates of Moll, Jack, and Roxana, but thin out the "density" of their narrative discourse. It is not merely that the proliferation of incidents is considerably diminished, though of course whole episodes are cut out, but that most of the epiphenomenal baggage is gone. Even the longer abridgements tend to radical simplifications of the narrative voice, discarding the "reflections," moral and otherwise, that Defoe salts through his texts, as the consciousnesses of his narrators play over the events they have experienced and are now relating. It is this sense of consciousness at play, so powerfully intimated by the textuality of Defoe's texts, that gives the reader "room" in which his own consciousness might "play," or, as Defoe says, to take these narratives "as he pleases." Criminal biography allows its reader no equivalent scope. Its "field" is too narrowly bounded to allow much play, or, alternatively, its boundaries so haphazardly drawn that a reader's consciousness soon plays out. In the next chapters we shall try to define the boundaries of Defoe's larger, more capacious fictions, and to understand how it is those boundaries can shift over time and yet still maintain a capacious integrity.

For, whatever Defoe says, his novels are not to be taken "just" as the reader pleases. If that were the case they would have no specific value intrinsic to themselves, and so, I would argue, no particular social or literary value to distinguish them from ordinary criminal biography. They might do a better job of its social and political "work" – and in their day I suspect in certain ways they did – but they would do little or nothing for us. We can still read and (with difficulty) interpret early eighteenth-century criminal biography, but it does not invite or require interpretation as Defoe's fictions do; it can be read and let be. It is this inviting, indeed this requiring, that validates Defoe's often discounted claim that his novels do have moral value, and that underpins their particular kind of coherence – a coherence which is not so much ideological or even ideational as formal (and so, I'd say, "literary") and without which they could not have survived the loss of their immediate context. How did Defoe bound "his delightful Field for the Reader to wander in"? And what could have been – what is? – the good of wandering there?

4

Intimations of an invisible hand: the mind exercised, enlarged, and kept in play by strange concurrences

It is in vain for me to run into a collection of stories, where the variety is infinite, and things vary as every particular man's circumstances vary .... my business is not preaching, I am making observations and reflections, let those make enlargements who read it.

Serious Reflections of Robinson Crusoe, pp. 213–14

The just application of every incident ... must legitimate all the part that may be called invention or parable in the story.

Preface to *Farther Adventures of Robinson Crusoe*, p. vii

Let the Naturalists explain these Things, and the Reason and Manner of them; all I can say to them, is, to describe the Fact.

Robinson Crusoe, p. 188

Should we ... say nothing of God is to be understood, because we cannot understand it? or that nothing in Nature is intelligible but what we can understand? Who can understand the reason, and much less the manner, of the needle tending to the pole by being touched with the lodestone, and by what operation the magnetic virtue is conveyed with a touch? .... Yet we see all these things in their operations and events; we know they must be reconcilable in nature, though we cannot reconcile them; and intelligible in nature, though we cannot understand them.

Serious Reflections of Robinson Crusoe, p. 207

There was a strange concurrence ... in the various providences which befel me.

Robinson Crusoe, p. 143

There is no Diversion so cheap and innocent as Reading; the Man who takes Delight in Books, passes a great many Hours agreeably, which lie heavy upon the Hands of those who have no Taste that Way. Sir Francis Bacon advises Reading for Health-Sake; for Reading which is the Exercise of the Mind, is as essential towards preserving a good Constitution, as Riding or Walking, which are the Exercise of the Body .... The Truth on't is, the Mind must have something to keep it in Play, otherwise it will prey upon it self.

?Defoe, *A Collection of Miscellany Letters Selected out of Mist's Weekly Journal*
(1722–7), 4: 194–5

The one thing that allows Defoe's novels to transcend the moral and explanatory power of criminal biography is the same thing that enables them to outlive their original context: they arouse readers' imaginations. In this respect their obvious deviation from "standard" criminal biography is not so important as their calling attention to the story-telling situation. The first would have put their original audience on the alert, but the second had a far more enduring effect; it was (and is) something readers could notice long after the conventions of criminal biography changed. Either way, Defoe's texts tease readers into trying to see through or around the particular story being told, to glimpse the reality behind it and its larger meaning. Thus readers provoked by the "ignorance" of Defoe's relators – their partiality and tendentiousness, in short their insufficiencies of consciousness – may find their own consciousnesses being raised as, seeking to compensate for that "ignorance," they come to see things the narrators do not see, and, concurrently, to experience a self-awareness, even a wholeness, the narrators apparently lack. Given the investment readers are encouraged to make in the text, they may even see things that, strictly speaking, could not have been "there" when the novels first appeared (feminism, for instance, or ego psychology, or the basis for a Marxist critique of nascent capitalism). They may even feel the presence in or around these texts of certain ideas or notions that neither they nor it can quite put into words.

By mobilizing readers as they do, Defoe's novels come to mean more than they say, and more than one or a few things. It would be foolish to try to specify all their meanings, as these, though finite, not only are quite numerous but change over time as readers change; the meaning of a text depends always (though not entirely) on the various bents or preoccupations of the readers who "actualize" or "realize" it.[1] If we may assume a readership agitated by the same issues and concerns that animate the two forms of criminal biography, however, it should be possible to speculate (reasonably, I think) on what these novels may have meant to significant numbers of Defoe's original audience.

Criminal biography sought to make its subjects "fit" for execution – or, rather, to render their executions fitting and proper – by representing them as saints or rogues, now beyond or beneath ordinary human concern. Before saying how they were severed forever from the human community, it either brought them back into it as shining examples of what humans might, after all, conceivably become, or else, reducing them to caricatures of one kind or another, it banished them to the farthest margins of imaginable human action. As serious criminal biography

---

[1] For "actualize," see Wolfgang Iser, *The Act of Reading: A Theory of Aesthetic Response* (Baltimore, 1978), pp. 18–27; "realize" is a comparable term used by Hans Robert Jauss, *Toward an Aesthetic of Reception*, tr. Timothy Bahti (Minneapolis, 1982), e.g., p. 21.

moved toward the first of these ends, it explored the mysterious and potentially embarrassing question of criminal motivation, important for what it might say of human nature generally. In cases of murder, it was also particularly concerned to show how even the most "private Murthers have been detected by Miracle," i.e., by "the Interposition of Providence . . . in the Most Extraordinary and Miraculous Manner."[2] For all its antic and apparently insouciant comedy, criminal rogue biography was also engaged with socially significant issues. Aside from justifying in its own oblique way the hanging of men merely for crimes against property, it dealt with the claim that thieves were just another variety of economic individualist, more glamorous than the general run of tradesmen, merchants, or other supposedly legitimate entrepreneurs, and certainly less hypocritical. The equation of trade with theft was not at all so mysterious a matter as men's motives in committing crimes, or God's in allowing them to happen, but it was potentially far more embarrassing for that segment of society it singled out. Given all the seeking after the main chance that marked the Whig ascendency, this group would have included far more than just the trading classes or any mere "bourgeoisie." Murderers at least were a scandal on the whole human race.

In dealing with all these matters criminal biography left much to be desired. Mishandling mysteries and muddling issues, not giving them the sustained and deliberate consideration they clearly warranted, it substituted simple, easily held ideas and feelings, or no particular ideas and feelings, for the difficult and complex affect that properly ought to have obtained. Defoe's novels seek to be more adequate to the phenomena they describe. None of his narrators, to be sure, tries as assiduously as murderers like Dramatti or Strodtman to explain how he (or she) came to do what he (or she) did, and while they have more to say about providence, even here their overt declarations fall far short of those uttered by the typically repentant criminal. Yet, on both these great matters, more is to be inferred from the situations of Defoe's criminal protagonists than criminal biography could ever have preached, even at its most strenuous and serious. Roxana in particular, though she does it unawares, displays to us an etiology of crime that is far more sophisticated and persuasive than anything to be found in actual criminal biography, and all Defoe's narrators, nearly as unwittingly, argue for the operations of providence with powerful effect, enhancing rather than diminishing its mystery.

Defoe's novels are less successful in coping with the vexing similitude of thieves to more legitimate economic individualists, but even here they outclass criminal biography at its own game, providing a sometimes exhilarating means of handling the problem for the moment at least

[2] Defoe, *Jure Divino* (1706), bk. 3, p. 2n.; Henry Fielding, from the title of *Examples of the Interposition of Providence in the Detection and Punishment of Murder* (1752).

(albeit in a peculiarly "literary" way). Defoe's response to the embarrassing equation of trade with theft, along with his version of the etiology of
crime – or rather what he supplies toward the imagining of such an
etiology – will concern us in the next three chapters. Here, although I
begin by considering his depiction of providence, my main concern is the
way his texts manage to sustain a variety of more or less appropriate and
sometimes contradictory interpretations, including some neither he nor his
original audience could ever have imagined.

Providence is the armature around which the most serious criminal
biography is wound. Giving shape and order to disparate and awful
events, making the seemingly random and accidental appear organized
and coherent, it powerfully supports the notion that even the worst and
most egregious human behavior is orderly and comprehensible because –
at some level – God wills it to conform to conventional moral values. The
"interposition of providence in the detection and punishment of murder"
particularly helped prop up society. All sorts of "admirable discoveries"
showed murderers reined in by God's presiding power. In the seventeenth
century ghosts not uncommonly appear to accuse their killers, or corpses
bleed afresh in their presence. By the turn of the century, with the advent
of a more "sceptical Age," such manifest miracles are much less frequently
reported. God's Hand is now laid almost exclusively on the murderer
himself, and, though it works less directly, it is no less obvious. No longer
an outward sign, "some visible mark in the face," the mark of Cain is held
to be an agitation within. "Some think it was Horror of Mind," says a
preacher at Lincoln's Inn, "others ... a continual creeping of his Flesh."
The operation of providence in cases of murder becomes, in effect, an
increasingly psychological phenomenon, the "exceeding shame and confusion" that murderers feel closely resembling or indeed being identical
with the involuntary operation of conscience itself, that "natural magistrate in the heart." Just as "the First Instance of Murther in the World was
followed closely by Perplexity, Oppression of Spirit, and the intolerable
Gnawings of Despair itself," so, too, with later cases. God could so
"infatuate the policy of the Murtherer" that he stood accused by his own
behavior and "so terrifie his Conscience with the horror and hainousness
of the Fact" that he might even be "his own Executioner." "The
murderer's Soul is filled with hellish Horror of Heart" – to quote a second,
widely disparate source – for "the Almighty has planted such a Witness
within [him] as will give [him] no Rest Night nor Day."[3]

[3] William Smythies, *A True Account of the Robbery and Murder of John Stockden* (1698), sing. sheet;
Zachary Babington, *Advice to Grand Jurors in Cases of Blood* (1680), p. 20; William Lupton, *A
Discourse of Murther, Preach'd ... at Lincoln's-Inn* (1725), pp. 8–9; Babington, p. 20; Lupton, p. 15;
Heavens Cry against Murder. Or, a True Relation of the ... Murder of John Knight ... by One Nath:

Condemned murderers testify to this phenomenon, as indeed do lesser criminals to the less dramatic operation of providence in their own cases. Whether their crimes are great or small, the subjects of serious criminal biography know unmistakeably just what providence has done for and to them, and – most important – they tell their audience this in the most explicit terms or, at least, allow them easily to infer it. "When he was escap'd to Mr. *Key*'s at *Shadwell Dock*," confessed Matthias Brinsden a wife murderer in 1722, "he felt that Uneasiness in his Mind, that he wish'd he might be taken up; and tho' he was then in Bed, the Apprehensions of his Mind, would not let him sleep, but he fancy'd he heard the *Constables* approaching to Seize him every Moment, even while he was safe on his Pillow." A burglar who "thank'd God he never committed Murder" spoke also for the clear operation of providence, as did, too, in their way, all those petty criminals who praised the Lord they'd been caught and were now to be hanged.[4] Even at their most penitent, Defoe's criminals never speak quite so unequivocally. God's ways are not so simple for them, or for the readers of their stories. Knowing far less of providence than they let on, they nonetheless suggest more than they could ever know.

The increasing "psychologization" of providence spoke as much in favor of human nature as of God's overruling power. So long as it operated "outside" human agency and comprehension, providence stood as a sign of human insufficiency, ultimately controlling individual action because individuals were in no position to control themselves. As God's voice speaking in our minds, however, it could carry a much more reassuring message. However obscurely, however distanced from one's immediate consciousness, it could nonetheless seem an "in built" part of one's own being. *Robinson Crusoe* certainly appears to embrace this tendency, with all its references to "secret Hints" and "strange Impression[s] upon the Mind, from we know not what Springs, and by we know not what Power" (175). Consistently seeing such "Hints" and "Impressions" as "secret Intimations of Providence" (176) – once he's on his island, at least – Crusoe argues in effect for the intermeshing of the human psyche with a transcendent, ordering power, "invisible" but "friendly" and aiming at "our Good" (250). The criminal novels take quite a different direction. Though all Defoe's criminals show an eventual awareness of "an Invisible Hand in Mercy to me," as Jack calls it (169) – or as Moll says, "the Hand of Providence, which had done such wonders for me" (336–7) – none, not even Jack (whom I take to be the clearest-minded and least immoral)

Butler (1657), p. 9; Increase Mather, *A Sermon Occasioned by the Execution of a Man Found Guilty of Murder: Preached at Boston* (1691), p. 10; *The Authentick Tryals of John Swan, and Elizabeth Jeffryes, for the Murder of Mr. Joseph Jeffryes .... With the Tryal of Miss Mary Blandy, for the Murder of Her Own Father* (1752), pp. i–ii; *Jure Divino*, bk. 3, p. 2n.
[4] Thomas Purney, *The Ordinary of Newgate's Account of the Behaviour, Confession, and Last Dying Speech of Matthias Brinsden* (1722); Paul Lorrain, Ordinary Account, 21 June 1704.

seems quite to recognize all that he or she owes to God's mercy and judgment, or His mere withholding of condign punishment. Even at their most enlightened, they illustrate the sadder, more perplexing implications of Crusoe's dictum that "nothing is more frequent than for us to mistake Providence, even in its most visible appearances" (*SRC*, 188). Their distance from God, their incomprehension of His ways, I'll be arguing here and later, make their narratives ripe occasions for analyzing and theorizing not only the operations of providence but human nature as well.

Roxana mentions providence more often than any of the others, which perhaps is appropriate, she being both the most guilt-ridden and the most likely to be damned. On seven separate occasions she speaks of the "Judgment of Heaven" and the "Justice of Heaven," as well as of "the Blast of Heaven" and mere "Providence" itself (see 253, 259, 260 [twice], 265, 297, 330). All these passages occur in the last quarter of her narrative. Up to this point "providence" has been mentioned by name only once, and that by the Dutch merchant, who credits it with freeing him to marry Roxana by arranging the death of his wife (141). The text plants numerous clues, however, whereby even the least attentive reader will see that something more than mere fate or accident is at work in Roxana's life. When the Dutch merchant saves her from the extortionate demands of the Paris Jew, Roxana is made to say that all she saw in the event was "the generous Friendship of my Deliverer ... by whom, as far as relates to second Causes, I was preserv'd from Destruction." This is all she has seen, she realizes looking back, because she had no "Religion, or any Sence of a Supreme Power managing, directing, and governing in both Causes and Events in this World." She should have been "very thankful to [this] Power ... but I had none of these things about me" (121).

Elsewhere Roxana's ignorance is not so highly marked, but it hardly needs to be. Within a page of being rescued from the Jew, she wishes for a storm to blow her ship toward England and gets more than she bargained for. Though in her fear she promises to repent, a resolve that quickly wears off, she never sees what almost all her contemporaries would have seen in such a storm, a judgment and the prospect of a deliverance.[5] When a series of "accidents" reunite her with the Dutchman and her long-lost daughter, Roxana never suspects that these may be more than mere coincidences, or that the way they combine is itself significant. She never has more than a partial inkling of the role providence plays in wrecking her hopes, and even this comes toward the end of her story. "What a glorious Testimony it is to the Justice of Providence," she says, "and to the Concern Providence has in guiding all the Affairs of Men, (even the least, as well as the

[5] See J. Paul Hunter, *The Reluctant Pilgrim: Defoe's Emblematic Method and Quest for Form in "Robinson Crusoe"* (Baltimore, 1966), pp. 29, 151–2.

greatest) that the most secret Crimes are, by the most unforeseen Accidents, brought to light, and discover'd" (297). But afterwards she fails to
realize that her daughter's good luck in tracing her to Tunbridge Wells
might itself be providential, especially given the Quaker's clever efforts at
misdirection. Nor is Roxana ever struck by the extraordinary coincidence
that, of all the cookmaids in London, hers just happened to be her
abandoned and soon-to-be embarrassing daughter.[6]

Captain Singleton is the least carefully contrived of all Defoe's novels, but
even it shows in relatively subtle ways the deficiency of its protagonist's
religious awareness. In giving Robert Knox's account of his captivity on
Ceylon, Singleton suggests it might be "profitable" to compare his story
"with my own, to shew, whoever reads this, what it was I avoided" (238).
Singleton says more than he knows, for Knox in his "extremity" (a word I
borrow from Singleton, who often uses it in describing his journey across
Africa) consistently relies on God "to comfort him . . . who is the Father of
the fatherless" (241). Knox mentions "God" eleven times in the approximately eleven pages it takes to print his account, and "providence" once.
This conventional piety contrasts sharply with the practice of the equally
(indeed literally) fatherless and supposedly penitent Singleton, whose
religious awareness comes to him late and via the dubious agency of the
equivocating Quaker William. "God" appears only ten times in the 266
pages of Singleton's own narrative, including four times on one page, and
"providence" only three times, twice in close succession.[7]

Captain Singleton does not do as much as the other novels to suggest God's
intervening hand; whatever He was to Knox, He certainly isn't Singleton's copilot. Two incidents, however, deserve mention, one for what it
indicates, the other for what it omits. Thus, to speak to the latter first,
though the English castaway they meet toward the end of their trek across
Africa sees Singleton and his party as heaven-sent, they do not return the
compliment, even when he leads them to a fortune in gold (122ff.). Then,
too, there is the sudden "Flash, or rather Blast of Lightning" over their
heads as they cruise the Pacific. This "was so terrible, and quiver'd so long
among us," says Singleton, that they all "thought the Ship was on Fire":
"It is not possible for me to describe, or any one to conceive of the Terrour
of that Minute." For the first time in his life Singleton reflects with

---

[6] To get the full sense of potentially providential interventions in *Roxana*, see pp. 121, 122–9, 196,
202, 206, 216, 217–18, 230, 235–7, 261, 266, 274–5, 282.

[7] Cf. *CS*, pp. 238–49, to pp. 45, 195, 266, 268, 270, 271; 9, 266, 267. For Knox's account of his
captivity and escape see Robert Knox, *An Historical Relation of the Island Ceylon . . . Together, with
an Account of the Detaining in Captivity the Author and Divers Other Englishmen Now Living There, and of
the Author's Miraculous Escape* (1681), pt. 4, pp. 117–89. Knox is pious, frequently mentioning
God, but not so frequently as he does in Defoe's version of his account; apparently, Defoe means
to heighten still further the differences between these two Bobs.

"Horrour" on his "former Life," believing that "God had taken me into his immediate Disposing, and had resolved to be the Executer of his own Vengeance." All this may stand without comment, but Singleton's aside to the reader before he goes on with his story ought also to be noted. "Perhaps many that read this," he suspects, "will be sensible of the Thunder and Lightning, [but] think nothing of the rest, or rather may make a Jest of it all, so I say not more of it at this time, but proceed to the Story of the Voyage" (194–5). Crude though this device may be, it brings the reader to a heightened awareness of God's presence in the world, and, once raised, such an awareness is bound to supersede Singleton's.

Jack is an altogether better person than Roxana or Singleton, and generally more self-aware and morally developed than Moll. By the middle of his story he realizes that he ought to thank God for his miraculous deliverances, but these "young Infant Thoughts, about the Works of Providence in the World" take a long time to develop into a fuller knowledge of "how an invisible over-ruling Power ... orders the Events of every Thing relating to us" (169, 308). Even as a thief and a slave he feels, to his credit, a "secret Influence," a "good Fate," "some strange directing Power" in his life (60, 70, 119). When he loses his "ill gotten Goods" just off the Virginia coast but prospers anyway with the help of his ex-master, he finds "a kind of Pleasure, in the Dissaster," seeing it as something "sent from Heaven" so that he might have a proper "Foundation" for his "prosperity" (157). When, returned to Virginia, he is reunited with his now "vastly improv'd" first wife, he quickly recognizes in this "odd Accident," too, the work of providence (260, 259).

Still, Jack is not so percipient as a careful reader might be. Thus, though he sees that his being made a slave by "some strange directing Power" is "a Punishment for the Wickedness of my younger Years," he notes neither the specific presence of God behind the event, nor its peculiar appropriateness (119). His being seized and sold into bondage for a term of years is just what would have happened had he been caught and tried as a thief, assuming of course he were lucky. The point is made abundantly clear as Jack describes the case of another young slave, "born a Thief, and bred up a Pick-pocket like my self." Jack is struck by a speech his new master makes to the "young Fellow .... for I thought all my Master said was spoken to me." He hears, among other things, that "God not only spar'd him" – i.e., the pickpocket, his semblable – "from the Gallows, but now had mercifully deliver'd him from the Opportunity of committing the same Sin again, and put it into his Power to live an honest Life" (121). Jack does not see that God has actually done as much, and more, for him. Though temporarily plunged into the "miserable condition of a Slave," he has been saved from hanging in a way that testifies still more powerfully to the justice and moral order of the universe (119). Jack, however, doesn't quite notice.[8] Even after thanking providence for having restored his first and now "better" wife, Jack makes the mistake of underestimating it. Thinking "my Fortunes were settled for this World," he cannot in the least imagine "how any thing disastrous could happen to us ... unless something should befall us out of the ordinary way of Providence." But this is just what happens, as his "short sighted Measures" are exploded by an "unseen Mine." To avoid being denounced as a Jacobite, Jack must go "wandring into the World again" (263–4).

Moll's insufficient awareness of what she owes God is the most interesting of all. She blesses providence twice in all her narrative, once for her reprieve and once for the bounty bestowed by her loving son in Virginia (291, 336–7). In the latter instance she leaves "the Reader to improve my Thoughts, as no doubt they [sic] will see Cause." This is a curious invitation, for what more might the reader say? Elsewhere Moll is not so circumspect, for, far from commenting on the role providence has played in her life, she seems entirely to miss its pattern. Meeting Jemy in prison, for instance, she gives him a somewhat fictive version of how she got there, and blames it all on "my ill Fortune" (298). This last phrase indicates no small tergiversation, following as it does so closely on Moll's first mention of providence and her claims to have undergone a spiritual change. Nor does Moll thank providence for getting her safely with all her goods across the Chesapeake Bay, or for the kind reception she meets with on the other side. This omission seems all the more striking, given her fears about that voyage (she doesn't worry, for some reason, about crossing the Atlantic), and her effusive praise of providence a few pages later (cf. 330, 336–7).

In certain respects Moll's experience parallels Jack's, but she doesn't see as much in it as he will. Her ship, too, founders just outside the harbor, carrying all her worldly goods. She, too, has her favorite spouse restored to her, and in circumstances that assure a better marriage this time around. Jemy, in fact, reappears with surprising suddenness (I'm paraphrasing Moll) on three separate occasions. Two of these are amazingly coincidental, thus her spying him outside the window just after she's married her honest citizen and at just the right moment to save his life, and thus also their being both confined in the same prison at the same time and both for a first offence (the last is important in that it contributes to their remissions of punishment). Moll remarks on these coincidences, but not so much as she should; surely she should realize, at least in retrospect, that all her future happiness depended on these two "chance" encounters. Not even the first of Jemy's reappearances, which is frankly the most mysterious, as

---

[8] Something else Jack fails to notice, and which we may, too, is that the Kentish Town widow and his master both have the same surname, "Smith" (84, 118). Jack's heart nearly broke to think "how this poor Creature work'd, and was a Slave" (85), and then, as if to pay for robbing her, he becomes a slave himself.

it is occasioned by his hearing her call him at a distance of twelve or fifteen miles (154), is enough to suggest to Moll that perhaps some supernatural force is at work in her life and aiming at her good. Finally, like Jack, Moll undergoes a mysteriously appropriate punishment when her third husband, a man with whom she otherwise could have been quite happy, turns out to be her brother. This can seem merely a curious quirk of fate until one realizes that the marriage has recapitulated, though to a closer, more painful degree, the crime she knowingly committed when she married Robin. The incest she notionally commits, still yearning after the elder brother – "I committed Adultery and Incest with him every Day in my Desires" (59) – and the notional incest she has actually committed, for by marriage her husband's brother becomes her brother, redounds against her in a way she could never have foreseen; and which in fact she never does see.[9] Moll is the luckiest and the blindest of all Defoe's criminal protagonists, which raises a powerful question.

Why has God been so good to her? Most modern commentators avoid this question altogether, perhaps because in proper post-Victorian fashion they see no God in the novel but Defoe, and he turns out benign. Defoe "sets out to be a moralist," says Peter Earle, "but the moral he makes is often a very doubtful one .... It is almost as if he got carried away by the exciting adventures of the characters he created and felt reluctant to give them their due .... despite his love of realism, [he] was reluctant to doom his creations." This is a slightly more diffident version of the argument that Defoe liked his characters "too much" to punish them, presumably because – in the most extreme version of this argument – they functioned as his surrogates in a fantasy life governed by anti-social, capital-accumulating, self-assertive bourgeois individualism.[10] As Earle's "as if" indicates, he is trying to explain Defoe's fictions by a further fiction. But the notion that Defoe couldn't bear to hurt his alter egos is unconvincing even in its own terms, for one may both identify with and punish the misdeeds of others (especially others, especially fictitious others). I myself

9 Providence can even show a sense of humor, for as Maximillian Novak points out, "it is suggestive of divine Providence" that during Moll's second attempt to steal at a fire (a rather dirty deed; see chapter 5, n. 13), "she is struck and almost killed by a mattress which is thrown from a window" (*Defoe and the Nature of Man* [London, 1963], p. 79). Ian Bell too readily discounts this and other examples on the grounds that Moll herself sees no such implications until she is arrested (*Defoe's Fiction* [London, 1985], p. 142), and that making Moll "into an ironically myopic figure ... would be wholly outside the realm of popular fiction" (p. 134). Leopold Damrosch, Jr., also sees an absence of "providential plan" in Defoe's fiction after *Robinson Crusoe*, offering this as a reason for its being "exceptionally episodic" (*God's Plot & Man's Stories: Studies in the Fictional Imagination from Milton to Fielding* [Chicago, 1985], p. 211).
10 Peter Earle, *The World of Defoe* (New York, 1977), p. 232, and more generally, pp. 230–2. The notion that Defoe's characters are mere extensions of the nastier – i.e., greedy, guiltless, and bourgeois – aspects of his own character gets its most recent and relentless incarnation in Bram Djikstra's peculiarly single-minded *Defoe and Economics: The Fortunes of "Roxana" in the History of Interpretation* (Houndmills, Basingstoke, Hampshire, 1987).

suspect Defoe was showing God's goodness mysterious beyond human comprehension. Even a sinner who does not, to other sinners, seem sufficiently repentant could enjoy His grace; this is what was meant when it was said to be "free." "God's ways are unsearchable," says one of Defoe's spokesmen in *The Family Instructor*, "sometimes our falls are made the first steps to our recovery; and the very particular sins that we commit, are the introduction to our deliverance from the domain of sin in general" (15: 296). This could certainly apply to Moll's case.

It almost looks as though providence were trying to get through to her via a series of disasters and lucky occurrences, not only to punish and warn but to give fresh starts and second chances. The foundering of the ship outside Bristol (if only she would know it) wipes the slate clean; as with Jack, the loss of her ill-gotten gains severs her connection with the sordid past. Her relation with the Bath gentleman, which recapitulates all her previous liaisons, provides her with an opportunity to prove herself. Like the Elder Brother, he gives her a handful of gold but, unlike him, exacts no sexual favors in return. He is a solid, decent man, as Robin was, who really cares for her. He has the real qualities of a gentleman, which her second husband, the linen-draper, only seemed to have. And finally, in a reversal of the situation with her brother, he is content to live with her as though she were his sister (he tells an innkeeper that they "are too near a kin to lye together" [115]). Her situation with him is ideal, he being all Moll has ever wanted in a man, and – given their respective marital situations – all she should want. But then, inviting him into bed, she ruins their relationship entirely on her own initiative. With the Elder Brother the blame was preeminently his, but here it is primarily hers. Moll puts herself back in the providential debit column, so to speak, being worse off now (first morally, then materially) than she has ever been before. Later, when she marries the honest citizen because she cannot have Jemy, she repeats, with greater culpability, the crime she committed against Robin. And here, too, the marriage is based on the violation of a natural, familial tie. Though not so glaring an act as incest, her willful surrendering of Jemy's son can seem far worse than anything she has done so far. The first incest was more notional than real, and the second was committed unawares. But this abandoning of her love child – it is this by virtue of her "honest Affection" for it, as well as her attachment to Jemy – is an act consciously committed against her heart's "Inclination." The unnaturalness of the act, and Moll makes it clear that mothers ought naturally to love and care for their children, causes a resurgence of her old melancholic "Disorder" – the same disturbance of mind she felt when she was forced to marry Robin against her will, and, later, when she was constrained to stay married to her brother (173–7).

Thus Moll falls ever deeper into sin's dark hole. Her marriage to the honest citizen – again all she should ever want in life, and now she knows it – is doomed from the start. He dies after five years and two children just as Robin did, falling into bankruptcy just as the linen-draper did, and succumbing to an immobilizing despair just as her brother did. Moll fails to see the comparisons, or even, quite, that she has completed a cycle. Of course she is worse off than when Robin died. There is less money, she is older, and there are no convenient grandparents in Colchester on whom to dump the children. The abandoning of Jemy's child leads to the abandoning of two more, under direr circumstances. These go to their "nurses" with no promise of future money to ensure their good treatment or even their being kept alive.[11] Still Moll does not see the light, any more than she did when her "ill Fate," as she mistakenly calls it, brought her to her brother's marriage bed (90; this by the way is the first mention of fate in the book). So Moll goes on to become a thief, "hardening" all the while and falling deeper still, until, in Newgate, the equivalent of hell on earth, she seems finally saved by the grace of God and the help of yet another good man (there are so many in Moll's life!).

This may be mysterious, but it is theologically sound and (*pace* Earle et al.) morally effective. Unlike the general run of criminal biographies, Defoe's novels do not whittle God's work down so men might carry it comfortably in their minds – either as an idea simply understood or as something equivalent to their own consciences. There is simply no reason *we* can understand for Moll's good fortune, and this becomes morally effective in two opposite but compatible ways. First, where criminal biography tends to encourage a certain moral complacency, almost a smugness, by making the distribution of divine mercy and justice seem so cut and dried, so easily understood, Defoe does no such thing. Grace may be had on certain terms, criminal biography as much as says, and though these are hard – "Think not a few Tears, Sighs, and Lord have Mercy on me, to be Repentance," says one Newgate ordinary, "This is nor so cheap and easy a performance" – they are efficacious. Or perhaps they are not so

---

11 The ugliness of Moll's treatment of her children – and Roxana's treatment of hers – cannot be overemphasized. Says a man of his sister who has abandoned her children, "[she] is a brute ... a devil incarnate .... she values her children no more than if they were a couple of calves from one of her milch cows; she is without natural affection, don't you see it?" (*FI*, 16: 91–2). In this case, it should be pointed out, the mother leaves her children in the care of her husband and a nurse. Defoe had harsher words for women like Moll, saying "those who cannot be so hard-hearted to murder their own offspring themselves, take a slower, tho' as sure a way, and get it done by others, by dropping their Children, and leaving them to be starved by Parish-Nurses" (*Augusta Triumphans* [1728], p. 10). For horror stories about such nurses not cited in Starr's edition of *Moll Flanders* (pp. 383–4, n. 4 to p. 173, and n. to p. 175), see Narcissus Luttrell, *A Brief Historical Relation of State Affairs from September 1678 to April 1714* (Oxford, 1857), 3: 205, 206 (14 and 17 October 1693); Read's *Weekly Journal*, 16 September 1721; and Applebee's *Original Weekly Journal*, 5 March 1726. Even the best sort of foster care, Defoe took pains to point out, could not match the "affections and tenderness of a mother"; that would be "a kind of natural impossibility" (*FI*, 16: 178–9).

hard: "God has made the *Terms* of *Salvation* such," says another Newgate ordinary, "as all Men might receive them and comply with them."[12] Allowing his readers no such facile inferences – there is no easy, necessary, or complete fit between the human psyche and the transcendent moral order – Defoe restores the relationship between men and God to a proper disequilibrium. Moll gets off scot-free and unscathed while others are caught and hanged. Virginia for her is just one happy discovery after another, thus the helpfulness of everyone she deals with, the generous love of her son, the growing gratitude of her husband each time she reveals she's been holding out on him. Her prosperity waxes even to the point that one of the indentured women servants sent over by her governess "come[s] double, having been got with Child by one of the Seamen in the Ship" (340). Moll lives to a ripe old age, preserving her good looks and spunk while others about her sicken and die, most notably the decent Robin, the honest citizen, and ultimately her addled and invalided brother, each of whom has fewer sins than she to account for.

At the same time Defoe weighs in against human arrogance, however, he encourages hope where, we should think, one ought most to despair. Thus when Moll's sole surviving child (so far as we and she know) proves to be so good a child, she feels overwhelmed by God's love. "Really my Heart began to look up more seriously," she says, "than I think it ever did before, and to look with great Thankfulness to the Hand of Providence, which had done such wonders for me, who had been myself the greatest wonder of Wickedness, perhaps that had been suffered to live in the World." "Even on all other Occasions of Thankfulness," she adds, "my past wicked and abominable Life never look'd so Monstrous to me ... as when I had a Sense upon me of Providence doing good to me, while I had been making those vile Returns on my part" (336–7). That God does not parcel out his rewards quid pro quo may be disheartening to Pharisees, but it is great and encouraging news to sinners for whom despair is no less dangerous than pride. Moll's great good fortune might be likened, perhaps, to Mae West's diamond ring: goodness, as we and Cary Grant discover, had nothing to do with it.

But I was careful earlier to say that it only seems God has been good to Moll; it is possible to see the novel in a very different light. Though the fortuitous events of Moll's life clearly show God's presence – "there should be a Motto over all the Amazing Occurrences of the World," says Defoe, "GOD REIGNS" – He may nonetheless have held Himself back from her heart.[13] There is more said about God's "unsearchable ways" in *The Family Instructor* than has so far been quoted. Having pointed out that salvation may come even by means of "particular sins," Defoe's spokesman

---

[12] Samuel Smith, Ordinary Account, 22 December 1690; Lorrain, ibid., 22 March 1704.
[13] The *Review*, 8: 746 (31 May 1712).

goes on to add that "therefore we cannot conclude ourselves reprobate, or anybody else, till we see them past the reach of sovereign grace" (15: 296). In other words, the books are open on us until we die; only then can we be sure of our own salvation or venture a guess about someone else's. As Moll is not yet dead, we should not even surmise she is home free. Her repentance may not have been efficacious. Or, as Defoe obscurely indicates, she may not be so great a penitent "as she afterwards pretends to be" – that word "pretends" being most problematic, as it ranges in meaning from "aspires" to "feigns." All such uncertainties are cleared up in contemporary revisions of the novel, each of which makes Moll unquestionably penitent and shows her living both happily and well ever after. Defoe's text does not necessarily lead its readers to any such conclusion. The ambiguity surrounding Moll's repentance can in fact seem quite ominous; she may only think she has made her peace with God. Repentance, says Defoe, "is a sense of, and sincere sorrow for, sin in all its parts, as well original and actual; and this sorrow must be always attended with a sincere desire of pardon and sanctification, and earnest endeavours after reformation and amendment" (*FI*, 15: 23).

Moll does not seem as earnest or sincere as she might be, especially when measured against the general standards her culture prescribed for people in her situation. No one ever "seemed to have a truer sense or a more quick feeling of his crimes, than this unhappy man," the author of *Remarkable Criminals* reports approvingly of one condemned felon, "his heart was so far from being hardened ... that he ... afflicted himself continuously and without ceasing." As a counter example it offers the case of a "young fellow" who "was so unaccountably stupid and wicked that though he made a large and particular confession of his guilt, yet it was done in such a manner as plainly showed his crimes made no just impression upon his heart."[14] For a repentance to be effective, as Defoe himself emphatically makes clear, "God requires the heart" (*FI*, 15: 23). The condition of Moll's heart is dubious in the extreme. When she gets her "full Swing of Liberty," her resolutions to reform seem to vanish "like most others made by such People when in Danger and Confinement." The phrasing here describes a thief who, though he had "determined to lead a new Life" after being tried and acquitted for one robbery (which he had in fact committed), was later hanged for another. Once Moll's death sentence has been commuted, it can seem that all the while she has "rather [been] concerned at the Punishment then Penitent for the Crime." Though she has shown herself "very attentive to ... Exhortations, and seemingly devout at Prayer," there is still "something" about her behavior "which [gives] great

<hr />

14 *Lives of the Most Remarkable Criminals Who Have Been Condemned and Executed for Murder, the Highway, Housebreaking, Street Robberies, Coining or Other Offences*, 1st pub. 1735, ed. Arthur L. Hayward (New York, 1927), pp. 281–2; ibid., p. 147, and see also p. 224, as well as *Select Trials for Murder, Robbery, Burglary, Rapes, Sodomy, Coining, Forgery, Pyracy, and Other Offences and Misdemeanours* (1764), 2: 198.

reason to think, that [she has] more lean'd on the Hope of Life here, than made due and timely preparation ... for Eternity." Chief among such indications is that she shows no desire "to make due Reparation." The Newgate ordinary describes one thief who, "with Tears in his Eyes, and I hope true Sorrow in his Heart," said that "he repented, and wish'd he could make full Satisfaction to the Persons he had wrong'd, but he had not wherewithal." Moll is luckier than this thief but only in the most limited sense. Bound for a new life in America with as much of her ill-gotten goods as she can bring along, she has still to "fit [her]self for Eternity."[15]

Defoe's own opinion in these matters was utterly conventional. Repentance "is not likely to be sincere," says Robinson Crusoe, unless there is "restitution as far as the possible power of the party extends" (*SRC*, 47). Jack provides an instructive contrast to Moll, feeling after visiting the Hampstead widow that "I ought to make Restitution to all that I had wrong'd." As he cannot figure out how to do this, "the Thought in time wore off," but at least he has "the thought" (87). No such idea ever intrudes itself into Moll's mind, either in Newgate as she prepares to die or, later, as she prepares to start life over in the New World. "But my case was particular," she says, "it was by no Means proper for me to go thither without Money or Goods," that is, like any ordinary convict (309). Even readers not wanting to begrudge Moll her carefully and dangerously accumulated "Stock" would have found it far easier to wish her godspeed had she made at least some token effort to undo the damage she has done. But Moll doesn't, and her case makes an interesting contrast, too, to that of "some felons" transported a little more than a year before the novel was published. Before embarking, they handed over "vast Numbers of Pocket-Books," which, though of no intrinsic value, contained "very useful Notes and Papers to the Owners." This gesture, they were reported to have said, was "the only Satisfaction they were capable of making their injured Country."[16]

---

[15] Guthrie, Ordinary Account, 7 April 1742; *An Exact and True Relation of the Behaviour of Edmund Kirk, John Bennet, Morgan Reading, and Andrew Hill during Their Imprisonment, and at the Place of Execution* (1684), p. 1: Lorrain, Ordinary Accounts, 24 June 1709, 22 March 1704, 18 May 1709, 24 June 1709. Another significant contrast to Moll is provided by the two narrators of *Street-Robberies, Consider'd*, both of whom want to make restitution at least to the extent of doing some good for their country; see pp. 48, 63.

[16] Applebee's *Original Weekly Journal*, 29 October 1720. According to the period's standard commentary on the Ten Commandments, restitution must be made, if not to the injured party, then to his heirs. If neither are to be found, then restitution ought to be made to the Church. And if restitution is beyond one's power, one must solemnly promise God to accomplish it as soon as possible, being humbly penitent all the while (John Dod and Robert Cleaver, *A Plain and Familiar Exposition of the Ten Commandments* [1635], pp. 298–300). Moll does not meet this test, nor does she seem sincerely penitent at her trial, where, "with Tears, yet not so many Tears as to obstruct my Speech," she pleads for mercy because "at worst" she's a first offender (286). My point is not that she ought to receive sentence of death supinely grateful – that would be abnormal even within the terms of criminal biography – but that her behavior in court is a bad prognosis for future spiritual recovery. She shows none of the "stupid infatu-ation" appropriate to the occasion, and which a properly repentant and subsequently hanged

If Moll is not truly repentant, her situation at the end of the novel might seem unimaginably horrible. "Many persons that have been in the condition you are now in," wrote the author of an "address" to prisoners, "have made most solemn vows and promises of amendment .... but when they have obtained a Reprieve, or Pardon, and been suffered to live longer, it has appeared their purposes were not sincere, or they have proved ineffectual; and the reason is, the heart was never changed or renewed."[17] God not only "requires the heart," Defoe took pains to emphasize, He "regards no prayers but what the heart joins in" (*FI*, 15: 13, 207). If Moll's heart is not in her mouth, it should be, one way or another. All her success as a thief, and, too, her final retirement with Jemy in "the greatest Kindness and Comfort imaginable," all "little Difficulties ... made easy" (342), may actually be no more than a sign of God's "severest anger." When He lets sinners "go on and does not punish them till last," Defoe chillingly suggests, "'tis a signal that he has no thought of mercy in store for them" (*FI*, 15: 11–12). But if Moll's heart remains as yet unchanged, it may still change. Thus her narrative ends with a declaration that she and Jemy intend "to spend the Remainder of our Years in sincere Penitence, for the wicked Lives we have lived" (345). These are the last words of the book, but – as Defoe in a variety of ways takes pains to indicate – the last word on Moll has yet to be written.

Whether she has been "saved" or punished is highly disputable, then, but neither should these seem mutually exclusive alternatives. It may be both have happened, and at greater cost than Moll can know. If virtue is its own reward, Defoe argues in *Conjugal Lewdness*, so too is vice. "Who enjoys an uninterrupted Health," he asks, "but the Temperate, the Moderate, and the Virtuous? Their Vitals are not exhausted; Nature is not oppress'd; the Vigour of the Spirits expended, and the marrow of their

highwayman describes when he says, "I made a most pitiful and shuffling defence; as indeed who could do otherwise under the vast load of guilt, I had to sustain .... I saw destruction before me, yet determined to make use of no means to shun it" (Charles Speckman, *The Life, Travels, Exploits, Frauds and Robberies of Charles Speckman ... Executed at Tyburn* [1763], p. 41). Moll seems insufficiently cast down during her trial; it is only afterwards, with "nothing before me but present Death," that she claims to feel "real signs of Repentance." But even then, her governess by comparison is far less equivocal. Though she experiences Moll's danger only at second-hand, it is enough to make her "a true penitent." Moll's minister shares this view, validating it, "and which is still more," says Moll, the governess was penitent "not only ... for the Occasion, and at that Juncture, but she continu'd so, as I was inform'd to the Day of her Death" (286–7). The various contemporary revisions of the novel attempt to repair Moll's moral deficiency, it seems to me, by giving her a charitable old age before she finally dies unambiguously repentant. This may have been a way, too, of retrospectively justifying the happiness of her experience in America, which stands sharply at odds with what was known of other criminals sent there. "They write from Maryland," reports Read's *Weekly Journal*, "that the Malefactors transported thither are kept in great Awe, and to constant Labour from six in the Morning to six in the Evening, being allow'd Beds to lie on, and sufficient Meat and Drink" (23 July 1720).

[17] *A Compassionate Address to Prisoners for Crimes; and More Particularly to Such of Them as Are under Sentence of Death* (1742), pp. 68–9.

Bones wasted: Their Youth has not robbed their old Age."[18] But Moll's youth has robbed her age, for all the remarkable resistance she shows to physical withering. Her vigor and her occasional capacity to feel affection are no small part of her attractiveness, offsetting her material greed. As the years go on, however, and her fortune waxes more than it wanes, these things undergo an irreversible decline. Her vigor is misdirected, and she never loves anyone again as she loved the Elder Brother. It was he who first gave her occasion to confuse love and money, and who taught her money was more important; she never forgets that lesson, and never escapes that confusion. This can seem a just and terrible punishment. Jemy is the second great love of her life, but her steady bestowal of gifts on him seems the only way she can express her love. Again and again she holds back on him, so that "he would often say, he wondred what he had done, that I would not Trust him" (325). When at one point he seems inconvenient, she even wishes that she had left him in England – where, very likely, he would have been hanged (335).

Nor is this the only indication that her happiness with Jemy is not all that it should be or could have been. Had they emigrated to Virginia after their first reunion, when she first suggested it, they would have been spared all the dangers and uncertainties of their latter years. Moll, for one, would never have become a thief, and they might have had a family. This last point might seem less important were Moll not so taken with her son, Humphry. Humphry is a piece of providence, to be sure, though it is hard to tell exactly how much Moll's pleasure in seeing him comes from true affection, and how much from the money and lands he gives her. Her effort to reciprocate is itself curiously ambiguous; she gives him a stolen watch. But Humphry stands also as a reminder of all those children she so casually discarded, including the son she had by Jemy, the one child she abandoned with any real reluctance. Moll's marital bliss at the end of the novel is literally barren; she has wasted her spectacular fecundity just as she wasted her beauty, trading on it until eventually it was gone and she had nothing much to show for it. Her last amorous encounter, undertaken after she has "past the Merry part of Life" and must employ "the baseness of Paint," serves to indicate both her failing beauty and her casual unawareness of what she has lost (226, 235–6). The man finds her attractive first because he is drunk, and later because she is convenient and clean. But he never offers her "a settled way of Maintenance, which was what I would have been best pleas'd with," and eventually he loses interest, "[leaving] it off altogether without any dislike, or bidding adieu." "So there was an End of that short Scene of Life," says Moll, never realizing that this last interlude is no isolated event but rather her Indian Summer (235–8). In her last significant encounter with a male before she

[18] *Conjugal Lewdness: or, Matrimonial Whoredom* (1727), p. 392.

is reunited with Jemy in Newgate, Moll sits in on a high stakes game at a gambling house. The gentleman sponsoring her offers nothing untoward; he only wants to change his luck (260–2).

All that is left of Moll's great energy at the end of the novel, it might well seem, is a certain irritable restlessness. She cannot stay secure in Virginia but must venture out again, back alone across the ocean. Though her lack of critical self-awareness conduces to a short-term happiness, it can also make her situation seem poignant, even sad. Moll verges on being one of "the Easy Ones," those "whose very Souls are indolent and asleep, who receive no Impressions of Grief or Joy, Pain or Pleasure, and whose Minds are, as it were perfectly passive." They "neither look before them or behind them, one Way or t'other . . . . to them 'tis all one to be happy or unhappy, bless'd or unbless'd, quiet or unquiet . . . they neither Taste the sour or the sweet; the Musick of the Viol, or the Scraping of a Kettle, is alike to them, and they distinguish not between Good and Evil."[19] I suspect Defoe meant Moll to speak a jolting but unconscious irony when, in summarizing her situation as she and Jemy start life over, she says that "our Affair was in very good posture," their plantation being "sufficient to us as long as we could either of us live." There is no need to think any farther, for "as for Children, I was past the prospect of any thing of that kind." This appears at the end of a paragraph, the next beginning, "But our good Fortune did not End here . . ." (332). What has it profited Moll to have gained, lost, and regained the New World?

Moll's experience, then, is clearly susceptible to a variety of interpretations. A punished Moll is a warning, a saved Moll an encouragement, and an exhausted Moll an admonition not to leave off repenting too long. Though these various interpretations conflict with each other, they are nonetheless coherent in that all gather around a single theme: the role of providence in human affairs, which cannot be known exactly. That this becomes a subject for serious deliberation is in itself sufficient; definite conclusions are hardly necessary and might well make the text less interesting, to say nothing of less morally useful. Is Moll, for instance, truly penitent? "A change wrought in the heart," Defoe wrote elsewhere, "will infallibly show itself in the conversation." Has Moll's conversation in fact changed? One's answer, and what one makes of it, might in fact be taken

---

19 *Conjugal Lewdness*, pp. 224–5. Moll's "easiness" should have other implications as well, at least for readers with hearts "less obstinate and insensible than an idiot" (for the use of the phrase in context, see *FI*, 16: 292). "Many, whom God has been pleased to prosper," says a letter in Mist's *Weekly Journal*, "attribute all to their own good Conduct, and prudent Management; they think grossly, and imagine, because they can, in some Measure account for this Affluence . . . that it is truly and properly their own acquiring . . . [they fail to] consider that . . . there's a main original Spring, which our short Views cannot discover"; they make "light Esteem . . . of Providence" (*A Collection of Miscellany Letters Selected out of Mist's Weekly Journal* [1722–7], 2: 14). A disregard for the role of Providence in human affairs, writes Crusoe, is "a kind of practical atheism, or at least a living in a kind of contempt of Heaven" (*SRC*, p. 199).

as an index to one's own religious state, for while "the symptoms of conversion are easily discovered by those who know the working of the Spirit of God, ... they are perfectly invisible to others" (*FI*, 15: 214). If there is a conversion, one might not have the spiritual wherewithal to see it; but, on the other hand, there may simply be nothing to see. Inferences about Moll's heart can only be made on the basis of collateral inferences about the state of one's own. Here, too, her narrative would have turned readers back on themselves, or, rather, on their sense of themselves.

Though efforts to pin the text down on so open and ambiguous a question are bound to fail, such efforts need not in themselves be fruitless. The point of the question becomes the questioning process itself, the intellectual and emotional exertion it produces and the effect of that exertion. Defoe himself may have indicated as much in praising reading as a healthy "diversion," as "play" and "exercise" for the mind. When we note Moll's references to providence and observe certain "strange concurrences" in her life, we are responding to a "program," as it were, for semi-directed imaginative "play." For all the reasons sketched out in this and the last chapter, the object of this "game" – and its chief challenge – is to understand Moll's experience in ways that transcend her own, quite limited point of view. This does not mean that somewhere beyond that point of view some larger, better, more "correct" way of looking at things is always or necessarily available. In Moll, it seems to me, Defoe at times presents problems without solution, problems, even, that might not yet have come quite to be defined as such.

Looking back at *Moll Flanders* from this side of modernity, many critics see it as a celebration of secularization without realizing that secularization can be felt as a negative process, a stripping away of old certainties and old guides to behavior. Though Moll's unawareness of providence as the manifest hand of God in the world may seem to some of us a sign of her liberation from old shibboleths, it marks, too, her loss of a traditional way of making sense of human experience and – in her case – the absence of anything to replace it. The world is filled with signs she might read, but she doesn't recognize them and indeed hardly even notes them; secularization for Moll involves loss of a double kind, for she lacks even an awareness of her loss. Looking beyond her account of what she's experienced, Defoe's original audience, I've suggested, could see there was still a transcendent, manifest, though not immediately or wholly intelligible order in the world. This in itself, however, would not have done much toward solving the practical, social problem she represents, which is what it means to have people like her – not all of them explicitly criminal – roaming the streets in search of what she calls "purchase" (e.g., 199, 257). Moll is ever the entrepreneur or at least the caricature of one.

Unable to see providence even as the inward haltings of the spirit in the face of monstrous deeds, though occasionally she feels such haltings, Moll fails to give much comfort to the idea of a "natural magistrate in the heart." Largely deaf and blind to God's guidance but hearing, sometimes, the devil at her shoulder, she is constrained in her criminal activities only by an occasional fear of hanging, and this is a weak constraint. How were people with so feeble and fitful an inbuilt sense of morality and who recognized no transcendent moral order to be dealt with, if the threat of capital punishment itself could not deter them? Defoe presents this problem with barely a hint at a solution, having Moll suggest at the very start of her narrative that there should have been an institution for children like her, to train them up to "an honest industrious Behaviour" (8). Eventually, of course, institutions having the same end would be developed for full-grown people of her type, though that type had first to be constituted. Giving up on the notion that criminality was essentially normal, English culture would develop the counter-notion that it was abnormal, tied to a specific "criminal class" or the product of a specific, even extraordinary pathology.[20] Rather than being killed or exiled, criminals would be consigned to penitentiaries to be "reformed," i.e., to have updated versions of the "natural magistrate" built into their foul or simply feckless hearts. The point was to develop a practicable as well as socially acceptable self-consciousness, so that criminals might actually be returned to society to lead socially productive, law-abiding lives. Held under close surveillance and punished for each infraction as if God Himself were their judge, they were to become what Moll confesses she is not, sufficient "monitors" of their own actions. Bentham's Panopticon was a machine designed, in effect, to do what God no longer could be trusted to do and, actually, to do it better. Without foreseeing this future shift in attitudes toward criminality, Defoe may nonetheless have helped it along by showing just how little there truly is in Moll and others like her to make them behave in a truly "civil" fashion. The word itself, or some variation, on it occurs occasionally in her narrative (e.g., 142, 197, 230, 244), but the values it stands for no more influence her behavior than her equally occasional fears of punishment. Only the prospect of something so terrible as being burned at the stake, the punishment prescribed for women caught coining, can kill her criminal impulse dead in its tracks (see 254–5).

The exact nature of Moll's relation or lack of relation to providence, with all its attendant implications, is just one of the many sets of themes readers' minds may "play" on – or with – as they work their way through

---

20 According to John J. Tobias, the "concept" of a separate criminal class "developed gradually after 1815" (*Crime and Industrial Society in the Nineteenth Century* [Harmondsworth, Middlesex, 1972], pp. 59ff.). Well before this, however, a profound shift in attitudes toward crime and

the text. What is most important about this "play" – especially from the standpoint of the novel's continuing "readability" – is that it is only *semi*-directed. Whether accidental or not, Defoe's "absence" from the narrative allows readers a freedom they would not have otherwise had to organize their reading in a variety of ways, to a variety of ends. There is no authorial voice – and so no clear "authority" – to say just what ought to be made of all the "concurrences," strange or not, that catch any particular reader's attention. It is up to readers to bring "authority" to the text, to provide it as best they can with a form and meaning significant within the givens of the particular "horizons" that shape or bound their consciousness. *Moll Flanders*, then, might appropriately be "organized" or "thematized" around a wide range of matters, e.g., the whole question of just what an adequate repentance requires; the significance of money in an increasingly mobile, commercial society; the situation of women; the causes of crime and its moral, social, and economic implications; the psychology of deviance; the growth (or rather deformation) of an interesting and vital mind; the individual vs. society; the contradictions between natural and social law, and so on.

But how can a novel seem to be about so many things, and yet not about every and anything? The answer to this question touches on one of the defining characteristics of texts we call "literary," i.e., their capacity to organize themselves extra-cognitively. The same "concurrences" that lead one to believe that *Moll Flanders* is in some significant way about providence, or indeed a variety of other matters important to eighteenth-century minds, encourage and legitimate the interpreting of it outside its original context. Thus while Moll's late, occasional references to providence call attention to it as a possible organizing principle in her narrative, these alone would hardly warrant the sustained consideration just given this theme. Nor is it merely the frequent mention of money, or Moll's complaints about the sad state of women that can make these themes seem important. All such organizing of the text around specific ideas is encouraged by the appearance of seemingly significant patterns in it, patterns which need not be interpreted in any particular way, but which suggest the text is one coherent structure susceptible to – indeed in need of – interpretation.

In a justly famous essay Roman Jakobson speaks of "the coercing, determining role" of "the regular reiteration of equivalent units."[21] He is

---

criminals had begun to take place in England, marked most visibly by the movement to the penitentiary system of punishment; see of course Michel Foucault, *Discipline and Punish: The Birth of the Prison*, tr. Alan Sheridan (New York, 1977), and also Michael Ignatieff, *A Just Measure of Pain: The Penitentiary in the Industrial Revolution* (New York, 1978).

[21] Jakobson, "Closing Statement: Linguistics and Poetics," in *Style in Language*, ed. Thomas A. Sebeok (Cambridge, Mass., 1960), pp. 350–77.

speaking primarily of the effect of rhythm, rhyme, and other phonic patterns in verse composition, such as assonance, consonance, and alliteration. "Words similar in sound," he says, "are drawn together in meaning." As his examples illustrate, the "meaning" he has in mind often transcends ordinary conceptual boundaries. That is, rhyme, rhythm, and other more or less arbitrary similitudes between words and phrases bind a work together in ways some critics used to call "organic," meaning by this metaphor that the work in question possessed for them an almost mystical coherence, something apprehended and deeply felt but which they could only approximately (if at all) describe in their own, sadly prosaic language. Jakobson is content to say that "equivalence in sound . . . inevitably involves" – he might better have said implies – "semantic equivalence." I suggest "implies" because, though semantic equivalence may seem powerfully suggested, we cannot always quite put our fingers on what such "regular reiterations" might actually mean.

Narrative has its own rhythms and even what might be called the functional equivalent of rhyme. Though perhaps less obviously and exactly, here, too, form affects meaning as palpable similarities between signifiers encourage the seeing of connections between otherwise disparate signifieds. It is possible to see providence at work in Moll's life because episodes across the text are juxtaposed in ways that attract attention, though not always conscious attention. I have relied on such juxtapositions in tracing connections between the Elder Brother, the gentleman at Bath, and Jemy; between the honest citizen, Robin, the linen-draper, and Moll's brother; and between Moll's earliest, notional violation of family ties, her actual incest with her brother, and her willful abandoning of her child by Jemy. But finding providence in or behind such juxtapositions is only one way of reading them. In Moll's three transgressions against family ties, for instance, one might also see a progressive hardening. The natural morality that recoils against marrying her lover's brother, and which makes it impossible for her to remain married to her own brother, eventually becomes so attenuated that it gives way to the devilish blandishments of Mother Midnight, who argues there is no harm in giving away her child. That Moll will not even countenance the idea of having an abortion means (within the novel's original context) she retains some residue of right feeling, but this, so powerful earlier, has become much weaker here. Little wonder, then, that the novel makes her marriage to the honest citizen seem but a brief hiatus in a long downward course. But one might also see in these same three transgressions something still different: the difficult situation of a woman out of her own dispose, who must do what she knows to be wrong or severely prejudice her material well-being. Moll is not without compunction, thus her leaving her brother despite her mother's counsel; nature has its limits. A woman alone is like "a Jewel dropt on the Highway," says Moll (128), but she's no easy pick-up. She will not knowingly and actually commit incest or murder, nor will she counterfeit the king's coin, though she comes close to doing all three. Moll draws the line at significant boundary points, thus avoiding, in the examples just cited, the worst crimes one may commit against the family, against others, and against the state (coining was considered a form of treason).

Several points require to be stressed. The first is that once we group Moll's three violations of family ties together, we can find a variety of implications in them, depending of course on how we compare or contrast them. The second is that, once we start thinking about them, we will inevitably be led to hook them up with other episodes which, very likely, will not seem immediately relevant to the original organizing principle, in this case incest or the violation of family ties. Thus, these three particular episodes might be linked to a whole series of episodes illustrating, to keep to examples already mentioned, on the one hand Moll's progressive hardening and on the other the desperateness of her situation vs. her reluctance to be utterly evil. Our original grouping keeps branching out, growing larger and more complex, and as it does the possible permutations between episodes grow, if not exponentially (for not all permutations will seem significant) at least according to some steeply accelerating curve. Needless to say, the organizing ideas behind such ensembles themselves keep changing, growing richer and more intricate as the ensembles enlarge so that, quite soon, they surpass simple description.

This brings me to a third important point. The episodes so far singled out from *Moll Flanders* are rather easily attachable to overall themes. It is not always possible, however, to say just what one episode's echoing another might mean in thematic terms. The relations between some episodes are best spoken of, perhaps, in formal terms only, that is as elements functioning to produce a sense of coherence and ultimately closure in much the same way as the repetition of, or variations on, a particular subject or theme might function in a piece of non-programmatic music. Only then can we begin to see the text as having something like an overall coherence despite – and in the midst of – its multiplicity of sometimes contradictory meanings. Consider, for instance, how Moll's story gets a certain definite shape though no definite meaning from the succession of men in her life. Thus Moll's men might be divided into two types, A and B, the first having a style which attracts her and the second a utility she falls back on in times of need. The first impress her as gentlemen and the second as men of substance. Moll moves from one to another in a pattern of alternation, thus:

A (Elder Brother)

                  B (Robin)

A (the linen-draper)

                  B (her brother)

A (the Bath gentleman)

                  B (the honest citizen)

A (Jemy)

                  B (the honest citizen)

         . . . . .

A (Jemy)

Far more complex arrangements (or "scores") might be possible, though these of course would only elaborate, and not alter, the basic patterning of this sequence. Thus the ellipsis is not unimportant, for it indicates Moll's whole career as a thief and includes, too, not only her last, brief interlude with the baronet she picks up at Bartholomew Fair, but the gentleman she meets at a gaming house (both these encounters, as I've already mentioned, are significant for what fails to happen).

Even so simplistic a rendering of the novel's action suggests two points quite plainly. The first is that the alternating pattern begins and ends on roughly the same note, and the second is that we have here not only an oscillation between two poles but, in Moll's succession of men, almost something of a rhyme scheme. Thus if we give each man his own lower-case letter, the sequence reads a,b,c,d,e,f,g,f,g. While these are very crude observations (more complex descriptions would doubtless allow us to find more elaborate patternings), even so, they lead to no simple conclusions about the meaning of the novel. The honest citizen/Jemy/honest citizen/ Jemy "quatrain" suggests some kind of resolution to Moll's search for the right man, but the ending of the series on an "A" rather than a "B" can indicate the opposite, for from this perspective the series remains open. Alternatively, the beginning and ending of the series on an "A" might give a sense of cyclic return, offering closure of a sort though (it would seem) no firm resolution. I don't wish to reargue my point that *Moll Flanders* can be understood in a variety of ways but to point out that these various understandings are predicated on our perception of seemingly significant concurrences in the text, reiterations that suggest some kind of regularity. The clarity, vividness, and coherence of patterns like those I've just sketched out make *Moll Flanders* seem richly meaningful, even when we feel at a loss (or should) to say exactly what it means.[22]

---

22 A quite interesting and too often overlooked discussion of Defoe's fiction makes the mistake, it seems to me, of trying to be too specific in assigning meaning to patterns it detects in *Moll Flanders*. Organizing the novel around Moll's relations with men in a way that has stimulated my own thinking, Douglas Brooks traces a series of parallels and contrasts – a "system of echoes

The same kind of structural equivalences (one might almost say narrative algebra) can be found in *Colonel Jack* and *Roxana*. That is, if we organize both novels around marital or sexual liaisons, certain patterns emerge which suggest coherence and closure. Thus Roxana's first and third lovers are diamond merchants, while her second and fourth are princes. Lover number five is a courtier (there seems no particular patterning here, except that – odd man out – he represents the low point of her amorous career). After leaving him, she re-encounters and agrees to marry diamond merchant number two (lover number three), which marriage she

and repetitions," he calls it, a "structural logic" – the elements of which hark back in one way or another to the two brothers in Colchester, and forward to Jemy in Virginia. Brooks's argument begins to go awry, however, when he tries to explain the novel's conclusion. Moll cannot be happy, he contends, until she is free of "the source of all her trouble," which is the guilt she incurred by marrying Robin. "The man might be dead," says Brooks, "but the guilt he left Moll with, concretized in the marriage to her own brother is not." With her return to Virginia, however, Moll is put into a position where that guilt can "be lifted by confrontation":

> Moll must face again her brother and the offspring of their incestuous union, must relive momentarily that part of her life which was an unsuccessful attempt at revenge for the injuries caused by the elder brother, and which forced her into physical incest. The first obstacle to peace of mind is passed when Moll meets her son and he not only fails to upbraid her for her incestuous marriage, but reveals a genuine affection for her .... The second, and last, passes with the death of her brother who, alive, is the very embodiment of Moll's guilt .... with his death her guilt, and life of deception, vanish. She is free to confess. Accepted by her son, she must now be accepted by her husband for what she is, and, far more important, for what she has been.
>
> He is surprisingly amiable .... Where the first Virginia episode (so intimately bound up with the affair of the two brothers) failed, the second, its re-enactment, succeeds. Through Jemmy the discordant notes of incest that have sounded through Moll's life achieve resolution; and when "all these difficulties [have been] made easy" Moll can return to England, and the novel come to an end.
>
> (Douglas Brooks, *Number and Pattern in the Eighteenth-Century Novel* [London, 1973], pp. 50, 52)

For all its apparent plausibility, this interpretation is highly problematic. Putting aside the whole question of whether Moll really is happy at the end of the novel (and whether indeed she confesses), what is all this talk about "guilt"? Moll does not seem especially burdened with it, and the almost magical process by which it is lifted – somewhere between old-fashioned psychoanalysis and the kind of advice an unscrupulous fortune-teller might give a sick old woman with money ("get rid of the source of all your trouble") – is in any case difficult to locate. Brooks seems to be offering a psychological reading of the novel, but is the psychology in question Moll's, Defoe's, or the reader's? (And if the last, an eighteenth- or twentieth-century reader?) He seems to be talking about some final settling of accounts, but where in fact does this transaction take place, and what is the medium of exchange? All these questions might be answered, but they and their answers, it seems to me, originate not in the text but in a particular kind of reader's response to the text. Insofar as the work itself is concerned, the kind of movement toward closure Brooks describes might better be represented schematically, as void as one can make it of heavily freighted terms like "guilt" or "happy." The "structural logic" Brooks invokes remains intelligible only so long as we try to keep it symbolic. Despite these criticisms, Brooks's two chapters on Defoe are well worth reading; they point to features undeniably in the novels, and hard to explain according to conventional interpretive strategies.

briefly regrets when it seems that prince number one (lover number two) might now want to marry her. His wife (like the second diamond merchant's) has died, and left him free. But then two things occur which assuage this regret. First, prince number one gets religion and changes his mind, and second, diamond merchant number two buys himself an English baronetcy and a Dutch patent of nobility. After moving back and forth between commercial men and courtiers, Roxana's future is fixed with a man who combines both attributes, a tradesman prince as well as an all around nice guy. Jack's involvements with the opposite sex are much simpler. All his wives eventually betray him, except the last, whom he marries with a great deal of circumspection and no romantic illusions. But even she turns out to have made an unmaidenly mistake in her youth, cuckolding Jack, as it were, in advance. Jack's search for a proper wife ends only when wife number one is fortuitously restored to him, reformed as he himself had been by the salubrious effect of being sold into slavery.

Such structurations, whatever we make of them, encourage us to see in these texts the sort of coherence that warrants interpretation. And here, too, implications of closure raise interpretive questions. Why, for instance, should slavery be a redemptive experience for Jack and his wife – and, come to think of it, why should slavery figure so prominently in that novel? Isn't it ironic that Roxana gets practically all she wants, only to have it go sour because her daughter won't leave her alone? Such questions tie into larger concerns, there being more capacious and interesting structures in *Colonel Jack* and *Roxana* than those having merely to do with spouses and lovers. Like those "strange concurrences" adumbrating God's Hand in *Moll Flanders*, these are less visible to modern readers than they would likely have been to Defoe's original audience. They suffer, moreover, the further disadvantage of being less assimilable to modern concerns than providence, a capacious theme which translates easily into current idiom; thus Darwin and Marx, even Freud and Einstein, have their own versions of it.

The ideas – or perhaps I should say constellations of attitudes – that stand behind the large narrative patternings of *Colonel Jack* and *Roxana* are not so easily renovable. Still, along with *Moll Flanders*, these novels open large windows into the past. Intimating the possibility of an order teasingly beyond comprehension, they continue to project not only a multiplicity of meanings but a mysterious coherence attractive even to godless, psychology-saturated moderns who, if they consider the morality of trade at all, incline to think it a settled question since Marx or Adam Smith. It is not so much that Defoe's novels hold the past in amber, reflect or refract it, as that their attractive but often elusive structures provide means by which attentive and moderately learned minds might reconstruct for themselves something of its patterns of thought and feeling. Or so it seems to me we are doing when we see God's mysterious hand behind or beyond the strange concurrences appearing in *Moll Flanders*. The "fields" these novels project allow only so much wandering; indeed, at times they are more like mazes. Armed with our readings of collateral, non-literary texts, we search for historically plausible themes as though they were threads leading back to the text's original meaning.

Still – and this is another of their great and special qualities, the qualities that make them "literature" – inasmuch as the controlling structures of these novels are large, diffuse, and partly of our own creating, we are allowed each of us a certain freedom to negotiate them differently. This freedom – this "room" for "play" – is doubtless part of their continuing appeal as, now, somewhat "aestheticized" objects. As I've repeatedly argued, however, an audience that read these novels against the background of criminal biography might well have found in the "Exercise" or "Work" these texts provided them a sense of personal empowerment and a simulacrum, at least, of moral authority. The "sober Reader" who makes "just Reflections" shows he is, for instance, what Moll is not: "Qualified to preach" and "capable of reading Lectures of Instruction to any Body" (268, 287–8). Offering rich opportunities to make "enlargements" and "applications," to "gather" up the "moral" of the "history" or otherwise "naturalize" what the text merely "describes," Defoe's novels, then, might be said to "legitimate" both themselves and (in an especially modern sense) their readers, too. They can even seem "equipment for living" in Kenneth Burke's sense of the phrase – apparatuses, that is, for the strengthening and diverting of minds that (as Defoe himself darkly might have hinted) could otherwise "prey upon" themselves.[23]

[23] Kenneth Burke, *The Philosophy of Literary Form*, 3rd edn (Berkeley, 1973), pp. 293–304.

5

The general scandal upon business: unanswerable doubts, and the text as a field supporting very nice distinctions

There is some difference between an honest man, and an honest Tradesman; and tho' the distinction is very nice, yet I must say it is to be supported.

The Complete English Tradesman, 1: 226

If no man can be called honest but he who is never overcome ... none but he who is sufficiently fortified against all possibility of being tempted by prospects, or driven by distress, to make any trespass upon his integrity—woe be unto me that write, and to most that read!

Serious Reflections of Robinson Crusoe, p. 46

[Trade] is like a hand-mill, it must always be turned about by the diligent hand of the master, or if you will, like the pump-house at *Amsterdam*, where they put offenders in for petty matters ... if they will work and keep pumping, they sit well, dry and safe, and if they work very hard one hour or two, they may rest, perhaps a quarter of an hour afterwards; but if they over sleep themselves, or grow lazy, the water comes in upon them, and wets them, and they have no dry place to stand in, much less to sit down in ... so that it is nothing but *pump* or *drown*, and they may chuse which they like best.

A Tradesman has Hazards ... and Fears and Anxieties ... all the Way he goes.

The Complete English Tradesman, 1: 48, 2 (pt.1): 237

Now, it is certain, a Man who lives in a Crowd ... be his station in Life what it will, can very rarely acquaint himself with the Truth of Things, because his Mind is seldom at Leisure to make a strict Enquiry into it: The Pleasures, or Business of Life possess him alternately, and deliver him over from one Amusement to another; so that he can with less Difficulty gain Admission to a Prime Minister, than to Himself. His Understanding is intrenched with so many Passions, Temptations, and Impertinences; there are so many Delays of Brocades and Hoops, and Linnen to be broke through, that before a Man can get at it, the Inclination grows cold. Whereas the busy swarm of vain Images which buzz about the Mind in the heat of a social State, always leave it in the Shades of a recluse and solitary one; there the Passions are laid, the Temptations are at a Distance, and the Impertinences chased away .... The Understanding is then easily come at, it lies naked and exposed, and represents Things to the Fancy, as they really are.

?Defoe, *A Collection of Miscellany Letters Selected out of Mist's Weekly Journal*
(1722–7), 4: 181–3

But I desire not to be the promoter of unanswerable doubts ... and therefore I
only name things.

Serious Reflections of Robinson Crusoe, p. 117

The last three chapters have considered the means by which Defoe sets his
texts apart from and "against" the general run of criminal biography,
indicates they are in need of interpretation, and opens them up to a variety
of more or less "legitimate" meanings. Another way of describing these
chapters is to say they offer an account of how his fiction would have
aroused readers' interest, given a push to their imaginations, and bounded
the movement of their minds. All this would have kept Defoe's readers
from settling into an easy relationship with his protagonists or the narratives they project. Neither monsters nor fools nor saints, as they would
have been within the conventions of ordinary criminal biography, Defoe's
criminals are often attractive and sympathetic. Still, they ought to have
given pause to readers trained up within such conventions, there being too
much in and about them to allow for easy identification with their sinful
pleasures or their pious resolves to reform. The texts force such a complicated awareness. Though the action in individual episodes is generally
easy to follow, the meaning of that action is often ambiguous. The large
structures in each text, too, are difficult to parse out; the novels seem at
first glance loosely episodic but their episodes are often curiously inter-
connected in ways suggesting some kind of extra or subcognitive "logic."

Within individual episodes, then, and in the way episodes follow one
upon the other, Defoe's texts seem various and open to the point at times of
near incoherence (perhaps this is too strong a term, but it seems to me
implicit in the common notion that Defoe writes with a kind of "journal-
istic" realism). This quality is especially apparent in contrast to the
monovalent and tightly sequenced form of serious criminal biography. At
the largest level, however, the diversity of Defoe's novels seems bounded
by a coherence which, being more formal than ideational, invites interpretation. Criminal rogue biography abolishes thought, stridently emptying
itself of ideas and emotions by destroying the structures that support them.
Defoe's novels offer structures somewhat – though not entirely – empty of
ideas and feeling, leaving readers free to fill these structures in with
feelings and ideas of their own, or, alternatively, to amalgamate what
feelings and ideas they find there with those they bring to the text. The
question before us continues to be, what was the good of these qualities?
This may seem a pointless question, and not the least because so speculative. The fact is, however, that we cannot fully appreciate – or in some
cases even see – the particular textures and overall architectures of Defoe's
criminal novels, i.e., their art, without proposing some notions of how they
may have functioned (or tried to function) for their original audience.

Along with trying to find order and meaning in the criminal act, criminal biography sought to provide an image of the criminal that would allow its audience to come to terms with him and, in some cases, with what society had done to him. It responded to the first of these problems by stressing God's providence, written even into the hearts of men; it did not do very well at offering an etiology of crime. It responded to the second by sanctifying criminals or debasing them, the case of thieves being especially problematic not only because of the inordinancy of their punishments but because their activities could seem so similar to those of their economic and social "betters." As we have just seen, Defoe's novels display the role of providence in human affairs with greater moral effect and theological correctness than the general run of criminal biography, and, as I hope to show in the final chapter of this book, one of them provides a sophisticated etiology of crime. Defoe had a much harder time dealing with the troublesome implications of theft. The freedom of writing fictions allowed him to skirt the problems raised by capital punishment – he could simply leave his thieves unhanged – but there was no simple "fix" for the prevalent suspicion that modern economic life was the pursuit of criminal ends by other means.

Decades after Adam Smith's updating of providence's "invisible hand," a commentator on the eighth commandment could still write that "nothing is more usual than for each side to try to over-reach the other in buying and selling, in other words to steal or cheat." Smith was one of the greatest of a series of eighteenth-century thinkers trying to imagine, in J. G. A. Pocock's words, "how society might operate rationally and beneficially" in the absence of "civic virtue." The "self interest" and concern with "personal profit" that a commercial or "speculative" society encouraged, it seemed all too clear, equally tended to prevent "the individual engaged with exchange" from "contemplat[ing] the universal good."[1] As Pocock's language suggests, the problem extended far beyond the immediacies of "buying and selling." Like crime, commercial life could stand as a handy sign for larger, more pervasive, less easily definable things. A clear example, and certainly the best known, is provided by one of the century's favorite plays. When *The Beggar's Opera* makes Peachum and Lockit particularly obscene examples of how business and crime could share a common ethos, its actual target is not businessmen or crooks but Walpole

---

[1] *The Explanation of the Ten Commandments*, (1796?), pt. 3, p. 7; J. G. A. Pocock, *The Machiavellian Moment: Florentine Political Thought and the Atlantic Republic Tradition* (Princeton, 1975), pp. 464–5, and 462–505 generally. For persistent efforts over the seventeenth and eighteenth centuries to make self-interested individualism seem not anti-social after all, but, rather – viewed largely, in terms of its aggregate effect – a firm basis for mutually beneficial social and economic interrelation, see also J. A. W. Gunn, *Politics and the Public Interest in the Seventeenth Century* (London, 1969), and Albert O. Hirschman, *The Passions and the Interests: Political Arguments for Capitalism before Its Triumph* (Princeton, 1977).

and the whole new, confusing, thoroughly corrupt – and very modern, as it turned out – political order he represented and helped create.

Criminal biographers like Defoe's contemporary, Alexander Smith, treated the equation of trade with theft in rather a careless but – I would say – peculiarly crafty way. Though criminals frequently charge their victims with a corruption equal to or greater than their own, their shots don't quite land home. "We are grown almost a nation of cheats," says one of Smith's rogues, and, "worst of all, men won't cheat upon the square." There is satire in this but also a certain comedy, achieved here as often elsewhere at the expense of the thief himself. How can he pretend to set up as a critic of public morality, or its lack? Note, too, the rueful quality of this particular thief's complaint. Caught and hanged as all such "little" thieves eventually were, he is finally and inevitably outclassed by the truly "great" criminals who, being too powerful and wealthy to be brought within the compass of the law, steal from the public with impunity. "Little thieves are hanged," the proverb went, "but great ones escape." Or, in Garth's much quoted lines, "little villains must submit to Fate, / That great ones may enjoy the World in State." But even here the satire of criminal rogue biography is not especially pointed. "Who is there now-a-days does not rob?" another of Smith's criminals asks, and goes on to name an almost encyclopedic range of trades and professions. Even taken seriously – something their context tends to prevent – such comments can have no particular impact. If practically everyone gets splashed by the muckraking highwayman, what he says is all the more easily shrugged off; no one ought to feel *particularly* embarrassed.[2]

Lacking the ideological wherewithal to lift "the general Scandal upon Business, (*viz.*) that a Tradesman cannot be an honest Man," Defoe was not above using similar methods to ward off attacks on the trading ethos. Arguing in *The Complete English Tradesman* that if all tradesmen are to be "censur'd as dishonest," then "almost all Mankind" must be so, too, Defoe insists that "in Fact, no Man that has any Thing to do in the World with the Poor, or with the Rich, with the Buyer or with the Seller, with a Labourer, or the Master, with one or with another, can be honest. But we are all K----s, and the Sons of K----s, Man and Mother's Child; not an honest Wretch left on the Face of God's Globe, no, not one." More desperate than ingenious, such an argument gives little relief or surcease from what one journalist called "the mercenary low-priz'd Humour of the

[2] Alexander Smith, *A Complete History of the Lives and Robberies of the Most Notorious Highwaymen, Footpads, Shoplifts, & Cheats of Both Sexes*, ed. Arthur L. Hayward (London, 1933), p. 491; the proverb was first recorded in 1639, according to D. C. Browning, ed., *Everyman's Dictionary of Quotations and Proverbs* (London, 1951), p. 482; Samuel Garth, *The Dispensary* (1699), 1: 9–10; Smith, ibid., p. 181. For anticipations and echoes of the proverb and Garth's rephrasing of it, see *Turned to Account*, p. 254, n. 12; for the curious inconsequentiality of writers like Smith as satirists, see especially its chapter 8.

Times we live in," and a preacher at an assizes the "general Spirit of sordid Selfishness and violent Covetousness, and consequently of Fraud and Injustice of all kinds [lately] gone out among us." Such comments flew especially thick after the collapse of the South Sea Bubble when, as one thief put it, "all Mankind were turn'd thieves." Given the wide participation of monied people of all sorts in the buying and selling of South Sea stock, he might just as accurately have said that all mankind had turned to trade. What Defoe called the "general . . . Duty" of "getting Money" was no peculiarly middle-class concern, any more than it is today.[3]

Defoe was never quite able to argue his way out of the "scandal" that trade was inherently dishonest and so comparable to theft. However much he tried to make it seem a heroic and worthy endeavor – *The Complete English Tradesman* with all its confused, ungainly, even tortured arguments is a monument to this effort – he could never quite erase its bad name. Having inherited and to some extent accepted an ideology antagonistic to individual economic enterprise, he could not remake that ideology all by himself. Still, he could defend against it, and in far more interesting and potentially more wholesome (or at least less noxious) ways than those proposed by criminal biography. Bringing the considerable resources of literary discourse to bear on the equation trade = theft, he wrote – not to obscure or confuse it, as, say, Alexander Smith did – but to disarm it, recontextualizing certain of its more vexing implications so these might be dissolved, attenuated, or at least contained.[4]

---

[3] Defoe, *The Complete English Tradesman*, 2nd edn (1727), 2 (pt. 2): 159, 2 (pt. 1): 45–6; the *London Journal*, 6–13 August 1720; George Bell, *A Sermon Preach'd at the Cathedral Church of St. Peter in York . . . at the Assizes* (York, 1722), p. 5; Applebee's *Original Weekly Journal*, 26 May 1722; Defoe, the *Commentator*, No. 46 (10 June 1720). For some time after the "plague of dishonesty" that led up to and characterized the South Sea crash, Maximillian Novak suggests, "the robberies of hungry and desperate men and women seemed almost heroic" compared to the "greed and self-interest" of "upper-class . . . crime"; he believes the event had an important shaping effect on Defoe's fiction (*Realism, Myth, and History in Defoe's Fiction* [Lincoln, Neb., 1983], pp. 129–30).

[4] The standard account of Defoe's views about business ethics is still Hans H. Andersen, "The Paradox of Trade and Morality in Defoe," *Modern Philology*, 39 (1941): 23–46, but it badly needs an update. Andersen takes too simple a view of Defoe's psychology and finds him, comfortably enough, putting trade into "an independent compartment with rules of its own" where "moral objections were virtually powerless" (p. 37). The tortured, inconclusive arguments of *The Complete English Trademan*, where Defoe returns again and again to the same moral objections against business practices, never quite able to set them aside, seem not to have impressed him. I'd not disagree with John J. Richetti's calling Defoe "a sort of poet laureate of the market system" (*Daniel Defoe* [Boston, 1987], p. 44), as he was certainly capable of praising trade and tradesmen to the skies. Still, his rhetoric can often seem quite odd. Charles Lamb noticed this when he said *The Complete English Tradesman* could be read in "an *ironical sense*, and as a piece of *covered satire*," though it was "difficult to say what [Defoe's] intention was in writing it" (letter to Walter Wilson, 16 December 1822, excerpted in *Defoe: The Critical Heritage*, ed. Pat Rogers [London, 1972], p. 86). A more recent admirer of Defoe as a defender of commerce, noting with some bepuzzlement a "tendency to weaken his own position," regrets that Defoe "at times lets his imagery confound his purpose." He doesn't much like, for instance, Defoe's

Literature, Kenneth Burke suggests, typically "deals" with the socially problematic by situating and labeling it. "Sizing things up" is one of his metaphors; "the strategic naming of a situation" is another. "Strategic" he defines after the *Concise Oxford Dictionary* – "one 'imposes on the enemy the time and place and conditions for fighting preferred by oneself' " – and by "naming" he means that a work of literature "singles out a pattern of experience ... sufficiently representative of our social structure, that recurs sufficiently often mutatis mutandis for people to 'need a word for it' and to adopt an attitude towards it."[5] Burke cites *Madame Bovary* and *Babbit* as examples of what he means, pointing out that each novel introduced a new word into its language. Defoe's novels might seem to do something similar, insofar as their protagonists – and many other characters in them as well – can be taken as emblems of the confused new state of men and women in the early capitalist world. But Burke's notion that literary works "strategically" name new situations can suggest quite another possibility: what might be called "the strategic situating of a name." If problematic situations need names in order to be dealt with, might not the opposite be true? Might not problematic names require to be situated – or, rather, resituated? I'm speaking here of the ways in which literary texts, especially, play with, rearrange, and so alter the meaning of socially, politically, and morally "difficult" ideas by stringing them (or, actually, the "ideologemes" that compose them) into new syntactical series, refiguring them by repositioning them with respect to each other and to heretofore unrelated ideas (or ideologemes). As John Frow points out, it is by this means that the "specifically literary" acquires its "extra-aesthetic dimension." Breaking or at least disrupting the "structured order of the [preexisting] semiotic field," literary texts can contribute to the creation of new semiotic fields, new orders within which the "reality" of "social authority," "social power," and "social structure" might be reencoded and, possibly, rethought.[6]

My argument in this and the next chapter will be that *Moll Flanders* and *Colonel Jack* pattern the experiences of their protagonists in ways that prevent readers from coming to any easy conclusion that trade = theft, and that they do this so differently from ordinary criminal biographies as

---

calling trade (or rather writing about it) "the whore I really doated upon" (Thomas Keith Meier, *Defoe and the Defense of Commerce* [Victoria, B.C., 1987], p. 97).

[5] Kenneth Burke, *The Philosophy of Literary Form*, 3rd edn (Berkeley, 1973), pp. 296, 298, 300.

[6] John Frow, *Marxism and Literary History* (Oxford, 1986), pp. 99–100, but see generally pp. 88ff. The earliest use of "ideologeme" I know is Bakhtin's, in *The Formal Method in Literary Scholarship: A Critical Introduction to Sociological Poetics*, tr. Albert J. Wehrle (Baltimore, 1978), where see pp. 17, 21–5. The term gets defined by Fredric Jameson as "the smallest intelligible unit of the essentially antagonistic collective discourse of social classes" (*The Political Unconscious: Narrative as a Socially Symbolic Act* [Ithaca, 1981], p. 76), but the argument might be made that this ties ideology too exclusively to class, ignoring other lines of division in relations of power and dominance like race, gender, and age.

to beggar comparison. *Moll Flanders* so enhances the individual terms of the equation, and sets them into such complicated motion, that the reductive relation the equation insists on cannot possibly be sustained. Readers may simply have been disoriented by this series of "moves," but they may, too, have found themselves provided with a heady, new, even empowering perspective on life in modern society. *Colonel Jack*, as I'll try to show in the next chapter, tries for more and achieves less, attempting to bind together a variety of seemingly disparate and contradictory concerns into an odd, often awkward, and possibly in its own way desperate *concordia discors*. One thing it does succeed in doing, however, is to make the merchant's life seem not so bad compared to other ways of making a living, or gaining social status. But let us begin with the *discordia concors Moll Flanders* presents, in an episode that might serve as a touchstone for the novel's special qualities not only *qua* novel but vis-à-vis its supposedly non-fictional analogues.

Toward the end of her long criminal career, Moll is seized in the streets and wrongly accused of minding her business; that is, she is arrested for a shoplifting she didn't commit. Dragged back to the mercer's shop where the crime took place, Moll vainly protests her innocence. She is badly treated, especially by the man who seized her, one of the mercer's journey-men. Only when the actual thief is caught do Moll's captors begin to think they might have made a mistake. The journeyman continues insolent, however, even in the face of mounting pressure from a gathering crowd and the intervention of a sympathetic constable. Finally they all go before a magistrate, who reprimands the mercer and commits his journeyman to Newgate. In the end, Moll gets some 200 pounds in order, as the mercer thinks, to avoid the bad publicity that would come from her suing him in court. During the dinner that concludes the deal, the freed but now abject journeyman cringingly begs Moll's pardon. She plays the gracious lady and accepts his gesture, though it means nothing to her "since there was nothing to be got by him" (see 241–53; 252). This episode invites consideration for a variety of reasons. It is one of the longest and most complex in Moll's criminal career, and one of only two that give extended attention to her victims. (The other, even longer, concerns the baronet she meets at Bartholomew Fair.) It is unusual, too, in that it involves dialogue between three or more persons simultaneously – we might call this trialogue – and of the few trialogues in the book it is the most fully realized. It echoes, moreover, an actual event described first in a sessions paper, and then in Smith's *Lives of the Highwaymen*, a point we might briefly consider.

When Moll returns to the mercer's shop to negotiate a settlement, she arrives in a rented coach and "good Cloaths" (250); when she comes to get her money and the dinner, she brings along her governess "dress'd like an old Dutchess" and a hired gentleman who pretends to be her suitor (252). These details suggest a vague but nonetheless teasing comparison to the final exploit of one Mary Jones, hanged in 1691 "for stealing 42 Yards of Gold and Silver Lace." "To put a better colour upon her Design," the sessions paper reported, she "came to the Prosecutor's Shop in a Sedan; and after having cheapened several pieces of Lace, she took away the piece of Lace abovesaid, and the next day she was found in another Shop, playing the same prank." Smith embroiders on this in his typical fashion: Mary Jones, according to him, "was apprehended for stealing a piece of satin out of a mercer's shop on Ludgate Hill, whither she went in a very splendid equipage and personated the late Duchess of Norfolk, to avoid suspicion of her dishonesty. But her Graceless Grace being sent to Newgate and condemned for her life ... she was hanged."[7] No direct influence need be assumed to compare these two texts fruitfully to Defoe's. Neither he nor Smith are content with simple facts as a sessions paper might describe them, but there resemblance ends. Smith goes for a quick laugh, here at the expense of the great with his wisecrack about "the late Duchess of Norfolk." Impersonating her was no good way to seem honest, for, "owing to her gallantries" (as the *Dictionary of National Biography* so delicately puts it), she was separated from her husband in 1685 and finally divorced in 1700; in 1701 she married Sir John Germain, her long-time lover.

Some dim memory of Smith may have influenced Defoe as he wrote about Moll and the mercer (thus the governess as an "old Dutchess"), but the resemblance could also be accidental.[8] Either way, the episode may be taken as an instance of the gulf that separates his fiction from the factitious, though often entertaining lies of criminal rogue biography.[9] For Smith,

[7] Old Bailey Sessions Paper, 9–11 December 1691; Smith, *Lives of the Highwaymen*, p. 276.

[8] To my knowledge there is no hard evidence that Defoe read Smith's *Lives of the Highwaymen*. Novak quotes a reference to this author and his "ingenious Volumes" from Mist's *Weekly Journal*, 16 September 1721, a paper in which Defoe had a powerful hand, but he need not have been the author of this particular item (Novak, *Realism, Myth, and History in Defoe's Fiction*, pp. 129–30). Two texts known to be his, however, refer to a murderer hanged in 1682 in such a way as to suggest Defoe's source was Smith, rather than his own memory of the case (cf. mentions of Captain Vratz in *SRC*, p. 182, and *CEG*, pp. 30–1, to Smith's *Highwaymen*, pp. 269–72).

[9] Ian Watt has singled out this very same episode as one among several in the novel that "offer the closest parallel to the staple materials of the rogue biographies." For this reason he finds it "not particularly plausible" but "contrived," by which he means that it is removed from "ordinary experience" (*The Rise of the Novel* [Berkeley, 1964], pp. 106–7). But how is "ordinary experience" to be defined? If it includes what one ordinarily *reads* about life as people are supposed, however extraordinarily, to be actually living it, then "anecdotes concerning trickery and deception" do have a certain plausibility, are part of "the norms of everyday life" (Watt, p. 106). Moll's roguish tricks are in any case far less bizarre and extravagant than similar feats reported in the rogue literature or even the newspapers. They seem more plausible, too, in that they have solid consequences, as such tales ordinarily do not. Consider, for instance, Moll's stealing a horse from in front of a tavern (p. 254) or her making away with a fellow lodger's trunk from an inn in the country (pp. 264–6). Moll is faced with the practical implications of

Mary Jones's arrest is but a final furbelow, a bit of truth added to a string of falsehoods perhaps to give them piquancy. For Defoe, Moll's encounter with the mercer is part of a larger, developing pattern. This pattern is actually quite complicated, for it includes not only her own behavior but her relation to the reader and his relation to the world she inhabits – and so, too, potentially, his relation to the world that he himself inhabits.

Before focussing on the incident itself, it is necessary to say some things about its context and its manner of proceeding. The novel prepares readers to appreciate the peculiar complexity of Moll's transaction with the mercer, first, by emphasizing the importance of its position in the overall arc of her life, and, second, by carrying so much of its action forward through dialogue, i.e., through the competing voices and points of view of the people around her. To begin with, we might note that Moll's false arrest is the first of what she calls her "finall broils" (241), i.e., the beginning of the end of her long criminal history. She emphasizes the point at the end of the episode, too. Counting up her wealth, noting that her governess believed her "the richest of [her] Trade in England," she observes "I was now in good Circumstances indeed, if I could have known my time for leaving off" (253). But Moll does not leave off, and a kind of suspense begins to develop, preparing the reader for the novel's climax and denouement. In her very next theft, significantly, she absconds with a horse, an item she is obliged to abandon, for "never was a poor Thief more at a loss to know what to do with any thing that was stolen" (254). Imprudence on so grand a scale is a clear symptom of that pride which inevitably goes before a fall, and of something else as well: Moll is losing control, failing to see what an ordinary person might see. The adventure with the mercer has all the marks of a providential sign, but Moll fails even to register it. Significant, too, is the fact that before stealing the horse she has disguised herself as a beggar, though she "naturally abhorr'd Dirt and Rags." Finding it "the most uneasie Disguise" she has ever put on, she abandons it as "Ominous and Threatning." Moll's criminal career is carrying her away from herself, and one way or another the consequences will likely prove disastrous. Eventually, after a series of very risky ventures, she is nearly caught in a goldsmith's shop and barely talks her way free. Nothing daunted, she is out at her old trade the very next day, which happens to be Christmas, and caught as flat-footed as any novice might have been.

In a broad, quite superficial way, this process of derangement conforms to patterns typically found in both kinds of criminal biography. Moll's growing imprudence and loss of perspective is an instance of the progressive intellectual deterioration thought to accompany prolonged or

such stunts: how to dispose of the horse? what to do with the trunk? These problems are as *real*, say, as those faced by Crusoe in his efforts to make bread.

egregious delinquency, and which was often called "infatuation."[10]
Defoe's presentation of this phenomenon is far more circumstantial and
slower moving than it would be in serious criminal biography and nar-
rationally more sophisticated, which of course makes for important differences. Thus the disparity between Moll's point of view then, when she was
embroiled in the events of the story, and that of her retrospective narrative
voice now, as she relates those events, prepares the reader to feel wiser
than she both then and now. As she increasingly loses control over herself
and the course of events, moreover, Moll verges on the condition of those
many criminal rogues, who – whatever their initial, crude attraction –
come eventually to seem no more than caricatures. Told in the right tone
of voice by the right kind of narrator – which is to say not her but a
wisecracking know-it-all like Alexander Smith – Moll's foolish theft of that
horse would drop her down to the same level of hapless buffoonery that
depersonalized and so prevented sympathy for a host of other Molls (e.g.,
Frith, Raby, King, as well as Jones), to say nothing of hundreds of other,
mostly male, petty criminals.[11] Here, too, Moll risks more than she knows.

Either way – or rather both ways – the reader acquainted with the
conventions of criminal biography is primed to feel an increasing distance
between Moll and himself, a certain disaffiliation. Normally, this setting
the reader "against" the criminal would serve to realign him with social
orthodoxy. In the case of Moll's dealings with the mercer and his journeyman, however, things are rather more complicated. Because the tradesmen are each interesting in his own way, as is the constable who intervenes
and even the magistrate and the onlooking crowd, Moll is not the only
attention-catching, attitude-defining "other" at hand. Turning Moll over
in one's mind, considering and judging her role in the affair, it is possible
also to consider and judge the roles of various other individuals, as well as
a fragment of the great social mass.

Dialogue (or, to be more exact, reported speech) plays an important
role in generating these additional possibilities. Here as elsewhere, it
establishes a dense and complex context for the protagonist's monologue,
keeping the reader's relation to the text dynamic and alive. By insinuating
other voices into the text (or in the case of indirectly reported speech, the
shadows of other voices), Defoe makes readers all the more aware of the
peculiarity of the voice they have been hearing and of the person that
voice represents. In hearing other people speaking, readers are suddenly,
if briefly, freed from the confines of the narrator's point of view. They hear
a "window" opening to an outside world, onto normal lives and normal

---

[10] See *Turned to Account*, pp. 76–8 and appropriate notes; also the texts cited in chapter 4, n. 3 and,
      in a slightly different context, the "stupid infatuation" mentioned in the same chapter, n. 16.
[11] For Molls Frith, Raby, and Jones, see Smith's *Lives of the Highwaymen*, pp. 282–90, 94–7, 273–6,
      respectively; for Moll King, transported to America, see Gerald Howson, "Who Was Moll
      Flanders?" the *Times Literary Supplement*, 18 January 1968, pp. 63–4.

concerns or, in some cases, onto lives and concerns which, by comparison, make the protagonist seem more normal than they might have thought. Dialogue hedges the protagonist about with comparisons and contrasts – or, more properly, with potential comparisons and contrasts, for Defoe's narrators rarely see as much as even the most casual reader can see. Dialogue, furthermore, prevents the reader from responding in a fixed mode to the narrator's voice, however complex that mode may be. As the text shifts from straightforward narration (monologue) to dialogue, and back again, it forces readers to shift gears continually, to keep up an ongoing readjustment of the various "ratios" they would otherwise tend to establish between themselves and his criminals.

Such complications of effect and affect are to be found in all Defoe's fiction, but especially where he employs dialogue. Its role in *Colonel Jack* and *Roxana* cannot concern us here, but much of what I am going to say about its functioning in *Moll Flanders* will apply, at least in principle, to them as well. Like all Defoe's protagonists (including Crusoe – H. F. is the lone exception), Moll is endowed with a sidekick or familiar, whose conversation defines and highlights her own special tendencies. In the criminal novels these sidekicks are more corrupt than the narrator, at least to all appearance. The corruption of Moll's governess is indicated by her greater experience and shrewdness at crime and by her horrific hintings at abortion. Up until she repents, the effect of hearing the governess's voice is to soften the impact of Moll's; Moll is not as bad as she, or as the still more wicked housebreakers and coiners whose gangs she refuses to join. When Moll reports the speech of normal people, however, quite an opposite effect is achieved. Their talk, so unlike Moll's, belongs to the ordinary, everyday world of the reader; her victims (or potential victims) are people like him and his friends and relations. Seen from this familiar perspective – though only for a moment and however incompletely – Moll must have looked strange, even dangerous and bad.

All this bears on Moll's exploitation of the mercer and his journeyman, particularly because the episode occurs toward the end of a series of similar, though simpler and briefer episodes, all of which describe more blatant and generally more dangerous ways of taking other people's goods and money. This series begins with Moll's theft of a tankard, the first crime she commits without the excuse of "necessity," and goes on to include her robbing the occupant of a burning house while seeming to help, her "narrow escape" when she attempts to steal a gentlewoman's watch outside a meeting house, her near capture when, disguised as a man, she is traced to her governess's house, and her stealing a bundle from a maid about to board the Barnet Coach with her mistress. It is at this point that the episode with the mercer occurs, and then four more follow, as Moll robs little Lady Betty and her sister in St. James's Park, cheats a gambler

at a gaming house, and makes her final attempts at the goldsmith's and the
silkdealer's. All these episodes report the speech of Moll's victims, and in so
doing stimulate curiosity about the cost of her crimes to them. The few
words the tavern boy calls out in the course of his duties, insignificant in
themselves, give him a certain solid reality; this is the sort of thing
eighteenth-century readers would have heard every day. What will
happen to him when his mistress finds he overlooked the tankard? Or how
will the woman at the burning house – so effusive in her thanks for Moll's
help – feel when she realizes she has entrusted her children to a thief, and
that, though safe, they've been parked uninvited at a neighbor's? And
then all her most precious possessions, gone![12] How are we to feel about
Moll's outsmarting these and other honest people, when such people could
just as well be us, our friends, clients, patrons, employees, or relatives? The
fact that Moll's victims come from all levels of society means that practically everyone who could afford the price of the book would have been in a
position to ask such questions. All these episodes (except perhaps that at
the gaming house) involve great dangers for Moll, but readers would have
seen these dangers in a context complicated by their awareness of her
victims' viewpoints, some of which would have been all too easy to share.[13]

[12] My point about the children being left uninvited at the neighbor's may sound farfetched, but it
is raised by Moll herself as she reflects on how "surpriz'd and afflicted" her victim would be to
find "that she had been deceiv'd . . . and that the Person that took her Children and her Goods,
had not come, as was pretended, from the Gentlewoman in the next Street, but that the
Children had been put upon her without her own knowledge." This, too, inasmuch as it
imposes on the civility of good neighbors – "they took the Children in very civily, pitied the
Family in Distress, and away came I with my Bundle," says Moll – forms part of the
"inhumanity of this Action" (206–7).

[13] Moll's theft from the burning house should by itself have been enough to bring readers over to
her victims' point of view. In an essay on the horrendously "frequent" house fires of London, a
writer styling himself "Philanthropus" excoriates those who can witness such events with "no
manner of Uneasiness." The very worst such people, he adds, are those who "reap . . .
Advantage" from these "Losses and Misfortunes": "such a Man has removed himself, as far as
it is in his Power, from his own Species, and got as near as he can, to be upon the Level with the
Beasts of *Prey*[;] that there are such savage Creatures, is . . . . a Scandal to Mankind"
(Applebee's *Original Weekly Journal*, 4 April 1730). An arsonist who stole goods out of a
merchant's house after setting it on fire confessed "himself guilty of a double Sin in committing
the Robbery at the Time the Family was in the greatest Terror and Confusion" (*A Genuine
Narrative of the Lives, Characters, and Trials of the Four Following Malefactors: viz. James Cotes, for a
Highway-Robbery; Richard William Vaughan, for Forging and Counterfeiting Bank-Notes . . . ; William
Stevens for Stealing . . . Woolen Cloth . . . ; and William Boodger for Forging an Inland Bill of Exchange*
[1758], p. 30). The victimized family's gratitude would also have had a certain effect. A thief
who made a practice of stealing from milliners – "women being less on their guard than men,
and always delighted with any one who will hear them prate and chatter" – and who found
himself on many occasions "treated with extraordinary marks of civility and politeness," said
that this "sometimes has squeezed my heart a little, but I was too far gone on the road of
perdition to think of returning back" (Charles Speckman, *The Life, Travels, Exploits, Frauds and
Robberies of Charles Speckman . . . Executed at Tyburn . . . the 23d of November 1763* [1763], p. 7).
Though Moll's heart is squeezed some by the "inhumanity" of her act, "the Reflection wore
off" (206–7). Not long after, in a second effort at stealing from a burning house, she gets

These instances of dialogue have a double effect, including readers as listeners in an "opened" narrative but making them at the same time all the more aware how much they stand apart, as silent, unobserved observers. The dialogues suggest a familiar world from which one is nonetheless excluded; to any two-party interactions they describe, the reader makes a third. The effect of this, and its potential value, can be seen quite clearly in Moll's account of her liaison with the baronet she picks up at Bartholomew Fair. This episode gets even more space than her victimization of the mercer and his journeyman, being in fact the longest single episode in her life as a criminal. It has a specific moral, and is clearly designed to push the reader into a viewpoint superior to that of any of the principals involved. When Moll tells her governess what they did in the coach and how she robbed him, her story, however implausibly, brings Moll's mentor nearly to tears. The governess is doubly pleased, she tells Moll, first for the loot but second because the experience "may do more to reform him, than all the Sermons that ever he will hear in his Life" (228). In a way the episode stands in the same relation to the reader, too, being as good as a sermon but more effective. What the baronet did with Moll was his "worst action," he tells the governess in a long central dialogue, his moral regrets compounded by fears of blackmail and venereal disease (232). When the governess assures him, however, that Moll is both clean and convenient, he loses little time in repeating his "worst action." His relapse, fool that he is, will seem all the more repugnant as readers regard it with a knowledge he doesn't and never will have. Moll is "past the Merry Part of Life," she has already said, and before he arrives for his second go 'round she tells us something else; for the first time in her life she is using paint. Whether he observes it or not, and it makes no apparent difference to his lust, the baronet is held in the embrace of a cold and aging whore (226, 235–6).

Moll's encounter with the mercer and his journeyman seems far more ambiguous in its intent, but then it is far more complex and has hardly so specific a "message" to communicate. Its "message," if anything, *is* its complexity. Around the two main actors, Moll and the mercer, cluster various auxiliaries, first his employees and later Moll's lawyer, governess, and hired suitor. The clustering is especially noticeable in the first part of the episode, as the three-way interplay between Moll, the mercer, and his journeyman comes under the separate regard of the constable, a crowd, the magistrate, and eventually the mob. In the course of a few pages eight separate speakers contribute to the ongoing action, seven of them present at once. These include Moll, the mercer, and the journeyman of course, plus the constable, a porter, two other journeymen, and, finally, the

squeezed more thoroughly by a mattress thrown out a window; "nor did the People concern themselves much to deliver me from it, or to recover me at all" (223–4). Poor Moll!

magistrate. During these few pages, moreover, the action is practically at all points trialogic, as first one threesome, then another, is formed out of the repertoire of individuals present, Moll being usually included but not always (there is one interaction she merely observes, where the mercer encourages his journeyman to resist arrest).

Nothing quite like this takes place in the book before or after. Though Moll's interactions with the family in Colchester involve her in at least two "triangles," and are, psychologically at least, far more complicated and nuanced than anything happening here, they are not as fast-moving or condensed. Nor do they – and this is most important – involve her in three-way dialogues. Moll never converses with both brothers at once (an interesting possibility which Defoe ignores), nor with either one of the brothers and anyone else in the family (it would have been almost as interesting to hear her speak with Robin and Robin's mother at the same time). Moll's relations with her husband/brother and mother/mother-in-law in Virginia are nearly as complex as with the family in Colchester, but there are no three-way conversations here, either; indeed, husband and mother never seem present at the same time. Trialogue does briefly take place when Moll, Jemy, and Jemy's supposed sister (actually his whore) realize the match they've just made is gone bust, but the "sister" doesn't say much. Even when Moll and the governess team up against the baronet, it might be noted, each shakes the man down separately. It is only in this affair of Moll and the mercer, then, that Defoe really introduces third and even fourth "actors" into the flow of his narrative. The effect is not so spectacular as Sophocles' great innovation – nor am I suggesting that Defoe is the first English novelist to write trialogue – but it is nonetheless curiously powerful. A great deal is put before the reader at once, and it is wonderfully multi-dimensional. The novel's "field of play" is enlarged exponentially, and so, too, the reader's opportunity to range imaginatively over the issues and questions it sets into motion. In any trialogue, after all, there are potentially six – even nine – different dialogues.[14]

The trialogic character of the episode involving Moll, the mercer, and his journeyman, along with the constable, the magistrate, and the mob, tends to make it especially difficult for readers to fix their attention solely on Moll or indeed on any of the other figures involved. Too much is going on in this three-ring circus for any one act, any one performer, to become a single focus of interest. The main performers in any case are each doing

[14] Thus in any set A,B,C, there are these three possible dyads: A–B, B–C, A–C, plus these three further combinations of two vs. one: AB–C, AC–B, BC–A. Each dyad, moreover, may be situated vis-à-vis a non-participating third, thus: (A–B) C, (A–C) B, (B–C) A. These last groupings would include conversations between any two of the parties that are overheard or otherwise observed by the third.

more than one thing at a time. As Moll's gameplan unfolds, her behavior toward the mercer and his journeyman undergoes a transformation; her differing behaviors toward each, however, are not seen simply by themselves but as each registers against the other. The mercer seems more sincere, but his behavior, too, has a double orientation insofar as he seeks to placate Moll for his own sake and to ease his journeyman's difficulties. Attempting to appease Moll in the presence of his employer, the journeyman for his part is likely acting at the latter's direction and to please him as well. My view of all this complexity is that it tends to encourage a certain disinterested attention. Because so much is going on, and because so little of it allows for simple interpretation, readers are kept from investing too much of themselves in a single character or interaction. As fascinating as Moll's encounter with the mercer and his journeyman may have been to eighteenth-century readers, Defoe's manner of presenting it would have prompted so many different points of view that it would have been hard to privilege any one in particular. How and why this should bear on the "scandal" of "business" – or, more largely, on the moral confusions of an increasingly commercial, i.e., modern society – will eventually be addressed.

Moll's encounter with the mercer and his journeyman has much greater emblematic potential than her encounter with the baronet. It doesn't at all, however, preach so clear and neat a sermon. The baronet's fate shows how ripe men like him are for plucking in a world where there are Molls; in absconding with his purse, wig, and sword, she almost literally (and certainly symbolically) takes him apart. His inability to control his physical appetites leads him to risk his bodily health and domestic happiness, to say nothing of his own good opinion of himself and perhaps something of the world's. The "hot-brain'd" mercer and his far less equable journeyman risk a great deal more, however, in not being able to control their tempers. The mercer risks, in fact, being reduced to the level of his journeyman, an altogether too intemperate character whose lack of self-control may be read as both a cause and symptom of his failure to achieve and maintain himself as an independent businessman. Moll winds up rubbing the journeyman's nose in the dirt of his own insignificance. It is a nice question who is morally worse, the journeyman or the baronet. Morally speaking, the mercer is clearly superior to them both; no matter, though. The baronet remains securely a baronet whatever else may happen; it is an inherited and inalienable privilege. Self-made man that he is, the mercer is what he is, and remains what he is, only through constant self-management. For this reason Moll threatens him far more than she does the baronet; it's not just his livelihood that's at stake but, as the fate of the journeyman shows, his sense of identity.

After the actual thief has been caught, the mercer tells Moll "very civily he was sorry for the mistake," and seeks to explain it by saying "they had so many things of this nature put upon them every Day" that he and his people could hardly help being suspicious (244). Moll is not at all moved by this, and, later, when he makes a long speech before the magistrate to much the same effect, she dismissively calls it a "Harangue" (247). For Defoe, however, and no doubt many in his audience, the mercer's complaint would have had some resonance. "Such is the slippery dealings of this age," he was to write in *The Complete English Tradesman*, "especially in mercers and drapers business, that the shop-keeper ought never to turn his back towards his customers; and this is the reason why the mercers and drapers in particular are oblig'd to keep so many journey-men, and so many apprentices in their shops, which were it not for the danger of shop-lifting, wou'd be a needless, as it is a heavy, expence to them" (1 [Supplement]: 44). Keeping shop could be an immensely difficult and ticklish business, requiring a great deal of alertness as well as self-control; it could also produce great psychic stress.

Defoe illustrates these points in a variety of ways. He supposes, for instance, a case where "a good customer," i.e., one the shopkeeper and his assistants "know and are satisfy'd in," wants to make a purchase. At such a time the journeyman serving her may have "on either hand a set of strange faces, tumbling and turning over his goods, and perhaps not yet determining whether they shall *buy* or *steal*." "Seeing his journey-man oppress'd with a crowd," the prudent shopkeeper ought to respond "like a General engag'd in a battle, ready to send troops to the assistance of any part of his army that may be overpower'd" (*CET*, 1 [Supplement]: 44–5). The military metaphor applies only so far, however, for the operation must be accomplished with tact as well as dexterity. Not only is the shopkeeper's property at stake, but his reputation, and the latter was in fact only a more fragile kind of property. Customers, Defoe points out, could be exceedingly touchy. Those ladies tumbling the goods might very well be honest, and could take offence should any indication be given they were under suspicion. London was not so big in Defoe's time that tradesmen could afford to offend anyone who might bring custom, or take it away. "In this gossiping Tea-drinking age," Defoe warns, "'tis not to be imagined how ... scandal will run, even among people who have had no knowledge of the person first complaining" (*CET*, 1: 86ff.).

Little wonder, then, that the mercer wants to patch things up with Moll outside of court. Enough damage has been done already. "Which is the Rogue? which is the Mercer?" the crowd cries as he goes along with Moll to the magistrate, in both cases meaning him, "especially the Women ... and every now and then came a good dab of Dirt at him" (246). In allowing his temper to get only the slightest bit the better of him, the mercer has put himself in a very bad spot. "The man that stands behind the counter," Defoe advises, "must be all courtesy, civility, and good manners" – even, it seems, when he suspects the people in his shop are robbing him. "A Tradesman behind his counter," Defoe urges, "must have no flesh and blood about him, no passions, no resentment . . . . 'tis his business to be ill used and resent nothing . . . . he must be all soft and smooth; nay, if his real temper be naturally fiery and hot, he must show none of it in his shop; he must be a perfect *complete hypocrite*, if he will be a *complete tradesman*" (*CET*, 1: 86, 85, 94).

The tradesman, in other words, can never quite be a whole, authentic person in and of himself; the self-discipline that makes him a "complete" homo economicus threatens, by its very nature, his larger identity as a social and moral being. Surveying a number of instances where this is the case, *The Complete English Tradesman* shows how business may require the suppression of what normally would seem not bad but good or generous instincts. The tradesman cannot, for example, pay too much attention to religious matters without having business suffer; too frequent a wish to pray, Defoe suggests, might actually be a temptation from the devil (*CET*, 1: 52–4). Though tradesmen have a duty to teach their apprentices the essential elements of their trade, they must be careful, too, not to teach them *too* well; they may become one's future business rivals (*CET*, 1: 12–13, 146–50). Nowhere, however, does Defoe more effectively describe the individual human cost of the tradesman's self-discipline than when he speaks, at length, of men he knows who have trained themselves up "by custom and usage" so that "nothing could be meeker and milder than they, when behind the counter, and yet nothing ... more furious and raging in every other part of life." What he has to say is so powerful, and so lurid, that it warrants extensive quotation:

nay, the provocations [such men] have met with in their shops have so irritated their rage, that they would go up stairs from their shop, and fall into frenzies, and a kind of madness, and beat their heads against the wall, and perhaps mischief themselves, if not prevented, till the violence of it had gotten vent, and the passions abate and cool. I heard once of a shop-keeper that behav'd himself thus to such an extreme, that when he was provok'd by the impertinence of the customers, beyond what his temper could bear, he would go up stairs and beat his wife, kick his children about like dogs, and be as furious for two or three minutes, as a man chain'd down in *Bedlam*; and again, when that heat was over, would sit down and cry faster than the children he had abused; and after the fit he would go down into his shop again, and be as humble, as courteous, and as calm as any man whatever; so absolute a government of his passions had he in the shop, and so little out of it; in the shop a soul-less animal that could resent nothing, and in the family a madman; in the shop meek like the lamb, but in the family outrageous like a Lybian lion.

Defoe does not condemn such behavior, seeming merely to set it out as an instance of how far some people have had to go to "subject" themselves to their "business." "The sum of the matter is this," he concludes:

it is necessary for a Tradesman to subject himself, by all the ways possible, to his business; his customers are to be his idols: so far as he may worship idols by allowance, he is to bow down to them, and worship them; at least, he is not any way to displease them, or shew any disgust or distaste whatsoever they may say or do; the bottom of it all is, that he is intending to get money by them; and it is not for him that gets money to offer the least inconvenience to them by whom he gets it.   (*CET*, 1: 94–5)

This straightforward, matter-of-fact laying out of the implications of the cash nexus – particularly the "subjection" (or *asujetissement*) it requires – can easily be taken to describe more than just the predicament of shop-keepers. In its light one rereads Defoe's solicitous, even fawning letters to his political masters with new interest, wondering at his state of mind as he tried to sell them on one or another of his ideas or projects. In a world of buying and selling – where buying and selling can stand as a metaphor for most public life – practically everyone trades on his personality, that is to say constructs and maintains a public persona (often at considerable variance from what is – or seems – really his own) in order to get his business done. However much he may value himself as a free individual, or a social individual, he is obliged to participate in this parody of true social interaction. It is not possible to be autonomous or authentic; that would require the achieving of a position somehow outside the world of buying and selling. And all the while it is necessary to keep swallowing the rage there is every reason to feel, given the constraints of one's situation; letting it out unseasonably might interfere with business. The psychic tensions implicit in all this may explain something of the attractions of *Robinson Crusoe*, as well, too, as the recurrent fascination with stories of tradesmen who, abandoning their shops and all concern with customer satisfaction, took to robbing on the highway.[15]

Though the novel does not probe too deeply into it, there is much more to this affair of Moll and the mercer than meets Moll's eye or may, at first, meet the modern reader's. Like all those others mentioned in chapter 3, the mercer has his story, too; like theirs, his might be told in a variety of ways. One way – and this immediately begins to raise problems – would be to try to make it into a simple cautionary tale, like the baronet's. Under the pressures of the moment, the mercer has forgot himself and jeopard-

---

[15] For tradesmen turned highwaymen, see *Turned to Account*, pp. 119, 252–3. Very interestingly, at one point in *The Complete English Tradesman* Defoe compares the young businessman sent out into "the world" insufficiently prepared by his apprenticeship to "a man out of a ship set ashore among Savages, who instead of feeding, are indeed more ready to eat him up and devour him" (1: 13). Crusoe's landing on a *desert* island, it seems, is no small part of his luck.

ized his status; because a tradesman has no business being "hot-brain'd," he loses out to the cool-headed Moll. She in fact proves better at her trade than he at his, getting top dollar for rather shoddy merchandise (her reputation) and leaving him (the more fool he) more or less pleased at the transaction. Moll has not allowed personal feeling to distract her from the main object, which is making money, while the mercer and his journey-man have; she is the better "hypocrite." In terms of the hard but necessary ethics of the business world, they have gotten what each of them deserves.

This is quite a different lesson from that to be learned from the baronet's predicament, and – quite apart from the unattractiveness of the ethic it relies on – not at all a comfortable one. Controlling physical appetites may not be easy, but the assumption is that it brings clear social and personal benefits and makes one generally a better person. Controlling your temper even under severe provocation, so as not to damage your livelihood, may make one *seem* a better person but – as Defoe so vividly demonstrates – underneath the smooth-seeming surface may lie a fractured personality, utterly at odds with itself and all that it loves best. One may veer between "madness" and "soullessness" and still be a good tradesman – indeed may need to do as much in order to be a good tradesman – which is to say one may be a good tradesman without feeling at all like or being a good person. The baronet's moral universe may not necessarily be simpler than the mercer's, but it is simpler to deal with. It is easier in his case to know what constitutes good conduct; one has more solid underpinnings for one's sense of identity.

But even setting these considerations aside (though I'll want to return to them later), the mercer's encounter with Moll resists "simple" construing. A good deal more is at stake here than the getting and giving up of money, and one can't quite measure who wins, who loses, and to what extent justice has been done, in only these terms. The constable, the magistrate, and even the mob raise the idea of a very different kind of justice – as does Moll, too, though only to exploit it. From this standpoint, there is much about the mercer's situation that can seem regrettable, unfair, undeserved. Given the true facts of the case (which no one but Moll and the reader can know) the man should not have been rebuked by the magistrate (at least not so strongly) nor called "rogue" or pelted with stones and dirt by the mob. If he has not acted well, neither has he done so badly as it appears to the world at large. Still, the fact that he comes around to suffering his embarrassment with good grace might tend, too, to mitigate the exigency of his situation, or at least not to play it up to the point where he seems grossly victimized. What happens to him is far from the worst thing Moll has done (remember the woman at the burning house, the child in the alley), and the mercer is a good loser. That the affair costs him only 200 pounds may seem even a victory of sorts, measured against the governess's prediction that it will cost 500. Moll's encounter with the mercer is not only multifaceted, but played out in a complicated sequence: Moll down, then up and triumphant; the mercer up, then down, but not down and out.

The reader's sense of the mercer's situation at the end of the episode might also be shaped by the fate of Moll's other main victim. He and the journeyman both come off badly against her, but the master does considerably better than his employee. The mercer may be "hot-brain'd," as Moll says, but he is also able to behave "civily"; nothing indeed could be more "civil" than his closing gesture of throwing a gown and a supper into the bargain he makes with Moll. The journeyman, however, can manage no such equability, no such grand gesture reconfirming his (masculine, it might be specified) strength and importance. Seeing he has no money, Moll gives him scant attention. Nonetheless, unknowingly and without caring to know, she actually extorts a great deal from him. The journeyman is, to be sure, an unattractive character: impulsive, surly, shortsighted, short-tempered, all bad qualities in a person but especially in a tradesman. He takes advantage of Moll, feeling her up under pretence of searching her because, as he wrongly thinks, she is in no position to complain. When the constable moves to arrest him, he resists and is knocked down, getting himself into further trouble and allowing the real thief to escape in the confusion. The journeyman has less excuse than the mercer for his "mistakes," his being not only more numerous and egregious but apparently less well-motivated; it is not his shop, after all. Why is the man so officiously self-important? Is this an instance of the worm turning? Or, in Defoe's language, of a "soulless animal" seeking "vent"?

Still, there are aspects to the journeyman's situation that keep him from seeming utterly antipathetic. In the first place, Moll is no innocent victim; she was not "innocently going along the Street" as she claims. Besides, she reciprocates in good measure, spitting in his face and getting him arrested; the man really is outmatched. Reduced to looking "like a condemn'd Thief," committed to Newgate and requiring to be bailed out by his master, he may even begin to generate some sympathy; perhaps Moll is carrying things too far. Coming to collect her money for having been treated like the thief she is, she learns he has "a Wife and several Children," is "very poor," and has "nothing to make satisfaction with." The man faces two assault charges and, if Moll sues him for damages, the prospect of debtor's prison. So now, though he had once "kept a Shop of his own, and been in good Business" (it's easy to guess why things changed), he offers to beg Moll's pardon "on his Knees" as "openly" as she pleases. Moll accepts this compliment, taking it, she tells her reader, as a sign of his "mean Humility" and "compleat baseness of Spirit." He was "imperious, cruel, and relentless when Uppermost, and in Prosperity," she says, but "abject and low Spirited when Down in Affliction." "However," she adds, "I abated his Cringes, told him I forgave him, and desir'd he might withdraw, as if I did not care for the sight of him, tho' I had forgiven him."

In this comment alone rather a great deal is being advanced for the reader's consideration. In the first place, there is the question of Moll's own state of mind. Is she now indifferent to the journeyman, or does she dislike him still, or for new and different reasons? The affair has long since come to seem a business deal to her; is some residual emotion stirring? The "as if" is peculiarly ambiguous. Obviously the phrase indicates a feigned distaste for the man, but does it govern the last clause of that last sentence, too? Is Moll feigning forgiveness, also? She may be relapsing once more into an indifference toward the journeyman, or pretending to have conquered a resentment while at the same time she conceals a deeper, newly stimulated revulsion. This ambiguity prevents any easy acceptance of Moll's point of view, for, of course, in order to accept it, readers would first have to determine it. And even if this finally could be done, the time spent on the process itself would tend to influence reader response, slowing down consideration of the episode just as it concludes. If Moll's final description of the journeyman confirms the bad impression he originally gave, the text in the meanwhile has given readers a chance to set that initial impression aside; and here there is a chance to rethink it. It is possible, after all, that the journeyman's bullying manner and general officiousness may have something to do with his own failed business, his cringing abjectness with his concern for his family.

Whatever the case, Moll has succeeded in puncturing the man's self-esteem without wanting or caring to; she leaves him more bereft than the drunken baronet half naked in his hackney coach. That she is the most recent disaster in the journeyman's life means "nothing" to her, nor does the emotional cost of the submission he offers with such great trepidation. Moll cares only for cash value. But then how should anyone so alone in the world, so oblivious to the threat of disgrace and imprisonment, conceive what prison might mean to a more or less honest man, with a family? In her treatment of the journeyman, Moll herself escapes seeming "imperious, cruel, and relentless" only because she doesn't care. And later, caught red-handed at the silkdealer's, and then pleading for her life at her trial, she escapes seeming "abject and low-spirited" only because her apologies are insincere and opportunistic. How much better is she than the mercer's journeyman? How much worse? Such questions cannot be definitively answered. Two antithetical value systems are at issue, business ethics (almost though not quite in Defoe's view an oxymoron) vs. "ordinary" ethics, and the conflict between them allows for a number of both "long" and "short" views. In triumphing over anger and fear, Moll proves better at wheeling and dealing than the journeyman or his master, but she also transcends shame, pity, and the simple human decencies that, in others, put them in a position that allows her to exploit them. In this respect the constable, the magistrate, and even the mob number among her victims. Furthermore, though Moll succeeds beautifully over the short term, who is to say that over the long run – retiring from her "trade" with 700 or 800 pounds and a one-way ticket to Virginia – she does better in her line of work than the mercer in his, or even the journeyman?

Once again this is to point to the ways Defoe's fiction keeps the mind in play; the weighing of Moll against her various victims is fraught with rich implications. The mercer and the journeyman are not easily categorized – the latter may finally be pitiable, but he's still a jerk – nor of course is Moll. The complexity of their interrelations and interactions is made especially clear by the contributions of the constable, the magistrate, and the mob to one's sense of what has actually happened. Each separately judges Moll to have been badly treated. Each, however, has only seen a fraction of the whole, and none knows Moll as the reader does. Their sympathies are misplaced, but then neither the mercer nor the journeyman quite deserves or needs sympathy. They suffer no great damage and in fact learn valuable lessons, while Moll, richer, more emboldened, becomes that much stupider and readier to fall. The misplaced sympathies of the various spectators make it seem that no particular sympathy for anyone involved is warranted, nor should any single point of view – except perhaps the reader's own – be privileged. As a whole, I'd suggest, Moll's encounter with the mercer and his journeyman finally invites neither sympathy nor antipathy, nor even judgment. The complex and shifting actions it displays are fascinating but best observed in a state of readerly abstraction; in this respect, the cooptation of the constable and the magistrate is especially monitory. Both these functionaries are admirably fair-minded and represent (at least in this instance) the best values of their society; still, they are no more percipient than the mob, which stands for the worst. Knowing better than they, knowing what is truly the case, the reader in the enjoyment of his readerly perspective stands *magister magistratum*.

The difficulties of siding simply with Moll or her victims, plus the sheer inadequacy of the viewpoint taken by the various representatives of society, tend, I'd suggest, to disaffiliate the reader not only from Moll but the whole transaction. Aligned with neither thief nor tradesmen, nor with those called upon (or volunteering) to judge the differences between them, the reader can escape the situation's "meaning" (whatever that may be). An effect parallel to that of criminal rogue biography is achieved, where high-spirited but empty gestures, grotesque comedy and Grand Guignol, promiscuous irony and unfollowable plots free one from feeling much of anything for thieves or their victims, or practically from thinking at all. But not by the same impoverishing means, nor to the same impoverishing ends. Here – encouraged to open wide the avenues of their minds, not shut them down to avoid their being choked with garbage or unbearable traffic – readers are given occasion to become (or at least feel like) disinterested observers. Art, said Henry James, offers "a miraculous enlargement of experience," permitting us to feel "for the time that we have lived another life." In this case, however, the feeling ought not to be confused with vicarious identification. Defoe's complex display of relations between Moll and her several victims is not designed to bring us into any of their lives, though these seem real enough; quite the contrary. The reader absorbed in the special pleasure of the text, according to Barthes, is "someone who abolishes within himself all barriers, all classes, all exclusions." Or, as Wolfgang Iser says, in the act of reading "we are preoccupied with something that takes us out of our own given reality"; "given," I'd say, is the operative word.[16]

In his preface to *Colonel Jack*, Defoe suggests the novel is something like a herb garden, "a delightful Field for the reader to wander in . . . where he may gather wholesome and medicinal Plants" (2). To the extent his audience shared Defoe's discomfort at "the general Scandal upon Business," to the extent they felt entailed by a world where everyone engaged in the exchange of goods and services might be called "knaves" (or, as the mercer discovers, "rogues"), they might have found something therapeutic in the distance *Moll Flanders* allows from such a world, and the special perspective it provides on it. In describing Moll's crimes the text comes very close to raising the nastier implications of economic individualism, but it keeps the two from bleeding together by promoting a certain objectivity in the reader and a high degree of discrimination. To balance out those "nice distinctions" between "honest men" and "honest tradesmen" which so vexed Defoe, it encourages the seeing and considering of equally "nice" distinctions between a full-fledged thief and the tradesmen she variously exploits. Thus the interactions between Moll and her victims in this particular episode show there are different degrees of complicity in the specious ways of the world, and that those who buy, sell, etc., are not so bad as those who take and give "nothing" in return. It also encourages its readers to see that all tradesmen are not alike in the way they do business, suggesting a scale of behavior which ranges from the scrupulous fair-mindedness of the constable, himself a cornchandler, to the sometimes "hot-brain'd" mercer, to the exploitive and irascible journeyman, himself a failed shopkeeper. (Nor are all thieves alike, thus the difference between

16 Henry James, *Theory of Fiction*, ed. James E. Miller (Lincoln, Neb., 1972), p. 93; Roland Barthes, *The Pleasure of the Text*, tr. Richard Miller (New York, 1975), p. 3; Wolfgang Iser, *The Act of Reading* (Baltimore, 1978), p. 140, and see also p. 79.

Moll and the actual thief, who gets caught and escapes only by a stroke of luck.)

At most, though, the mere proliferating of such distinctions could only blur or "fuzz" the equation of trade with theft, making it harder to "see"; this is the sort of thing Defoe called "raising a Dust."[17] The text worked more powerfully, I'd suggest, by giving readers a chance to feel above and beyond such matters, "removed" from the equation and all that its problematic linkage implied. The various problems facing the mercer and his journeyman are similar not only to Moll's but to those of any reader trying to keep his head above water in a market economy. The need to compete to survive, the moral compromise this entails along with the inevitable cost to one's own sense of self, the threat one might falter financially and/or psychologically (for the two are terribly inter-dependent), the need to placate those in positions of power and authority: all these and more are agitated here. So long, however, as the reader is engaged in contemplating these matters disinterestedly, as problems impinging on others, they do not impinge on him. (He might even gain distance from the problems of trying to be disinterested, by considering the cases of the constable and the magistrate.) The "wholesome" and "medici-nal" value of such distancing would involve more than mere escape, however, an important point to be made in comparing Defoe's fiction to criminal rogue biography.

In imagining the world evoked by a text, Iser points out, we are "temporarily isolated from our real world." The value of this is that, "for a brief period at least, the real world appears observable . . . . Suddenly we find ourselves detached . . . able to perceive it as an object. And even if this detachment is only momentary, it may enable us," as we "awaken" from the text, "to . . . view our own world as a thing 'freshly understood.'"[18] In Defoe's time, such detachment from the exigencies of "the real" would have had more than simply aesthetic value. (Indeed the term "aesthetic" was yet to be invented.) As John Barrell has observed, an increasing premium was being put on writing that could offer "a 'panoramic' view of society," that could represent "as wide an 'expanse of life' as possible." Barrell relates this to the rising concern, documented by Pocock and others, about whether a basis for social and political order could be found in a polity where "self-interest" seemed increasingly a source of "corrup-tion." As British society became ever more "highly differentiated in terms, particularly, of occupation," says Barrell, there was an "increasing belief . . . that those whose living depends on their success in the specific occu-pation they practise will tend to place their own interests, or those of that occupation, before those of Britain as a whole." It was not at all easy to see

---

[17] Defoe, *The Secret History of the Secret History of the White Staff, Purse and Mitre* (1715), pp. 5, 31.
[18] Iser, *The Act of Reading*, p. 140.

how such men could practice the "civic virtue" supposedly available to the landed aristocracy. "A devotion of the self to the universal good," to quote Pocock himself, seemed something "only a highly autonomous self could perform," and such selves, it further seemed, could only develop in "a real and natural order" based on the possession of inherited, "real" and "natural" property. Given such assumptions, Pocock goes on to explain, "the rise of forms of property seeming to rest on fantasy and false consciousness" – that is to say, property "seen to have a symbolic value, expressed in coin or in credit" – brought with it "an element of existential fear." "The foundations of personality themselves appeared imaginary or at best consensual: the individual could exist, even in his own sight, only at the fluctuating value imposed upon him by his fellows."[19]

Just such a notion seems amply evident in the transactions that go on between Moll and the mercer and his journeyman. For all its very real difference from Moll Jones's actual swindle in 1691 (still a frequent sort of crime in 1722), the episode says, at base, very much the same sort of thing about a world where so much depends on "credit." Given the fact that a large part of the business of everyday life involves strangers sizing each other up, this is a world where appearance is as good as reality if it can be sustained. (If it can't, of course, some people go to jail and others feel cheated; and not always the right people go to jail.) Moll takes full advantage of this situation, passing herself off in a variety of guises that allow her to escape the boundaries of her sex and class; she visits Oxford as a countess in a coach and six, and steals, for a while, as a man. Such plasticity has been celebrated, for instance by John Richetti, who values Moll's ability to "overcom[e] the limitations of coherent psycho-social identity."[20] But it can have its downside, too. Moll can range as widely as she does only because she lives in a "slippery" world, one where people often don't really know each other and can't, but must nonetheless act as though they do. This, enhancing their sense of vulnerability, inevitably affects their sense of themselves; eventually it undermines even Moll.

Enough has already been said about the difficulties of living within these circumstances, and how, ranging from high to low, they could include not only shopkeepers dealing with actual or potential shoplifters but investors with stockjobbers and company directors, and the nation as a whole with placeholders and politicians. Given a social world comprised of competing subjectivities, and the inadequacy, not to say partiality, of any individual point of view, how could there be any notion of "the common good"? A "wide range" of mid-century writers representing "a variety of

19 John Barrell, *English Literature in History, 1730–80: An Equal, Wide Survey* (London, 1983), p. 14; Pocock, *The Machiavellian Moment*, pp. 484, 463, 463–4.
20 John Richetti, "The Family, Sex, and Marriage in Defoe's *Moll Flanders* and *Roxana*," *Studies in the Literary Imagination*, 15 (1982): 29.

political persuasions" addressed this question, Barrell argues, by trying "to negotiate for themselves a position from which they would describe, or argue for, the unity of a society apparently separated by the separation of trades and professions." Though they represented "a variety of political persuasions," all were "concerned to suggest" that this "position" was properly that of "the gentleman, in one form or another," who, because his virtues were not "defined . . . by his occupation," was "still adequate to the task of comprehending" the "complexity and variety" of social organization "as a unity." This effort at rescuing the notion of civic virtue, Barrell adds, was a way of supporting and preserving "the privileges and the authority . . . of the ruling class." Their "wide," "comprehensive," and disinterested "vision" of the social was meant to stand as the mark and warrant of their claim to hegemony.[21]

No such argument is extractable from *Moll Flanders*. Though Defoe believed that, of all men, "gentlemen" were the likeliest to have the widest, most capacious views, he was not especially interested either in "civic virtue" or in supporting the claims of a hereditary ruling class.[22] The baronet is a poor advertisement for either the disinterest or perspicacity of his kind. Nor can one find anything like a total, comprehensive view of the workings of society in Moll's narrative – insofar as it is Moll's, of course, one would hardly expect to find such a thing – though there are certainly frequent intimations of such a view in Defoe's commercial and political writings.[23] *Moll Flanders* does, however, provide rich opportunities for "recluse and solitary" readers – as by definition practically all readers of novels must be – to rise above "the busy swarm of vain Images which buzz about the Mind in the heat of a social State," above its "Passions," "Impertinences," and "Temptations," to a position where "the Understanding . . . represents Things to the Fancy, as they really are."[24] In this chance to take up a position of disinterested observation, readers may experience, whether they fancy themselves gentlemen or not, something like the supposed autonomous authority of gentlemen. No one on view in the episode of Moll and the mercer is as good at disinterested observation as they, not even the magistrate; no one, as I've already said, sees as much. Such a privileging of the reader *qua* reader involves, too, a privileging of

[21] John Barrell, *An Equal Wide Survey*, pp. 40, 33, 50.

[22] See, along with his surrounding commentary, Barrell's quoting of Defoe in *The Complete English Gentleman* on the tendency of a "scholastick education" or "trade" to "so fix a man in a particular way, that he is not fit to judge of any thing that lyes out of his way, and so his learning becomes a clog to his natural parts" (*CEG*, p. 216, as cited in *An Equal Wide Survey*, p. 33).

[23] On this subject see John Richetti, "The Novel and Society: The Case of Daniel Defoe," in *The Idea of the Novel in the Eighteenth Century*, ed. Robert W. Uphaus (E. Lansing, Mich., 1988), pp. 47–66.

[24] ?Defoe, *A Collection of Miscellany Letters Selected out of Mist's Weekly Journal* (1722–7), 4: 181–3; more extensively quoted, this passage stands as this chapter's fifth and longest epigraph.

him over all those involved in the episode. Their various senses of virtue, identity, and being are defined necessarily in terms of their relation to the rough and tumble of economic exchange; his, for the moment, is not. Barthes's "classless" reader pleasuring in the text may, after all, be only a bourgeois (or embourgeoisified) reader *sous rature* or, more simply, just *en vacances*. Still, insofar as he may feel he's abolished "within himself all barriers ... all exclusions," he may be able to escape the daunting sense – so hard, as Pocock says, on "the ego's confidence in its own integrity and reality" – that as an individual he exists, "even in his own sight, only at the fluctuating value imposed upon him by his fellows."[25]

Returning from his reclusive, solitary, seemingly autonomous experience of the world *Moll Flanders* projects – a world of complex interactions (even now) inevitably homologous to his own – the reader might almost seem his own little Robinson Crusoe, in a better position now, by virtue of his long isolation, to reflect upon, enlarge, and apply what he's experienced to "real life" as he goes on to live it. Something is obviously wrong if the pressures of business can make men behave so badly, and if the law, even when fairly administered, can go so oddly awry. Moll's false arrest – with all it involves and as the text prompts the reader to imagine it – might put a whole range of matters affecting him into clearer focus, which might then start him toward solving (at least for himself) some of the problems that come with living in a society that, opportunistic and money-centered, is immensely wearing on one's sense of self even as it encourages and rewards self-interest. Still, and here is an important difference from the serious form of criminal biography, Defoe's fiction requires no such thing. Beneficiaries of what might be called (to turn the jargon back on itself) a

---

[25] Pocock, *The Machiavellian Moment*, pp. 465, 464. In the sort of readerly affect/effect I'm describing, it might be possible to see an early example of something D. A. Miller believes to be a "fundamental" attribute of "the Novel, as a cultural institution," i.e., its encouragement of its reader into a state of mind – a "constitutive fantasy" – where he may luxuriate in the feeling that he, at least, enjoys "an integral, autonomous, 'secret,' self":

> Novel reading takes for granted the existence of a space in which the reading subject remains safe from the surveillance, suspicion, reading, and rape [figurative or literal] of others. Yet this privacy is always specified as the freedom to read about characters who oversee, suspect, read, and rape one another .... We enjoy our privacy in the act of watching privacy being violated, in the act of watching that is already itself a violation of privacy. Our most intense identification with characters never blinds us to our ontological privilege over them: they will never be reading about *us*.

For Miller, writing about mid-nineteenth-century novels and powerfully influenced by Foucault, the novel-reader's peculiar privacy and privilege confer a sort of "panoptic immunity," it being "built into the structure of the Novel that every reader must realize the definitive fantasy of the liberal subject, who imagines himself free from the surveillance that he nonetheless sees operating everywhere around him" (*The Novel and the Police* [Berkeley, 1988], p. 162). Whether Miller is right or not about "the liberal subject," "surveillance," the nineteenth century, or "the Novel" with a big "N," the "ontological privilege" *Moll Flanders* confers would of course have to be very differently defined, given the undeniable fact that it precedes all these things, even "the liberal subject."

"*re*interpellative" encounter with the text, products of a "*counter*-assujetiss-ement," readers are put in a position (a reading position, to be sure) where they're free to remain innocent bystanders, undogged by any feeling that if not part of some solution they must be part of some problem. The text from which this chapter's longest epigraph is taken, after talking about the need for leisure and solitude to see "Things . . . as they really are," goes on to quote certain coffee-house "*Literati*" who "affirm, till they are black in the Face, 'That it's impossible for any Man to be honest, who has Rogues to deal with, that a Man's Interest is to be the Measure of his Actions; that the Necessity of Affairs is an Excuse for any Thing.'" Though this writer (and it may be Defoe I'm quoting) understands the basis for such feelings, he refuses to share them. "It is from [such] Mens walking so much in the Dust of publick Life," he says, "that they don't see the Absurdity of their own Notions."[26] Alone with his book, the reader of *Moll Flanders* might want only to kick that dust from his heels, to stretch, like any leisured gentleman, his legs down the new, "delightful" perspectives its "garden" supplies.

Such may have been (at least in part) the effect of *Moll Flanders*; we cannot know for sure, of course. If we stick only to the text before us, the most we can claim is that it keeps a tension up between Moll and its reader, and that this tension comes not only from his relation to her but from his relation to her relation with others. Sometimes these relationships get very intricate. That they achieve so high a degree of complexity when her victims are tradesmen, however, seems to me significant, as does the fact that tradesmen figure so infrequently among her "realized" victims and are introduced so late, after so much else will have shaped readers' attitudes. Shoplifting, after all, is one of Moll's great pastimes. There seems, too, some teasing meaning in the fact that shopkeepers are the targets of her last two criminal attempts. Here again there is trialogue, though the effect is somewhat different, the dramatic interaction being less complex and encouraging less objectivity and balance. The man across the way from the goldsmith's is impetuous and awkward, and so makes a bad collar. But the alderman who intervenes and settles the matter is quite shrewd and nearly catches Moll out; she is lucky to get off. When Moll tells the silkdealer a hastily concocted sob story, he and his wife are almost fool enough to let her go, but his shopgirls insist she be arrested and are right to do so. Moll calls them "sawcy Wenches" and "hard Hearted," "hard Mouth'd Jades." She can't understand why they refuse a hundred pounds not to appear against her, when three pounds is about all they'd earn in a year (273, 276, 284).

[26] ?Defoe, *Miscellany Letters*, 4: 181–2.

Here, particularly, readers should feel the great gulf that has opened up between Moll and them, even as they may believe they've grown accustomed to her. For these shopgirls, at least, there is no difference between honesty in the ordinary meaning and honesty in trade; in this respect, they might just be the most moral people in the whole book, or rather the most simply and clearly moral. Perhaps, by stopping Moll as they do, they offer a more direct and even somewhat romantic response to "the general scandal upon trade." Certainly, being single-minded and pure of heart, they are a credit to their *métier*. But why – I have no certain answer – do we find this ethical simplicity in shopgirls, and nowhere else in the world of buying and selling? Is it because they stand only at the threshold (too literally in Moll's case, for they catch her going out the door) of the commercial world? In their simple knowledge of what is right and wrong and how they should act upon such knowledge, they, too, stand apart (though in a way quite opposite to that I've been imagining) from the ambiguities and ambivalences of a social world where nothing seems clear or immediately the case, certainly not virtue, where artifice can be taken for actual fact, where people's identities can rest on nothing more than the "credit" they give each other, the confidence one can sustain in oneself.

Whatever the fate of all such speculations, the fact remains that in dialogue, and especially trialogue, Defoe discovered means to keep his criminal protagonists always before his reader's eyes as dynamic figures, rich in potential meaning. Even Singleton becomes interesting by virtue of his association with the casuistical and split-tongued Quaker William. Dialogue plays an important part in *Colonel Jack* and *Roxana* as well, though in these novels there is nothing like the exquisite equilibrium achieved out of multiple points of view that I find in the episode of Moll's false arrest. Both present episodes of comparable dialogic complexity, but their affect is more tendentious, a matter that will concern us in chapter 7. In the next chapter, shifting attention from *Moll Flanders* to *Colonel Jack*, my concern will be not the thief vis-à-vis his or her victims, but the various social, political, and economic functions Defoe makes one of his thieves assume. Here I have been interested in "fine" textures; there the focus will be on larger, wider-ranging structural features. Having the luck to be about God's providence – if actually it is "about" anything at all besides its protagonist – *Moll Flanders* remains an open, various, and yet more or less coherent text. *Colonel Jack* and *Roxana* are not so happy in their programmatic tendencies. Pressed to say what these novels are "about," I would suggest that *Colonel Jack* is a meditation on the situation of men in a commercial society nostalgic for the values of its past but in need of a new ethos to deal with its changed situation. It is a confused and confusing book because that ethos – call it ideology, if you will – is not yet available. *Roxana*, which among other things seems to me to illustrate a particular psychology of deviance, risks on the other hand being almost too programmatic, too narrow and defined. The next two chapters will elaborate on each of these admittedly cryptic descriptions.

6

The frontiers of dishonesty, the addition and concurrence of circumstances: more on the strategic situating of names

Custom indeed has driven us beyond the limits of our morals in many things, which trade makes necessary, and which we cannot now avoid; so that if we pretend to go back to the literal sense of the command, if our yea must be yea, and our nay nay; if no man must go beyond, or defraud his neighbour; if our conversation must be without covetousness, and the like, why then it is impossible for tradesmen to be Christians, and we must unhinge all business, act upon new principles in trade, and go on by new rules: in short, we must shut up shop, and leave off trade, and so in many things we must leave off living .... But this is a subject would launch me out beyond the bounds of a letter, and make a book by itself.

The Complete English Tradesman, 1: 234–5

There is ... little visible Difference between the lawful Applications of Industry and Business, and the unlawful Desires after exorbitant Wealth .... getting Money is so general a Duty, that it seems to be one of the Ends of Life; how then shall we distinguish the Vertue from that Extreme? And where are the Bounds between the Duty and the Crime? The Confines of Virtue reach to the Frontiers of Vice, and where this ends that begins.

Defoe, the *Commentator*, No. 46 (10 June 1720)

Disputes about what is or is not honesty are dangerous to honesty itself, for no case can be doubtful which does not border upon the frontiers of dishonesty.

Serious Reflections of Robinson Crusoe, pp. 33–4

Something struck me with a kind of Wish ... that I might leave off that curs'd Trade; and [I] said to my self, O! that I had some Trade to live by, I would never rob no more.

Colonel Jack, p. 83

Writing upon trade ... was the whore I really doated upon.

The *Review*, [9]: 214b (11 June 1713)

It is certainly true, that few things in nature are simply unlawful and dishonest, but that all crime is made so by the addition and concurrence of circumstances.

The Complete English Tradesman, 1: 241

By itself the first fourth of *Colonel Jack* would stand as a brilliant revision of
standard criminal biography. Some paragraphs might have come little
altered from actual accounts, but others offer a vivid, sympathetic picture
of social and economic deprivation practically unmatched by anything
else in eighteenth-century literature. In passages like Jack's description of
being rousted out of the warm glasshouse ashbeds in the middle of the
night (9–10), we see the "lives of the indigent Vulgar" (to quote Mandeville again), so many of which were "sport[ed] away" at each month's
sessions.[1] My concern here, however, is not with just one part but with all
the novel and how, in its entirety if not its "wholeness," it constitutes a far
larger, more sweeping revision of criminal biography – or, rather, of the
tactics criminal biography typically used in trying to deal with the social
and political embarrassments of theft – even as it seems to leave criminal
matters behind.

In allowing Jack to escape the gallows and go on to live additional lives,
Defoe does something unprecedented in criminal biography and even in
his own fiction. He launches Jack out into the large social order, so that
Jack as thief becomes part of a field of potential comparisons and contrasts
which includes Jack as Virginia exile, as would-be gentleman, and as
trader to foreign shores. At one swoop, Defoe thus enhances and complicates the conventional comparisons between thieves and supposedly more
honest men. For where criminal biography tends, finally, to make these
comparisons operate in only one direction – measuring thieves by the
standards of the "honest" world, it defends those standards by discrediting
and debasing the thief – the overall structuring of *Colonel Jack* allows for
multi-directional comparisons, with multiple implications.[2] The sequence
of the novel itself contributes to this effect, inasmuch as it reverses the
normal pattern of criminal biography. Because Jack moves from crime to a
more or less honest life, his criminal career becomes a standard or "base"

---

[1] For Mandeville, see chapter 1, n. 25. For an account of the London underclass worth setting
against Defoe's, see Henry Fielding's *Enquiry into the Late Increase of Robbers* (1751). After quoting
Saunders Welch's description of the houses that accommodate "idle Persons and Vagabonds"
in St. Giles and St. George, Bloomsbury, Fielding describes what he himself once saw in
Shoreditch, "where two little Houses were emptied of near seventy Men and Women; amongst
whom was one of the prettiest Girls I had ever seen, who had been carried off by an *Irishman*, to
consummate her Marriage on her Wedding-night, in a Room where several others were in Bed
at the same time." "Such is the Poverty of these wretches," Fielding continues,

> that, upon searching all of the above Number, the Mony found upon all of them (except the
> Bride, who, as I afterwards heard, had robbed her Mistress) did not amount to One Shilling;
> and I have been credibly informed, that a single Loaf hath supplied a whole Family with
> their Provisions for a Week .... This Picture, which is taken from the Life, will appear
> strange to many; for the Evil here described, is I am confident, very little known, especially to
> those of the better Sort. Indeed, this is the only Excuse, and I believe the only Reason, that it
> hath been so long tolerated.   (pp. 140–3)

[2] For the methods by which thieves were discredited and debased, and the possible motives, see
Turned to Account, chapter 8.

against which his subsequent, more "honest" careers may be measured. And, by the standard of Jack's career as a thief, each of his later careers seems somehow tainted – though, curiously, this is least true of his career as merchant.

Viewed simply, *Colonel Jack* may seem a success story. Of all Defoe's criminals its protagonist is closest to a classic type, yet he avoids the usual fate of robbers who aspire to be gentlemen. He goes straight, winds up wealthy and at peace with the world, a good woman at his side and God his acknowledged benefactor. Soldier, scholar, capitalist, self-made man, he might even seem Defoe's own *beau idéal*. Actually, there is ample evidence he is not. Despite his best efforts Jack fails to meet Defoe's criteria for "the complete English gentleman," and his trading ventures in the Caribbean are not only illicit but contrary to Defoe's own view of England's best interests.[3] Only as a planter in Virginia does Jack achieve an "honesty" he can be proud of, and even here there are signs in the text suggesting that perhaps he is prouder than he should be. Jack seems successful only if his story is viewed simply, something the novel tends to prevent in a variety of ways.

It is not that Jack at the end lacks anything his heart desires, quite the contrary. He gets all he wants, and has come to want no more than he can have. Unlike other robbers with genteel pretensions, he finds – at last – a place in the social order and is more or less content with it. It is rather that the peace the novel finally gives him to achieve leaves in its wake large, dangling disquietudes. Jack's story sets into motion many more questions than it answers, and though the overall structure of the novel brings to these questions a certain kind of closure, the patterns it establishes are at best only quasi-coherent. More obviously than most literary texts, and most obviously among Defoe's novels, *Colonel Jack* fits together better as a collecton of signifiers than it does as a collection of signifieds. In fact as a collection of signifieds it hardly adds up at all, "what it does not and cannot say" being in many ways more interesting than what it can and does say. What "order it professes" – to continue quoting Pierre Macherey – "is merely an imagined order, projected on to disorder, the fictive resolution of ideological conflicts, a resolution so precarious that it is obvious in the very letter of the text where incoherence and incompleteness burst forth."[4] Much of what follows, necessarily, will involve the tracing out of hints and partial, not whole, often confused and contradictory meanings.

---

[3] On Jack's failure to achieve true gentility, see Everett Zimmerman, *Defoe and the Novel* (Berkeley, 1975), pp. 139–42, and David Blewett, *Defoe's Art of Fiction* (Toronto, 1979), pp. 104–10; both offer persuasive and needed corrections to earlier, less critical views. On the illicit nature of Jack's trading ventures, see n. 18 below.

[4] Pierre Macherey, *A Theory of Literary Production*, tr. Geoffrey Wall (London, 1978), p. 150.

Even by Defoe's usual standards, *Colonel Jack* does not have – or seem to have – much of a plot. It falls into four parts, the first two following, at least internally, a more or less plausible sequence of events. The internal sequences of the last two parts are often problematic, however, and so, too, the connections between all four. Having ended his career as a thief (part 1), Jack is abruptly transported to Virginia by a gang of kidnappers, where he rises from slave to planter (part 2). Then, instead of settling down to a life of piety and quiet prosperity, he returns to Europe, where he seeks to become a proper gentleman. After living in London, then in Europe as an officer in the French army, and again in England, losing three bad wives and a fourth good one, Jack returns to Virginia (part 3). One motive for this return, introduced abruptly and out of chronological sequence, is his fear of being arrested as a Jacobite rebel. While waiting to be pardoned Jack makes a trading voyage to the West Indies, which, by a series of twists and turns, leads him into a highly lucrative and dangerous trade with the Spanish in the Caribbean (part 4).[5] There is, to be sure, an "invisible hand" behind Jack's kidnapping, and his return to Europe may be explained psychologically, but the return to Virginia is handled very awkwardly, and his trading voyages in the Caribbean seem little more than a series of appendices to a story pretty much over. Even *Captain Singleton* looks better plotted than this, resolvable as it is into two large, looping voyages away from England and then back, two sets of hardships overcome and two great fortunes made.

Nonetheless, *Colonel Jack* gives certain intimations of wholeness. It does this by endowing its protagonist with what might be called "categorical completeness," and by suggesting all sorts of comparisons and contrasts across its text. Jack enjoys (if that is the word) a variety of social and economic functions so large as almost to hold the novel together by itself. Rejecting Will's suggestion that they "buy a Couple of good Horses, and ... take the Highway like gentlemen" (67), he turns down a chance to become the usual sort of highwayman and embarks on a course of life that carries him through practically all levels of society.[6] He is in this order orphan, beggar-boy, thief, soldier, overseer, planter, prisoner of war, man

[5] For the same four-part division, described in slightly different terms, see Blewett, *Defoe's Art of Fiction*, p. 104.

[6] Mounted robbery was a great move up in thieves' self-estimation, as indicated by the complaint a condemned highwayman named Wager made against his partner, a certain Horsenail, who had "us'd him ill, in turning Evidence against him." Horsenail "ought to have consider'd," said Wager, "that he was the Person that put him into a more Gentleman-like Way of subsisting himself than meanly on Foot ... that he provided them with Horses, and equipp'd them for Highwaymen" (James Guthrie, Ordinary Account, 3 March 1736/7). Read against the conventions of criminal biography, Jack's refusing Will's suggestion looms as a great turning point in his life. He could have wound up there with Wager and Horsenail, moving from foot to horseback to the gallows.

of means, officer in the French army, a rebel in the service of the Pretender, once again an independent man of means, a rebel, a planter, and then, initially as a fugitive from English justice, a trader in the Caribbean. Once again he is taken prisoner, frees himself, and then once again becomes a fugitive, this time from Spanish law. (He thus manages, long after having given up thieving, to fall foul of the legal systems of all three of the great European powers, for in fighting the duel with his second wife's lover he has made himself a fugitive from French justice, too.) Finally Jack returns to England a much magnified man of means. For most of this time, until his first return to Virginia, Jack chases after an ever-changing and receding notion of what it means to be a gentleman. He is also, during his time in Europe, four times a husband. Jack is many more things than a thief, and much more than criminal biography makes even its most favored thieves. From glasshouse blackguard up at last to what he believes to be a proper gentleman, Jack moves through the whole spectrum of lower and middle English society and, in France, lives briefly among aristocrats. Jack enjoys, moreover, as wide and various a set of relations to the means of economic production and distribution as he does to the social order. As beggar and thief, he is a parasite; as slave, a worker; as overseer, a manager; as planter, an entrepreneur and capitalist; and as gentleman living in Europe, a rentier. Eventually, in his final calling as merchant, he participates in the transfer of wealth from one hemisphere to the other.

Jack's touching all these bases endows the novel with an air of completeness if only because readers are hard-pressed to imagine any other role for him to fulfill, anything else for him to do. Viewed at the widest angle and all at once, Jack's life seems more or less all of a piece despite its variety and often awkward movement from episode to episode. It would seem still more awkward were it not for a second main unifying effect, one which binds together widely dispersed and disparate episodes into networks of seemingly significant though often covert and sometimes mysterious relationships. All sorts of comparisons and contrasts are suggested by the many parallelisms and analogies which riddle the text. The metaphor is doubly appropriate because it is hard to say what many of these analogies mean, and because they cut across and threaten to perforate the cognitive schemes by which Jack's narrative might otherwise be ordered. The relationships they indicate have a double effect, binding the text together at one level and disrupting it at another; this is what I mean by saying the novel fits together better as a collection of signifiers than of signifieds.[7]

---

[7] This phenomenon has not gone unnoticed. G. A. Starr observes that "a yoking together of opposites permeates the whole story," but doesn't quite know what to make of it. Actually, as I shall argue, this aspect of the text fits intimately in with another of Starr's astute, but

Consider, for instance, the similarity between the Captain's saving his life by crossing a river on horseback and the Colonel's doing the same nearly two hundred pages later (97, 99; 265). The Captain is traveling north to Scotland, pursued by Englishmen he has robbed; Jack is traveling south, away from Scots who have risen against King George, and pursued by the English army. The similitude between these two events may have been stimulated by Defoe's remembering, at some level, the first as he was writing about the second, rather like an improvising musician reaching back to replay, with some variation, a few bars played earlier in his performance. The second event in any case echoes the first, and like all echoes it gives the sense of two moments united across space. Thematically, the analogy is trivial or even disturbing (what can it mean?), but in purely formal terms it might be seen as a subset of a more numerous body of events, all involving perilous passages across water. Jack crosses the Atlantic four times and makes three voyages to the Caribbean. He makes his first Atlantic crossing as a kidnap victim, his second is interrupted by French privateers, and on his third the ship is robbed by pirates. The outward legs of his first and third Caribbean voyages are also menaced by pirates, and Spanish ships intercept the homeward legs. Such events may seem somehow symbolic ("sea changes," etc.), but quite apart from any such inferences they stand as boundary markers. Each time Jack crosses water his life, and his narrative, take on a new direction (or threaten to). This is not at all a surprising feature in a text which speaks of his first wife's having "pass'd the Rubicon" (197). The value of this larger set of recurrences – whatever the two river crossings may mean in conjunction with each other – is that water crossings become a kind of signal to the reader, an aid to his following shifts in the action. This, in turn, may help him integrate the text, boundary markers indicating points of connection, of course, as well as divisions.

Other recurrent motifs can seem more important thematically. Whippings, beatings, and fights figure frequently in the novel, and in ways that almost force comparison. Some of these comparisons are obvious, others more subtle; some make "sense" or can seem to, others don't. Jack, for instance, is disinclined to whip slaves because he hated seeing the Captain whipped in London. He is all the more inclined to fight a duel with his second wife's lover, however, because he was in no position to fight his first's, and so lost face (or at least a quantity of nose). Less obvious, though still possible to understand in psychological terms, is the similarity between the beating he gets from his first wife's lover and the beating he

---

undeveloped impressions: "in this book Defoe's gift for perceiving incongruity seems . . . to have exceeded his ability to control and interpret it" (*Defoe and Casuistry* [Princeton, 1971], pp. 83, 82).

gives his third's. Much less obvious, and not at all explicable in terms of Jack's psychology or any other "natural" phenomenon, is the similarity between this first beating and the attack he and Will make on the woolen-draper's apprentice. Both occur in Grace-church Street, and follow nearly the same scenario (cf. pp. 57–8 and 203–4). Taken by themselves, these whippings, fights, and beatings form a sequence which has effects both centripetal and centrifugal; at one level the episodes are forced together but, at another, they threaten to fly apart by virtue of their real differences. Readers may be confused but also intrigued by the possibility that some meaning may lie behind this set of concurrences.

One such meaning (or set of meanings) may be suggested by the notion that one of the novel's major themes is Jack's growing adaptation to the world. Thus, over the course of his life, Jack risks loss of selfhood in a number of ways, this being generally indicated as some attack on or threat to his individual autonomy and freedom of action. Whipping seems significant in this connection because of its association with kidnapping and slavery – the Captain is whipped because he was part of a kidnapping ring – and because of the association of slavery with kidnapping and crime, both being means by which people are made into slaves. Jack's position at either end of the whip, cane, fist, or sword stands as an index to his personal status or significance. As a slave, and later as a prisoner of the French or Spanish, he risks becoming a commodity, an object exchangeable for cash. As a thief or Jacobite he risks being hanged and so becoming an object lesson for (and on behalf of) others. As someone beaten or menaced with violence he serves as a means by which his first wife's lover and, potentially, his second's might vindicate their questioned honor. Even as a cuckold he is threatened with becoming a means, or adjunct, to another's pleasure.

The greater Jack's material worth, the more significant he becomes vis-à-vis society; but the more he becomes, the more he risks losing. This is made clear from the start, when his first significant sum of money seems lost down the hollow tree. It is made clearer still, when, getting a reward of 25 guineas for the papers stolen at the customs house, he finds that "the Care of preserving [his money] brings Tears into his Eyes, and Fear into his Heart" (38). Jack never quite escapes such fear until he has given up chasing after gentlemanly status, got himself a wife he can trust, patched up his quarrel with the king, and made more money than he will ever need. Thus, once he knows the Spanish will not re-enslave him, their holding him for ransom is no great cause for concern. Nor, despite its inconvenience, is he very much bothered by having to hide out on the Mexican coast. In both circumstances, as he had done when kidnapped, then as a slave in Virginia, and then as a captive of the French privateers, he finds means to manipulate those who hold the upper hand, to gain an advantage sufficient to prevent his becoming utterly their client, tool, or object.[8]

There is discoverable in the set of recurrent motifs we've just been discussing, then, both pattern and coherence. To find the particular coherence I've just suggested, however, one has to ignore certain elements of the pattern. There is more form here than "recoverable" meaning, or, one might say, more cohesion than coherence. A further problem for any reading of the novel which sees it as a single rising curve toward increased autonomy and freedom – call this reading #1 – is that large and powerful counter-currents in it suggest other forms as well. The jumpiness of its plotting aside, the novel's overall movement might just as easily be seen as a rise and then fall, as a series of ups and downs, or even, somewhat disturbingly, as an ongoing, never quite successful series of efforts to escape the dog-eat-dog competition of social and, particularly, economic struggle. A good deal of this variousness derives from Jack's double status as both sympathetic hero and ideological stalking horse, as well as from the doubleness of Defoe's concerns as a defender of his class. Some of it, too, may come from Defoe's inability to speak straightforwardly about the moral and social implications of economic individualism.

As ideological stalking horse, Jack is not of much interest in himself but important – and to a certain extent expendable – as a sign. Though his range and variety far transcend those of even the most richly symbolic thieves in criminal biography, in some ways he is very much like them. Like Whitney and many other notorious robbers of the period, Jack has Jacobite sympathies; like all the better class of thieves he has aspirations to live like, even to be, a gentleman.[9] Endowed richly by nature, he has had the misfortune to have been born into the wrong milieu. "If he had come into the World with the Advantage of Education," Defoe remarks in his preface, highlighting this last point, "and been well instructed how to improve the generous Principles he had in him, what a Man might he not have been" (1). Similar things are said of actual criminals, though not, ultimately, with much sympathy.[10] Jack escapes their usual fate not only

---

[8] Cf. John J. Richetti's reading of Jack's narrative, which sees it showing "as a whole a pattern of development from dependence ... to self-containment" (*Defoe's Narratives: Situations and Structures* [Oxford, 1975], p. 150, also p. 161). This seems proposed as an unspoken corrective to Starr's view that the novel, having no overall moral theme, lacks an overall structure, or to James Sutherland's claim that Jack "knocks about the world, engaging in a series of miscellaneous and unrelated adventures" (Starr, *Defoe and Casuistry*, pp. 87, 99–100, 110; Sutherland, *Daniel Defoe* [Boston, 1971], p. 205). My argument aims not at refuting these various points of view, but at integrating them into a larger concept of the novel.

[9] For the first of the notable Jacobite crooks – and what the phenomenon may have meant in terms of larger social and political concerns – see my article, "King William, 'K. J.,' and James Whitney: The Several Lives and Affiliations of a Jacobite Robber," *Eighteenth Century Life*, n.s. 12 (1988): 88–104.

[10] Even so attractive a thief as Benjamin Child – whose "Deportment" in prison "could [not] be more worthy of Pity, and good Usage," and who had "the good Wishes of all Persons

through an abundance of providential (i.e., authorially arranged) good luck, but because of his "strange Rectitude of Principles." This "rectitude" puts an immense distance between him and the commonest sort of thieves (the Captain, for example), and it separates him as well from even relatively attractive criminals like the Major. Jack is not one of those "Highspirited Fellows that would sooner accept the Gallows than a mean Trade," thus his pride at the "honesty" he achieves in Virginia though he starts out as a slave.[11] Despite Will's prompting he never mounts the highwayman's high horse.

Jack's "rectitude" is, nonetheless, "strange"; it is not the seeming randomness of the world alone that is to blame for his curious sequence of careers. His "strange kind of uninstructed Conscience," his "strange, original Notion of . . . being a Gentleman" (55, 60) themselves play a role, and it is not an altogether happy one. Thus his strange "Original something" (155) – a complex of attributes which ought perhaps to be compared with common, original sinfulness – exerts a positive influence over the first half of the novel but, over the last, leads Jack into social and economic misconduct. This second way of looking at the overall structure of the novel — call it reading #2 – will suggest at least two further "readings," each requiring revisions and transformations of #1 and #2, and each progressively more difficult to set out.

Like all Defoe's fictive protagonists (with the possible exception of H. F.), Jack's life reaches a point where – or so it can seem – he would have done well to sit tight and be content with a quiet, modest happiness. As with the other criminal novels, this moment occurs dead center in his narrative, when – having achieved "Honesty" and feeling "Ransom'd from being a Vagabond, a Thief, and a Criminal," but wanting to go on to become a gentleman (156) – Jack decides to return to Europe.[12] Once there, he discovers being a gentleman involves more than he'd imagined. Mere wealth, education, manners, and the personal conviction that one is a gentleman are not sufficient. Humiliated because he cannot handle a sword and has never tested his courage in combat, Jack repairs these

(Numbers of which were of the best Fashion) that came to see him" – could not expect to escape hanging. Though even "his Prosecutor was . . . taken with his engaging Demeanour and Complacency of Temper," and he was widely admired for freeing several debtors with the money he had on him when caught, such feelings, says the source of all this information, could "have no Impression on the Letter of the Law, that directs the bringing of all Malefactors to Justice, be their Manner of Address and Behaviour, their Discourse and Conversation, ever so like that of the compleatest Gentlemen" (*The Whole Life and History of Benjamin Child, Lately Executed for Robbing the Bristol Mail* [1722], pp. 26–7).

11 *Memoirs of the Right Villanous John Hall, the Late Famous and Notorious Robber*, 4th edn (1708), p. 29.
12 For an extensive discussion of center-point "symmetry" in Defoe's fiction, see Douglas Brooks, *Number and Pattern in the Eighteenth-century Novel* (London, 1973), pp. 20–4, 27–8, 31–5, 41–50.

deficiencies by buying a commission in the French army and serving with distinction. He earns an actual colonelcy, turning a once ironic (even mocking) nickname into a proper title. Here, too, Jack's wish to become an actual gentleman – to prove to the world and himself that he is what he feels himself intrinsically to be – might seem to exert a beneficial effect; his ambition leads him to ever wider and greater accomplishments. In this phase of his life, however, there is a powerful discrepancy between the letter of his achievements and their true meaning, both personally and socially.

There were two kinds of gentlemen according to Defoe, "born" and "bred," and by either standard Jack's status is ambiguous. Even if we accept his nurse's claim that his father was "a Man of Quality" and his mother a "Gentlewoman" (3), the genteel blood that flows in Jack's veins is not enough by itself to make him a gentleman as Defoe preferred to define the term. Defoe had little patience with the notion that "born" gentlemen were inherently different from other folk merely by virtue of their "blood." That "unhappy Humour" – which, he satirically observed, was in any case easily diluted by wetnurses' milk – was far less important than personal virtue and education. Defoe was insistent that even "the sons of mean persons" could become gentlemen, so long as they were born into sufficient wealth to support a gentlemanly upbringing. Unhappily for Jack, he is not born into money but makes it, a qualification which, in Defoe's view, would at best suit him to father a line of gentlemen (*CEG*, 3–4, 17–19, 75–6, 257–8). Nonetheless, the novel makes Jack's birth an important factor in shaping his future. If his gentle blood is a fiction, it is an enabling one, for it encourages him to rise higher in the world than he otherwise might, and it certainly keeps him from the gallows. Jack's father was not wrong when he said that Jack would act like a gentleman if he believed himself "to be so" (3). It might also be noted that Major Jack, who is one-half a gentleman by blood, is not so bad a character as Captain Jack, whose blood is entirely base. Jack's birth is a highly ambivalent sign, as is his rather remarkable set of personal accomplishments.

Defoe set high standards for "bred" gentlemen, and Jack fails to meet these, too. Along with "an originall fund of wealth, wit, sence, courage, virtue, and good humor," "bred" gentlemen had the distinction of being "set apart by a liberal education for the service of their country." They marked themselves out "by the greatest and best actions," and led lives "of glory and true fame" (*CEG*, 4). Far from serving his country, Jack does the opposite. He fights for the French against England's allies and, as an eventual Jacobite, commits treason not once but twice. When Jack's quest for gentility makes him a renegade, it takes on an unwholesome cast. What originally led him away from outlawry leads him back into it, and the stakes for society are now a good deal higher.

Though Jack sees nothing meretricious in his French colonelcy, or in pretending, back in England, to be a French gentleman, there are ample indications that all is not well. Becoming a gentleman has been Jack's life goal, but now (as he thinks) he's achieved it, his life is no better or happier than before; indeed, in some respects it is worse. Defoe is unkind to him, or, as Defoe might prefer to have us think, providence fails to bless Jack's enterprise. As Jack goes through three bad marriages, losing each of his wives to other men, the one thing that changes is the increasing gentility of his style. Thus he learns to live up to, and even administer, what his first wife's lover calls "Gentleman's Law" (201). Declining to fight a duel with that man, he gets beaten in the street. But he deals more *comme il faut* with his second rival, wounding him in a sword fight outside Paris, perhaps mortally. Where Jack's first rival was a mere gentleman (and self-proclaimed, at that), his second is a marquis; he moves up in the world as both cuckold and man of honor. Jack treats his third wife's lover just as he was treated by his first's. Concluding that the "villain" is no gentleman despite his being called "the Captain of a Man of War," Jack confronts him, invites him to draw his sword, and, when the man refuses to fight, beats him into insensibility (241–3; cf. especially 201).

Though Jack grows increasingly gentleman-like over these three episodes, his personal well-being remains at a standstill. He learns how to use a sword and to kill, if need be, to defend his honor. From being judged no gentleman and beaten up, he arrives at a point where he can judge someone else no gentleman and beat him up; so what? For all his additional attributes, Jack is no more a man, certainly no better at keeping his wives. All three confrontations in any case end with his having to leave town in a hurry and start being gentlemanly all over again, some place else. It is only in his fourth marriage that Jack achieves the happiness he has sought so long, and he gets it by lowering his gentlemanly sights. "I had Married two Gentlewomen, and one Citizen, and they prov'd all three Whores," he says, but thinks "I should now find what I wanted in an innocent Country Wench" (246). Actually she is not as innocent as she seems, he later finds out, but his grief at her death is so great that he returns to Virginia, "the only Place I had been bless'd at, or had met with any thing that deserv'd the Name of Success" (250). This is as close as Jack gets to acknowledging that his efforts at living like a gentleman have failed.

The whole question of Jack's class status is finally left to peter out, never brought to closure nor even framed (as is the case with "open" endings) by a final question mark. Like his analogues in conventional criminal biography Jack is a gentleman yet no gentleman, but, unlike them, the ambiguity of his status never gets resolved. His pretensions to gentility are not ironized or brutally dismissed. He doesn't suffer what the law prescribes for even "the compleatest Gentlemen" who steal: "After a few Jirks and unmerciful Thumps, they expire the Contempt, and hardly the Pity, of any that behold 'em." But neither is there any romantic discovery of his true parentage as other novels of the period might offer – no strawberry birthmark on his shoulder, for instance, for some chance stranger to recognize. "The Robbers upon the High-way, by their own Heraldry intitl[e] themselves Gentlemen of the Road," scoffs a late seventeenth-century writer, but if you "look into their *Pedigree* . . . the best of them [are] but *Cadets*" and the rest "most commonly the spawn of broken Tradesmen and worst of Debauchees."[13] For all the novel indicates – or fails to indicate – the same dismissive cry might be raised against Jack. Defoe's unwillingness to make him an unequivocal gentleman was rooted, I suspect, in his own class attitudes. Defoe vehemently disliked the notion that "born" gentlemen were "a different Species from the rest of Mankind," to be rated "above the ordinary Price" and ranked "in a higher Class than [their] Neighbours." His aim in *The Complete English Gentleman*, he makes clear, is to "undeceive the World, divorce their Minds from an espoused Error, and set the real Gentleman in a true Light, that we may no longer make a Harlequin of the Man we should admire [but set] up a new Class truly qualify'd to inherit the Title" (16–18). Jack may seem part of this project, but actually he is only constrained by it; it is in Defoe's own interests to keep him an ambiguous sign.

Consider the strong implication were Jack to rise unmistakeably to gentlemanly rank, either by some romantic vindication of birthright or even (and perhaps most especially) by virtue of his own efforts. One way or another, it would seem that blood had indeed been the crucial factor, that it "tells" by one means or another. One great advantage in the final ambiguity of Jack's class status is that it prevents any such inference, while at the same time it keeps the notion of gentility open: blood alone does not make a gentleman. Given the prejudices of his audience (at least some of it), and perhaps certain deep and contradictory convictions of his own, Defoe was willing to go no further.[14] But why give Jack gentle blood in the first place? I would guess that here, too, Defoe was respecting the prejudices of his audience, and turning them to advantage. Jack's origins endow him with a mysterious allure and raise pity for all he has lost; they

[13] *Memoirs of Hall*, p. 19; J. M., *The Traveller's Guide; and the Country's Safety, Being a Declaration of the Laws . . . against High-Way-Men* (1683), pp. [iii–iv].

[14] That "the boast of birth and blood is all a cheat, and there is nothing at all in it, nothing convey'd from the noble spring by the channells of nature," is something Defoe "cannot grant neither." "The word gentleman," he points out (but perhaps with some irony), "is understood to signify men of antient houses, dignify'd with hereditary titles and family honours, old mansion houses, old advousions, the right of patronage to churches, establish'd burying places, where they shew the monuments of innumerable ancestors, names deriv'd from the lands and estates they possess, parks and forrests made their own by prescripcion and usage time out of mind, and such like marks of the antiquity of the race" (*CEG*, pp. 76, 257).

also set him apart from the other two Jacks and most of the would-be gentlemen in criminal biography. Obviously, too, if Jack is to illustrate the limitations of mere genetic endowment as a basis for class rank and privilege, he has to be a "born" gentleman according to the strictest – and for Defoe – the most trivial meaning of the term. Jack's birth makes him the poor, bare thing itself, unaccommodated gentleman.

If, then, there is something intrinsic in "born" gentlemen, Jack's life shows it is not of much account. The notion that gentlemen are nonetheless somehow a species apart can have great effect, and this is not always good for society. Jack's flirtation with Jacobitism might be taken to illustrate the latter point. Here Defoe doubtless wanted to advance certain immediate political concerns, but other, subtler initiatives are involved as well.[15] For one thing, the lack of any particular reasons for Jack's Jacobitism makes it seem merely conventional. Thieves with genteel pretensions commonly show such a tendency, and, significantly, it is a sign of gross vulgarism. "All the *Rogues, Whores, Pimps, Thieves, Fools,* and *Scoundrels* in the Kingdom" were Tories, trumpeted the leading Whig weekly – a charge the Tory press did not bother to refute – and Jacobites, in the terms of this polemic, were merely hardcore Tories.[16] In his politics as in other things, Jack's inability to distinguish the genuinely genteel from the *demodé* or bogus calls into question the efficacy of his blood; he is no gentleman by instinct. Jack thus risks his claim to genteel status twice over by rebelling against the crown, legally (he might once more be made a slave) and socially (he commits a *faux pas*). At least as important as its social or political significance, however, is the formal value of Jack's slide into Jacobitism. This becomes a resource Defoe can exploit to bring the novel to some sort of conclusion, much as he exploits Jack's unhappy string of marriages. Defoe may not have cared to provide Jack with a strawberry birthmark or the equivalent, but in reuniting him with his first wife he gives him, and the novel, the next best sort of coincidence. Though Jack never regains his patrimony, he does recover something else he had lost and, with it, a satisfaction he had never expected. Jack gets a happy ending after all, if not the one he originally wanted.

With this, needless to say, readers might come to feel a sense of closure. The gentility theme has gone nowhere, really, but a theme which the novel ties into it has. The same point can be made about Jack's Jacobitism, another outgrowth of his quest for gentility but which, like his search for a good wife, admits of a definite conclusion. Defoe was pleased to say,

---

15 The social and political significance of Jack's Jacobitism is also discussed by Zimmerman, *Defoe and the Novel*, pp. 130–1, and Blewett, *Defoe's Art of Fiction*, pp. 95–101.
16 Read's *Weekly Journal*, 29 August 1719. This same newspaper had fun, too, telling the story of a failed haberdasher forced to flee to Calais to escape his creditors, and who then occasionally would come back across the Channel to rob on the highway; during his time in France he, too, became "a great Favorer" of the Pretender (16 April 1720).

quoting Charles II, that a king "could make a knight, but could not make a gentleman" (*CEG*, 25); a king can, however, *un*make a Jacobite. Instead of the personal fulfillment and social recognition that comes with being a gentleman, Jack gets a king's pardon to add to his marital success. Both reconciliations – with wife and monarch – allow Jack to close out that part of his life which was most concerned with the chimeric pursuit of gentility, if not directly then at least metonymically. One almost suspects Defoe of introducing and heightening Jack's marital and political problems so as to have something in the novel that would admit resolution.

The sense of closure that comes with these two reconciliations is all the more enhanced by their formal homology. In the first instance Jack pardons, in the second he is pardoned, and in both instances gratitude provides the basis for a strong bond between the subordinate, pardoned person and his or her superior. Jack's wife will be a better wife because she has recognized the errors of her ways and because Jack has so graciously forgiven her; in the same way Jack will be all the more loyal a subject to George I. Both relationships produce still greater closural effect by virtue of their homology to Jack's situation in Virginia vis-à-vis the black slaves on the one hand and his master on the other. These relationships made Jack part of what seems – on the face of it – an ideal social hierarchy. The Great Master and his servants are united not by fear or cruelty but a sense of mutual obligation, the master being grateful for good service, the servants for good treatment, and both feeling an affection for the other that might almost be called love.[17] When Jack departs from Virginia he leaves this behind, never quite to regain it. No more is heard of Mouchat and the other loyal slaves, and Jack's relationship with his "tutor" goes a bit sour when, upon his return, they both compete for the same woman. What Jack lost in leaving Virginia is in a way regained, however, when he remarries and makes his peace with the king. His wife – his slave, too, after all – in effect replaces Mouchat, even to the extent that she solicits his pardon from Jack's new Great Master, the king.

Had the novel ended at this point, which it might have done conveniently, it would have achieved – barring extensive revision – a rough but sub-stantial coherence of form and meaning. Turning his back on crime, Jack would have moved toward social integration in two ways, first, by positive economic participation and, second, by seeking a valued class status. Spurning the world of work in favor of becoming a gentleman, but then finding gentlemanliness a dead end, Jack would have returned to Virginia and managed his plantation happily and honestly ever after. Instead of offering such an ending, however, the novel goes on to raise a whole new

[17] For the general importance of gratitude in all these social relationships, see Maximillian E. Novak, *Defoe and the Nature of Man* (London, 1963), pp. 118–21.

set of questions, the effect of which, intentionally or not, is to unravel its form and "unmake" such meaning as it so far would seem to have achieved. The first and most obvious casualty of the novel's continuing into part 4 is the shape of Jack's life, which loses its "curve." The rise, fall, and upward recovery displayed through part three becomes instead an oscillating rise/fall/rise/fall/rise, with Jack's eventual return to England bringing a less definite sense of an ending than his earlier return to Virginia. A less obvious but potentially more disturbing and interesting casualty is Virginia itself, or rather the meaning of Jack's life there. Barring the addition of part 4, this would seem his peak experience, and the "center" of the novel. Reconsidered from the vantage point of the novel's actual ending, however, Virginia no longer appears quite the idyllic place it otherwise might have done. By continuing into part 4, the novel may be said to "de-center" itself.

The damage part 4 does to the novel as a whole – or rather to its "wholeness" – is not immediately apparent, part 4 seeming merely a new phase in Jack's ongoing, miscellaneous life, similar in certain respects to the others. Here Jack turns his energies once more to economic matters, making a second fortune on top of his first. Though trading in the Caribbean gives him an opportunity to act like a Spanish gentleman, as once he had acted like a French gentleman, money, not class, is now Jack's main concern. Nonetheless, his behavior is once again socially ambiguous and, if inquired into closely, highly dubious. He shows considerable courage and skill in dealing with the Spaniards, but, as Maximillian Novak has pointed out, Jack's trade was forbidden by treaty. Defoe, moreover, repeatedly denounced such trade on the grounds that it "destroyed the normal circulation of goods and money between England and Spain." Novak concludes on the basis of this information that Jack as merchant is no better than Jack as thief; indeed, "in violating the rules of mercantile morality he has committed a far worse crime than any of his petty thefts as a hungry young pickpocket on the streets of London." Jack is "both a 'Trade Thief' and a 'Trade Lunatick,'" Novak goes on to add, "terms that Defoe applied to capitalists who pursued immoderate wealth by circumventing the established rules of trade."[18] Here, too, it seems, Jack is denied a final legitimacy. In part 4 of his life, just as in part three, he falls back into the outlawry it seemed he had escaped, and again there is more at stake for society than when he was merely a thief.

All this appears the more curious in that Jack's economic status seemed to have been healthily resolved by his accepting and making the best of his surrogate punishment in Virginia. "And thus," he says, "I was Set up in the World, and in Short, removed by the degrees that you have heard

---

[18] Maximillian E. Novak, *Economics and the Fiction of Daniel Defoe* (Berkeley, 1962), pp. 123, 125, 127.

from a Pick-pocket, to a Kidnapp'd miserable Slave ... then from a Slave
to a Head Officer, and Overseer of Slaves, and from thence to a Master
Planter" (151–2). In the course of this changeover Jack shifts from the
worst kind of economic parasitism to the best kind of entrepreneurship (or
so one might think), i.e., from stealing property to actually creating it as
Locke describes the process, transforming nature via the application of
labor.[19] What more powerful display could there be of the difference
between thief and honest man than this, to show the same man first a thief
and then a planter? Why go on, then, to make that same man a "Trade
thief"? Why not leave the whole question of Jack's honesty alone, rather
than re-opening it? A number of plausible hypotheses may be advanced
for the addition of part 4 to the novel but, while some are better than
others, none has the force of a conclusive explanation. All we can speak of
is the effect part 4 has on any effort to construct a view of the novel as a
whole, as it shifts readerly perspective on each of the previous parts, and
vice versa. The juxtaposition of Jack's careers as thief and trader is
especially interesting, not only for the light they cast on each other
(reading #3), but for the repercussions of their combined effect on his
career as a planter in Virginia (reading #4).

   Jack's new wealth from illicit trade may have been meant as yet another
consolation prize. It may have been intended, too, as a counter to the
absurd notion, held by some gentlemen, that their birth put them above
profitable economic employment (CEG, 64–6). Here, also, Jack would
stand as a test case, showing (in this instance positively) how much a
"born" gentleman might do. Nonetheless, even the most direct implications of the episode make it seem a great, dangling loose end. Jack
doesn't need the money, he risks a great deal to get it, and the illicit nature
of the enterprise damages the good standing he has begun to win back as a
character. Nor does the basic structuring of part 4 do much to make it
seem part of the rest of the novel or even of a piece by itself. Each of Jack's
three voyages to the Caribbean stands as a discrete narrative unit, any one
of which might well have ended the book. That is, Jack could have been
made to settle down in Virginia after his second voyage, having more than
made good his losses from the first. Or the first voyage could just have
easily ended his story, especially had Jack, now pardoned by the king, got
back from St. Nevis without being captured by the Spanish; Jack's Cuban
interlude, like the account of his campaigns in Italy, seems a way of
spinning the novel out. Even the voyage to St. Nevis seems arbitrarily
tacked on, particularly as its main motive – Jack's fear of becoming known

---

[19] It is this that Jack describes when he speaks of "curing" land, p. 155; see also pp. 152–3,
especially for its description of the way that tobacco, a product of the earth, becomes "money."
The reference to Locke is to *An Essay Concerning the True Original, Extent and End of Civil
Government*, chapter 5, "Of Property."

as a Jacobite – is so awkwardly supplied. To find an excuse to get Jack back on the move after he's settled him down, Defoe is forced to contradict what he'd already written about Jack's role in the '15, to revise his novel on the run, so to speak.[20]

It may be that Defoe wrote the last part of *Colonel Jack* as an afterthought, without any overall plan. There is a kind of providential logic linking parts 1 and 2, and the connection between 2 and 3, along with the ending of 3, can be understood psychologically. But it is difficult to see how providence or psychology can explain Jack's onset of avarice, particularly as he doesn't start trading with the Spaniards until after he's been pardoned by the king. There are, moreover, frequent indications in the novel's first three parts that Defoe was looking forward to future events as he wrote. For example, the Captain's involvement with kidnappers toward the beginning of the novel prefigures the kidnapping that ends part 1 and begins part 2. Similarly, Jack's presence on the battlefields near Ghent toward the beginning of part three anticipates his later service in the French army, and even his Jacobitism. During this visit he has reason to be glad he's not a soldier, because otherwise he'd have been made a prisoner of war; later, two of the more notable events in his careers as French officer and Jacobite involve the same fate narrowly escaped. This battlefield visit also serves to link part three back to the end of part 1, for these are the very same wars to which – by virtue of an extraordinary time warp! – Jack would have shipped out some twelve years earlier, if the Captain hadn't persuaded him to desert the army.[21] The English troops cheer King William but Jack is not among them; when, eventually, he does return to soldiering, it is to fight for the King of France and the Pretender, the two greatest enemies of Protestant monarchy. It is clear, too, that by the time Defoe was halfway through the novel he had decided to bring Jack back to Virginia (see 173). Not much later, as he works his way through the details of Jack's first marital break-up, there is an indication he will try at some future point to bring Jack's wife back into the narrative (see 198). Though part 4 occasionally looks back to the preceding text, nothing in parts 1 through 3 (so far as I can tell) hints forward to part 4.[22]

Possibly, after getting Jack back to Virginia, Defoe felt some need to

20 Thus the awkward backtracking on p. 264 to change what had been said on p. 250 about Jack's participation in the 1715 uprising against the king: "I must now return to a Circumstance of my History, which has been past for some Time ..."

21 If Jack were born c. 1672, as Monk convincingly suggests in his edition of the novel (n. 1 to p. 10 on p. 311), then Jack's desertion from the army has to have occurred during the War of the League of Augsburg (1689–97). It is clearly this same war which is being fought while he visits the English troops at Ghent; thus "the Prince of *Orange* had been made King of *England*, and the *English* Troops were all on his Side ..." (183).

22 Thus the threat of Jack's being made a slave in Peru harks back to his kidnapping, and the hospitality of the Mexican planters compares to that extended by the French at Bordeaux.

bulk the novel out to justify its original price of six shillings (one shilling more than his other novels) and did this piecemeal, adding on bits at a time until he felt he had enough.[23] If this were the case, Defoe may have backed into his attack on Jack's honesty, with none of the particular intention he had in part three with respect to his gentility. I suggest this only as one possible explanation for the novel's not falling as hard on the one as it does on the other. Jack's climb toward gentility, in any case, threatens to get him hanged (223) or at best to reduce him "to Misery and Poverty again"; the Jacobites he sees in Virginia, and whom he fears for more than one reason, have been "sold after the usual manner of con-demn'd Criminals" (266–7). The text thus insists on a kind of congruity between Jack's thieving and his quest for gentility which, somehow, leads him into thoughtless rebellion against the crown. It does not insist on a similar congruity between Jack's trading voyages and his adventures as a pickpocket in London; quite the contrary. Novak's scholarly view of the essential similarity between these two phases of Jack's life is highly useful, though not quite in the way he suggests. Jack's trade with the Spaniards may have a relatively clear and simple meaning outside the novel, but its meaning inside the novel is another matter. This is not to say that it is any the less illicit or immoral, but that in the overall context of his narrative other considerations surround it and modify its meaning.

   To begin with a very simple point: insofar as Jack has won the reader's sympathies, the great individual benefits that accrue to him from trading with the Spaniards count for more than the diffuse and relatively small losses it involves for English society as a whole. The fact the text never mentions these losses, failing to develop the full legal and moral impli-cations of Jack's behavior, makes them seem even more diffuse. Whom is he hurting, and to what extent? To compare Jack's behavior with that of more honest merchants, one has, in effect, to introduce those merchants into the novel, along with a concern for them; to feel he is behaving badly, one must have or develop an opinion on the Caribbean trade. The novel makes it far easier to compare Jack as merchant with Jack as thief; the fact that these are the first and last of his careers by itself tends to encourage the comparison. Still, the comparison does not hold in quite the way Novak suggests. It is true that Jack's "Restless pushing at getting of Money" (40) as both merchant and thief jostles other, more scrupulous men aside, disrupting the larger economic order. Thus all Jack's thefts, except the last (which involves the Kentish Town widow), directly interfere with the commerce that is London's lifeblood. In robbing a customs-house broker,

[23] If this were Defoe's intent, he failed. Within a week of publication, the price of *Colonel Jack* dropped from six to five shillings, and this apparently became its permanent price; see the novel's title page (which may have been set in type even before the novel was completed), and advertisements for it in Applebee's *Original Weekly Journal*, 22 December 1722 (date of publication), 29 December 1722, and 5 January 1723.

a collier master, a Jewish diamond merchant, an old man in from the country selling bullocks, and a woolen-draper's apprentice just come from depositing money at a goldsmith's, Jack and Will (though not in this order) impede the importation of food and fuel into the city, attack a representative of one of its major industries, and threaten the security of its banking and trade arrangements. In light of the last it is especially significant that they steal so many papers. These are of far greater value than they realize (in either sense of the term), their preferred booty actually being the small sums of cash they generally get with them. Without such papers, commerce within and beyond the city would be difficult if not impossible. Nor are such papers easily replaced, as the anxiety of the customs-house broker and the Jewish merchant indicate, the two victims in this series who get the most attention. Lacking their bills of exchange and notes of deposit, such men find their affairs at a stand; in robbing them, Jack interferes with international trade long before his stint in the Caribbean, and in ways that strike closer to home.[24]

One might better reverse the terms of Novak's comparison, then, and say – quite commonsensically – that Jack's career as a trader is only as bad as his career as a thief. But actually the text makes his thieving seem far worse. The difference hinges not on the magnitude of his thefts, nor even on the intentionality behind them, but on their objects and effects. Jack gives good value to the Spanish, judging by their eagerness to deal with him, and what he skims off the Caribbean trade will hardly be noticed by English merchants. The people he robs in London, however, are sorely affected. Jack may not mean to hurt them as badly as he does, knowing no better, but even where no violence is used and sums are stolen that might seem unimportant, he injures his victims – and society – more than he knows. Jack is at least as much a vandal as a thief, and his economic vandalism strikes at the very existence of the metropolis. For without trade, as Defoe wrote, "this great City [would have] to dismiss two thirds of its People, and send them into the Country to Till the Land, and get their Bread as Adam did ... where they must disperse too, and scatter up and down, for they must live no more of them in a place than the Land could maintain, if they did they must starve" (*CET*, 2, part 2: 117). In their small, brutish way, Jack's thefts tug London back toward post-lapsarian chaos; his later economic delinquencies, by comparison, seem distant and tame. What, after all, is a little "corporate crime" here and there (especially "there") to muggings on the way home or at one's very door?

24 Defoe may have meant to emphasize this point by making the diamond merchant a Jew, as Jews were important participants in international trade. When Jack robs this "gentleman" – and everyone around him scrupulously allows him this title – he commits an act that might in current terms compare to the mugging, say, of an OPEC minister on Wall Street or a Japanese banker in Smyrna, Tennessee.

Nor is Defoe content to leave matters at that. Following Novak, Samuel Holt Monk compares the first and last parts of the novel in an effort to find a function for its seemingly "dull" and "careless" conclusion. Defoe "probably had one more moral to point," he suggests, for just as "Jack had violated the law of nature by stealing from the old woman of Kentish Town ... he violates a law of mercantilist economic theory [by] disrupting the flow of gold from the New World to the Old, merely to satisfy his own excessive avarice."[25] The relative gravity of these two "laws" and the heinousness of violating them might well be disputed, but there is no need to become entangled in such arcana. The fact is the two cases display a simple, powerful difference that far outweighs any theoretical similarities. Though in grand economic terms Jack's robbing the widow of her mite may seem the least considerable of all his crimes, and though it is done out of moral ignorance and provides the one occasion where he tries to make recompense, it is nonetheless the worst thing he does in the whole novel.[26] As such it demonstrates the clear iniquity of his life as thief, for it is to this that thieving has led him. However analogous his merchandizing may seem, it eventuates in nothing remotely comparable. The fortune Jack gains from trade is not squeezed from the poor and vulnerable but the product of mutually profitable exchange.

It would seem (whatever else his motives) that in writing part 4 Defoe had actually a "moral" to blunt – i.e., the conventional claim that economic individualism was hardly different from theft. Criminal biography confers on its most celebrated thieves a certain paradoxical status. "He never practised pilfering, stealing, Shop-lifting, Street-robbing," one highwayman claimed in a bid to escape the death penalty, "nor any of those little Ways used by petty Thieves." Thieves and yet not like other thieves, such criminals invited comparison with their supposedly legitimate but equally liminous opposites: the "not-thieves" who were nonetheless like thieves. Even a Whig newspaper could refer to highwaymen as "Equestrian Merchants," a comparison doubly to the disadvantage of merchants, inasmuch as it sets highwaymen literally and figuratively above them.[27] As he did in setting out Moll's dealings with the mercer, though less clearly and exactly, Defoe encourages the making of some very "nice" yet powerful distinctions between Jack as thief and Jack as not so honest a tradesman. Where the novel had called the standard definition of "gentleman" into question by making Jack a "born" gentleman and then ambiguating his status, its strategy here is exactly the opposite; it aims to

<hr>

[25] Monk, preface to *CJ*, pp. xvii–xviii.

[26] The pain Jack causes in robbing the widow is shown in a contemporary engraving, for which see Capt. Charles Johnson, *A General History of the Lives and Adventures of the Most Famous Highwaymen, Murderers, Street-Robbers, &c.* (1734), facing p. 120.

[27] Guthrie, Ordinary Account, 3 March 1706/7; Reed's *Weekly Journal; or, British Gazetteer*, 20 August 1720.

sort out, rather than muddle further, the already muddled but easy, popular, and of course anti-bourgeois notion that all businessmen are crooks. It does this by making Jack a "Trade thief," but in a context where the metaphor is difficult to sustain. Jack, too, is a thief and yet no thief, the difference being that the novel makes him first one and latterly the other, keeping his "trade thefts" as far from his actual thefts as its full length allows. So long as the reader is kept from confusing Jack's business dealings with more or less ordinary street crime, illicit and avaricious though these dealings may be, he is in no position to confuse far more legitimate businessmen with out-and-out thieves. He may compare such businessmen to Jack, of course, but this will be to their advantage, any such comparisons tending to raise the notion that there is in fact a trade morality, which Jack violates and other men observe.[28]

But one cannot end novels on such *aperçus*, something Defoe well enough understood. Even a story given over to the subversion or destabilization of inconvenient but popularly held ideas has to come to some kind of conclusion and, at some level, seem all of a piece. Defoe tries in awkward ways to achieve both effects, and the results are appropriately shaky. Part 4 exerts an especially divisive effect on the novel, threatening to split it into two parallel and unrelated lines of action. By themselves, parts 1, 2, and 3 organize around Jack's efforts to rise toward gentlemanliness. From the vantage point of part 4, however, parts 1 and 2 reorient themselves, combining with 4 to make Jack's main thrust in life seem the getting of money; Jack becomes more important as economic man than as gentleman. The novel itself becomes almost like one of those either/or optical illusions, the rabbit/duck, for instance, or the vase/two facing profiles, except the effect is not so witty. If the novel is mainly about gentility, part 4 seems awkward and adventitious; if it is about economics, part 3 is a blind alley. Either way, substantial parts of it are made to look irrelevant and digressive. Defoe tries to finesse this difficulty by connecting the last two parts of the novel via Jack's Jacobitism, this being both the end point of his gentility and the starting point of his mercantile adven-

---

28 A kind of negative argument for the morality of trade could be made on other bases as well; thus Defoe argues in *CEG* for the "honesty" of many in trade by saying, in effect, they are neither so bad as some others or as they might be (2 [pt. 1]: 28–52). Such negative, but advantageous comparisons could reach high as well as low. Albert O. Hirschman suggests that "commercial and money-making pursuits" could seem relatively "harmless and innocuous" when compared not only to "the looting armies and murderous pirates of the time" but to "the passionate pastimes and savage exploits" favored by "the long-dominant aristocratic ideal": "The very contempt in which economic activities were held led to the conviction, in spite of much evidence to the contrary, that they could not possibly have much potential in any area of human endeavor and were incapable of causing either good *or evil* [his emphasis] on a grand scale .... In a sense, the triumph of capitalism, like that of many modern tyrants, owes much to the widespread refusal to take it seriously or to believe it capable of great design or achievement" (*The Passions and the Interests: Political Arguments for Capitalism before Its Triumph* [Princeton, 1977], pp. 58–9, 63).

tures. If only metonymically, Jack's two great errors – social and economic – are linked by and to his one great political error, rebellion against the king. Upon this metonymy one might build one or more interpretations, but the novel gives no clues as to how to proceed. Jack's Jacobitism connects plausibly with his failed or bogus gentility, the connection having a long history in criminal biography, but how is one to connect it with his avarice?

Equally problematic is Jack's sudden religious awareness, which comes late and arbitrarily, as though saved for this moment. In conjunction with his remarriage and pardon it suggests that Jack's life is at last straightened out on all levels, religious as well as political and domestic. Only when Jack makes his last, great reconciliation with God, it seems, is he finally able to profit from the other two, making a second return to England for a second reunion with his wife. This last great diapason sounds rather thinly, however, for while it puts an end to Jack's shady dealings in the Caribbean, it does not resolve them; there is nothing equivalent here to the effect of the king's pardon on Jack's quest for gentility. Nor (though the temptation is strong) can one extend the metonymy that holds Jack's social, political, and economic errors together quite far enough to make the pardon include his trade with the Spaniards, for the pardon (as noted earlier) precedes the trading. Had it come later, it might have seemed to offer Jack a state of economic as well as political grace, freeing him to make yet a third try at life in Europe and, as it happens, his marriage. But as things stand, Jack's life as merchant peters out, too, with a few scant closural gesturings to reinforce the effect of his getting right with God. Thus Jack gets a real attack of the gout and makes some final comments on the growing vogue for writing lives, the first harking back to the beginning of part 4 where, needing an excuse to hide from his fellow Jacobites, he only pretended to have the gout, and the second resuming a theme sounded at the very beginning of the novel. Here, too, for whatever reasons, Defoe misses a chance to achieve greater closural effect.

So much for reading #3, which contradicts reading #2 by denying that Jack's career as merchant is the moral equivalent of either his life as a thief, or his failed and treasonable efforts to become a gentleman, or both. Reading #4 moves beyond this point by making Jack's experience in the Caribbean seem – albeit backhandedly and only on balance – the least unsavoury and most attractively simple of all his social and economic roles. Of all the "readings" I am proposing, this is the most tenuous but also the most intriguing. It comes as the inevitable consequence, however, of the novel's effort to make Jack "honest" by showing him rising from slave to overseer to slaveholder. Virginia for Jack is seemingly the great good place. His experience there stands opposite his career as a thief and –

insofar as this seems the one wholly legitimate period in his life – what he does there pales all his subsequent achievements. There for the first time in his life he becomes part of an overall social hierarchy, his position in it definite, solid, and ultimately important. Wealth and social class are the same thing in Virginia, something we and Jack fail to appreciate until his first return to England, where it is not. In Virginia careers are open to talents, and Jack rises to his proper level. There is (or need be) no difference between his individual sense of himself and what – with appropriate help, which he gets – he can become. No similar opportunities are available in London, except possibly – and briefly – in crime.[29] When Jack turns his back on Virginia, first to become a gentleman and then a merchant, his separate, successive pursuits of social and economic standing once more threaten to exclude him from society.

Jack's time in Virginia, however, is not entirely non-problematic. For one thing, he is not so good a master to the slave he calls his tutor as his Great Master was to him. But this falling off is not so troubling as another, larger phenomenon. Defoe loads Jack's rise from slave to slavemaster with more than biographical significance, heaping it with political and even religious implication. In doing so, he inevitably starts his reader thinking emblematically, perhaps even allegorically, and the further such thoughts extend the more disturbing they become. Of the secondary meanings that attach to Jack's experience in Virginia, the clearest and most coherent – up to a point – is political. In discovering how to manage slaves by making them "Grateful ... for their good usage" (149), Jack illustrates an important principle in Defoe's own theory of governance, and one which, we've already noted, serves later in the novel to bind husband and wife as well as king and subject. There is something powerful in this demonstration of a general political principle operating through all the important social relations, but something ominous, too. The homology is grand but also self-subverting. The fact that it includes slaves, instead of the servants more usually included in discussions of the "relative duties," taints the whole equation, tending to imply that the subordinate parties in domestic and political as well as economic relations have no choice but to feel gratitude for the kindness extended them by their superiors, the only alternative being a balder, more ruthless form of subjection. It is better for both slaves and masters, the text suggests, if neither is forced to confront

---

29 Thus, despite the real concern the customs-house broker shows for Jack, he doesn't intervene in his life in any crucially useful way. I don't think this is accidental. "If we see a youth among the poor people of good natural parts, quick thought, strong memory, sharp wit," says Defoe, "we are generally apt to say 'tis pity the boy should not be put to school, 'tis pity he should not be well taught; and some times such a youth has been pick'd up and taught in meer charity by some man of learning and estate who has so pityed his circumstances; and some great men ... have been rais'd from such beginnings" (*CEG*, 109). Defoe might easily have made Jack's life just such a romance, but he doesn't.

the harsh implications of the institution that binds them together. When slaves feel gratitude, even love toward their masters, more work gets done with less cruelty, and there are fewer hard feelings all around.

Thus Jack's "Gentle usuage and Lenity" has "a Thousand times more Influence" on his master's slaves, "to make them Diligent, than all the Blows and Kicks, Whippings, and other Tortures could have" (149). Which does Jack's heart good, for he is not by nature a cruel man, and which makes his master practically ecstatic. "Nothing has so much robb'd me of the Comfort of all my Fortunes," he tells Jack by way of congratulation, "as the Cruelty used in my Name, on the Bodies of those poor Slaves" (145). "Cruelty," he had told him earlier, "is the Aversion of my Nature; and ... the only uncomfortable thing that attends me, in all my prosperity" (133). The master speaks as if cruelty and his prosperity were two separable things, but in fact the one is the foundation of the other; it is cruelty – the commission, the threat, even the mere withholding of it – that has made him rich and continues to make him rich. When Jack first suggests one might manage slaves without cruelty, his master asks, "but how then can my business be done?" (133). It is Jack's genius to put – or to seem to put – his master's business on another footing. Mere slaves – who could not "be mannag'd by Kindness, and Courtisy; but must be rul'd with a Rod of Iron ... or they would Rise and Murther all their Masters" (128) – are, through his efforts, made practically "the same as ... Christian Servants, except [they are] the more Thankful and Humble, and Laborious of the Two" (150). Jack calls what he does "managing" (149) and "Government" (134), but it could also be called the production of false consciousness.[30]

The slavery Jack experiences, observes, profits from, and risks in Virginia becomes almost too powerful a metaphor for what is at stake in social relations. If Jack's first and last wife did not become his grateful spouse and faithful servant, she would nonetheless have remained his slave. Given her disadvantage before him, it is in her own best interest to give herself selflessly to him. Similarly, it is in Jack's own best interest to become King George's loyal subject, the alternative being, possibly, to become yet again someone else's slave in Virginia. Needless to say, the novel values both submissions, going so far as to make them both seem marks of redemption. Nonetheless, neither submission can seem unambiguously admirable, insofar as it bears comparison to Jack's slaves' grateful

---

[30] Thus see Althusser on the way that ideology variously "interpellates" individuals into subjects who "'work,'" and "'who work by themselves' in the vast majority of cases, with the exception of the 'bad subjects' who on occasion provoke the intervention of one of the detachments of the (repressive) State apparatus": "the individual *is interpellated as a (free) subject ... in order that he shall (freely) accept his subjection*, i.e. in order that he shall make the gestures and actions of his subjection 'all by himself'" (*Lenin and Philosophy and Other Essays*, tr. Ben Brewster [New York, 1971], pp. 181–2).

appreciation of their slavery. This homology can seem still more complicated and disturbing as it extends beyond politics into religion.

For some reason – perhaps to make slavery as Jack and the Great Master practice it seem more acceptable – Defoe wants to suggest that the Great Master (who is by no means accidentally so named) is in some ways like God. Thus, though inherently kind, he is sometimes obliged to be cruel because it is the only way to get his "business" done given the nature of the human materials he works with. Jack's advent, however, brings a new dispensation for both master and slave, as Jack finds a new way of going about his master's business. Standing as mediator between slaveholder and slaves, partaking of both their natures, Jack saves his fellow slaves from dire punishment by interceding with their master. He even goes so far as to test their sentiments by spreading a false story of his own execution. If the Great Master is like God, and Jack like Christ, and the slaves like sinners to be redeemed, then somewhere on a plantation in Virginia, it might seem, the New Jerusalem is abuilding. This is heady stuff, and strange. Everett Zimmerman quite properly calls the whole episode "unsavoury," but it's dangerous as well.[31] To the extent the analogies sketched out hold, they open the door to terrible blasphemies; insofar as they cannot, they make Jack's narrative vulnerable to interpretations that might otherwise have been unimaginable.

Colonel Jack is not an anti-slavery novel nor does it want to suggest that a simulacrum of God, though now dead, was once alive in Virginia. Most certainly it does not want to suggest that Jack (CJ) is or was the type or anti-type of JC. What it does want to do, apparently, is to link Jack's various social, economic, political, and religious relations up into one unified field of analogies: Jack is to the slaves as the Great Master is to Jack, as King George is to Jack, and as God is to Jack – the last relationship being of primary importance because, ultimately, all authority ought to be aligned with God's – and (in not the least interesting of these comparisons) as Jack is to his wife. This pattern of analogies is valuable in formal terms – thus the novel ends when Jack, having worked through each of these relations, finally squares things with God – but it raises vexing problems when we try to discover its meaning. Each relation is problematic enough in itself, but, when an effort is made to consider them all together, they become unimaginably complex or too dreadfully simple. It is either all too difficult or all too easy to answer the riddle, how are a husband, a king, and God all like the Great (Slave)Master? Defoe does not want the easy (and embarrassing) answer, but the text presses in its direction. The pressure may be inadvertent. In its effort to achieve wholeness of meaning and form, *Colonel Jack* may be saying more than Defoe knows, can admit, or even wants to say about social hierarchy,

[31] Zimmerman, *Defoe and the Novel*, p. 137.

politics, economic struggle, the dreadful position of men before God, or of men with respect to their wives.[32]

In situating Jack in Virginia, Defoe seems to have opened a considerable can of worms, the implications of the situation being more than he (or we) can sort out and digest. By comparison Jack's life in the Caribbean is much simpler, if less licit. Up to the time he commences as merchant, Jack has had a hankering after the social, evidenced in part 1 by his joining up with and then quitting the anti-society of the London underworld, in part 2 by his climb up the Virginia social ladder, and in part 3 by his desire to become a complete, if not entirely English gentleman. Nonetheless he remains all the while an outsider, even in Virginia feeling a gap between himself and the larger world that beckons. When he commences trading with the Spanish in the Caribbean – at first out of exigency and then with an increasing, positive excitement perhaps not entirely describable as "avarice" – the excitement may have something to do with a newfound freedom vis-à-vis the social. In the Caribbean the social complexities that elsewhere press on Jack, and on the reader's awareness of him, are comparatively absent. Jack has no friends, no wife, no master, no king to contend with, no victims to placate, bully, or bamboozle. Nominally an outlaw, he is welcomed wherever he goes as someone who gives good value for value received. Once more it might be said, this time with reference back to his "managing" the slaves in Virginia, that Jack's good fortune is not achieved at the cost of others' misery. Here is no expropriation of

[32] On the subject of slavery, too, it is possible Defoe knew or felt more than he could say, or even order in his mind. His description of the institution in *Colonel Jack* is contradictory, but also complex and rich; whether Defoe intended the effect or not, we can see Jack, "liberal" to start, becoming racist before our eyes, with all the usual racist rhetoric. Thus when his first efforts to treat the black slaves decently fail to make them properly compliant, he begins "indeed to see, that the Cruelty, so much talk'd of ... in Whipping the *Negro* Slaves, was not so much owing to the Tyranny, and Passion, and Cruelty of the *English*, as had been reported ... But that it is owing to the Brutallity, and obstinate Temper of the *Negroes*, who cannot be mannag'd by Kindness, and Courtisy; but must be rul'd with a Rod of Iron, beaten with *Scorpions*, as the Scripture calls it." This realization brings with it a comfort, i.e., that "the *English* not being accounted to be of a Cruel Disposition ... really are not so" (128). Defoe's treatment of the rebellion on the slave ship in *Captain Singleton* is curious, too, in that, momentarily, he seems not unsympathetic to the enterprise. And what are we to make of Crusoe's selling Xury, despite his promise to the contrary, and of his being wrecked during an illicit voyage to buy slaves cheap in Africa? That these were relevant questions in Defoe's own time is indicated by Charles Gildon's reference to "that infamous Trade of buying and selling of Men for Slaves," and what he finds to be Crusoe's peculiar lack of "Conscience" in the matter: "one would have expected him to have attributed his Shipwreck to this very Cause" (*The Life and Strange Surprising Adventures of D— De F—* [1719], p. 14). As Defoe's authorship of the text has recently been powerfully questioned, Captain Misson's magnificent denunciation of the enslavement of Africans may not be directly relevant; such speeches, however, do not come out of the blue (see *A General History of the Pyrates*, ed. Manuel Schonhorn [London, 1972], pp. 404–5, and, on Defoe's authorship, P. N. Furbank and W. R. Owens, *The Canonisation of Daniel Defoe* [New Haven, 1988], pp. 100–9). Defoe's complex views on slavery remain to be examined in detail; in the meanwhile, for a useful survey see Peter Earle, *The World of Defoe* (New York, 1977), pp. 67–71, 131–3.

others' property, as in part 1, or, as in part 2, of their labor (which, Locke says, is – or ought to be – a form of inalienable property).[33]

In a curious way, once Jack accommodates himself to being an outsider, reordering his life to pursue purely economic goals, he reaps unanticipated social advantage. He finds himself, as he says, "in a very odd Condition indeed." Taking him in and protecting him from the authorities, his trading partners on the Mexican coast become "Friends" and make him "perfectly easie" (299, 301). Not since he and the other Jacks roamed the London streets has Jack enjoyed such simple, unencumbered relations with others.[34] In part 3 of the novel he had no friends, and in part 2 his only friend was the Great Master. The kindness of the Spanish planters might be compared to that of the customs-house broker, and Jack's living with them at the edge of legality might be compared to his life among the glasshouse boys. Of course he is in a better position now to exploit the help he gets, being wiser and more autonomous. Conceivably Jack could settle down and, living the life now of a Spanish gentleman (see 301–2), make a third try at establishing himself in the New World. For all his pleasure in Mexico, however, certain things make this impossible. He misses his wife, comes to a proper awareness of God (a Protestant God), and is mindful of the wealth he has left behind. Like Moll and Singleton, like Crusoe at the end of his *Further Adventures*, Jack feels a second yearning toward home and concludes his narrative with a second voyage back to England, in hopes that a third effort at making a go of life there, and nowhere else, will this time succeed.

This return has closural effect, of course, but less than it might. The fact is that Jack fares best away from England. Though abortively, Scotland and France offer greater scope to his talents, and his ventures in Virginia and the Caribbean make him wealthy. England has given him nothing but an unslakeable and self-diminishing desire to be other than he is. Jack has great entrepreneurial talents, even as a thief. Unlike Moll, whose great forte is technique ("the Greatest Artist" of her time, etc.), his great talent lies in negotiating deals, in selling things back to his victims that would otherwise get him nothing. He is a skillful manager of workers, too, and takes to the Caribbean trade like a duck to water. Everything he puts his hand to, except trade, he has to learn, sometimes at the cost of painful mistakes, but Jack knows how to buy and sell from the very first. He is a born tradesman, who wants instead to be a born gentleman. Why, having allowed him to discover his natural environment, does Defoe then turn him homeward? The novel's conclusion may owe something to its author's nationalism, as might, too, the various returns of Moll, Singleton, and

---

[33] Locke, *Concerning Civil Government*, chapter 5, para. 27.
[34] Thus, giving his chief benefactor's family presents, which they appreciate, Jack significantly pronounces them "not at all Mercenary" (306).

Crusoe. Though Defoe was strongly interested in encouraging the coloni-
zation of Virginia and Maryland, even South America and Madagascar,
deep down he may have felt such distant climes were no place for him and,
presumably, for his comfortably moneyed readers finally to repose their
imaginations. Or, more simply, to have kept his characters abroad may
have seemed in some way to impugn England. Of all the novels, *Colonel
Jack* might most have seemed to support this inference. To have allowed
its protagonist to live out his days as a French, Spanish, or even Virginian
gentleman might have pushed too hard against the English caste system,
with all its fragile mystifications. Even letting Jack carve out a secure and
happy place for himself in the New World may have seemed, to Defoe, to
imply too great a criticism of the Old.

"In the beginning," Locke famously declares, "all the world was
America ... Right and conveniency went together." Because "no such
thing as money was anywhere known," there could be none of what Jack
calls "the Restless pushing" after it.[35] Defoe is not nostalgic for a moneyless
world, quite the opposite. The great attraction of America for him is that
so much money can be made there, so relatively easily, which is to say
merely by hard work. If Defoe is nostalgic for anything, it is a world where
wealth stands in direct relation to work, and where earned wealth and an
individual's status – which is to say, economic activity and perceived social
worth – are exactly congruent. If Defoe felt any such nostalgia, however, it
was only as part of a larger, clearer-eyed, and consequently somewhat
disordered view of current social and economic realities. Defoe had his
doubts about the social value of trade, a residual respect for gentlemanly
"blood," and, very probably, an audience not too susceptible to the notion
that tradesmen were as good as gentlemen. The most this novel can be said
to assert – and it is a partial, hesitant, contradictory assertion – is that
economic men are certainly no worse than gentlemen. Indeed, in some
respects, gentlemen may pose greater threats to society than even the
worst kinds of economic men, whether these be thieves, slavemasters, or
illegal traders.

At a larger, still vaguer level, *Colonel Jack* is "about" thieves, merchants,
gentlemen, slaves and the masters of slaves, none considered alone but
each situated vis-à-vis the others. The effect of this is to prevent any one of
Jack's divers social and economic roles from being judged by a single,
possibly absolute standard. Though the chief beneficiary of this "situating
of names" is the notion "merchant," and the chief victim the notion
"gentleman," the potential meaning of the text exfoliates beyond these
probable intentions, almost uncontrollably. If only by virtue of the fact
that all Jack's functions are linked together by a single lifeline, the novel
suggests a complex of teasing but ultimately confused and confusing

[35] Locke, *Concerning Civil Government*, chapter 5, paras. 49, 51; *CJ*, p. 40.

comparisons and contrasts. Thieves and gentlemen are opposite and yet alike; merchants and thieves are alike and yet opposite; merchants and gentlemen are most definitely not alike, but both are clearly different from thieves. All three, moreover, enjoy an autonomy that sets them apart from slaves. And yet, as Jack's overall experience shows, the pursuit of all three forms of autonomy – the thief outside, the gentleman inside, the merchant at the verge of society – risks eventual slavery at the hands of other, more powerful men, all of whom operate with some kind of socially sanctioned authority. (Even Jack's kidnappers are sanctioned by society, insofar as the Virginia planters who buy their cargoes ask no questions.)

Autonomy, which is to say freedom from social authority, tends to shade toward outlawry; but then in this novel socially sanctioned authority itself is ambiguous. The various people who expropriate Jack, or try to, have no real right to his person: not his kidnappers, not the French privateers, not the Spanish authorities in Havana, not the Great Master himself, perhaps not even (and this verges on political blasphemy) the dubiously entitled king. George I, after all, has come to be Great Master of Britain as questionably as Jack's master in Virginia gains sovereignty over him.[36] In both instances, however, a *fait accompli* is legitimated by the subordinate's accepting and acknowledging his superior's authority. Jack submits to the king just as he submits to the Great Master, or, alternatively, is brought to submit to the king just as he brought his fellow slaves to gladly serve their owner, i.e., by the waiving of a threatened punishment. Somewhere in Whitehall the king's ministers are "managing" Jack and other restive Britons (the thought, I'd guess, if not conscious would have been very close to the surface of Defoe's mind) by the same techniques Jack used to "manage" *his* Great Master's unwilling, sullen, and potentially rebellious subjects.

In *Robinson Crusoe*, too, Defoe shows his protagonist managing restive and potentially dangerous men by means of plausible and persuasive fictions. The mutineers surrender, finally, because Crusoe leads them to believe that they're outgunned and outmatched, that they've landed on an island with an established political order headed by a "Governor" whom he merely represents. This playing on their credulity is entirely necessary, if they're to be subdued and brought under rule with the minimum of blood and fuss. Defoe's fascination with such matters is easily explained. He, too, had gone about telling stories to credulous people for political reasons, first as Harley's secret agent in Scotland and over wide areas of England, then for later ministries; he was a veteran of numberless pamphlet wars and for

36 For what it's worth, we might note that George I is no "born" king, like the Pretender, but king by virtue of his social attributes; here is another instance where "blood" does not quite "tell."

years had engaged in a covert, undercover "management" of Mist's and Applebee's journals.[37] None of the stories he told, though, could have been so successful, so literally enthralling, as those Jack tells the slaves. Putting them into a position to think, actually, they're freer than they really are, Jack makes them into the very best sort of slaves, i.e., cheerful, willing, credulous, unmindful of their domination, objects who, believing even they are "free" subjects, freely accept their subjection all by themselves. Dancing within "circles" of Jack's "drawing," literally and figuratively enthralled, they "dance" – as do "indeed the greater Part of the Inhabitants of the Globe" – "to the Musick of their Chains."[38]

Does *Colonel Jack* itself aim at "managing" its readers? It is worth noting the novel actually shows – and, I'd say, allows for – two kinds of enthrallment. Jack is freed by his experience of slavery, as is his wife, too; under the rule of the Great Master he begins to consolidate himself into an effective personality (which is to say "subject," in all appropriate senses of that term). Slavery for him – he's a *British* subject, after all – is an opportunity to look around and take stock of things, to measure himself against his possible places in the world. Promoting similar effects – not credulity and acceptance but perplexity, curiosity, and critical engagement – Defoe's novels might similarly seem, even at their most compelling, a way of preparing readers for a certain kind of freedom. "Just as it was not possible in the West itself, from a certain stage of interdependence onward," says Norbert Elias, "to rule people solely by force and physical threats, so it also became necessary, in maintaining an empire that went beyond mere plantation-land and plantation-labor, to rule people in part through themselves, through the moulding of their super-egos."[39] The most credulous sort of readers, I suppose, might be as molded by a novel as the slaves are by Jack. Better, cleverer, more critical readers might also fall prey to the far more subtle stratagems of a great

[37] By the time he wrote *Colonel Jack*, Defoe had been nearly two decades in "a secret management" (his own phrase) of a variety of potentially dissident political elements: Scots, Dissenters, Tories, and anyone else who might possibly embarrass first Harley and then, after 1714, a succession of Whig ministers. Coerced into this activity by the threat of long imprisonment, yet seeming to warm to his task, Defoe was placed in a situation not unlike Jack's vis-à-vis the Great Master. For the above, and other like uses of "manage" and "management," see *The Letters of Daniel Defoe*, ed. George Harris Healey (Oxford, 1955), pp. 68, 140, 272. In one letter to Charles De la Faye (26 April 1718) the word appears no less than five times (see pp. 452–3). Apparently it could have something of a bad odor, for, in complimenting a powerful political figure on his "managing" of the Sacheverell affair, Defoe asks him to "pardon ... the word" (Letter to Lieutenant-General James Stanhope, 8 March 1709/10, p. 265).

[38] It is Captain Misson in *A General History of the Pyrates* who declares that "the greater Part of the Inhabitants of the Globe," by which he means practically everyone except him and his fellow pirates, are "born and bred in Slavery, by which their Spirits were broke." "Ignorant of their Birth-Right," he says, "and the Sweets of Liberty," they "dance to the Musick of their Chains" (ed. Schonhorn, p. 394).

[39] Norbert Elias, *Power and Civility*, *The Civilizing Process: Volume II*, tr. Edmund Jephcott (New York, 1982), p. 314.

master like Defoe, but hardly, since he gives so much of the show away, with equal unawareness. There may finally be no escaping the invisible, insidious disciplining of "the subject" Foucault calls the "government of individualization." Still, it would seem better to dance (if dance we must) in wider rather than narrower circles and, if not without chains, then at least alert to their weight, heft, and clink.

Colonel Jack draws its circles quite wide indeed, projecting no single pattern or meaning because, it seems, Defoe himself had no single pattern or meaning to give it and so, finally, none to impose on his readers. Like all the other criminal novels, as well as *Robinson Crusoe*, it ends ambiguously, inviting a double view. On the one hand there is material and even personal happiness, on the other a quality of loss. Jack's losses are not so bad as those of the other criminal protagonists, and so his end can seem happier. He is older but wiser, has been cuckolded but now is happily married, has rebelled against the king but been pardoned, has ignored God but now recognizes and praises His mercies. Beneath all this, however, there is all through the novel, and especially at the end, an ill-defined but pervasive sense of disequilibrium, of basic disharmony. First, there is the highly ambiguous status of Jack's character, always, and second, a recurring implication that between this character (however we define it) and the larger social world there is a lack of "fit" not entirely Jack's fault.

Like the best sort of highwaymen, his virtue consists of "generous principles," which themselves are not enough. Unlike those highwaymen, however, Jack does not close his life climactically, in a flurry of struggle, assertion, triumph and debasement; there is no final settling of his account. He survives as none of them do, but, despite his royal pardon and all his eventual wealth and social polish, he never quite achieves the legitimacy he once had wanted, and which a hero should have, if not death. What equilibrium he may seem to have achieved is belied by his continuing motion, the novel ending with Jack (quite literally) neither here nor there. He is an arriviste who never arrives, left by the novel in transit where of course he forever remains. Having cast away the status he enjoyed in Virginia, he has yet to find his proper niche, a status that answers to his full range of special qualities. Looked at from this angle, *Colonel Jack* can seem yet another of Defoe's unhappy meditations on the insufficiency of human nature. What makes it more, however, is a still more disturbing intimation. Jack is like the best sort of highwaymen, too, in that his virtue is somehow wasted. There was something in him, once, which his world let go unrecognized and unused, and the best parts of it have somehow dissipated. For all his great range and variety – "what a man might he not have been" – Jack is no man for all seasons. But, the novel comes close to suggesting, the climate around him is wrong, too. He

finds no proper place in the world because the world as currently constituted can afford him none.[40]

If, as Bakhtin claims, "the artist has a keen sense for ideological
problems in the process of birth and generation," it would seem that
Defoe's keen sense for such things has led him – and his readers – into a
morass of confusions and contradictions. His effort, faute de mieux, to
achieve order at the level of the signifier via analogies, cross-comparisons,
and the plenitude of Jack's functions, serves only to emphasize the chaos of
the novel at the level of the signified. Nonetheless, some value may be seen
in this achievement. Bakhtin prizes literature because it "often anticipates
developments in philosophy and ethics," a high standard and one by
which *Colonel Jack* can hardly be said to succeed.[41] Another way of looking
at literature in relation to the history of ideas, however, is offered by Pierre
Macherey. "Literature challenges ideology by using it," he says. "If
ideology is thought of as a non-systematic ensemble of significations, the
work proposes a *reading* of these significations, by combining them as signs"
(emphasis his).[42] I take this to mean that while ideology seems to add up,
it doesn't, and that its incompleteness and incoherence are exposed when a
given work of literature tries to make it add up, if need be by using all the
devices for cohesion and closure it has at hand.

Thus, the more impressed we are by Defoe's efforts to make *Colonel Jack*
seem "all of a piece" (Macherey's phrase), the more aware we become that
"it is fissured, unmade even in its making" by the ideology out of which it
is formed and which it seeks to transform: "the disorder that permeates the
work is related to the disorder of ideology (which cannot be organized as a
system)."[43] The triumph of literature, in this view, is that the silk purse it
tries to make out of the sows' ears of one or another set of socially provided
ideas has always some salutary defect. And this defect – optimally – turns
the mind back not on the artist but on the insufficiency of the materials

[40] For a differing view of the significance of Jack's never "acquiring a concrete social identity or a
particular and defining location in society," see Richetti, *Defoe's Narratives*, p. 174, and
pp. 145–91 generally.
[41] P.N. Medvedev / M. M. Bakhtin, *The Formal Method in Literary Scholarship: A Critical Introduction
to Sociological Poetics*, tr. Albert J. Wehrle (Baltimore, 1978), p. 17.
[42] Macherey, *Theory of Literary Production*, p. 133.
[43] Ibid., pp. 154–5. Cf. the following comment by Hayden White on the problem of closure in
historical writing (which he regards as a variety of fiction), when there is no clear consensus on
what is just and proper: "If every fully realized story, however we define that familiar but
conceptually elusive entity, is a kind of allegory, points to a moral, or endows events, whether
real or imaginary, with a significance they do not possess as a mere sequence, then it seems
possible to conclude that every historical narrative has as its latent or manifest purpose the
desire to moralize the events of which it treats. Where there is ambiguity or ambivalence
regarding the status of the legal system, which is the form in which the subject encounters most
immediately the social system in which he is enjoined to achieve a full humanity, the ground on
which any closure of a story one might wish to tell about a past, whether it be a public or a
private past, is lacking" ("The Value of Narrativity in the Representation of Reality," in *On
Narrative*, ed. W. J. T. Mitchell [Chicago, 1981], pp. 13–14).

with which, and against which, he was forced to work. It is at such points
we might begin to hear the dissonant jinglings of the "chains" that –
binding, defining, restraining our subjectivity – still, and inevitably,
"subject" us. "Established against an ideology as much as it is from an
ideology," says Macherey, "the [literary] work contributes to an exposure
of ideology, or at least to a definition of it."[44] *O tempora, o mores, o* varieties
of false consciousness: it is no small part of Defoe's great genius that he
projects these unflinchingly, with all the flaws, contradictions, and
inconsistencies that riddle them. Because Dante and Milton "conferred
upon [the] modern mythology [of Christianity] a systematic form," said
Shelley, they would keep it from being "utterly forgotten."[45] It is only
slightly to parody this pronouncement to say that Defoe keeps the ideological disarray of early capitalism alive in *Colonel Jack*, and so – however
he may have affected his original readers – in our minds, too, by conferring
upon it an essentially *un*systematizable form. Such naivity as he shows is
neither easily come by nor easily sustained, perhaps reason enough to
value it. It is not for nothing, then, that *Colonel Jack* passes up its several
chances at achieving greater coherence and a more powerful sense of
closure.

[44] Macherey, *Theory of Literary Production*, p. 133.
[45] Shelley, *Defence of Poetry* in *Selected Poems, Essays, and Letters*, ed. Ellsworth Barnard (New
York, 1944), p. 555.

7

Notions different from all the world: criminal stupidity, the self, and the symbolic order

It will be impossible to bring vice out of fashion if we cannot bring men to an understanding of what it really is; but could we prevail upon a man to examine his vice, to dissect its parts, and view the anatomy of it; to see how disagreeable it is ... how despicable and contemptible in its highest fruition; how destructive to his senses, estate, and reputation; how dishonorable, and how beastly, in its public appearances: such a man would certainly be out of love with it.

Serious Reflections of Robinson Crusoe, p. 87

I was in a kind of Stupidity ... I had a Mind full of Horrour ... but my Thoughts got no Vent ... I had a silent sullen kind of Grief, which cou'd not break out either in Words or Tears.

You go upon different Notions from all the World; and tho' you reason upon it so strongly, that a Man knows hardly what to answer, yet I must own, there is something in it shocking to Nature, and something very unkind to yourself.

Roxana, pp. 129, 156

Such is the power of words, that mankind is able to act as much evil by their tongues as by their hands; the ideas that are formed in the mind from what we hear are most piercing and permanent.

Serious Reflections of Robinson Crusoe, p. 81

The knowledge of things, not words, makes a scholar.

The Complete English Tradesman, p. 212

Perhaps if we could but artfully enough describe the Ugliness and Deformity of the Thing it self, we might stamp some Aversions in Mens Minds to it.

The *Review*, 7: 25 (11 April 1710)

With the growing complexity of social interaction in modernizing societies, Norbert Elias argues, "foresight" becomes as valuable a characteristic as "self-control." As "the number of ... people [increases] on whom the individual constantly depends in all his actions, from the simplest and most commonplace to the more complex and uncommon .... more and more people must attune their conduct to that of others." This growing, ever wider and more tightly reticulated "web of interdependence" puts "the individual who gives way to spontaneous impulses and emotions" in a situation where his "social existence" is increasingly "threatened." "Those able to moderate their affects," on the other hand, gain "greater ... social advantage." Indeed, it can seem – as with Moll and the mercer – that "the different structure of society now punishes affective outbursts and actions lacking the appropriate foresight with certain ruin." "Each individual," consequently, is "constrained from an early age to take account of the effects of his own or other people's actions on a whole series of links in the social chain." Along with "the formation of a more complex and secure 'super-ego' agency," Elias points out, this concern with "subordinat[ing] ... short-term impulses to the commands of an ingrained long-term view" encourages the development of "what we would today call a 'psychological' view of man." That is, "a more precise observation of others and oneself in terms of longer series of motives and causal connections" emerges from an increasingly felt need not only to exercise "vigilant self-control" but to engage in "perpetual observation of others" as essential and "elementary prerequisites for the preservation of one's social position."[1] One way in which "the civilizing process" shapes the psychology of the individual subject, then, is to make it increasingly more interested in itself and others as interactive "psychological" beings.

Much about criminal biography may be made to fit into Elias's overall schema. Its writers invest a great deal of energy into showing how small, seemingly insignificant bits of behavior can have very large consequences for both individuals and society. Separate acts combine into what Elias calls "chains of action," and individuals can be implicated in sometimes surprisingly extensive "chains of dependence."[2] Thieves rob, defraud, and hoax practically everyone from high to low; filled with all sorts of unforeseen encounters, their "lives" show that any given string of events can interconnect the humblest with the greatest persons in the land and, moreover, temporarily reverse their usual social positions. Murder can be the end result of drinking too much, of staying out too late, of having skipped church as a child; there is no knowing in what small dereliction of one's duty it all might have begun. All this may have served to bring readers to a greater self-consciousness about the potential range, scope, and effect of their individual behavior on themselves and the larger world, and so further supported self-control, but it would not have done much to explain just how and why certain people could go so badly wrong as, finally, to wind up hanged. Such insights, had they been available, could

---

[1] Norbert Elias, *Power and Civility, The Civilizing Process: Volume II*, tr. Edmund Jephcott (New York, 1982), pp. 232, 236, 280, 236, 248, 274. In her own way, Moll, too, is a valuer of foresight: "I was seldom in any Danger when I was by my self," she says of her criminal ventures, "or if I was, I got out of it with more Dexterity than when I was entangled with the dull Measures of other People, who had perhaps less forecast, and were more rash and impatient than I" (220).

[2] Elias, *Power and Civility*, pp. 234, 236, 242–3.

have contributed powerfully to the "foresight" Elias describes, to the
defense and enhancement of self against competing selves that it and
self-control aimed at achieving.

The primary concern of this last chapter will be Defoe's last novel, his
most psychological and – certainly among the criminal novels – his most
pointedly moral. These two aspects combine powerfully, each enhancing
the other. Thus, by itself, the novel's "moral" would seem little more
(perhaps even less) than the usual set of clichés. Roxana pays tribute to the
"Justice" of providence and the watchfulness of conscience in language
that might almost have come from the usual pamphlet. "The most secret
Crimes are," she says, "by the most unforeseen Accidents, brought to light,
and discovered." "Sin and Shame," she claims, "follow one-another so
constantly at the Heels, that they are ... like Cause and Consequence,
necessarily connected one with another ... 'tis not in the Power of humane
Nature to conceal the first, or avoid the last" (297–8). Without her
psychological density, and the complexity of affect that psychology pro-
vokes, Roxana herself would hardly seem more than an overblown cliché,
a "domestic" or "familiar" murderer who – corrupting her servant,
deceiving her spouse, sharing in her daughter's murder – had managed to
violate all the relative duties in an elaborate but not especially meaningful
pattern of action.[3] Roxana is not demonstrably struck down by God, nor
even caught and punished according to law. Nonetheless, her story
achieves a significance far beyond that of any ordinary criminal biography, showing (among other things) how the self can ruin itself quite
spectacularly though in an utterly private way. Had she only chosen to
recognize her daughter, her "social position" would probably not have
been threatened much at all. As she shows at the end of her narrative,

---

[3] For the categories "domestic" and "familiar," see, respectively, J. A. Sharpe, "Domestic
Homicide in Early Modern England," *The Historical Journal*, 24 (1981): 29–48, and *Turned to
Account*, pp. 4, 21–41, 43–51, 66–8. While the first term has wide usage in criminology, the
second, I'd argue, speaks more closely to patterns of eighteenth-century thought. For the
"relative duties," see, for instance, William Fleetwood, *The Relative Duties of Parents, Husbands,
Masters, Wifes, Children, Servants* (1705). As Maximillian Novak points out, Roxana's story can
also be seen as a version of an oft-repeated tale about "a person who is haunted by a crime
committed in the past and who is eventually destroyed by the secret gnawing at his conscience"
(*Realism, Myth, and History in Defoe's Fiction* [Lincoln, Neb., 1983], p. 20; see also *Turned to
Account*, pp. 76–7, and pp. 237–8, n. 13). Or, barring consideration of Susan's murder, Roxana's
career might be described in much the same terms routinely applied to the case of a woman
eventually hanged for theft: "The cause of her following such a wicked course as she had done,
was her pride, which raised in her a desire of living above her condition and circumstance in the
world .... But therein she found herself mistaken, for instead of growing rich and great, and
able to live at ease, she brought poverty, shame, misery and ruin upon herself by those very
wicked practices from which she expected to reap great advantages and satisfaction" (Alexander Smith, *A Compleat History of the Lives and Robberies of the Most Notorious Highwaymen, Footpads, Shoplifts, & Cheats of Both Sexes*, ed. Arthur L. Hayward [London, 1933], pp. 374–5).
Roxana's situation differs from this "standard" paradigm only in that, the last we hear of her,
she's not poor.

however, coming up to the moment just before the bottom drops entirely out of her life, guilt alone can be a terrible, disabling punishment, as destructive of the self as public execution and savoring – far more than Moll's Newgate, perhaps – of the inevitable miseries of hell.

But it is not merely the scope of Roxana's crime or the nature of her punishment that sets her apart from Defoe's other criminal characters and even the most interesting of actual murderers. More than any other redacted criminal in the period, fictive or not, her life seems all of a piece, a complex but largely comprehensible string or "chain" of deleterious causes and effects, with the worst of these the product – to an extent she never quite realizes – of a "Distemper . . . in my Head" (239). As, prodded by the novel, the reader examines and dissects the various "parts" of this distemper, he can begin to feel a highly self-conscious, self-probing reflexivity, an almost squeamish curiosity about the way his own mind works. But this is often the case with "anatomizing" (to use Defoe's metaphor), that the opening up of another makes us all the more anxiously aware of our own interiorities. Even late or post-modern readers may feel something of this anxiety if not its attendant moral effect, primed as we are by the recurrence in our own culture of certain notions the text presents about the frailty of consciousness: not only its susceptibility in a large, complex, intricate society to dark and errant impulses of its own, but its dire dependence for its sense of self on what some now call the symbolic order, i.e., that which enables and governs the ever lengthening "chains" of our interactions with others as well as our sense of self.[4]

Criminal biography does not offer much in the way of "psychology." Criminals' motives are generally made to seem inexplicable except, finally, as expressions of general human depravity. Crimes are committed either as the result of some sudden absence of mind (thus Strodtman's insensate wielding of the tobacco-beater, Dramatti's fatal outburst toward his wife), or else they proceed from irrational calculations. The latter case is illustrated by all those failed or would-be gentlemen who "resolve" to become highwaymen after weighing the advantages of what they mistakenly take to be a "merry life" against the one, major disadvantage of "a short one." Claude Duval was one of them. Unable to "confine himself in

[4] Over the past few decades *Roxana* has drawn increasing attention from a number of astute scholars and critics. In developing my own view of it, I have found the work of G. A. Starr especially useful (see the relevant chapters in *Defoe and Spiritual Autobiography* [Princeton, 1965], and *Defoe and Casuistry* [Princeton,1971]), as also Novak's "Crime and Punishment in *Roxana*," *Journal of English and Germanic Philology*, 65 (1966): 445–65 (the essentials of which have been absorbed into his *Realism, Myth, and History in Defoe's Fiction*), and Everett Zimmerman's "*Roxana*: The Verbal World" in his *Defoe and the Novel* (Berkeley, 1975), pp. 155–87. Also of interest for what it says of "the curious role of language within *Roxana*" is Janet E. Aikens's "Roxana: The Unfortunate Mistress of Conversation," *Studies in English Literature*, 25 (1985): 529–56.

his Expenses and Attendance, within the narrow bounds and limits of a Servant," and realizing that "he must have some new way to get money," he is "not long unresolved what course to take," for, making the acquaintance of a gang of highwaymen and "having before observed their way of living[,] a little persuasion now serves his turn; he resolves to make one with Them." What was that "little persuasion," and how did it determine Duval's "resolve"? As it rushes through a few brief preliminaries before getting down to its main business, this text doesn't say; nor do, in fact, much more serious, considered efforts to depict the criminal impulse. For all its seeming reference to a considered course of action, the term "resolve" typically did nothing more than mark the sheer depravity of criminals; that they could seem to reason, and reasoned so badly, was a sign of "their stupify'd Minds."[5]

Such stupidity – the exact opposite of anything like "foresight" – must at times have seemed itself stupifying; thus the utterly incomprehensible "resolve" of John Palmer, who decided to kill his mother. Having wasted his inheritance and "musing within himself how to carry on his further Revels and wicked and Worldly Enjoyments, which he knew very well could not be done without money; he presently bethought himself of the Estate which his poor Mother enjoy'd." It would have gone to him when she died, "but considering that she might ... live a great while longer, being a very healthful Woman, ... he resolv'd to shorten her Days." For all his musing, knowing, bethinking, and considering, Palmer's "barbarous and unheard-of" crime – which he expects to net him 50 pounds a year – seems hardly rational at all. The narrative, giving full attention to its "cruel and unnatural" details, decides it was something "the *Devil* (the inventor of all Wickedness) put him upon."[6] The same non-explanation for monstrously criminal behavior is offered by Nathaniel Butler, one of the earliest murderers to feature in English criminal biography. He, too, uses the word "resolve" as he describes how he murdered his friend and bedmate, another apprentice, and exactly how he felt and what he thought – or didn't feel and didn't think – all the while he was doing it.

"About (when he poore ignorant soule as void of death, as I of good[,] sweetly sleeping, and having committed his soule to God, as I had given up mine to Satan) the 14 or 15 night I had lyen with him, at 4 of the clock in the morning," Butler confesses in nearly unfollowable syntax,

---

[5] Smith, *Lives of the Highwaymen*, p. 304; *The Life of Deval. Showing How He Came to Be a Highway-Man ...* (1669/70), p. 3; George Olyffe, *An Essay Humbly Offer'd, for an Act of Parliament to Prevent Capital Crimes, and the Loss of Many Lives* (1731), p. 5. The idea that thieves stole out of choice after having given the matter careful consideration, and not out of necessity or derangement, could have the effect, too, of making their crimes seem a sort of wager against society. The value of this was that it could make hanging them seem not so much a "sporting away" of the lives of the indigent and vulgar as, rather, the end result of a sporting proposition.

[6] *The Cruel Son; or, the Unhappy Mother. Being a Dismal Relation of One Mr. Palmer and Three Ruffians, Who Barbarously Murder'd His Own Mother and Her Maid* (1707), pp. 6–7, 2.

I resolved to act my bloody tragedy, better becoming a fi[e]nd, then a friend, I
gave him a stob in the face, whilst he was asleep, and the young man awakening,
and put in a great fright, by this so sudden a cruelty, by a common desire, strove
for his life, and caught hold on the haire of my head, indeavouring if he might, to
keep that I resolved to bereave him of, and plucked a lock from the same, and
though I had great relentings of heart, and checks, feares, and horrors of conscience, upon this proceeding, which convinced me of the barbarousnesse of the
act; yet considering that I had given him a stob in the face, which would have
been looked upon by all, as an intended Murther, and thinking (being blinded by
the Devil) that by adding to my cruelty, and perfecting my sin, to counsell my
cruelty, and so avoid the shame. He being acquainted with my friends, and the
place of their residence, I fear'd he would by his means make it known to them,
and that make me odious amongst them to my great disgracement, therefor I was
tempted of the Devil, and my base heart by nature prone to wickednesse as a child
of wrath to dispatch him forth with out of the way that so my cursed intentions
might be the more secret before the eyes of the world, thus did my own blindnesse
of heart, cheat me of, and so destroy my life, whereupon I claped my hands on his
mouth, and so by violence kept him down, and stop his breath, by which means he
was strangled to death ...

Later confessions would at least be cast into clearer, more easily readable
prose. "O Sir!" said Elizabeth Chivers, "I am lost! I cannot pray, I cannot
repent, my Sin is too great to be pardon'd! I did commit it with Deliberation and Choice, and in cold Blood; I was not driven to it by Necessity
.... out of my wicked Heart [I] destroy'd the Child, and cast my self
away." Chivers had killed her three-month old baby despite the fact that
its father, her lover not husband, had agreed to support them both. "The
Devil putting it into her cruel Heart to destroy the poor Infant, which she
suckled," the ordinary reported, she "carried it to *Hackney*, and drown'd it
in a Pond there. And this she did without being driven to it by any
Necessity, or feeling any Remorse for it then."[7]

Phebe Ward had similarly been moved to "the commission of the most
crying Sin" by Satan's mysterious, imponderable instigations. Though she
"had receiv'd good Education from her Parents, who were honest and
religious Persons," at age sixteen she began "at several times, and with
several Men" to commit fornication. Nothing too extraordinary here, but
how was one to explain the fact that, luckier than Chivers, "tho' she was
courted by One of them to marry him, yet she would not consent to it"?
"Nor indeed could [she] endure the Man ... disliking him more than any
other; and yet," the ordinary adds with some astonishment, "he was the
Father to that Child of whom she (as an unnatural Mother) prov'd the
cruel Murtherer." Leaving her native Yorkshire and coming to London,

---

[7] *Blood Washed Away by Tears of Repentance: Being an Exact Relation of the Cause and Manner of That
Horrid Murther Committed on the Person of John Knight ... by Nathaniel Butler* (1657), pp. 5–6; Paul
Lorrain, Ordinary Account, 1 August 1712.

Ward "got into good Service in a worthy Family, where being suspected to be with Child, and ask'd the Question, she positively deny'd it, not only once, but several times." Here again Ward was more fortunate than most women caught in her situation, for "she was kindly and charitably offer'd by her Mistress (with whom she had not liv'd above a Month) to be taken care of, and well provided for, in her Lying-in, if she would own (as it greatly appear'd) that she was with Child." Yet still "this miserable Wretch" unaccountably denied the fact, stifling the baby when it was born – "(she could not well tell how)" – and throwing it into the privy. Years later, asking questions close to the central concerns of *Roxana*, another Newgate ordinary would still be wondering how any woman "could deal in Blood and Slaughter? How a Parent could tear to Pieces the Life of her own Infant? How she could bear its Cries, Innocent and Helpless, without relenting?" He got no answers to these questions, the woman having escaped justice in this case – and readerly attention – by dying in jail.[8]

Either the criminal's mind ceased functioning entirely, leaving only the basest, most brutish instincts, or else, parodying rational calculation, it flew off (some screws getting loose) into ever widening and ultimately nasty eccentricities. But how was mind disabled, how did it become maladjusted? Necessity, bad company, and occasionally cruel treatment are sometimes shown to have brutalized people to the point they become criminals, though the mechanism of this "hardening" process is never itself explained. All of us may become criminals, but at the same time criminals look – and sound – very strange people indeed. Even those whose behavior is explained (or explained away) in the usual economic, political, or crudely psychologistic terms are often made out, finally, to seem utterly uncommon, quite beyond the bounds of normal humanity or even human comprehension. Thus, while the better sort of thief wants to cut a gentlemanly figure as well as get money, and on occasion robs (or so it is claimed) out of a sense of social grievance, he frequently winds up committing unaccountable, even incredible acts of buffoonery or brutality.[9] There is no sense of a specific "character" behind such actions, even though, within the psychology available to the era, it would have been possible to suggest at least something along these lines. The "Comical Frolicks" and "whimseyes" of a famous late seventeenth-century burglar, wrote one of his biographers, might be "conceived" as things done "meerly to allay and pacify some troubles within, for that they were rather like fits of a possessed person, then the results of innocent mirth." It is not said what these interior "troubles" might have been – "there are questionless

---

[8] Lorrain, Ordinary Account, 22 December 1711; Thomas Purney, *The Ordinary of Newgate's Account of the Behaviour, Confession, and Last Dying Speech of Matthias Brinsden* (1722), pp. 3–4.

[9] See *Turned to Account*, chapter 6.

some Concealments and Depths, which will never be fathomed here by any Line or Research" – but this text is unique, to my knowledge, in suggesting as much as it does.[10] Thieves seem to have been interesting primarily as wild and crazy "guys" – that is, as objects to tease, guide and twig readers' fancies along a number of clearly set out lines – not as victims of poverty, miseducation, bad company, bad luck, or, particularly, their own bad minds. And if money was the greatest, the most easily understood and most visible motive for theft, then it was clear, too, that many people without money did not steal, and this despite the recurrent implication that some of them actually might have grievances against society.[11]

The motives of criminals are mysterious on those rare occasions when criminal biographers seriously consider them; mostly they don't. Their main business is to preserve the moral complacency of their audience by consigning their subjects (ecstatically born-again or not) to perdition. Thus the narrator of *The Counterfeit Lady Unveiled*, one of the few substantial criminal biographies before Defoe, offers a range of explanations for his protagonist's behavior. She read romances, wanted to rise in the world, needed money, enjoyed crime as a means of exercising her wits, or, maybe, it was just her "inclination" or "Fate" to be a criminal. In any event she was hanged, seeming "not only very willing, but also very desirous to dye." His lack of any real interest in her character is made apparent when, midway through the narrative and wondering at one of her more "unhandsome ingrateful" actions, he just says, "Well, let her go for a base lewd woman." Defoe's practice is so entirely different as nearly to prevent all comparison. Criminals' motives in his novels begin to seem

10 *The Life and Death of James Commonly Called Collonel Turner* (1664), pp. 36, [iii].

11 Moll suggests as much at the beginning of her narrative, in her remarks about the lack of provision for children of convicted criminals, and Jack's early life in itself is enough to indicate that society bears some responsibility for his turning to a life of crime. "The Wonder in fact is," says Fielding commenting on the miserable circumstances of the poor and the very bad example set for them by the upper classes, "that we have not a thousand more Robbers than we have; indeed that all these Wretches are not Thieves, must give us either a very high Idea of their Honesty, or a very mean one of their Capacity and Courage" (*An Enquiry into the Cause of the Late Increase of Robbers, &c.*, 2nd edn [1751], p. 143). While a hard view was typically taken in print of criminals' efforts to excuse their behavior by, say, appeals to necessity, there is evidence to show that sometimes these could mitigate decisions reached by the courts; see Douglas Hay, "War, Dearth and Theft in the Eighteenth Century: The Record of the English Courts," *Past and Present*, 95 (1982): 117–60, esp. pp. 154–5, John Langbein, "*Albion*'s Fatal Flaws," ibid., 98 (1983): 96–120, esp. 111–12, 113, and Peter King, "Decision-Makers and Decision-Making in the English Criminal Law, 1750–1800," *The Historical Journal*, 27 (1984): 25–58, esp. 41–2. Whatever was said in print, people seemed to have entertained at some level the notion that crime was not always a matter of individual responsibility but sometimes the product of larger social and economic factors. "If there was no Property," says a character in a dialogue somewhat though not entirely stacked against him, "there could be no Theft." "Some People would Farm out the Air, and *Enclose* the Sun and Moon, if it were in their Power," he says, "[in order to] wallow in Superfluities and seize much more than Nature requires"; "I would gladly know who gave them the Privilege to starve out and distress their Neighbours" (Jeremy Collier, "Of Theft," in *Essays upon Several Moral Subjects. Part IV* [1709], pp. 266–7).

substantial, even lucid. Tracing "Actions ... to their Motives and Springs," his fiction offers what criminal biography often advertised but rarely achieved.[12] It escapes, nonetheless, the frequent side effects of psychological explanation. *Tout comprendre* (were we ever to get that far; we don't) would not be *tout pardonner*, for the more we see and understand of his characters, the more difficult it is to come comfortably to terms with them. Defoe's criminal protagonists are not easily filed away and forgotten. All of them, most especially Roxana, develop a special tension in the reader as he works his way through their stories. They being but other versions of us (the novels give readers ample means to think), it is not difficult to sympathize with them, and yet they do such terrible things, Roxana the worst of all.

In the context of Defoe's other criminal characters, Roxana seems something of a mutation. She has a psychic history as the others do not, and we see that history playing out against the psychologies of other characters in her narrative. Moll and Jack present rich characterizations (I omit Singleton purposefully), but chiefly by virtue of the complex claims they make on the attentions of their audience. Though both escape the usual banality of redacted criminals, neither offers more than a brief insight into the onset or outcome of criminal behavior. Why does Moll go bad, and Jack turn good? Such questions have greater resonance in these two novels than in actual criminal biography, but – it is almost correct to say – they are not answered much differently. Moll's slow-moving, highly circumstantial account may seem at first to challenge the "stale plea of misfortune" typically made by thieves, inasmuch as it solidly grounds her behavior in social and material conditions the reader can understand.[13] Rather than standing merely as an explanation for her criminality, Moll's "stupid" or "hardened" state of mind becomes itself a phenomenon susceptible to explanation. There is no need here to spin out the ways the novel makes her crimes intelligible. Her lack of family and friends, the fact she is a woman, the power of money in an often anonymous and increasingly mobile society, the absence of anything like an adequate social safety net – all these are made vividly present. Still, Moll is no mere creature of circumstance, and, at the broadest, most general level, her criminality develops according to lines set out by criminal biography. So, too, does Jack's, at least at first.

Moll's earliest crimes, she says, were prompted by "the prospect of my

---

[12] Francis Kirkman, *The Counterfeit Lady Unveiled. Being a Full Account of the Birth, Life, Most Remarkable Actions, and Untimely Death of Mary Carleton, Known by the Name of the German Princess* (1673), pp. 6–7, 9–10, 11–12, 129, 100, 112, 214, 118; Charles Johnson, *A General History of the Lives and Adventures of the Most Famous Highwaymen, Murderers, Street-Robbers, &c. To Which Is Added, a Genuine Account of the Voyages and Plunders of the Most Notorious Pyrates* (1734), p. 304.

[13] Thomas Manley, *Usury at Six Per Cent. Examin'd, and Found Unjustly Charged ...* (1669), p. 24.

own Starving," which "harden'd my Heart by degrees." Her subsequent thefts, however, admit no such excuse. Moll leaves off stealing awhile, earning her living by needlework, and then resumes for no other reason but that the Devil "resolv'd I should continue in his Service" (199). Actually, Moll robs for bread only briefly. The point her honest citizen makes about his first wife – she was "a Whore not by Necessity, which is the common Bait of your Sex, but by Inclination, and for the sake of the Vice" – might just as well apply to her (135). The truth of it is that Moll likes stealing, at least once she learns how, thus her boast about becoming "the greatest Artist of my time" (214). Moll doesn't need to steal, even if, given the way of the world, she needs money in her pocket to have a friend wherever she goes. As her encounter with the baronet at Bartholomew Fair indicates, she could have continued trading on her person well into old age. Alternatively, she might have made a good living by informing on lace smugglers. Though underhanded, the latter at least would have been within the law. Or, more narrowly, Moll might have lived simply but honestly in the north of England. Even her claim that her first thefts were acts of necessity is undercut by the temptation she feels to murder her second victim, the child whose necklace she steals in an alley. "The Devil put me upon killing the Child," she says, echoing the language of felony indictments before going on to congratulate herself for the "tender Thoughts" that blocked this impulse and kept her from doing "nothing but what, as I may say, meer Necessity drove me to" (194–5). Like all rationales, this is meant to obviate a sticking point; even so early as her second crime there is more than mere necessity behind Moll's thieving. There is, to take her language literally, something devilish in it.[14]

"Necessity is the Touchstone of Honesty," Defoe insisted, by which he meant not only that honest people would steal if they had to, but that truly honest people would stop once they had risen "above Want."[15] By this standard Moll's criminality derives from her nature, not her need, just as Jack's nature leads him to give up crime. Where Jack, a born gentleman

---

[14] Bills of indictment for felony typically employed a formula that ran more or less like this: "Not having the fear of God before his/her eyes, and being seduced thereunto by the instigations of the Devil," the prisoner to be tried had committed such-and-such a crime. Given the peculiar insularity of legal rhetoric, it is hard to know what this really may have meant, but Defoe certainly believed that the devil is "not . . . always the agent in our temptations . . . 'tis our own, corrupt, debauched inclination, which is the first moving agent"; we lay "thousands of crimes . . . to his charge . . . . he is not guilty of . . . calling him our tempter, and pretending we did so and so as the devil would have it, when on the contrary . . . we were only led away of our own lusts" (*SRC*, 258). Moll's claims along these lines might well have seemed as convincing to contemporary observers as an explanation given by a certain murderer: "the Devil (as he fancy'd) put it into his Head, that he cou'd not possibly rob the House with Safety, till the Maid was dispatch'd" (*Select Trials, for Murders, Robberies, Rapes, Sodomy, Coining, Frauds, and Other Offences. At the Sessions House in the Old-Bailey* [1742], 1: 53).

[15] *Street-Robberies, Consider'd* (1728), p. 63; and, for the same idea, *Serious Reflections of Robinson Crusoe*, p. 46.

endowed with "generous principles," is eventually able to rise above the temptations imposed (or sharpened) by necessity, Moll seems a born criminal (indeed is born of a criminal in Newgate, the quintessential milieu of criminals). Nonetheless, if we look back to the earliest part of *Moll Flanders*, it is possible to see her later life of crime as an expression of something more than inborn tendencies triggered by the fear of want.[16] The Elder Brother ruins Moll in more ways than one, but perhaps the worst thing he does is to confuse her about love and money. In what amounts to a single, repeated gesture, he indicates affection and gives her cash, with the effect that money becomes eroticized for her.[17] "I ... thought of nothing, but the fine Words, and the Gold," she says, "I ... was taken up ... with the Pride of my Beauty, and of being belov'd by such a Gentleman, as for the Gold I spent whole Hours in looking upon it; I told the Guineas over and over a thousand times a Day" (25, 26). Awakening Moll's pride and narcissism, as well as a real feeling for himself, the Elder Brother binds all these up with money. Thus Moll gazes on the gold as she might gaze on her lover or her own image in a mirror, and toys with the guineas as lovers might toy, hour by hour. The Elder Brother's betrayal not only shatters her pride but sours her on love for the rest of her life; all she has left is an awakened, injured narcissism, and a powerful feeling for money. After Robin dies she will have other suitors, "and such as call'd themselves Lovers," but she trusts not a one: "I understood too well to be drawn into any more Snares of that Kind: The Case was alter'd with me, I had Money in my Pocket, and had nothing to say to them: I had been trick'd once by *that Cheat call'd* LOVE, but the Game was over" (60).

For the rest of Moll's life money will matter too much, becoming almost a fetish, and love (though from time to time it will raise its dangerous head) too little. All this is implicit long before she begins to steal, in the description she gives of the completion of her ruin. Offering a hundred guineas as an "Earnest" of his love, the Elder Brother promises to marry her eventually: "My Colour came, and went, at the Sight of the Purse, and with the fire of his Proposal together; so that I could not say a Word, and he easily perceiv'd it; so putting the Purse into my Bosom, I made no more Resistance to him, but let him do just what he pleas'd; and as often as he pleas'd." The purse in her bosom both warms and chills, but finally it

---

[16] Similar considerations apply to the Jacks; even at his simplest Defoe is no crude sociobiologist, believing nature all and nurture nothing. While the unlucky Major is only one-half a gentleman by birth, and acts it, the still less lucky Captain's situation is more complex than it might otherwise appear. "Every Body said he had the very look of a Rogue, and wou'd come to be Hang'd," says the Colonel, which means "in a Word he got nothing of any Body for good will," which means in turn that he "was as it were oblig'd to Turn Thief, for the meer Necessity of Bread to eat" (9). In another environment the Captain may well have turned out differently, which is to say that Defoe sees his characters not as genotypes but as phenotypes.

[17] See Juliet McMaster, "The Equation of Love and Money in *Moll Flanders*," *Studies in the Novel*, 2 (1970): 131–44.

chills; anaesthetizing her to love, as the last two phrases indicate, it usurps the place of her heart. "And thus," Moll continues, "I finish'd my own Destruction at once, for from this Day, being forsaken of my Vertue, and my Modesty, I had nothing of Value left to recommend me, either to God's Blessing, or Man's Assistance" (28–9). "The temper of a child, misled by vice or mistake," Defoe observed elsewhere, is "like a dislocated bone"; it "is easy to be reduced into place, if taken in time; but if suffered to remain in its dislocated position, a callous substance fills up the empty space, and, by neglect, grows equally hard with the bone, and resisting the power of the surgeon's skill, renders the reduction of the joint impossible." Children need "instruction" to have their "[natural] bent or inclination [to evil] rectified or driven out," he believed, but Moll's childhood is characterized more by dislocating jolts (*FI*, 15: 65–6). Her experience with the Elder Brother, the last she allows to damage her, calcifies her beyond repair.

Jack's criminal career poses a very different question. Why he becomes a criminal is not so interesting – abandoned to survive as best he can, he has every reason or excuse in the world – as why he stops. His crucial turning point is also a painful experience, but the psychology of it is far less clear-cut than the stimulus-response behaviorism (almost Pavlovian conditioning) of Moll's episode with the Elder Brother. His "generous principles" uppermost, Jack approaches the widow he had robbed a year before, pretending to have been sent by the thief, now in Newgate, to make restitution. When he sees that his victim is "an honest poor industrious Woman," Jack feels all the more "a Villain." But when he finds the money he had taken was all the wealth she "had in the World," and that she had "work'd hard" for it by "keeping a Nurse Child," he begins to speak strangely and finally breaks down and weeps. He does not comment on the woman's likeness to his own surrogate mother, but what he does say warrants close attention, for it reflects a great crisis of mind and spirit. In the passage about to be quoted, Jack's use of the third person to refer to himself deserves close attention. Though his shifting back and forth between "he" and "I" begins simply, as the byproduct of a simple subterfuge, it rapidly escalates into something far more complex. To help the reader follow this process, all personal pronouns appear in bold print:

I Thought it would have broke **my** very Heart, [Jack says,] to think how this poor creature work'd, and was a Slave at near Threescore, and that **I** a young Fellow of hardly Twenty, should Rob **her** of **her** Bread to Support **my** Idleness, and Wicked Life; and the Tears came from **my** Eyes, in spight of all **my** strugling to prevent it, and the Woman perceiv'd it too; poor Woman, *said* **I**, 'tis a sad thing such Creatures as these should plunder, and strip such a poor Object as **thou** art; well, **he** [meaning the thief, i.e. himself] is at Leisure now to Repent it, **I** assure you; **I** perceive Sir, *says* **she**, **you** are very Compassionate, indeed, **I** wish **he** may

Improve the time God has spar'd **him**, and that **he** may Repent, and **I** pray God give **him** Repentance, who ever **he** is, **I** forgive **him**, whether **he** can make **me** Recompense, or not, and **I** pray God forgive **him**, **I** won't do **him** any Prejudice, not **I**, and **she** went on Praying for **me**.

Well, Dame, come hither to **me**, *says* **I**, and with that **I** put **my** Hand in **my** Pocket, and **she** came to **me**: Hold up **your** Hand, *said* **I**, which **she** did, and **I** told **her** Nine half Crowns into **her** Hand; there Dame, *said* **I**, is **your** 22s. **you** lost, **I** assure **you**, Dame, *said* **I**, **I** have been the chief Instrument to get it of **him** for **you**; for ever since **he** told **me** the Story of it among the rest of **his** wicked Exploits; **I** never gave **him** any rest till **I** made **him** promise **me** to make **you** Restitution: All the while **I** held **her** Hand, and put the Money into it, **I** look'd into **her** Face, and **I** perceiv'd **her** Colour come, and go, and that **she** was under the greatest Surprize of Joy Imaginable.

Well, God bless **him**, *says* **she**, and spare **him** from the Disaster **he** is afraid of, if it be **his** will; for sure, this is an Act of so much Justice, and so Honest, that **I** never expected the like; **she** run on a great while so, and wept for **him**; when **I** told **her**, **I** doubted there was no room to expect **his** Life: Well, *says* **she**, then pray God give **him** Repentance, and bring **him** to Heaven, for sure **he** must have something that is Good at the Bottom; **he** has a principle of Honesty at bottom, to be sure; however, **he** may have been brought into bad Courses, by bad Company, and evil Example, or other Temptations: But **I** dare say **he** will be brought to Repentance, one time or another, before **he** Dies.

All this touch'd **me** nearer than **she** Imagin'd, for **I** was the Man that **she** pray'd for all this while ...   (85–6)

Jack's frequent use of "I," "me," and "you," linguists would say, is phatic; it is an effort to open, and keep open, a channel of communication between him and the old woman, to establish a personal connection. Still more interesting, however, is his use of "him" and "he." Unwilling to confess, Jack pretends the crime belongs to some unnamed third person, a convention his interlocutor naturally and unwittingly (I think) picks up toward the end of the first paragraph. This gives Jack's subterfuge a substance which he then goes on to exploit. Emphasizing the difference between the "he" who committed the robbery and the "I" who is making reparation, Jack tries to put emotional and moral distance between himself and what he later calls "one of the vilest Actions, in the World" (86). But all the while, his sense of his crime is exacerbated by his growing awareness of his victim's decency. And, too, he wants increasingly for her to forgive him. These various feelings are strongly at odds with each other, nor can Jack maintain his distinction between "he" and "I." Both mean "me," as the end of the first paragraph reminds both him and us, and, to still more powerful effect, as does the very end of the quotation. Nonetheless, Jack seeks to maintain and elaborate the distinction, trying by his repetitions of "me" and "my" (note especially the beginning of paragraph two) to cut these pronouns loose from the problematic "him" that he was, or the still more problematic combination of "him"-and-"I", which – if allowed to obtain – would imply a schizoid, unwhole, and unwholesome self. Jack wants to limit the reference of "me" and "my" to the "I" that he is while speaking to the old woman *now* – the "I" that is repeatedly stressed in the second paragraph, as if utterly to displace "he" and "him." Ironically, the more Jack says "I" in an effort to draw the woman's attention to his present generosity of spirit, the more she speaks of "him," offering her forgiveness away from the "I" he wants simply to be, toward the "he" whom he has disavowed. And all the while, in her simple goodness, the old woman makes him feel all the more guilty for what he has done (and possibly, too, for what he is doing).

If Jack wants to be forgiven he cannot sustain the distinction between "he" and "I," but he cannot escape it either. As the text continues beyond the quoted passage, Jack asks the old woman to forgive "the Thief," though of course she has done so already. Apparently the forgiveness has not "taken," the old woman's speech act (in Austin and Searle's terminology) not having met conditions for "felicity," the chief of which is that she offer him her blessing, full knowing what he has done, as he stands before her.[18] "Will you Sincerely and Heartily forgive him, Dame?" Jack asks, "I do desire it of you; and with that I stood up, and with my Hat off, ask'd her Pardon." Willingly she complies, but her sincerity of heart cannot mend the duplicity of his. Not ready to believe he is anything but what he claims to be, or that the "him" of whom they have been speaking can have any real connection with the fine figure before her, she does not accept his gesture of respect: "O Sir, *says she*, do not stand up, and with your Hat off to me, I am a poor Woman, I forgive him, and all that were with him, for there was one or more with him, I forgive them with all my Heart: and I pray God to forgive them." The simplicity and purity of the old woman's "I" – so prominent here and at the end of the first quoted paragraph – stands in poignant contrast to Jack's. The "I" he presents still remains unrecognized as the "he" who robbed her, and, more ironically, even that "he" risks getting lost as the woman's simple, undiscriminating goodness now promiscuously forgives an undifferentiated "them." Jack's criminality redounds against him, paradoxically, even as he tries to escape it. Little wonder, given the distress this occasion makes him feel, that he never risks robbing again.

This remarkably complex episode warrants more extensive analysis than I can give it here. It provides so full a sense of the disjunctions in Jack's mind, for one thing, because it is so artfully situated. This is not the first time Jack has referred to himself in the third person in the course of a

---

[18] See J. L. Austin, *How to Do Things With Words*, 2nd edn, ed. J. O. Urmson and Marina Sbisà (Cambridge, Mass., 1975) and the first of John R. Searle's many books, *Speech Acts: An Essay in the Philosophy of Language* (London, 1969).

dialogue – alerted to the phenomenon, the reader is prepared to think what it may mean – nor is it the first time he has suddenly felt a strange, new, unnerving sense of himself vis-à-vis another.[19] The episode is remarkable, too, in that its affect can be at once so simple and so complicated. Clear enough to be deeply touching, it may also make us wonder, with all its flurry of personal pronouns, how in fact it is possible to make sense of what Jack says. Somehow, amidst all the "I's," "me's," "he's," "him's," and the occasional "you," readers manage to sort out referents and constitute two people speaking, one of whom is himself two people (or three, if we count the "I" who is speaking now). Pronouns are mysterious, as any linguist will aver, and never more so than when they function as "shifters," switching referents again and again in the full stream of speech, never (or almost never) missing a beat.[20] But then identity, and our consciousness of it, are themselves mysterious. The prose of this passage registers Jack's emotional strain as he flounders at the edge of an identity crisis, his "I" (Freud's *das Ich*, though Lacan's *je/moi* construct might be more relevant) sliding away from his "him" (i.e., his notion of how he appears to the Other), and both threatening to break loose from their larger referent, which is Jack's unspeakable (so it is with us all), elusively extra-linguistic sense of self. At the same time it shows this strain, the passage can impose an analogous (if only cognitive) strain on the reader. As Locke said in an apposite context, "we must here take notice of what the Word I is applied to."[21]

Moll's seduction and Jack's efforts to make amends are among the most memorable episodes in Defoe's fiction. The one allows readers to understand and appreciate the moral numbness – or "stupidity" – that falls on Moll, and the other the painful disorientation of Jack's conscience-stricken soul; those who fail at "managing" themselves risk falling into one or the other of these two terrible states. There is nothing quite like either passage in any criminal biography I have read.[22] But then, too, there is nothing

19 See especially Jack's dialogue with the customs-house broker, pp. 33–40, where, as the broker asks a series of questions, Jack realizes he ought to have a surname and to have had a mother (36); that he has no proper place to put his money, and nowhere at all to call home (37); that he doesn't know his age (38); and that now, because he has money, his companions at the glasshouse might rob, cheat, or even kill him (38–9).

20 For "shifters," see Roman Jakobson, *Shifters, Verbal Categories, and the Russian Verb* (Cambridge, Mass., 1957), pp. 1–3.

21 Locke, *Essay Concerning Human Understanding*, 2: 27: 20, ed. Peter H. Nidditch (Oxford, 1975), p. 342. For Locke's influence on contemporary views of personal identity, see Ernest Tuveson, *The Imagination as a Means of Grace: Locke and the Aesthetics of Romanticism* (Berkeley, 1960), pp. 5–41; John Dussinger, *The Discourse of the Mind in Eighteenth-Century Fiction* (The Hague, 1974), pp. 31–43; and Christopher Fox, "Locke and the Scriblerians: The Discourse of Identity in Early Eighteenth Century England," *Eighteenth-Century Studies*, 16 (1982): 1–25, which has been subsumed into his *Locke and the Scriblerians: Identity and Consciousness in Early Eighteenth-Century Britain* (Berkeley, 1988).

22 The closest possible analogues in criminal biography to the corruption of Moll's psyche by the Elder Brother are perhaps the description of John Stanley's brutalization by his father or the

like either episode again in either of the two novels. Once Moll goes numb, that's pretty much it, and Jack, reformed, never again experiences the lacerating dissociation from self that comes from a consciousness of his crimes. Neither episode becomes part of a larger, developing picture of the particular operations of either character's mind. Though Moll's and Jack's natures may, to some extent, be framed by circumstance, once framed they take on a fixity seemingly immune to subsequent circumstance. This limits the potential meaning of each episode, as does, too, the strong implication in both novels that criminality (or the lack of it) owes much to heredity. If Moll's crimes are foredestined and Jack's redemption predestined, the psychological interest of each character is correspondingly diminished, and so, too, their value as moral examples to readers anxious about their own moral – and social – position, now and in the future.

Where *Moll Flanders* offers only a glimpse at the origins of a criminal mentality and *Colonel Jack* a brief, vertiginous sense of how powerfully self-alienating it might feel to be a criminal, *Roxana* provides an extended opportunity to develop both kinds of insight. Moll suffers from what she calls "a deprivation of thought" (281), but Roxana's thinking shows actual depravity. That is, her mind does not contract so much as go increasingly wrong. Each misstep she makes prepares the way to her next, while conscience, powerless to halt the process, nonetheless intervenes with sufficient force to make her life intermittently, then permanently miserable. *Roxana* builds its history of moral and psychological decay on a character who is much more clearly a *tabula rasa* than either Moll or Jack, and, from the beginning, it makes its audience highly conscious of the way such tablets get inscribed.

Nothing in Roxana's background suggests an inherent tendency to vice or virtue. Her nature is "malleable," like that of children in general, or, to use another of Defoe's pungent metaphors, "like some vegetables ... when taken green and early." Nor do any manifestly bad experiences deform her

account of Charles Drew's unhappy homelife as a child; see, respectively, *The Life of Mr. John Stanley* (1723) or *Lives of the Most Remarkable Criminals Who Have Been Condemned and Executed for Murder, the Highway, Housebreaking, Street Robberies, Coining or Other Offences*, ed. Arthur L. Hayward (New York, 1927), pp. 136–142, and *The Suffolk Parricide, Being, the Trial, Life, Transactions, and Last Dying Words, of Charles Drew* (1740); both criminals are discussed in *Turned to Account*, pp. 59 (Stanley) and 56–60 (Drew). Jack's dizzying loss of a sense of self might be compared to the strange alienation from themselves and others that comes over many murderers at the time they commit their crimes, or shortly afterwards (for examples, see the confessions of Strodtman, quoted in chapter 1, and of Butler, quoted at the beginning of this chapter, as well as *Turned to Account*, pp. 76–8). The main effect of such inexact and approximate comparisons, however, is once again to emphasize the distinct difference between Defoe's fiction and the "real" thing, which is of course to say the conventionally redacted thing.

childhood. She becomes "hard and brittle" only when "condensed by time and age," a process the novel depicts over most of its length (*FI*, 15: 65). Still, Roxana's early experience is not entirely normal, as the opening of her narrative makes clear by emphasizing, paradoxically, her apparent normalcy. Born in France – "*as my Friends told me*" – and brought to England as a child, Roxana fits quickly into English society – or at least seems to. "I went to *English* Schools," she says, "and being young, I learnt the *English* Tongue perfectly well, with all the Customs of the *English* young-Women; so that I retain'd nothing of the *French* but the Speech; nor did I so much as keep any Remains of the French Language tagg'd to my Way of Speaking, *as most Foreignors do*, but spoke what we call Natural *English*, as if I had been born here." Contradicting this last claim, however, or rather more narrowly defining it, is another made a few lines later. "Being *French* Born," Roxana notes, "I danc'd, as some say, naturally" (5–6). Both claims make us nicely aware that what "we call" or "some say" is "natural" may actually be socially defined, a matter of custom, indeed may require to be socially defined. Roxana would never have known she was French without being told, and she dances "naturally" insofar as she seems (from an English perspective) not-English.

From the very beginning of the novel, then, Roxana is presented not merely as an individual in relation to other individuals, or to absolute values, but in relation to social norms or "codes." Inasmuch as the latter are learned, human behavior – however much it may seem "natural" – is a combination of inherent and acquired characteristics. As it continues, the novel goes on calling attention to the variousness of human custom and language. It makes reference to the speech and manners of the Italians, the Dutch, the Persians, the Turks, and "Eastern people" in general (102–4, 141, 179–80, 247). It notes not only the differences between France and England, but that Paris has certain characteristics marking it off from the rest of France, and that differences of custom or language in England are attributable to class or sect. London is thus at least two separate cities, as Roxana indicates when she moves from the West End to the Minories, for there she is "as much out of the way of . . . the Gang that us'd to follow me, as if I had been among the Mountains in *Lancashire*" (67, 211). Nor is English simply one language among others, but rather a variety of sub-languages (or sociolects) within itself. Thus, aside from "natural" English, there is also the discourse of Quakers (who also dress and behave differently) and the speech of the sailors in the storm, which Roxana finds so frighteningly unintelligible. Sailors' jargon is one language Roxana does not master, but that, probably, is only for lack of opportunity (in an earlier, parallel instance, she heard Dutch being spoken without understanding it, but then goes on to learn it; see 112–14). Adept at learning "codes" of all kinds, Roxana moves with ease through all the cultures she inhabits – English, French, Italian, Dutch – and is as skillful in dealing with princes and courtiers as with bankers, merchants, and Quakers.

Against this variousness of language and custom, a peculiar sense of Roxana begins to emerge. She does not quite belong to any of the categories in which she participates, which is to say that while she speaks or behaves "naturally" according to one or another standard, it remains the case that much of her behavior is "naturalized" rather than natural. Though she claims both France and England as her "Native Country," she does not quite belong to either, as in fact these contradictory claims make clear (cf. 51, 122, 233). As a French refugee who grows up in England, she partakes of both nations but fits into neither entirely, even though in each place she speaks "the Language perfectly well" (51). At heart Roxana is a perpetual foreigner, wherever she may be, an impression sustained all through the novel by her alertness to the peculiarities of the social milieux in which she is involved, and a self-distancing reflexivity. Thus from the first she speaks of herself "as if I was speaking of another-body" (6). No matter how firmly Roxana is (or seems to be) placed in a given social situation, she remains nonetheless an outsider. Moll and Jack are also outsiders, to be sure, but Roxana's status is far more teasing. Cut off from society at (and by) their births, they clearly *seem* the outsiders they are. Roxana, however, *seems* like everyone else – and in possibly more than one sense. Are not all human beings "seemers"? Where in social life, or the life of the mind for that matter, is the dividing point between authentic being and behavior that, seeming "natural," is actually put on? Who or what is Roxana if, neither French nor English by nature, she is not even (the name is a pseudonym, but then in a sense all are) Roxana? Her true name, we learn by careful reading, is not the one we know her by (and which, so casually imposed, is the one that sticks) but Susan (180; 205). Or is it Suzanne? Like her name, Roxana's true identity is difficult to pin down, it being defined as much by "the World" – a phrase which recurs more than seventy times in the novel – as by any individual essence. Nor is "the world" itself one fixed, determinable thing, the novel recurrently suggests, being in large part the various product of human ideas, desires, and practice.[23]

All this gives *Roxana* a much greater density and resonance than the earlier criminal novels. In some way or another we may all feel orphaned at birth like Moll or Jack, that is, cut off from a context proper to our sense of what we are or would like to be; some would say this is an inescapable aspect of modernity. But in Roxana's situation it is possible to see a far more definite, elaborate, and so in certain ways richer emblem of our own

23 In *Roxana* "the world" almost always means the social world; cf. *Moll Flanders* where the same phrase frequently appears, but not with quite the same effect, not having the context to become an organizing theme for that novel (or at least a major theme).

(and the modern human) condition. But what do I mean by "we" and "our"? Can I be speaking from a standpoint accessible to Defoe and his original audience, or am I being parochially post-modern? By one of those curious accidents of history, certain post-modern conceits about the individual's situation vis-à-vis society – or, more particularly, the socially provided symbolic order – have come to resemble ideas current in the seventeenth and eighteenth centuries. The French post-structuralists are merely the most recent to speak about the position of the individual psyche with respect to language (the chief component of the symbolic order). Bacon, Hobbes, and Locke each had intriguing and highly influential things to say about the lack of fit between words and reality, and the ways this lack of fit may impinge on the understanding.

"*Words*," says Locke, "*in their primary or immediate Signification, stand for nothing, but the* Ideas *in the Mind of him that uses them*, how imperfectly soever or carelessly those Ideas are collected from the Things which they are supposed to represent." This means that words ought not to be confused with reality, which is a separate order. By definition, then, we cannot hope to speak "of Things as really they are": "it is a perverting the use of Words, and brings unavoidable Obscurity and Confusion into their Signification, whenever we make them stand for any thing, but those *Ideas* we have in our own minds." The truth is, men "talk *barely* of their own Imaginations." Locke even has something to say about the potential language has for opening up, unnoticed, an abyss beneath our feet. Men not only mistakenly suppose "*their Words to stand . . . for the reality of Things*," they also "*suppose their Words to be Marks of the Ideas in the Minds also of other Men, with whom they communicate*: For else they should talk in vain, and could not be understood." Strictly speaking, both assumptions are unwarrantable. Given the assumption that no "natural connection" obtains "between particular articulate sounds and certain ideas," our interlocutors may in fact fit ideas different from ours to the words we use, or no ideas at all.[24] Had Locke lived three centuries later in France, his slogan might well have been "les noms dupeurs."

[24] Locke, *Essay Concerning Human Understanding*, 3: 2: 1–5, pp. 404–7. Cf. Bacon: "The ill and unfit choice of words wonderfully obstructs the understanding . . . words plainly force and overrule the understanding, and throw all into confusion, and lead men away into numberless empty controversies and idle fancies" (*Novum Organum*, 1: 43, in *The English Philosophers from Bacon to Mill*, ed. Edwin A. Burtt [Modern Library, 1939], p. 35; for a fascinating account of Defoe's marginalia in a copy of Bacon's *Advancement of Learning*, see Paula Backscheider, "Daniel Defoe as Solitary Reader," *Princeton University Library Chronicle*, 46 [1985]: 178–91.). In the context of Bacon's and Locke's comments on words it's worth considering (and re-considering) Hobbes's marvellously rich metaphor: "Words are wise mens counters, they do but reckon by them; but they are the mony of fooles" (*Leviathan*, 1: 4, ed. C. B. Macpherson [Penguin, 1968], p. 106). For a stimulating discussion of Puritan concerns about the lack of fit between words and the world, see Michael Clark, "The Word of God and the Language of Man: Puritan Semiotics and the Theological and Scientific 'Plain Styles' of the Seventeenth Century", *Semiotic Scene*, 2 (1978): 61–90.

It would be all too easy, however, to overstress his similarity to the host of recent writers concerned with the peculiar relation of language to human consciousness. Where, typically, they see language as limiting or undermining individual autonomy, Locke emphasizes its value as a means of enhancing the individual, conscious subject. As "sensible Marks of Ideas," words allow each of us to fix and communicate thoughts that otherwise might be lost or have no outlet: "The use Men have of these marks [is] either to record their own Thoughts for the Assistance of their own Memory; or as it were, to bring out their *Ideas*, and lay them before the view of others." Language for Locke is a mighty support to individual autonomy, defining and extending it. This is so much the case, in fact, that far from being an instrument to enforce social cohesion, it can set men at odds when nothing really divides them. Thus, in a highly significant anecdote, Locke describes a dispute among physicians which he amicably settled by pointing out that it "was about the signification of [a] Term . . . which when each considered, he thought it not worth the contending about"; there was no "real difference in [their] Conception of Things." Though Locke is highly cognizant of the mischief produced by "the Imperfection and Abuse of Words," he has faith – in the most literal sense of the term, else he himself "should talk in vain, and could not be understood" – that we may somehow rise above the slipperiness of language and, through language, achieve mutual understanding.[25] So apparently does Defoe. I note this because our main problem in tracing out what I've been calling Roxana's "psychology" will not be being modern but knowing when to quit.

Though no slavish disciple of Locke, Defoe, too, was very much aware of the insufficiency of words, which after all represent conventions for the most part unacknowledged and only arbitrarily fit the world. He, too, was suspicious of them, as he indicated by claiming (in a most unLockean fashion) that "the knowledge of things, not words, makes a schollar." As if to illustrate this point, *Roxana* shows its protagonist falling prey to the difference between words and things, the victim at first of others' fictions and then of her own. Roxana's first moral crisis introduces the theme. Skillful at "Circumlocutions," the jeweller insists that he considers her "not as a Mistress, but as his Wife" (41, 43). He denies they are committing "Adultery," claiming instead they are "as he call'd it Marry'd" (38, 45). In this business Amy also has "too much Rhetoric," vividly describing the dire "Misery" her mistress will face without the jeweller's financial assistance, and filling her ears with "Cant, of its being Lawful" to "Marry again" (39–40). Exploiting the difference between words and ideas, Amy and the jeweller detach the one from the other so as to escape the usual

25 Locke, *Essay Concerning Human Understanding*, 3: 2: 1, 2; 3: 9: 16; and 3: 9–11 passim, pp. 405, 484–5, 475–524.

definition of the behavior they urge on Roxana. Their tactic (as if to parody Defoe's dictum) is to emphasize the thing itself, its essence, not the word attached to it; then they attach a new word to it. Amy tells Roxana that she ought not to consider herself and the jeweller still married to their original spouses, as both these have refused their proper "Office." While they cannot "marry formally," their relationship, she urges Roxana, would be "allow'd by the Custom of the Place, in several Countries abroad" (37–8). When for his part the jeweller proposes "a Wedding Supper," causing Roxana to start "at the Word Wedding," he laughs and says, "Well ... you shall call it what you will, but it may be the same thing" (36).

The assault on Roxana's morality is double-edged. Amy and the jeweller rename adultery so that it will not seem discrepant with her value system, and they also try to get her to change her value system. Instead of standard English they propose their own version of the language, and, instead of "the Laws of the Land," their own notions of legitimacy. In effect, Amy and the jeweller aim at erasing what is inscribed on Roxana's psychic tablet, and reinscribing it. They try to sanction what they're doing by grounding it in some sort of wider social practice, thus Amy's reference to "the Custom ... in several Countries abroad," but actually they're "romancing" Roxana, encouraging her to exchange the real truth of her situation for cheap, specious, and ultimately quite dangerous fictions. They are dangerously bad company and all the more as they seem sincerely to believe what they say. Once Roxana and the jeweller have been bedded, Amy acts as though they are husband and wife in fact, thus her distress after Roxana establishes a *ménage à trois*. In an effort to console her, Roxana says they are both whores now, but Amy replies, "no, you are not, for you are Marry'd" (47). The jeweller, too, having "argued himself into" the idea they are married, faithfully upholds it (43). "To outward Appearance, we liv'd as chearfully, and as agreeably, as it was possible for any Couple in the World to live," Roxana comments, "the grand Exception only excepted." As the last phrase indicates, she cannot escape feeling the falsity of her situation. "I was a Whore, not a Wife," she insists, "nor cou'd I ever frame my Mouth to call him Husband, when I was speaking of him" (49, 45).

The question of what this connection with the jeweller ought to be "call'd" focusses attention for the first time on a recurrent theme in the novel, which is how things are named – or renamed – so as to suit the needs of the namer. The word "call" appears more than forty-five times in the text in one form or another, almost invariably in circumstances which alert the reader to a disparity between the actual nature of the thing being named – or, perhaps not quite the same thing, its name in "ordinary usage" (141) – and the term being applied to it. When the jeweller is murdered and his property distributed, Roxana makes "no Scruple of calling myself Madam —, the Widow of Monsieur —, the *English* Jeweller" (56). The child she has by the Prince de — is no bastard but, "as they call it, a Natural Son" (and the Prince himself is "call'd ... the Count de Clerac," so as to keep his true identity from the servants [76, 77]). The Quaker Roxana befriends is so "courteous" and "agreeable" that Roxana decides she "must call her [a] Gentlewoman ... tho' she was a QUAKER," and not "call her Landlady," which is "too course a Word for her" (210, 212). In each of these cases a euphemism replaces a correct name, just as Amy and the jeweller try to rename the act of adultery. This phenomenon is rampant, and by no means restricted to Roxana.[26] Still, as these examples indicate, Roxana's crisp sense of what things ought properly to be called does not long survive her relation with the jeweller. Barely twenty pages after his "Circumlocutions" and Amy's "Rhetorick," she is using comparable "Absurdities" to justify her adultery with the Prince de — "as a lawful thing." Her aim, though she doesn't realize it at the time, is to keep "Conscience from giving me any considered Disturbance." "I was the easier to perswade myself," she adds, "when it was so much for my Ease, and for the Repose of my Mind" (68–9).

Roxana and practically everyone around her "make the world the bond-slave of human thought," as Bacon put it, "and human thought the bond-slave of words."[27] They do so either to justify or rationalize bad behavior (such as, additionally, the Prince de —, the Jew who accuses Roxana of murder in order to get her jewels, her Quaker ally), or else, with dangerous innocence, they misconceive the world to their own advantage (thus the Dutchman who believes her basically honest, her daughter who thinks she is – or will be – a "mother," and, again, her Quaker ally). Either way, the human mind attempts to refashion realities, or rather its ideas of reality, by renaming those ideas. It is important to insist on Locke's distinction because we might otherwise underestimate the complexities of the resulting dialectic, at least as it takes place in Roxana's mind. Reality remains the same whatever it is called, nor (since words are not the same as ideas) can we change our ideas of it merely by altering our lexicon.[28] Though at one level our minds may admit such alterations, at

---

26 As Maximillian Novak says, Roxana's "narration is a continuous denunciation of the ways that human beings conceal reality in a miasma of words" ("The Unmentionable and the Ineffable in Defoe's Fiction," *Studies in the Literary Imagination*, 15 [1982]: 99). For a sampling of instances, see pp. 6, 7, 12, 14, 26; 70, 76, 77, 78, 86; 182, 202, 210, 212, 214; 281, 282, 290, 302, 306. As if to mark Roxana's point of departure from the world of fact into the world of words, the text has her say, of her sudden plunge into poverty, "the truth was, there was no Need of much Discourse in the Case, the Thing spoke itself" (17).

27 Bacon, *Novum Organum*, 2: 69, p. 48.

28 Says a wealthy but unhappy nobleman in *The Compleat English Gentleman*, "I have some things you call enjoyments, and you may call them by as great names as you will. Make up the

another level they leave a blot. Especially when it comes to moral values, *Roxana* suggests, there is something inscribed in the mind that never can be erased; this, of course, is conscience, "the natural magistrate in the heart."

Even if considered only in the context provided by Amy and the jeweller, Roxana's first unequivocally immoral act would seem far more than just another instance of the ill effects of necessity. Her tempters in effect enlarge the "norm" for deviancy, making its onset more elaborate than it would ever appear in criminal biography and its mechanism more easily comprehensible. That Roxana does not meet their "standard," refusing the rationalizations they offer for becoming a "whore," makes behavior that might otherwise seem stereotypical into something highly anomalous. Though more precisely aligned with the moral code than they, she stands at a double remove from it, Amy and the jeweller (who stand at one remove) marking the distance. This curious situation, in which Roxana is both more wicked *and* more ethical than her would-be tempters, initiates a process of moral deterioration several degrees more complicated than the usual "hardening" and, potentially, more affecting. Choosing evil "with my Eyes open ... knowing it to be a Sin, but having no Power to resist," Roxana creates a division in her person that grows more acute as time goes on, sickening her within and rendering her relations with others increasingly problematic (44). Roxana's reaction to her new situation illustrates and carries forward this division of self, emphasizing still more the strangeness of her state of mind.

Her having sinned "against the Light of ... Conscience," Roxana believes, makes her "fit for any Wickedness." Conscience "left off speaking," she explains, "where it found it cou'd not be heard" (44). As much in possession of a "strange, original something" as Jack, however, she nonetheless retains a peculiar regard for normal moral values, thus her curious reasons for putting Amy to bed with the jeweller. "Had I look'd upon myself as a Wife," she says, "you cannot suppose I would have been willing to have let my Husband lye with my Maid, much less, before my Face, for I stood-by all the while." Also, "as I thought myself a Whore, I cannot say but that it was something design'd in my Thoughts, that my Maid should be a Whore too, and should not reproach me with it" (47). Roxana's acting the bawd seems an effort to force Amy and the jeweller down to her level, to make them see things her way, and so to end once and for all the rub she feels between her situation as it really is, and the words they would apply to it. Roxana wants to simplify her life, to re-establish her relations with paramour and servant on terms more to her own liking, to close the gap between their sense of her and her own sense of self. The act done, Roxana believes she "need say no more": "this is enough to convince

account with all the fine words you can, but words will never make up things: one is imaginary, the other real" (pp. 160–1).

any-body that I did not think him my Husband, and that I had cast off all Principle, and all Modesty, and had effectually stifled Conscience" (46). Her gesture fails to achieve its intended effect, however, and proves costly in ways she cannot anticipate. Amy and the jeweller remain impervious in their fictions. The jeweller continues to call her "wife" even as he openly consorts with her maid, and, while she and Amy find themselves bound all the more closely together, their new domestic arrangement does nothing to re-establish Roxana's authority; quite the opposite. The debauching of Amy, who was "less Vicious than I" (47), marks the servant's first step toward becoming Roxana's own version of the Frankenstein monster, or (considering she was as "faithful to me, as the Skin to my back" [25]) perhaps the analogy ought to be to Mr. Hyde.

As this future cost is preparing, Roxana experiences another closer to hand, but just as unforeseen. Her disruption of "the pretended marriage, &c." is soon smoothed over, she and the jeweller living together "as merrily, and as happily, after this, as cou'd be expected." But, "harden'd" as she is – "and that was as much, as ever any wicked Creature was" – Roxana nonetheless finds "Intervals," "dark Reflections," and "Sighs" interrupting all her "Songs." "There would be, sometimes," she says, "a heaviness of Heart, which intermingl'd itself with all my Joy, and which would often fetch a Tear from my Eye." "Let others pretend what they will," she concludes, "there can be no substantial Satisfaction in a Life of known Wickedness; Conscience will, and does, often break in upon them at particular times, let them do what they can to prevent it" (48–9). Thinking to have "stifled" conscience, she finds it draws new breath; though it no longer speaks, it still can make her sigh. The very act supposed to show it dead has only re-aroused it, perhaps because Roxana's effort to pull servant and lover down to her level has only sunk her lower, into an active, predatory wickedness. "I was now become the Devil's Agent," she says, "to make others as wicked as myself" (48). Where before she at least could claim a kind of moral superiority to servant and seducer, now she is unequivocally worse.

Roxana's interaction with these two "others" not only illustrates an "improved" (though still general) psychology of crime; it initiates the novel's concern with her particular psychology. The distinction it presents between her private self-awareness and her public persona is of course crucial to the complex sense readers now begin to have of her, but equally important is the picture it gives of that persona addressing others, seeking to achieve a *modus vivendi* the private self can live with. In sum, the novel puts on view a complex set of relations in which Roxana's private self stands vs. her public self, vs. the public selves of others, vs. social norms as these are variously constituted and articulated by interacting individuals (Roxana, Amy, and the jeweller making up a minimal social unit), vs.

moral law, the last being both absolute and, conventionally enough, inscribed in Roxana's heart. "I sinn'd, knowing it to be a Sin," she says, and "thus made a Hole in my Heart" (44). The complex interaction of all these elements as forces grounding and shaping Roxana's behavior – particularly the sense one has of her as an individual made up of various conflicting parts – grows powerfully as the novel progresses. Eventually readers are left not only with an elaborate impression of Roxana's internal psychodynamics but with the implication, too, of a larger sociodynamic, the latter as one dimly glimpses (or suspects) analogous psychologies behind the actions of other characters in the novel.[29]

[29] Roxana and the characters around her may be "psychologized" in a number of ways. For various recent examples, see Zimmerman, *Defoe and the Novel*, pp. 155–87; John J. Richetti, *Defoe's Narratives* (Oxford, 1975), pp. 192–232; Wallace Jackson, "*Roxana* and the Development of Defoe's Fiction," *Studies in the Novel*, 7 (1975): 181–94; Steven Cohan, "Other Bodies: Roxana's Confession of Guilt," ibid., 8 (1976): 406–17; David Durant, "Roxana's Fictions," ibid., 13 (1981): 225–36; Terry J. Castle, "*Amy*, Who Knew My Disease": A Psychosexual Pattern in Defoe's *Roxana*," *ELH*, 46 (1979): 81–96; and James H. Maddox, "On Defoe's *Roxana*," ibid., 51 (1984): 669–91. Defoe would appear, however, to be working out of a very different kind of psychology than the Anglo-American Freudianism generally represented by the above examples; nor does he quite anticipate Lacan. For an argument that Defoe actually owes his psychology to the medical writer Thomas Willis (1621–75) or, as there's no particular evidence he read Willis, to medical theories like his, see Raymond Stephanson, "Defoe's 'Malade Imaginaire': The Historical Foundation of Mental Illness in *Roxana*," *Huntington Library Quarterly*, 45 (1982): 99–118. I myself would propose that the psychology presented in *Roxana* owes a good deal to the views of Robert South, a writer whose works Defoe knew and approved of (see *The Protestant Monastery* [1727], p. 30, and, though Defoe may not have written this particular item, *A Collection of Miscellany Letters Selected out of Mist's Weekly Journal* [1722–7], 4: 183). South's views merit a brief setting out.

According to the faculty psychology Defoe and his contemporaries inherited from the previous century, "the *Will* ... has no power to chuse *Evil*, considered absolutely as *Evil*; this being directly the Nature and Natural Method of its Workings." South, whom I've been quoting, solves this problem by blaming "that other governing Faculty of the Soul, the *Understanding*." Thus, if "the *Will* chuses, follows and embraces, things *Evil* and destructive ... it is, because the *Understanding* first tells it, that they are good, and wholesome, and fit to be chosen by it." The understanding is like "one Man [who] gives another a Cup of Poyson ... but, at the same time, he tells him, that it is a Cordial; and so he drinks it off, and dies." While this is typical of contemporary opinion, South is particularly interesting for his pursuit of the notion of how things get misrepresented in the mind, or, more largely, of the whole matter of representation itself. It is not merely that the understanding often fails to encode the world properly, but that the whole encoding process itself is slippery, and so potentially dangerous. "The way by which *Good* and *Evil* generally *operate upon the Mind of Man*," he asserts, "*is by those Words or Names by which they are notified and conveyed to the Mind*." Or, as he says elsewhere, "the greatest Affairs, and most important Interests of the World are carried on by Things, not as they *are*, but as they are *called*"; "Words and Names pass for Things themselves." One problem with this is that words are faulty and misleading instruments, and often carelessly applied. Another is that "there is a certain *bewitchery*, or fascination in Words, which makes them operate with a force beyond what we can naturally give an account of." A third is human nature itself: "nor are Men prevailed upon at this odd, unaccountable rate, by bare Words," says South, "only through a *defect* of Knowledge; but sometimes also do they suffer themselves to be carried away with these *Puffs of Wind*, even contrary to Knowledge and Experience it self." In other words (excuse the phrase) "that besotting Intoxication, which this *Verbal Magick* ... brings upon the Mind of Man" is such that "Words are able to perswade men out of what they *find* and *feel*, to reverse the very Impressions of Sense, and to amuse men with Fancies

Roxana's first misstep situates her (and her audience) in a psychologically complex world; her second puts her (and them) into motion with respect to that world. The two episodes would inevitably have to be considered together, if only for their reciprocal structure. Amy puts Roxana to bed with the jeweller, and she returns the favor. But these episodes are causally linked as well, and initiate a sequence of causes that shape the outcome of the novel. Roxana has done more than prepare her destiny in the person of Amy, who, utterly corrupted save for her intense loyalty to her mistress, will finally perform for her the ultimate favor; she has begun a terrible process in her own mind. "Sin and Shame follow one-another ... like Cause and Consequence," we have already quoted her saying. Put together, these two episodes offer the first illustration of that point, which turns out to mean far more than it would in ordinary criminal biography where sin occurs in the absence of shame, and then, sometimes at the last, shame reasserts itself. Sin and shame breed on one another, Roxana's history shows, the connection between them is not discrete and unidirectional. Shame not only follows sin, but – and this is most interesting – it prompts Roxana into further sin. Thus her reaction to the shame of becoming a "whore" – a callousness that may be real or affected, or both, which is to say she may overestimate how little she seems to care – leads her into the commission of a greater, more culpable crime, which then produces a renewal of shame. The sheer enormity of putting Amy to bed with the jeweller against her will (and staying to watch!) stings the conscience Roxana thought she'd silenced back into life. Her "holed" heart, we might say, reminds her that it still exists, and is wounded. Roxana herself describes the overall process, as it recurs during the course of her relationship with the Prince de —. It involves the build-up of "intellectual" – and moral – "Stupidity" until, at its height, she is "perfectly easie to the Lawfullness of [that relationship], as if I had been Marry'd ... and had had no other Husband." "So possible is it for us to roll ourselves up in Wickedness," she adds, "till we grow invulnerable by Conscience; and that Centinel once doz'd, sleeps fast, not to be awaken'd while the Tide of Pleasure continues to flow, or till something dark and dreadful brings us to ourselves again" (69).

Thus, succinctly, is summed up the recurrent pattern of Roxana's life – to the darkest, dreadful thing that closes her narrative, which, if not the murder of her daughter, is the series of heaven-sent calamities that (still darker, more dreadful) she leaves unspecified. As Roxana spirals down-

and Paradoxes even in spight of Nature, and Experience." Given "the absurd Empire, and Usurpation of Words over Things," and the fact that "the *generality of Men* are wholly govern'd by Names, and Words," it is hardly surprising, then, that "there is nothing, in which they are so remarkably, and powerfully govern'd by them, as in matters of *Good* and *Evil*" (Robert South, *Forty Eight Sermons and Discourse on Several Subjects, and Occasions* [1715], 2: 376–7, 395, 400, 404–5, 407, 408, 410–11).

ward to damnation – never quite brought back to herself again despite what she says – each new descent is prompted, ironically, by her efforts to avoid feeling shame or, finally, at her worst, merely to avoid its being imposed on her from outside.[30] Roxana's debauching Amy is only the first of three great turning points in her life, each of which brings her closer to the murder of her daughter. The second occurs midway through the novel, when she rejects the Dutchman's marriage proposal, and the third, of course, is her repeated refusal to acknowledge she is Susan's mother, which would also mean admitting she is the famed Roxana. In both these later episodes, Roxana's concern is to conceal her wickedness, rather than flaunt it as though she didn't care. The impossibility of cauterizing shame, one might say, has taught her to fear its recurrence. Yet all the time her conscience builds up layer upon layer of "callous substance," thickening with each seemingly healed scar.

Roxana does not merely refuse the Dutchman's offer of marriage, she attacks the whole institution of marriage. "A Woman [is] a free Agent, as well as a Man," she argues in a ringingly feminist speech, and as "fit to govern and enjoy her own Estate, without a Man, as a Man [is], without a Woman." Roxana does not begin by meaning to say so much, or meaning to mean anything in particular. The speech starts as an empty gesture, a screen to hide her real motive for saying no, which was a suspicion "really too gross ... to acknowledge," i.e., that he was after her money. When the Dutchman pre-empts this suspicion, Roxana feels "oblig'd to give a new Turn to [my refusal], and talk upon a kind of elevated Strain, which really was not in my Thoughts at first, at-all" (147ff.). By the time she finishes, however, she has come to believe in what she is saying. The Dutchman warns that her views are "shocking to Nature" and "very unkind to yourself," but Roxana is unimpressed. She has gone looking for an excuse, and found what she thinks is a rationale. Actually, to paraphrase Moll, she has only "reason'd herself out of reason" (*MF*, 57, 173). Carried away in a cloud of high-sounding but specious rhetoric – the Dutchman says she has "Notions different from all the World"; Roxana later calls these "my Platonicks" – she thus comes to do the very thing she found so intolerable in Amy and the jeweller (156, 232). That is, Roxana talks herself *into* behaving immorally, a significant step beyond trying, as she had earlier, to talk herself *out* of feeling bad about her immoral connection with the Prince de —. It is the Dutchman here who plays her original role, and it is to his credit that he continues to insist, as she did not, on the existence of a

---

[30] Grieving that "I cou'd not make myself known to my own Children, or form Acquaintances in the World," Roxana finds sudden solace in the thought that while "the thing cannot be remedy'd now ... the Scandal of it ... may be thrown off." But this is mere "fancy," and doesn't prove out (208).

natural moral order underlying speech, custom, and individual imaginings.[31]

Leaving the Dutchman (for whom she still has a hankering), Roxana returns to London, her "heart ... bent" – bent indeed! – "upon ... Independency [and] Liberty" (170–1). There, as if to prove the Dutchman wrong, she finds a world where notions like hers seem neither "shocking" nor unnatural, but then it is a world that cannot tell the specious from the real. Roxana's great success as a "Turkish" dancer shows as much. Only her costume is authentic, and, even then, the diamonds on it are false. "I was now in my Element," Roxana declares, but the feeling doesn't last (181). Eventually she recoils from her "scandalous" life, the worst part of her career so far, but not without having done irrevocable damage to herself, which is to say, to her sense of self (206). The Dutchman's warning proves prophetic. Wealthy beyond all conceivable need, disgusted by the perverse practices of her last lover and yearning after her lost children, Roxana decides "to shift my Being." This large phrase conceals a remarkably narrow idea; "not able to live in this Manner any longer," Roxana wishes to become respectable. But even this notion is remarkably narrow. Knowing that her having been "at best but a Whore, a common Whore .... cannot be remedy'd now," she fancies that "the Scandal of it ... may be thrown off" with a change of "Figure and Circumstance" (208–9). She will "shift" her being by moving from one end of town to another and, adopting a new style of life, pretend to be a

[31] Modern readers easily sympathize with Roxana's feminist declaration of independence, but, as it falls into a libertine tradition that was highly suspect, the original audience would likely not have been similarly inclined. One of the devil's general rules, according to Defoe, was "to infuse notions of liberty into the minds of men; that it is hard they should be born into the world with inclinations, and then be forbidden to gratify them" (*SRC*, 281). Such notions infused into the minds of women could border on pornography: "Ah! how I am ravished to hear you! ... that Liberty of Conscience which you begin to give me by your Discourse," says Agnes to Angelica in a book still locked safely away in a British Library cabinet, "hath rid me of almost an infinite Number of Troubles which tormented me" (*Venus in the Cloister: or, The Nun in Her Smock. Translated from the French by a Person of Honour* [1725], p. 15). Having published a dying declaration in which a criminal presents himself as an atheist or at least an agnostic, a major anthologizer of criminals' "lives" assures his readers that he has done so only because "the Reasonings in it were too weak to do any Hurt"; the intent instead has been to "fill the Soul with Horror" at "the Picture that this gives" (Johnson, *Lives of the Highwaymen*, p. 336). His chief predecessor, a good deal more uncouth, explains that he's occasionally allowed "these wicked offenders [to vent] a profane oath or curse" but only "to paint them in their proper colours"; their "words are always so odious, detestable and foul," he adds, "that some ... would be apt to conclude that Nature [set] their mouths at the wrong end of their bodies" (Smith, *Lives of the Highwaymen*, pp. 1–2). For an explanation of how it is possible "to represent a Conference betwixt two Parties" so as "to trapan and win the Opinions of the Vulgar ... under a Pretence of making the most vigorous Assaults [on] Behalf" of "that Side [one] has an utter Aversion to ... (tho' really to expose its Weakness)," see *Miscellany Letters Selected out of Mist's*, 4: 157–8. "Turning the narrator into an ironically myopic figure" was most definitely *not* – *pace* Ian Bell, *Defoe's Fiction* (London, 1985), p. 134 – "wholly outside the realm of popular fiction"; it was in fact a standard ploy in popular writing of all kinds.

Quaker. (The literal meaning of "shift" is to change one's dress, which in fact is all the real change she makes.) Better still, she thinks when it seems for a while that she may yet marry the Prince de —, she will go abroad "to live where all that had happen'd here, wou'd have been quite sunk out of Knowledge, as well as out of Memory, (*Conscience excepted*)" (234). The hoped for marriage does not materialize, but the afterthought in that last, intrusive parenthesis proves more telling than Roxana expects; it is not so easy, she discovers, to shift one's being as she thought. Once more, to her great pain, Roxana finds that conscience is not so easily written off. The threat of "scandal" sticks to her so long as she retains a residuum of moral sense. Her conscience may be weaker than it once was, but she has committed greater crimes. Her situation is no less painful now than when her holed heart first spoke up, after she put Amy to bed with the jeweller.

Thus, despite the tidy closural patterning provided by her eventual marriage to the Dutchman, Roxana's story ends (or seems about to end) nearly where it began.[32] Here, too, as when she lived in all apparent comfort with the jeweller, her inner feelings stand terribly discrepant with her outward appearance. "Let no-body conclude from the strange Success I met with in all my wicked Doings," she says, these "doings" seemingly past and her narrative gathering to a close, "that therefore I either was happy or easie: No, no, there was a Dart struck into the Liver; there was a secret Hell within, even all the while, when our Joy was at the highest; but more especially now, after it was all over, and when according to all appearance, I was one of the happiest Women upon Earth" (260). "Conscience," Defoe believed, "though for a time oppressed and kept under, yet upon all occasions tells [wicked people] plainly what their condition is, and oftentimes they repent. 'Tis true, sometimes they do not; God is pleased sometimes to treat them in the vindictive attribute, and they are cut off in their crimes, insensible and stupid, without a space or a heart to repent" (*SRC*, 166). Roxana is not entirely "insensible and stupid" (at least not yet), but what is left of her conscience nags at her, leaving her in a state of febrile exhaustion. Amidst "all humane Felicity," she cannot escape "Reflections" on her past, and these in fact affect her far worse than when she committed her first great sin: "They might be said to have gnaw'd a Hole in my Heart before," she says, "but now they made a Hole quite thro' it" (264). What she said earlier, when she turned the Dutchman down and then regretted it, holds truer now when she has him and all

---

[32] Thus this sequence of liaisons: marriage to a bad (in both senses of the term) merchant; then a non-marriage to a good jeweller; then an illicit relation with a prince/nobleman; then a near-marriage to a good jeweller/merchant; then an illicit relation with a prince; then a still more illicit relation with a nobleman; and then finally a marriage to a good jeweller/merchant turned nobleman.

the wealth and independence she could want: "I had a safe Harbour presented, and no Heart to cast-Anchor in it" (162).

Such is Roxana's situation just before the beginning of the last and longest section of the novel. As she tries to "shift" her "being" and finds she cannot, readers can be made all the more aware of the complexity of that "being," and of the potential complexity of "being" in general. Her crimes having split her into a number of irreconcilable parts, the private Roxana is at odds with the public and at war with itself. Increasingly, as her story continues to its awful close, noxious vapors will rise from somewhere beneath her consciousness, seeking "vent." She will want to express what she feels, but there will be no one to whom she can safely open herself, not even Amy.[33] Had the novel ended thus – Roxana's life trickling down to a secretly mean and unhappy conclusion – it would be notable for offering a highly sophisticated and more than usually interesting etiology of crime, along with a powerful vindication of conscience. Roxana would be notable enough as one of the major *bêtes noires* of Calvinist theology, the sinner so weakened by sin as no longer able even to wish for repentance. However disturbing such an ending would have seemed, it may nonetheless have been too quiet and inconsequential for the moral effect Defoe declaredly seeks. If, as I believe, one of his chief aims is to make his readers "out of love" with vice – with all that implies for the raising of their individual self-consciousness not only as moral but as social beings – then his chief means to this end must be to make them out of love with his protagonist. But this is something the novel has yet to do once and for all, having up to this point done it so frequently. *Roxana* owes its moral power to more than just its thematic complexity; both in fact depend quite heavily on the text's increasing "difficulty" both as narrative *and* as story, which is to say on the rising "load" it places on readers trying to follow the one and construct the other.

In moving from sin to shame and shame to sin, denouncing her crimes and then committing new ones, Roxana has alternately inspired repugnance and sympathy. Or, as G. A. Starr observes from a slightly different perspective, "emotional involvement with Roxana and critical detachment from her occur successively, not simultaneously." Here, "rather than balancing opposed attitudes" as he does in his other novels, "Defoe often engages unreservedly in his heroine's thoughts and actions, and then

---

[33] "My passion was so great," she says during her daughter's visit to the Quaker's, "that for want of Vent, I thought I shou'd have burst .... I had no vent; no-body to open myself to, or to make a Complaint to for my Relief" (284, for similar usages of "vent" see 298, 323, also 291). During an earlier crisis, Roxana feels "a violent Fermentation in my Blood" (235). This last metaphor seems especially appropriate given her one-time status as a brewer's wife, but then, on second thought, so does "vent."

abruptly recoils."[34] To repudiate Roxana readers must first feel some kinship toward her, especially if that repudiation is to be anything more than what it typically is in criminal biography, a complacent closing of social ranks against a convenient victim. The novel makes its readers feel that kinship again and again, along with Roxana's difference, as it describes her progressive hardening. Such recurrent changes of attitude alone are enough to make *Roxana* significantly more "difficult" than ordinary criminal biography, which allows for only one attitudinal change toward its subject, if any. (In the "serious" version this change is from repugnance to sympathy, the "other" being made kin; in the "comic" it is exactly the opposite.) This oscillation of feeling is very different, too, from the "cooled out" distance *Moll Flanders* allows its readers.

Because it swings readers' feelings back and forth, *Roxana* is an emotionally demanding and potentially tiring text. To feel disgust at, say, Roxana's putting Amy to bed with the jeweller, readers have to put aside the sympathy generated by her desperate circumstances and her clear-eyed rejection of their "cant." To feel sympathy at any subsequent point, and there are more than a few, they have to put aside an amply warranted disgust. To a certain extent this shifting back and forth ensures that each feeling is powerfully felt against its contrasting predecessor. In repeating the process as often as *Roxana* does, however, there is a risk that the opposing feelings will eventually cancel each other out or become muddled. In the first instance Roxana would lose most of her power as a monitory example; in the second, she might inspire feelings Defoe would have considered inappropriate. As she bewails her inability to repent, for instance, it is not difficult to pity her or even to feel she is a better person than she thinks. Even from the strictest possible eighteenth-century point of view, Roxana's sufferings (not the least of which is severe self-hatred) may seem greater than her sins require. In any case, there is more than enough in her situation at this point in the novel to make her seem both pathetic and, from a moral and even philosophical point of view, potentially unnerving. If at core (or heart) she is quite another person from the public or (shall we say?) epiphenomenal Roxana, and if the notions she propounds are not so different from those of *all* the world, then whom or what are we to blame for her bad deeds, and why should she be singled out? Because neither God nor the law writes *finis* to her case, these questions remain peculiarly open. Roxana's self-devouring heart might leave readers *too* amazed and wondering. What a finely Romantic heroine she could have been: Prometheus on the rock *and* the great carrion bird eating at her vitals!

It is not so much to prevent such musings as to control them, I'd suggest, that the novel continues, moving back over ground seemingly already

[34] Starr, *Defoe and Casuistry*, pp. 166, 165.

covered to display, with considerable suspense and tension, the heinous consequences of Roxana's loss of "heart."[35] What Roxana truly *is* becomes a question not of essences or psychology merely, but of the effect (and affect) she has on her reading audience. The basis for this closing effort is the active role the text has allowed (or imposed upon) readers up to this point – a role that involves more than moving back and forth between opposite feelings, and which, even as one's sympathies or antipathies are engaged, promotes a special kind of distance from Roxana and her story. The growing ability to trace a steadily developing pattern in Roxana's behavior brings with it a form of observation not possible in Defoe's other criminal novels, and this in turn prepares readers to encounter the dialogues which, as her narrative ends, divide them from her as completely as any drama staged at the gallows.

In displaying a pattern of psychological causality rather than the mysterious workings of God's invisible hand, *Roxana* not only sets itself apart from Defoe's other works but makes a special contribution to the history of the novel. Like most psychological novels, it offers its readers much more than a look at the particular processes of its protagonist's mind. The ways of God (or self-absenting authors) are beyond our ken, but the psychology of an individual is a more local phenomenon. Even when it baffles, it remains a thing potentially understood. *Captain Singleton*, *Moll Flanders*, and *Colonel Jack* proceed, as it were, by jumps. Because it is God (or Defoe) who orders their plots, moving their protagonists through life by various providential or fateful events, it is difficult to know just where these novels may be going. They are driven by forces impinging from the "outside," by which I mean that while certain powerful events determining the future course of the narrative can be seen as a consequence of the main character's behavior, they do not derive from that character. Typically such events are significant coincidences. This is not the case with *Roxana*, where the course of events is mainly shaped by the chief character's motives, or by her responses to what she takes to be other people's motives. That is to say (and this alone would make her very "modern"), Roxana's character becomes her fate.[36]

---

[35] Defoe's disruption of straightforward chronology at the end of *Roxana* is not unprecedented in his other narrative writing; thus see *The Family Instructor*, vol. 1, Dialogues 4–6, and vol. 2, pt. 1, Dialogues 2 and 3; and also *Religious Courtship*, Dialogues 2 and 3. In these earlier texts there are solid, readily visible rhetorical reasons for Defoe's manipulation of temporal sequence, which leads me to believe that the ending of *Roxana* was more premeditated than it may seem.

[36] It is worth noting in this connection that coincidence plays a fairly trivial role in *Roxana*. Only two chance occurrences play any part in shaping the course of her life, and neither is crucial in itself. In both cases – her re-encounter with the Dutchman in London, and her daughter's having been her cookmaid – the event becomes important only insofar as Roxana is able or unable to deal with it. Thus, to speak to the more important instance, the novel gives ample room to believe that Susan's turning up need not have been the threatening, and ultimately tragic situation it becomes (more on this later). The novel's first great coincidence, in fact – the

A special tension builds as readers accumulate information on Roxana, developing a clearer notion of how her mind works. Though no particular "theory" of her behavior will be entirely adequate, any such theory brings with it the possibility that readers may be able to predict what will happen next, or to understand how some past action has contributed to the one they are now considering. Few if any equivalent opportunities are offered by the earlier criminal novels. Moll's seduction by the Elder Brother, for instance, sets the pattern of her life ever after; no subsequent sexual encounter has any apparent effect on those that follow it. One may be interested in Moll's motives in each case, in the practical constraints that force certain behaviors, in the morality of what she is doing, and even possibly in the rationalizations she offers to justify herself, but there is little point is asking how the event unfolding now will relate to the large course of events in the novel. If notional incest can lead to unwitting, actual incest, anything might happen; our fortunes lie in God's hands, not our own. Or, to take a less dramatic example, while Moll's seduction of the Bath gentleman and her last fling with the baronet from Bartholomew Fair both warrant complex consideration, the first exerts no influence on the second, and neither impinges on her final relation with Jemy. Moll has a taste for gentlemen, but her exercising that taste in one instance has no consequence for her exercise of it in another. Moll has clear motives and even a rudimentary psychology, but that psychology is static, by which I mean that it is generally limited to an ongoing present. It is flat, without perspective; it has no cumulative force. Roxana at any particular moment, however, is what she has been and is on her way to becoming. Another way of saying this is that where Moll does B in response to situation A, Roxana does C as a consequence of having done B and, before that, A. Her doing C, moreover, is likely to put her in a situation where she may feel obliged to commit D.

No single event in Roxana's life can be as freely considered by itself as, for instance, a comparable event in Moll's. Not everything Roxana does leads to her doing something else, but the ligatures between her actions are a good deal more developed than in any of Defoe's other novels, or in contemporary fiction generally. To put the difference crudely, it is as

chance appearance of Roxana's husband in Paris – comes to mean nothing at all. It has no impact on her, once she has sent Amy to sound him out and decides to leave him be, and little impact on us. Consider the very different effect of Jemy's appearance at Brickhill, just after Moll has married her honest citizen (185–7). Where this seems a sign from some overruling power, a reminder to us (if not Moll) of her past and an index (however indecipherable) to her future, the reappearance of Roxana's husband serves only to indicate her current state of mind with respect to what she once was. If we make anything more of Roxana's husband's reappearance than she does, perhaps we might take it as a sign of her increased brazenness, a portent of too much future self-confidence. Though chance events occur in *Roxana* (thus the storm in the Channel), they affect the plot of the novel only insofar as they affect its protagonist.

though Moll were shooting dice and Roxana playing cards. The odds in such cases are to be calculated differently, for while each throw is a discrete event, the various hands in a cardgame can affect the odds for future hands. Only in the latter instance is there a possibility of the player employing various strategies (such as card counting), which is why it is possible to kibitz at blackjack, say, and not at craps. What I am suggesting with this inelegant (and inexact) analogy is that *Roxana* makes its readers more active spectators, or at least gives them that opportunity. Because readers are better able to guess at what is coming, and because Roxana's behavior is important in determining what is coming, the novel disposes them to pay particular attention to the way she plays out her hands. Much more than in the other novels, thinking what they might have done in similar circumstances, readers are allowed and encouraged to exercise what Elias calls "foresight," an attitude or ability essential to the technique of "self-control." Only in *Robinson Crusoe* does as much hinge on the protagonist making the right decisions, but Robinson (at least once he's on his island) generally makes them, leaving little room for second guessing.

The distinction I have been making between *Moll Flanders* and *Roxana* may seem to put the latter at a disadvantage, at least insofar as the most modern sort of reader might tend to value multiplicity and variety over programmatic consistency. Within the context of Defoe's expressed motives for writing, however, the value of the difference between the two extends beyond the mere representation of long "chains" of "action" and "dependence." It allows *Roxana* to be more pointedly moral, without at the same time sacrificing reader interest. That "various qualifying circumstances" typically prevent the "drawing of any simple moral" from *Moll Flanders* is a great bait to readers' imaginations.[37] For Defoe, however, such lability may well have proved an embarrassment. Thus it seems significant that both *Colonel Jack* and *Roxana* take harder lines on criminality, and that the latter, especially, gives its protagonist all sorts of harsh judgments to make on herself. Still, *Roxana* offers no simple moral, if by that one means a set of propositions readily apprehended and digested. No more than Defoe's other novels does it seek to achieve its moral effect by preaching at its readers; it does, however, differ in the extent to which it prompts moral reflection. Let us consider, for instance, the ways in which it and *Moll Flanders* handle highly similar events.

At the mid-point of both novels the protagonist rejects a proposal from a man she likes, and with whom she could have settled down into a kind of respectablity (at least she wouldn't have gone on to commit her most notable offences). Moll chooses instead to marry the honest citizen, whom she finds more convenient, and, when he dies, she becomes a thief. Roxana

37 Starr, *Defoe and Casuistry*, p. 138.

returns to London, breaks into high life, and becomes a "Queen" among courtesans.[38] Both come later to realize their mistakes, and, when opportunity offers (in both cases by happy coincidence), each tries to pick up where she left off. Roxana's refusing the Dutchman, however, evokes a very different kind of response from Moll's leaving Jemy. Though notionally the latter is the graver violation – a marriage contract is broken rather than merely waived – affectively it is not. Moll makes a bad choice but, given the circumstances, it is hard to see how she might have done otherwise. Jemy is generous and kind, but hardly someone to rely on, especially where money is concerned. After they are temporarily reunited, Moll is so overcome with feeling that she proposes they go to Virginia and live off the proceeds of her estate. At first Jemy agrees, but then he gets what he thinks is a better idea. His suggestion, however, that they cash out her Virginia holdings and buy land in Ireland, does not sit well with Moll, nor should it; she might end up with nothing. No similar conditions obtain when the Dutchman makes his offer. Roxana has every reason to believe that he is a good and sensible man, indeed "one of the honestest compleatest Gentlemen upon Earth" (158). It is in fact this very belief that causes her to lie about her motives for not wanting to marry. Because the objective situation here is simpler, it is very much easier to see what Roxana should have done, and very much easier to fault her. Roxana herself steers us in this direction, saying that she was "one of the foolishest, as well as wickedest Creatures upon Earth," declaring that "here I might have settled myself out of the reach even of Disaster itself" (158).[39]

The consequences of Roxana's behavior, too, tend to make the reader more judgmental with her than with Moll. The rejection of Jemy delays and (considering Moll can have no more children) perhaps diminishes the happiness she finally finds, but Roxana's rejection of the Dutchman poisons her future forever.[40] Where Moll simply sloughs off her life of crime (or so it seems), Roxana so damages her person that she cannot just resume where she left off. Trying to return to her moral status quo ante, she only makes her current status worse. It is not merely the futility and sordidness of the enterprise that encourages readers to view it askance, but the strong possibility it may be unnecessary. Thus all during the last part

---

[38] "I was Queen of the Day," says Roxana on the occasion of her second Turkish dance (179). All through the novel she yearns after noble status, though in the most meretricious way, finally to be satisfied with speciously acquired titles (see also pp. 70, 159, 161, 170, 234, 235, 239, 240, 242, 261–2).

[39] Compare this – or the paragraph on p. 161 where Roxana calls herself "a standing Monument of the Madness and Distraction which Pride and Infatuations from Hell runs us into; how ill our Passions guide us" – to Moll's saying "the Moral indeed of all my History is left to be gather'd by the Senses and Judgment of the Reader; I am not Qualified to preach to them" (268). *Roxana* is the most directive of all Defoe's novels, criminal or otherwise.

[40] On this point see Robert D. Hume, "The Conclusion of Defoe's *Roxana*: Fiasco or Tour de Force?" *Eighteenth-Century Studies*, 3 (1970): 481.

of the novel, as Roxana tries so sedulously to conceal her identity from her daughter – deceiving her husband, implicating the Quaker woman, and inspiring a murderous frenzy in Amy – it may easily be wondered whether the discovery of her past would be so terrible as she thinks. Had "the whole Affair" been "blown-up," Roxana says after a narrow escape from her daughter, "I must for-ever after have been this Girl's Vassal, *that is to say*, have let her into the Secret, and trusted to her keeping it too, or have been expos'd, and undone; *the very Thought fill'd me with Horror*" (280).

But neither exposure, nor the onset of a relation with her daughter, can seem to the reader quite the horrible fate it seems to her. Roxana's daughter loves her (poor creature!) and means her no harm. All she really seems to want is to throw herself at her mother's feet.[41] In all likelihood it would take very little to swear her to undying fealty, and what if Susan did reveal what she knew? Roxana is convinced that her husband "must have abhor'd me, and the very mention of my Name" (301), but this leaves out of account his general complaisance and pointed lack of curiosity about her affairs. The ship's captain with whom they were to have gone to Holland, the husband of Susan's friend, as much as lets the cat out of the bag when he tells him, "I hear your Lady has got a Daughter more than she expected" (296). Roxana nearly goes to pieces when her husband repeats this to her, but he no more notices her suspicious behavior than he did the captain's hardly cryptic implication. The Dutchman is not looking for cats in or out of bags, perhaps because he already knows enough of her past to suspect it will not bear examination. There is more than enough evidence, too, to suggest the Quaker suspects the truth and that it makes no difference to her, either. Indeed, like Susan, she is if anything impressed, even awed, by the notion that the Lady Roxana was once the king's mistress. All through the last part of the novel Roxana feels as though she will "burst" – the pressure builds inside and she cannot "vent" it – but to the people around her, who know more of her "secret history" than she thinks (or could bear them knowing), she is more an item of friendly gossip than of scandal. Only Amy shares Roxana's exaggerated view of what is at stake, but Amy is of course Roxana's creature, even more cut off from ordinary life than she (284; also 291, 298, 323).

The manifest sign of Roxana's moral and social isolation as the novel ends – and the chief means of getting readers to see the psychic decay which is both its cause and symptom – is an increased reliance on dialogue to carry forward the action. Practically all Roxana's narrative, now, is made up of either reported conversations or her musings on what these conversations might mean. As I've already pointed out, dialogue in Defoe's novels allows readers to see "around" or "beyond" his narrators, to

---

[41] For an opposing and quite negative view of Susan's motives, however, see Novak, *Realism, Myth, and History in Defoe's Fictions*, p. 108.

apprehend their worlds in ways they do not, and to judge the effects and qualities of their actions from more "normal" points of view. Other voices, even if only briefly overheard, help readers to define and judge more closely the voice speaking directly to them. Toward the end of *Roxana*, especially, this effect operates quite powerfully. Earlier on, Roxana participated vigorously in dialogue, and there was often something to be said for her point of view (thus, for instance, her discussions of marriage, morality, and sexual politics with the jeweller, the Prince, and the Dutchman). As the novel winds down, however, Roxana becomes relatively passive, a great deal of her talking being done for her by others. Most of the conversations she presents or describes, in fact, she relates at second-hand, they (and with them much of the novel's final action) taking place away from her as Amy and, latterly, the Quaker act as her proxies in prosecuting or defending her interests, primarily against Susan. Roxana sticks close to home, where she has only to deal with these two confidantes and her husband. There are two perilous occasions, however, when she is forced out into larger company. The first occurs when Roxana unexpectedly encounters Susan on the ship which is to take her to Holland, and the second immediately thereafter, when Susan pays a quick return visit to the Quaker's, nearly catching Amy and Roxana together. These, significantly enough, are the only two occasions when Roxana speaks with her daughter or even sees her close up. Both encounters, it is particularly worth noting, evoke the longest dialogues in the last part of the novel, and the most complex and intricate of all its dialogues. Each involves four interlocutors (elsewhere there are never more than three), and both might make one wish for another narrator; they are a first step toward making the reader's forced intimacy with Roxana unbearable.

Both dialogues are complex not only in the interactions they describe, but in what they show of Roxana's state of mind as she follows, interprets, and seeks to limit what happens. Though in no way to be condoned, her behavior throughout is plausible and comprehensible, and at first glance her interpretations seem valid. Seeking to conceal her inner disturbance, she studies Susan's speech and behavior to see how much, if anything, she really knows. The first encounter, Roxana thinks, goes well enough. Leaving her daughter, she is "thorowly convinc'd . . . that the Girl did not know me, which was an infinite Satisfaction." "It was evident," she adds, "that had she suspected any-thing of the Truth, she would not have been able to have conceal'd it" (279). But this conviction proves short-lived. When the Quaker is sent back to Susan and her friend to prevent a second encounter, Susan asks a series of pointed questions. The news of this puts Roxana "upon the Rack again," causing her now to suspect "that the Jade had a right Scent of things, and that she knew and remember'd my Face, but had artfully conceal'd her Knowledge of me, till she might perhaps, do it more to my Disadvantage" (280). Roxana's imputation of motive may be wrong, but, as one realizes in retrospect, her reassessment of the situation is clearly right.

The suddenness of this realization, and the importance of the information it carries, puts a special, hitherto unfelt strain on the reader's relation to Roxana as narrator. Though long chary of her value judgments, he has had no reason as yet to doubt her acuity as an observer. Here, however, it is possible to feel *as* one reads (not afterwards, as previously) the gross impediment of her filtering consciousness, even in something so simple as trying to know just what is going on. "I thought I perceiv'd that the Girl did not know me," Roxana has said in a revealingly worded passage, "because I did not perceive the least Disorder in her Countenance, or the least Change in her Carriage; no Confusion, no Hesitation in her Discourse." Yet very soon after taking comfort in this "Notion," she hears the captain's wife feed Susan a line that allows Susan to say "she was sure she had seen me before, but she cou'd not recollect where." Though this bit of discourse hits Roxana like a "Thunder-Clap," she does not (at the time, at least) suspect it has been contrived; her "Fancy" that her daughter doesn't know her remains intact (278–9). In another way as well Roxana proves an unreliable observer. All during this encounter, she believes her behavior gives nothing away, yet this is not true either. The Quaker, for one, has noticed something, the importance of which may be judged by the fact that it, too, is held back for maximal effect. Back from her follow-up visit to Susan, the Quaker tells Roxana she turned the girl's prying questions aside because "I saw by *thy* Answers on-board the Ship, when she talk'd of *thee*, that *thou* did'st not incline to let her be acquainted with *thee*" (281). Roxana did not know she was giving away so much, nor did the reader, until this moment (once burned, though, twice shy). No wonder Susan, better able to interpret Roxana's behavior than the Quaker, feels emboldened to stage yet another encounter.

So long as Roxana stands between the reader and the story she tells, this first dialogue begins to show, it is impossible to know for sure what Susan's game is or just how well Roxana plays her public role. "What my face might do towards betraying me," she says describing her second meeting with her daughter, "I know not, because I cou'd not see myself" (284). What Roxana cannot see, readers themselves can only see obliquely or inferentially, if at all. The crucial importance of knowing something so simple as the way she and Susan look during their two tense encounters, and the tantalizing inaccessibility of such knowledge, appear more strongly after their second dialogue. Of all the novel's dialogues, this is by far the richest and most complicated, especially now that the reader has been alerted to Susan's hidden motives, the role of the captain's wife as her "straight man," the Quaker's perspicacity, and Roxana's limited ability to gauge what is going on. Exploring even a few of the inferences this episode allows would lead us far afield, so I shall merely point out that again, and with unmistakeable plainness, Roxana simply fails to see something of major significance.

Thus, after the intrusive visitors are gone, and Roxana has had a chance to collect herself, she probes the Quaker to see "what she imagin'd *the Girl* had in her Head." Roxana has a double purpose, to cross-check her own impressions and to see what "the good Friendly QUAKER might have in her Head," too. So far the Quaker has played a cagey game. "I can't think," she had said just after Susan's departure, "but she had some other Drift in that long Discourse; there's something else in her Head ... I am satisfy'd of that." Now, when Roxana pretends that she herself cannot "imagine what it was [that Susan] aim'd at," the Quaker shows her own capacity to be disingenuous. "'Tis plain ... what she aims at," she replies, "she believes *thou* are the same Lady *Roxana* that danc'd in the *Turkish* Vest, but she is not certain." Once more the Quaker's insight surprises, especially as here again Roxana has underestimated her, just as she has done her daughter. Still more surprising, however, are some more or less hard-edged facts the Quaker communicates; these greatly alarm Roxana about her daughter's ultimate intentions. "Several times," the Quaker says, she "perceiv'd [Susan] to be in Disorder, and to restrain herself with great Difficulty; and once or twice she mutter'd to herself, that *she had found it out*, or, *that she wou'd find it out*, she [the Quaker] cou'd not tell whether; and that she often saw Tears in her Eyes" (292–3). That all this has escaped Roxana's notice is, in its way, quite shocking. How could she not have seen her daughter's tears, or heard the tremors in her voice? (The indistinctness of Susan's mutterings, incidentally, is rather a nice touch; readers are reminded here, too, that their only view of the event is filtered through another perceiving subject.)

The Quaker's description of Susan comes as a revelation, raising all sorts of questions about her motives, first in seeking to speak with her mother, and then in saying what she does when she gets the opportunity. Most simply, however, it makes one feel not only the insufficiency of Roxana's point of view but its increasing cruelty. As, newly aware, the reader reflects back on her version of what happened, Roxana's moral and perceptual "stupidity" become inextricably linked. The brilliance of this tactic is that, simultaneously, it alienates readers from Roxana both as moral beings *and* as readers. Roxana is no good as a mother and hardly better as a reporter of events. The same "stupidity" which allows her to damage her daughter, in effect, "damages" her narrative (though actually, of course, it enhances it). Even if the last part of the novel is being read only as an increasingly suspenseful "thriller" (Roxana having hinted from its start that something terrible is going to happen), Susan's tears and mutterings will seem important clues her mother ought not to have missed. Defoe makes readers feel the deficiency of Roxana's mind all the more powerfully as they try, and fail, to see through it. In this way Roxana can be exasperating even to those who, given her rich and complex fictiveness, might otherwise be willing to exempt her from the hard and fast rules of everyday morality.

Roxana may nonetheless retain some residual sympathy. She and the reader, after all, have spent considerable time together. For anyone struck by Susan's tears, however, Defoe administers the *coup de grâce* a few pages from the end of the novel. There he presents a last pathetic colloquy, at about the length of a page and a half, between Susan and the Quaker. As this is the third in a series, readers are used to the situation. Roxana is not present, having ducked out at the Quaker's suggestion. The dialogue is reported directly, marked for each speaker as it might be in a playscript, making it as present, as "taking," as reported speech can be in a novel.[42] No other dialogue is so marked in the book; nowhere else is the text as free of the narrator's intervening consciousness. Susan, as usual, gets no help from the Quaker, who answers her with a series of equivocations that allow her to pretend she's not lying. The dialogue is not especially dramatic or complex, but at one point, clearly at the end of her rope, Susan cries out: "If you knew my Distress, you cou'd not be so cruel" (320). The line could just as well be addressed to her mother as the Quaker, but her mother, maintaining a cold distance, is not there. The Quaker answers with still more equivocation, little realizing how corrupted an instrument she's become. Roxana, whose voice of course frames this dialogue, passes it on without comment even at the end. Susan is in an agony of pain, the Quaker bent to a wicked purpose, and Roxana's heart "holed" thoroughly through. Only a reader sharing in her "stupidity," one is tempted to say, will fail to see the full evil of her being.

And yet, too, the mysteriousness and pathos of that being remain undiminished. With the full weight of the text behind them, readers cannot quite lapse back into the "stupidity" of criminal biography, either, with its insistence on abolishing, ignoring, or grossly simplifying human complexity in order that *its* readers might comfortably rally themselves around tolerable (if not "easy") and always disposable notions of criminals and their crimes. There remains something unfathomable but eminently ponderable in Roxana. At the end of the novel she is trapped in an increasingly empty and (for the reader almost as much as her) inhospitable solipsism. As conversations whirl around her head, determining her fate,

---

[42] For Defoe's view that dialogue was more easily followed and made a greater impression on readers than straight narrative or other forms of expository writing, see *FI*, 15: ix.

she stands helpless by, unable to "vent" what builds inside because there is no one to whom she can speak her deepest, most private thoughts. And yet all her main interlocutors – Amy, her second "skin"; the Quaker, whose dress and speech she has adopted; Susan, who bears her name – seem almost other versions of her, extensions of her personality cut off from the main and at odds with each other as well as with her "own" self. Amy's destruction of Susan is, for Roxana, the equivalent of an unwitting and involuntary suicide. Helpless to avert the event, Roxana succeeds only in corrupting the Quaker, who was to have been the chief prop of her new-shifted "being." What Roxana has instead is a fractured, scattered, alienated being that ranges beyond and then turns back on her sense of self, a being that reaches down to depths she cannot imagine, where pressures build she cannot cope with.

All this is complex, but as her narrative closes readers may be led to ponder still greater complexities. We have already seen how Roxana is the sum total of certain intrinsic characteristics (e.g., her "French" aptitude for dancing), plus her education (which makes her a "naturalized" Englishwoman), plus the choices she has made over the course of her life (which have hardened and "holed" her conscience), plus what the "world" at various stages of her history has told her she is or seems to be (e.g. "French," "wife," "Roxana," "mother"), plus her reactions to these dictates. All these elements interact in very complicated ways, positively as well as negatively. Thus Roxana's rejection of the term "wife" and her efforts to avoid being called "Roxana" or "mother" are much more crucial in determining her ultimate fate than the things she does to warrant these terms in the first place. To all this, the last part of the novel adds a rich sense of the intricacies of Roxana's social context, especially of its implications. By this last term I mean the ways that social interactions entangle and embarrass, even long after they may seem to have been concluded. As the novel begins its close, readers can see quite clearly something they may not yet have noticed, that Roxana's increasingly immoral behavior has had permanent consequences beyond its bad effect on her mind; she has all the while been leaving a "trace" in the larger world. Thus her abandoned children, the liaison with the Prince de —, and most importantly the name "Roxana," all threaten to re-enter her life and so disturb her "being" just at the point she hopes to "shift" it. They threaten to do this, it is important to note, quite apart from any disturbance caused by stirrings of conscience. For yet another reason Roxana is not so free as she sometimes may have seemed; it is not only her "heart" (or psyche) that impinges upon and so limits her "being," but also her history, which is to say her long string of interactions with other "beings." In a particularly cruel twist, certain of these boomerang back on her just when – by virtue of all that she has done – she is at her weakest to fend them off. Roxana's plight at the end of the novel shows too, then, that one cannot simply dissever one's being from what one has meant, and may still mean, to other "beings."

Other "beings," moreover, can have psychologies fully as complex as hers and be nearly as mysterious. As more is heard from other characters via the closing dialogues, and readers pay close attention to what they are saying in their efforts to understand what is actually going on, it becomes increasingly obvious that Roxana is not alone in being divided into public and private personae, and that, with them as with Roxana, this distinction admits of further gradations. The Quaker is "deeper" than Roxana thinks. The face she turns toward Susan is not the same she turns toward Roxana, but the latter, too, is put on; the Quaker possesses a privacy Roxana does not delve into, just as Roxana does vis-à-vis the Quaker. Susan is still more complicated. She shows something of her private self to the Quaker when, finally, she confides in her, but she never reveals to anyone – not even, it would seem, her friend the sea captain's wife – the source or exact nature of the deep, almost obsessive need she has to reunite herself with an unloving mother. Even Amy, Roxana's closest "other" self, possesses more than one level of privacy. As Roxana's secret sharer, she lives a duplicitous life congruent with her mistress's; that is, apart from enacting their public roles together, they share a common privacy. Beneath this mutuality, however, there is a dimension to Amy's character that neither Roxana nor the reader can fathom – i.e., that aspect of Amy's self which so identifies with her mistress that, in the service of Roxana's own best interests, it does away with her flesh and blood against her explicit wish. One more reason Roxana cannot simply "be" what she wants to be, then, is that Amy herself is no simple "being." Nor, for that matter, is anyone else around her.

All this complexity is dizzying, but it may be valuably so. "Life is, or ought to be, but one universal act of solitude," Defoe thought in one of his somberer moods: "Everything revolves in our minds by innumerable circular motions, all centering in ourselves .... All reflection is carried home, and our dear self is, in one respect, the end of living .... we love, we hate, we covet, we enjoy, all in privacy and solitude. All that we communicate of those things to any other is but for their assistance in the pursuit of our desires; the end is at home." All Defoe's novels are epics of solitude, for their readers perhaps as much as their protagonists, but it is *Roxana* that illustrates its perils most powerfully: "Here we have no restraint upon our thoughts but from ourselves, no restraint upon our actions but from our own consciences, and nothing to assist us in our mortifications of our desires, but our own reflections, which, after all, may often err, often be prepossessed." "In solitude," Defoe points out, "a man converses with himself, and as a wise man said, he is not always sure that he does not converse with his enemy" (*SRC*, 4, 11). Though in Defoe's terms it is finally impossible to escape solitude, one might enlarge, nonetheless, one's conversational circle. In the solitude of reading, for instance, we also talk to ourselves, but (as Defoe realized) with other people's words. It is one of the great achievements of *Roxana*, I'd suggest, that it exploits this situation not to seduce or "subject" us as Moll, Roxana, and Jack's slaves variously are – not, as Moll might say, to "wrap" us up in its story – but, rather, extending our converse with ourselves, to enlarge and enhance our "privacy and solitude," which is to say what we are "at home."[43]

Such a state of mind would be quite different from the quasi-transcendent, "proto-aesthetic" abstraction I've suggested as a possible effect of the reader's encounter with Moll, the mercer, and his journeyman. This novel is more sobering and less flattering to the self-conception of would-be disinterested, "superior" observers; it is not a text that much supports any readerly sense of "ontological privilege."[44] Thus, as Roxana turns increasingly inward, readers may find themselves turned increasingly outward, away from any narrow, complacent notion of their own and others' identity, toward a heightened awareness of how complexly they and other individuals are constituted – not only within themselves but vis-à-vis each other and the language they use to describe and regulate their interrelations as well as their own states of being. In thinking about Roxana's "being," to borrow an elegant phrase from Locke, "we let loose our thoughts into the vast ocean of Being." Who or what is she if, being among other things a creature of language – of others' use of it as well as her own – language seems nonetheless to have carried her away from her true or at least original self? Where is *she* amidst all her discourse (which includes of course her representation of others' discourse), amidst all the actions and interactions imposed on her by specious values and social exigency?

Such questions are more easily asked about fictive criminals, for in the practical world the premises on which they rest may seem moral and socially unaffordable luxuries. "All the Right and Justice of Reward and Punishment," says Locke, require firm notions of "Personal Identity," "Human Laws not punishing . . . such an one [who] *is not himself*, or is *beside*

---

[43] Thus see the passage quoted in chapter 2 from his *Essay on Projects* (1697), and cited in n. 62 to that chapter, on readers being "forced" to "repeat" the "thoughts" they read. "Never poor vain Creature," says Moll of her falling victim to the Elder Brother's seduction, "was so wrapt up with every part of the Story, as I was, not Considering what was before me" (26). Moll is "romanced" in more than one way, her situation here adumbrating the dangers romance readers (especially women and children) faced of becoming "a real Slave to Fable and Fiction" (William Darrel, *The Gentleman Instructed, In the Conduct of a Virtuous and Happy Life . . . . To Which is Added, A Word to the Ladies*, 5th edn [1713], pp. lxx–lxxi, cited by J. Paul Hunter, "The Loneliness of the Long-Distance Reader," *Genre*, 10 [1977]: 466–7).

[44] For "ontological privilege," see D. A. Miller, *The Novel and the Police* (Berkeley, 1988), p. 162, cited more extensively chapter 5, n. 25.

himself," i.e., persons who are "Mad."[45] Roxana is by no means mad, but what readers see of her as she narrates her story, speaking as though she were "another-body," should keep them from adhering to any simple notion of who this "I" is that she (and each of us, for our parts) continually refers to. Perhaps this is yet another reason why the novel ends with Roxana suffering – as yet – no socially sanctioned punishment. All that one sees as her story trails off is a self-devouring heart that – baffling sight! – actually, gradually, disappears into the hole it makes in itself; and yet Roxana somehow continues to live. No Prometheus, and certainly no pelican rending her breast to nourish her young, she seems more like that fabled bird who, disoriented and confused, flies in ever tightening circles until it presents (to make my own attempt at elegant phrasing) a fundamental problem in ontology. But so, then, may we all.

"'Tis no Wonder," to quote Locke yet again, that "Men, extending their Enquiries beyond their Capacities, and letting their Thoughts wander into those depths where they can find no sure Footing ... raise Questions and multiply Disputes, which, never coming to any clear Resolution, are proper only to continue and increase their Doubts, and to confirm them at last in perfect Scepticism." *Roxana* is in its own way an essay concerning human understanding, and, like Locke's great work, concerned with setting out the limits as well as the powers of the human mind. It, too, launches readers on depths where they can find no sure footing, but with salutary effect. "'Tis of great use to the Sailor to know the length of his Line," says Locke, "though he cannot with it fathom all the depths of the Ocean. 'Tis well he knows, that it is long enough to reach the bottom, at such Places, as are necessary to direct his Voyage, and caution him against running upon Shoals, that may ruin him. Our Business here is not to know all things, but those which concern our Conduct." As a fitting motto for *Roxana*, this might stand with Defoe's remarks on the value of anatomizing vice. Roxana's not knowing the length of her line puts her and her audience in over their heads, but the "line" of her narrative hauls readers back even as she founders. Though Roxana falls prey to the "bewitchery in words" (to borrow a phrase from another of Defoe's contemporaries), the novel's reader is made its beneficiary.[46] "Chimney-corner romance" and other forms of "lying" may make a "hole in the heart," as we noted several chapters back, but not – to be sure! – a novel which alerts its readers to that very phenomenon.

"We live in an age," Defoe wrote, more sanguine here, "that does not want so much to know their duty as to practise it; not so much to be taught, as to be made obedient to what they have already learnt ... men will frankly own a thing to be their duty, which at the same time they dare

[45] Locke, *Essay Concerning Human Understanding*, 2: 27: 18, 20, pp. 341, 342–3.
[46] Locke, ibid., 1: 1: 6–7, pp. 46–7; "bewitchery in words" is South's phrase, quoted n. 29 above.

omit the practice of; and innumerable arts, shifts, and turns, they find out to make that omission easy to themselves, and excusable to others" (*FI*, 15: 1–2). So Roxana lives, her discourse carrying her away not only from duty but, finally, from a proper sense of the real. At the end of her narrative she hardly knows what is going on around her, or the effect of what she does and says, or who or what she really is or what she wants. But the novel which presents her discourse, which shows its operations and effects, which indicates that hers is only one possible discourse among many, directs its readers to a sense of things as they really are – or should be – behind the screen of language, offering in particular a full, rich sense of the human mind and heart amidst other human minds and hearts. "As men abound in copiousness of language," Hobbes believed, "so they become more wise, or more mad than ordinary."[47] This, too, might serve as a fitting motto for a novel that turns the dangerous power of language back on itself, displaying the perils of the petty fictionalizing, the romancing, it allows within the larger scheme of its own, grand fiction – and which, in so doing, to quote its narrator, "brings us back to ourselves again" (69). The last, *Roxana* is in some ways the most impressive of Defoe's several experiments at writing fictive but "anti-romantic" criminal biography – which is to say, novels that would tell larger, truer, more useful lies than the purported non-fictions of the actual thing.

[47] Hobbes, *Leviathan*, ed. Macpherson, 1: 4, p. 106.

Closing comments

Truth, complexity, common sense, and empty spaces

The dialogic means of seeking truth is counterposed to *official* monologism, which pretends to *possess a ready-made truth*, and it is also counterposed to the naive self-confidence of those people who think that they know something, that is, who think that they possess certain truths. Truth is not born nor is it to be found inside the head of an individual person, it is born *between people* collectively searching for truth, in the process of their dialogic interaction.

> Mikhail Bakhtin, *Problems of Dostoyevsky's Poetics*, ed. and tr. Caryl Emerson
> (Minneapolis, 1984), p. 110

The novel's spirit is the spirit of complexity. Every novel says to the reader: "Things are not as simple as you think." That is the novel's eternal truth, but it grows steadily harder to hear amid the din of easy, quick answers that come faster than the question and block it off. ∖

> Milan Kundera, *The Art of the Novel*, tr. Linda Asher (New York, 1986), p. 18

I would not have you ... complain ... of the Contradiction of your Character, since that is of a Piece with the whole Design of my Book.

I hate all that's common, even to common Sense.

> Defoe to Robinson Crusoe, in Charles Gildon, *The Life and Strange Surprising Adventures of Mr. D— De F—, of London, Hosier* (1719), pp. xvi, xv

Since ... we think it vain, to persuade People of Fortune, to employ those vacant Hours of Life, which lie burthensom upon their Hands, in the Study of some Art or Science, because the acquiring of an Art or Science, will demand Labour and close Application, and Men of Fortune must not take Pains; however we may prescribe to them both for their Health and Diversion, to fill up those empty Spaces in Reading good Books.

> ?Defoe, *A Collection of Miscellany Letters Selected out of Mist's Weekly Journal*
> (1722–7), 4: 194–5

Taking up an oft-reiterated theme, a recent book speaks of *Roxana* as a reaching out toward "novelistic possibilities."[1] This study of Defoe in context has avoided large teleological schemes in an effort, or so I'd hope, to escape some of the restrictions and premature foreclosures that come with thinking about the past as if its future had already happened. Defoe

[1] Michael M. Boardman, *Defoe and the Uses of Narrative* (New Brunswick, N.J., 1983), pp. 139–55.

245

was not reaching toward the writing of novels, probably not even toward the writing of literature. He was improvising, making complex gestures in a complex moment with little aim beyond that moment; it is the complexity of his gesturing, the quality of his improvisation, that marks him off from almost all other writers of prose fiction in his time, and from all other writers about criminals. Let us not overvalue him, or undervalue him either. Defoe's impact on the great novelists who defined the genre after him is extremely difficult to assess and may have been negligible. Richardson, Fielding, Sterne, Austen made their starts elsewhere, and each went his or her own way. Nor is it obvious that Defoe exerted any significant influence on subsequent writers of criminal biography. Though one is sometimes struck by a Defoe-like passage here or there, these can be found, too, in texts that appeared long before his novels were published. Defoe produces greatly enriched versions of criminal biography but does not seem to have enriched, or much changed, his society's attitudes toward criminals. The popular literature of crime continued, if not unchanged, then following its own lines of development. Defoe no more dictated its agenda than he did those of later novelists.[2]

But Defoe is important as a historical phenomenon nonetheless. Whether he meant to be a novelist or a social reformer, and whether he was successful in either or both these roles (whatever we may mean by "successful"), his criminal novels remain highly significant *as novels* – that is, as instances of a discourse that, setting itself against other discourses even as it includes and builds on them, produces a sense of "indeterminancy, a certain semantic openendedness, a living contact with unfinished, still-evolving contemporary reality."[3] One last opportunity to gauge this quality, which I take to be the key difference between his narratives and the common run of criminal biography – that difference from which all other differences follow, and to which all tend – can be found in the ordinary of Newgate's account of the last words and dying behavior of yet another petty shoplifter, hanged 31 October 1712. To convey as fully as possible its overall tone, thrust, and demeanor, I quote

[2] Contrary assertions have been made by Maximillian Novak in *Realism, Myth, and History in Defoe's Fiction* (Lincoln, Neb., 1983) and John Bender in *Imagining the Penitentiary: Fiction and the Architecture of Mind in Eighteenth-Century England* (Chicago, 1987). Though Novak claims that "the way criminal narratives and criminal behavior were perceived was influenced by Defoe's shaping of them [in his fiction]," when he gets down to cases he winds up talking about Richardson instead (pp. 131, 135–7). It is Bender's notion that the late eighteenth-century "rise" of the penitentiary was influenced or "enabled" by the earlier rise of the novel. His chief concern is with representational practice generally, not the representation of criminals *per se*. Consequently *Robinson Crusoe* and *A Journal of the Plague Year* – particularly as they represent the moral and psychological effects of confinement – get far more attention than *Moll Flanders* (thus see, respectively, pp. 49–60, 73–84, 45–51).

[3] M. M. Bakhtin, "Epic and Novel: Toward a Methodology for the Study of the Novel," in *The Dialogic Imagination: Four Essays by M. M. Bakhtin*, ed. Michael Holquist, tr. Caryl Emerson and Holquist (Austin, 1981), p. 7.

Paul Lorrain's text in its entirety. In its vexed, weak, and almost inadvertent reenactment of a stubborn, indecisive struggle that, by the ordinary's own admission, could be resolved only through the ultimate, unanswerable intervention of the state's full authority, it is not one of his more usual productions.

"*Eleonor Gravenor*, alias *Gladmore*, alias *Lovemore*," Lorrain writes, was condemned for privately stealing out of Mr. *Henry Barton*'s Shop, a parcel of Gold and Silver Fringe, and out of Mr. *John Peel*'s Shop, a piece of Callicoe, on the 11th instant. She confess'd, That she was guilty of both these Facts, and of several others of the like nature: That she receiv'd Sentence of Death on the 6th of *July* 1711, for having privately stoln 6 yards of Silver Lace, out of Mr. *Henry Hicks* and Mr. *Arthur Robinson*'s Shop in *Covent-Garden*, on the 23rd of *May* before; That afterwards she obtain'd the Queen's Pardon, and pleaded to it no later than the 6th of *June* last, but took no care to improve it as she ought to have done; saying, That her great Poverty and Inability to get Bread for herself and four small Children had made her give way to the Temptation by which she fell again into this her old wicked Course of seeking to supply her Wants by unjust Means. She told me, She was 50 years of age, born at *Shrewsbury*: That about 12 or 13 Years ago she came up to *London*, and lived first near *Tower hill*, afterwards in the Parish of St. *James Westminster*, where she married, and then remov'd to St. *Martins in the Fields*; in which last Parish she lived above four Years as a Housekeeper: That for the most part of all the time she had been in *London* and *Westminster*, she got her Livelihood (as she did before in the Country) by making Plain-work: That she was very sorry she had not kept to it; and heartily repented. She further said, That after she had pleaded the Queen's Pardon in *June* last, she was discharged from *Newgate* (where she had then lain 13 months) and sent to the Work-house in *Clerkenwell*; and there being sick and weak, and wanting Food, she follow'd other Prisoners who had made a Hole in the Wall of the Room she lay in, and so went out at that Hole and made her Escape with them; and presently betook herself to her former wicked Trade of Stealing, by which having supply'd herself with Cloaths (for She was even naked before) she appear'd more boldly abroad, and in that dress went upon some new Expedition: For one Morning having called at a certain Tavern for Wine to refresh her Spirits, she did from thence direct her way as well as she could, first to Mr. *Barton*'s, and then to Mr. *Peel*'s Shop, where she found her head swimming, and hardly knew what she did, because she was then in the power of the Wine she had drunk but a little before; and therefore could not do her business so dextrously, as not to be discover'd in this last Place; for not only the Callicoe she took at Mr. *Peel*'s, but also the Gold and Silver Fringe she had just before stoln out of Mr. *Barton*'s Shop, were found upon her; who thereupon being apprehended, and brought before a Magistrate, was immediately committed to the House of her former Abode, namely *Newgate*; and this happen'd about a Fortnight after she had (in an irregular manner) deliver'd herself from a less unhappy Confinement, and less severe punishment, than that she is now brought under by her own Folly and Wickedness. All this she declar'd; and added, That if she were now to live, she would lead a better Life, and would contentedly yield to have her right Hand cut off, which had done so much Mischief, and pick up a poor

Livelihood in gathering of Rags with her left Hand, which ever was honest, and therefore should not suffer with the other. Thus, it seem'd, she look'd upon that Member only, which was made the Instrument of Evil, to be punishable; but she was better informed afterwards, by being shewn, that when any Member does amiss, by the direction of the Mind, the whole Body must suffer for it.[4]

There is much here that invites casual comparison to Defoe. Related in far greater detail, emphasizing what she saw and how she felt at certain crucial moments, Gravenor's final adventures might even seem to anticipate Moll's last brushes with the law. Here, too, something seemingly authentic might be heard about life at the margins of society.

"Might" because this is not what is actually heard; the comparison to Defoe is more notional than real. Though Lorrain's account of Gravenor is interesting for what it allows her to say, it is just as interesting for its stolid refusal to pay her much attention. She gets all the space that custom and common decency entitle her to, perhaps more, but is shut up just as soon as she challenges the authority Lorrain represents as servant of the state. Gravenor may be allowed to plead extenuating circumstances – an unusual concession for the Newgate ordinary – but then all her talk of poverty, her inability to find work, her very nakedness, is countered with an overbearing insistence (or so he means it to be) on her "irregular manner," "her own Folly and Wickedness," her ignorance and even stupidity in assuming that what the hand has done to feed the mouth might not involve "the whole Body." What little impression we get of Gravenor as a separate being with her own distinctive voice comes, faint and attenuated, through the thick overlay of the ordinary's wholly ordinary rhetoric. There is no dialogue here, only the trace of an argument that Gravenor was bound to lose, if not to Lorrain then to the gallows. How could it be otherwise?

Showing how it could be otherwise, Defoe's novels do a great deal to prompt this question's being asked. Allowed to speak as Gravenor is not, his characters, though fictive, come to seem in a number of ways more "real" than she. What shows through Lorrain's prose accidentally, from either fatigue of office or, just simply, rhetorical incompetence – the authentic life story of a person inviting, indeed necessitating, judgment but still difficult to judge – is directly present in Defoe's. The necessary precondition for this effect is, of course, the deletion of the official, sanctioned voice of standard criminal biography, which allows criminals to say only so much as can be absorbed or rebutted, overwhelmed or discredited. Criminal biography may frequently invite its audience to come to its own conclusions about the meaning of the people and experiences it represents, but such judgments – if indeed they are to be the

---

[4] Paul Lorrain, Ordinary Account, 31 October 1712.

audience's *own* – require that criminals be given full voice or, at the least, permitted to speak without contradiction. What seems monologue is actually Defoe's way of opening up his texts and making them more dialogic, of freeing up relations between his protagonists and his readers.

Gravenor is not allowed to make her case, either on grounds of justice (couldn't there be another form of punishment? what she suggests, curiously, has precedent in Islamic law) or of sympathy. Moll and Jack, each in her or his own way, are allowed to plead extenuating circumstances and to suggest, inadvertently or not, how social institutions might be changed to produce less crime and greater social justice. (Compare Moll's idea about educating children of the poor to Gravenor's suggestion for an alternative punishment for theft.) It is possible to feel a sympathy for them, even for Roxana, that most writing about actual criminals was concerned to prevent. Moll, thus, might seem Gravenor writ large – a full, convincing, and not unsympathetic instance of the feckless many who, through bad luck and no overlarge degree of compunction or nicety, choose or are driven into lives of crime. Jack, abandoned to rear himself as best he can amid the savageries of urban life, appears more sympathetic still. Defoe's achievement in this respect seems all the more considerable in comparison, say, to Fielding, who, for all his supposedly greater humanity and generosity, all his genial capacity to forgive imprudent heroes, wasted remarkably little sympathy on petty criminals in real life or fiction.[5]

Lorrain's account of Gravenor's dying words, then, can lead us yet again to marvel at how "real" – how solid and actual, how full of affect, how free from the dead, oppressive weight of official attitudes and rhetoric – Defoe's novels make fictive criminals seem. Lorrain provides an especially good counter-example because of what he notes but fails to follow up or even quite actually to register. What Gravenor's ignored aliases indicate she might have been ("Gladmore," "Lovemore" can hardly be accidental; there must have been some history behind them) Moll is, and more. Criminal biography denied real people their authentic, individual reality, inadvertently as well as purposefully, while Defoe's

---

[5] Faced with the horrific conditions of London lodging houses for the poor, startled particularly by the presence in one of them of "one of the prettiest Girls I had ever seen," Fielding is careful to keep a certain ironic distance. The girl in question has been "carried off" into marriage by an Irishman (note the locution, also the ethnic identity of her heart's passion) and, Fielding adds, not before robbing her mistress (*An Enquiry into the Causes of the Late Increase of Robbers, &c.* [1751], pp. 140–3; see chapter 6, n. 1, for a more extensive quotation). *Amelia* (11: 7) offers a comparable but somewhat opposite instance. When a servant girl absconds with two of his wife's shifts, Booth is outraged that her "breach of trust" cannot be prosecuted as a felony. His own breaches of trust have cost his family much more than the few shillings the girl got from her theft, but the text itself makes no such point and seems to share its hero's opinion. There is a marvellous opportunity for irony here wholly in keeping with the aims of the novel but, harder on the perfidy of servants than the sins of their masters and apparently unwilling to make them seem comparable, Fielding curiously misses it.

fiction, ever artful, confers such status on imaginary beings. But this is not
where I want to rest my case. Though I find it an attractive position – it
certainly privileges the literary – it seems nonetheless too simple, too
uncritical, and, very likely, too sentimental. It takes, moreover, too hard a
view of the ordinary.

The difference between Moll and Gravenor is not merely the difference
between Defoe and Lorrain as writers, any more than it is the relative
lengths of the texts in which they appear; the basic and crucial difference
is that the one person is fictive and the other real. Defoe was immeasura-
bly richer in talent and imagination than the ordinary, but he had the
further advantage of being free from the constraint of the occasion which
Lorrain and his audience – along with Gravenor – were about to meet or
just had met. Whether the ordinary wanted to hear her (or even could) is
not so much the question as whether he and his public could afford to.
Moll can seem more "real" because she is in fact fictive, because none of
the etiquette or protocol that comes with hanging need be invoked; no
particular apologies, before or after, are due from her or the writer who
presents her. Defoe's novels give readers a much greater sense of proximity
to criminals' thoughts and attitudes, a much greater intimacy with their
voices, but it must also be observed that at the same time they offer
readers a certain privileged distance.

Defoe's sympathy with and possibly for criminals was not the sort to
make him a "liberal" reformer, at least as we would understand the term.
That role might better be assigned to Paul Lorrain as he treats with and
tries to shape the behavior and attitudes of people like Gravenor. His
account of her shows not so much a lack, I'd argue, as a consistent
suppression of sympathy. It is not that he is indifferent or coldhearted,
quite the opposite; he aims to make things easier and more comfortable
for everyone. Gravenor has had a hard life and it is about to be ended
with great cruelty, a cruelty which, for all the special pleading in favor of
the increasingly severe penalties in the statute books, was nonetheless
difficult to enforce.[6] Lorrain would put a good face on her situation,
would persuade her, if she'd only listen, that justice is not necessarily or
only retributive, as she seems to imagine, but potentially a matter in
which she might play an active, positive role. That she does not prove
cooperative is something of a disappointment. It is not only his deafness to
her which is important here, but, because he wants her to abandon her
position and accept his, her deafness to him as well. His looking forward to
her being "better informed afterwards" (i.e., at the gallows) carries with it
a certain ruefulness, it seems to me, as well as malice. Though Gravenor
may be "stupid" by his standard, even brutally so, he does not quite write

---

[6] See *Turned to Account*, pp. 153–67.

her off.[7] The hanging will shut her up and so end their speaking at cross-purposes, but it still will not entirely serve his purposes. His effort to make her agree with him is in a way a recognition of Bakhtin's point about truth being collectively established. He wants her to join in his officially sanctioned (which is to say not really *his*, or any*one's*), socially valuable (because it masks or erases difference), ready-made and in a sense already written monologue. Why, when it all might be so easily done, does she so perversely refuse? Lorrain is seeking to advance a "truth," but it will be incomplete without Gravenor's assent to it.

Like serious criminal biographers in general, Lorrain is engaged in a rescue operation. It is not the petty shoplifter herself that interests him – by the time his paper appears she is dead, and on her own she was never a considerable object – but (as I've argued elsewhere) a favored conception of what it is to be an ordinary human being. Gravenor is a bad example but Lorrain would prefer her to be a good one. It is not only that he wants her to submit to state authority willingly, as criminals were routinely exhorted to do. He wants her to confirm a particular view of its basis. Failing any dramatic display of moral regeneration, she ought at least to agree to the point he emphasizes at the end of his account: that she is a whole human being, and so wholly responsible for her behavior. That is, he wants her to endorse (quite literally, to sign off on) the notion that individuals are necessarily possessed of an essential and – however much they may seem to have turned against themselves and all notions of right conduct – an ultimately inalienable integrity. Thus, though he allows her to mention the desperate, miserable circumstances in which she's lived, as well as her claim to be some sort of compound, divided being – good on the one hand (no metaphor here, either), bad on the other – he denies these any significance. If Gravenor has been lacking in personal integrity, the state will in a sense restore it to her, albeit with extreme prejudice.

Society, as Lorrain and his audience would apparently like to imagine it, requires whole people – or people, at least, who seem and may be treated as whole and unitary subjects. And such people, as he describes them, are rather like societies in miniature; all their "members" form one body which is collectively affected by the actions of any one part. This reversal of the old body politic metaphor makes Gravenor's body itself political, and in rather sophisticated as well as all the obvious and crude ways. Gravenor will be hanged in the name of good government, her body being inscribed, as Foucault would have it, with all the signs of state authority. Her attitude toward that event, however, is potentially far more important than anything physically done to her, for, properly managed, it might contribute to a far less (obviously) repressive and so more attractive

---

[7] Lorrain doesn't apply this term to her, but it would have fit his customary usage; see, e.g., his account of Susan Perry (13 March 1713), quoted in chapter 2.

idea of how social order is (or might be) maintained. Insisting the self is a whole as society is a whole, Lorrain's metaphor carries with it certain implications, not the least of which is that the self is the basic unit of government, and that governance of the self might be seen as a model for social authority at large. This is rather different from the traditional view, which, seeing the king as supreme *pater familias*, modeled the sovereignty of the state on paternal authority. Good behavior is not only like civil government, but indeed its starting point; unlike despotism, civil government necessarily relies on the "civility" of each of its individual subjects. People may comply with the law out of terror, inasmuch as even partial infractions bring down penalties on the whole, or they might behave lawfully out of a more positive, which is to say mutual, sense of collective responsibility.

Gravenor's fault is that she fails to recognize either possibility, neither repenting (as best she might) so that her death might do some good to the community, nor even understanding (and this would be the barest minimum) why her punishment must take the form it does. She refuses the bargain by which, according to Unger, "the individual [gains] an illusion of coherent personality in exchange for his submission to the demands of the group," not understanding why (what good, in her dying moments, would it do *her*?) she should need or have such a personality.[8] Gravenor's problem, which is to say, the problem she makes for society at large, is that she lacks self-consciousness in more than just one sense. If only she could show an appropriate sense of self, a less fractured self-reflexivity! If only, freely accepting her subjection, she could be the subject her society needs her to be!

Here and elsewhere, Lorrain is engaged in something of a social experiment – an experiment, it has to be added, which eventually failed in more than this particular case. By the last third of the eighteenth century criminal biographers would cease adducing to low lives like Gravenor any possibility of reforming on their own or, rather, with a little help from the prison chaplain and a prospective swing on the gallows. The sovereign selves that made up society did not, even at the farthest reaches of imagination, include the likes of her; imagination had shrunk, becoming more class-bound even as (or so until recently it was generally thought) it grew more "humane." The shift to the penitentiary system saved lives, to be sure, but it did so at the cost of denying criminals any claim to individual autonomy. Insofar as it replaced transportation, the penitentiary denied criminals the chance to start over in a new place more or less on their own. Insofar as it led to a reduction in hangings, it replaced one great, simple brutality with an attenuated but newly elaborated set of

---

[8] Roberto Mangabeira Unger, *Law in Modern Society: Toward a Criticism of Social Theory* (New York, 1976), p. 146.

others, the aim of punishment being now to break the will not redirect it, to reduce the psyche by a variety of means so overwhelming as to burke all resistance to its being rebuilt from the ground up. Appeals to conscience, that representative in the breast of God's all-seeing eye, gave way to totalitarian fantasies like Bentham's Panopticon.[9]

Though in many ways the reform of punishment might be said to represent an "advance," it represents, too, a dropping of earlier hopes; it stands, in a curious way, as a diminution of decency and respect toward criminals, a dehumanization of them. In criminal biography as well as the prison system, the criminal and the criminal mentality were divided off from the norm. Criminals no longer were made to seem people like you or me, who might have something to say to us, but radically different in origin, upbringing, motives, and outlook. "Few violators of the law ... are not the offspring of the poorer classes of the people," declares a late eighteenth-century criminal biographer to his presumably well-heeled audience, and he partly attributes this "fact" to a lamentable difference in child-rearing practices, it being "but too common with women of the lower ranks ... to ruin their children by an extravagant tenderness."[10] Prisons, along with factories and schools, would soon move to correct this state of affairs. For all the consciousness of social gradation that existed in Lorrain's (and Defoe's) own time, serious criminal biography practically never considered its subjects a class apart. Concerned with touching something in criminals' souls which they shared with all other human beings (or at least making a display of such concern), it could show them a certain respect even as it justified despatching them. Lorrain may have been incompetent and insincere, he may even have been a fool and was certainly the servant of gross injustice, but he was not the monster Bentham was.

Neither fool nor monster, Defoe was content to do without the simplicity, ease, or quickness of the "ready-made" answers of writers like Lorrain, and seems, for all his "projectorial" boldness, constitutionally incapable of the "clear" and "complete" thought of later social reformers. All his novels are meditations on the incompleteness of truth, or, rather, on the incompleteness of our ability to recognize and grasp what truths we encounter. What Gildon, the first significant critic of his fiction, sneeringly but percipiently said of *Robinson Crusoe* – that it is an "incoherent Piece" and "will not bear the Eye of a rational Reader" – would be true of the later fictions as well. Gildon, it is worth noting, was especially offended by

[9] See of course Foucault's *Discipline and Punish: The Birth of the Prison*, tr. Alan Sheridan (New York, 1977). The appallingly systematic authoritarianism of late eighteenth- and early nineteenth-century English penology and prison practice is far more richly illustrated, however, in Michael Ignatieff's *A Just Measure of Pain: The Penitentiary in the Industrial Revolution* (New York, 1978).

[10] *The Malefactor's Register; or the Newgate and Tyburn Calendar* (1779), 5: 295, 1: 325.

Defoe's "irrational" and "superstitious" representation of providence, by which he meant that Defoe did not make it conform to "the Dictates of Reason" but allowed it "either contradictory Offices, or an unjust Partiality."[11] A failed Catholic and one-time Deist, Gildon speaks here with something like the voice of secular humanism; it is his line of thinking not Defoe's (despite a recent suggestion) that leads to Bentham's wholly secular, utterly materialist, super-rational, and soulless re-creation of providential design by means of prison architecture.

Even as Defoe founded state sovereignty on the consent of the governed, believed in mutual exchange as the basis of social interaction, and powerfully encouraged self-consciousness through his fiction, he was not optimistic about human nature or how it might be remade. "Conservative" in his ideas of sinfulness, concerned with reinvigorating notions of providence, he critiqued the belief that society might depend on the "civility" of its members by subverting the very notion of individual identity on which it was based. Defoe's criminals have no solid sense of self and, it might well be argued, no characterological core. At its fullest and most elaborate, serious criminal biography shows how people can fall away from their best possible selves, ceding control to the devil, their own bad appetites, bad company, whatever, but it also allows them an opportunity to regain themselves, to reconstitute their being even as they consent (and because they consent) to its dissolution. The protagonists of Defoe's criminal novels become increasingly alienated and fragmented, and are not offered comparable opportunities to snatch themselves from the abyss. Their material fortunes wax and they rise in social status, but, viewed within the terms of their immediate historical context, they do not quite achieve the self-sufficiency and autonomy so many modern critics have attributed to them. Defoe was not in his own time quite the celebrator of individualism he has been made out to be, but then he escapes most such simple categorizations.

Challenging the idea that human beings are or can really be "whole," Defoe seems also to be greatly suspicious of the method criminal biography took to advance it, i.e., by attempting to establish (or re-establish) a sense of moral consensus between the criminal and his audience, and so, too, between members of that audience. It takes more than words (to quote a poem he may have written) "to make a *Sheep-stealer* a *Saint*."[12] Moral truth, as *Roxana* so clearly indicates, is not a matter of what people can be brought to agree upon among themselves but something apart. The great danger of social convention is that it can usurp identity. The only defence

[11] Charles Gildon, *The Life and Strange Surprising Adventures of Mr. D— De F—, of London, Hosier* (1719), pp. 37, 33.

[12] *A Hymn to the Funeral Sermon* (1703); David Foxon's doubts about John Robert Moore's assignment of this poem to Defoe are endorsed by P. N. Furbank and W. R. Owens, *The Canonisation of Daniel Defoe* (New Haven, 1988), p. 39.

against the social construction – or, rather, *mis*construction – of one's own being is the strictest possible adherence to an absolute, "God-given" or "natural" morality. Inasmuch as Roxana becomes increasingly enmeshed in a socially created "world," her sense of self turns vaporish and insubstantial. In this respect she is exactly opposite to Robinson Crusoe, who, insofar as he becomes whole and puissant, owes this to the time he spends alone in the directest possible contact with nature and God. Even so, as Gildon was the first to recognize – correct despite himself – much in Crusoe's character remains "rambling" and "inconsistent."[13]

Robinson Crusoe burdened Gildon peculiarly. There seems some truth in his saying he is writing against it out of "Indignation, not Malice or Envy" (though malice and envy are obviously in play). His attack on its irrationality and incoherence – his objection that it does not "naturally" and "plainly" present "an evident and useful Moral," which ought to be "the very Nature of a Fable" – seems by its very vehemence to show the novel has somehow powerfully challenged him.[14] Perhaps the greatest affront it offers this would-be rationalist is its presentation of God's will and the human mind operating in ways that he (and by implication the most progressive thinkers of his time) cannot readily understand. His ridiculing the book, the scurrility of his personal attack on Defoe, seem ways of quelling the disturbances it has raised. As it has with its hero, Defoe's novel appears to have thrown Gildon uncomfortably back on first principles. The criminal novels, I've already argued, would have produced similar effects, would have tested readers in similar ways. The contribution they make to the "rise" of individualism – if any – comes (I'd claim) not so much from their offering models of individual striving and achievement that passive, impressionable readers might take to their hearts, fantasize about, even emulate, as from the ways they challenge readers' received ideas, making life as they and others live it seem more various and complex than "common" or "official" sense can ever allow it to be, encouraging them to ask their own questions, to come up with their own, always (I'd say) provisional answers.

In denying "the absolutism of a single and unitary language," says

---

[13] Gildon, *Life and Adventures of D— De F—*, p. x. Crusoe of course never does accommodate to an asocial or unsocialized nature, for he brings with him a great deal of cultural baggage (not the least of which are the artifacts from the ship), and the island has already been seeded with goats; a wholly natural environment may have driven him mad and probably would have killed him. Nor does Crusoe ever get any clear, unambiguous message from God; despite his conviction that he's doing what God wants for him, God remains at a distance, elusive, absconded even. From a modern standpoint, of course, "God" and "Nature" are social constructs, too, categories that societies project beyond themselves so as better to define their own, "human" domain.

[14] Ibid., pp. 32, 35.

Bakhtin, the novel promotes what is "in fact a radical revolution in the destinies of human discourse."[15] This may well seem too "hortatory" in the present context, for criminal biography itself marks a departure from absolutist discourse, if only minimally and inadvertently. Allowing audiences an anonymity and privacy they could never have experienced as witnesses to the actual facts, as part of the crowd at public trials or executions, or simply gossiping among themselves, it offered a chance ("let the reader judge") to stand separate and autonomous. Defoe's novels allow a still greater remove from the pressing questions criminals raised, and readers – offered a wholly anonymous, highly unconstrained vantage-point on their subjects – may, if they choose, pry themselves quite loose from all that official sanction or simple social pressure would define as appropriate and normal response. Still, as the case of Gildon shows, opportunities do not constitute facts, and Gildon – judging from the various rewritings that "normalize" the criminal novels as well as *Robinson Crusoe* – was no isolated example.[16] In challenging "common sense" novels do not always or necessarily reconstruct readers' attitudes, and, if and when they do, those attitudes may not long outlast the reading experience; the point is worth making given the recurrent attractions of "idealist" (and idealistic, idealizing) literary history.[17] The novel's "spirit of complexity" can be rejected or (the reception of Sinclair's *The Jungle* possibly offering the most famous case) perverted to the narrowest, most self-interested ends. And if the "dialogism" of the novel does succeed in planting itself in the minds of some readers, will this necessarily make them more open to other voices in the future? Perhaps they will become proud of containing multitudes.

It is better in the end to speak of Defoe's achievement more modestly. "Reality is beyond fiction," a writer in Applebee's *Journal* declares, having witnessed in the playhouse something that moved him powerfully: the presence in the audience of a formerly virtuous old man with his fifteen-year-old mistress, the daughter of this man's intimate friend.[18] He writes in the hope this man "may see [at the theater] what bloody Catastrophes have been caused by ... unlawful Love"; possibly "the Fate of the Stage Criminals represented before him" will keep him from becoming "a real

---

[15] Bakhtin, "Discourse in the Novel," in *The Dialogic Imagination*, pp. 366, 367. For the adjective in the next sentence, see Wayne Booth's introduction to Mikhail Bakhtin, *Problems of Dostoevsky's Poetics*, ed. and tr. Caryl Emerson (Minneapolis, 1984), p. xxvi.

[16] Gildon in fact claimed that the abridgement of *Robinson Crusoe*, which Defoe so disliked, was "more valuable than the Original" as it no longer contained so many "clumsy and tedious Reflections" (*Life and Adventures of D— De F—*, p. 35).

[17] On this subject see, for instance, Edward Pechter, "The New Historicism and Its Discontents: Politicizing Renaissance Drama," *PMLA*, 102 (1987): 292–303; David Simpson, "Literary Criticism and the Return to 'History,'" *Critical Inquiry*, 14 (1988): 721–47; and Carolyn Porter, "Are We Being Historical Yet," *South Atlantic Quarterly*, 87 (1988): 743–86.

[18] Applebee's *Original Weekly Journal*, 27 February 1731.

Victim like them on the Theatre of the World." It is not these pious and wholly conventional hopes that are of interest here, but the posture this particular writer takes, telling his story in an almost novelistic way against the story on stage. Playing the clichés of the playhouse off against a supposedly real but probably fictive event, he seeks to make it seem *realer*, in this case not only authentic but poignant. What he saw at the theater that night took away all his pleasure in the comedy on stage, he says, and "affected me . . . more than the deepest Tragedy I ever saw . . . in my Life." Several dialogues are indicated here over and against the discourse of the stage: the writer and reader vis-à-vis the old man and the girl vis-à-vis the conventions of a literary form which – however much for moral reasons this writer wants it to – fails to measure up to reality. Thus, glad of the chance to "unbosom" himself "Incognito," he seeks to supplement what might be seen at the theater, aiming by his own discursive intervention to help things along with his "mistaken Friend." To that man's experience at the playhouse he adds his own experience of that man in the playhouse, hoping that in reading him the man will realize what he might not otherwise learn despite the lessons of the theater: where he stands in the larger "theater of the world." And, of course, in a further level of complication, this writer is addressing not only one particular old man (who may well be fictive) but all readers who might see something relevant to their own situations in his.

The point of theatrical realism, Dr. Johnson observed, was not to persuade spectators that what they were seeing was real but "to bring realities to mind."[19] Obviously the writer in Applebee's has doubts about the theater's ability to do this, even as he advances the usual notions about the power of plays to change moral attitudes. Though his own discourse falls short of the kind of representation possible on stage, it means to indicate the real and, getting the reader to reflect back upon himself, to achieve the morally valuable effect of bringing the real to mind. In this writer's dissatisfaction with conventional modes, in his opening up of a gap between literature and actual life that makes room for his own writing, he seeks to speak actually and directly to all that literature leaves out of account. In his own small way he is doing, then, what Defoe does and – the gravid center of social commentary shifting increasingly from drama to prose fiction – what a great succession of English novelists began to do in the eighteenth century each with his or her own "new kind" of writing. This piece in Applebee's was published while Defoe was still alive, and it may be that Defoe contributed something to its writer's frame of mind. Or perhaps not; there may have been something in the very air of his rapidly changing, restive, divided, and clamant age suggesting that truth, like

---

[19] Johnson, "Preface to Shakespeare," in Samuel Johnson, *"Rasselas," Poems, and Selected Prose*, 3rd edn, ed. Bertrand H. Bronson (New York, 1971), p. 277.

ignorance, was a matter of gaps, that the mind best filled its empty spaces by exploring the interstices between socially provided modes of thinking and feeling, of writing, reading, and talking. For all his faults, Defoe was a great creator of interstices.

Index